ALL MY WORLDLY GOODS

For Ben and Thomas

All My Worldly Goods

A Feminist Perspective on the Legal Regulation of Wealth

ANNE MORRIS
The University of Liverpool

SUSAN NOTT
The University of Liverpool

Dartmouth

Aldershot • Brookfield USA • Singapore • Sydney

© Anne Morris and Susan Nott 1995

Published by
Dartmouth Publishing Company Limited
Gower House
Croft Road
Aldershot
Hants GU11 3HR
England

Dartmouth Publishing Company
Old Post Road
Brookfield
Vermont 05036
USA

British Library Cataloguing in Publication Data
Morris, Anne E.
  All My Worldly Goods: Feminist Perspective
  on the legal Regulation of Wealth
  I. Title II. Nott, Susan M.
  344.102878

Library of Congress Cataloging-in-Publication Data
Morris, Anne E., 1952-
    All my worldly goods : a feminist perspective on the legal
  regulation of wealth / Anne Morris, Susan Nott.
        p.   cm.
    Includes bibliographical references and index.
    ISBN 1-85521-370-2
    1. Property–Great Britain. 2. Women–Legal status, laws, etc.-
  -Great Britain. 3. Women–Great Britain–Economic conditions.
  4. Wealth. 5. Feminist theory. I. Nott, Susan, N., 1948-
  II. Title.
  KD811.M67   1995
  346.4204'082–dc20
  [344.2064082]   95-19399
                                                                 CIP

ISBN 1 85521 370 2

Printed and bound in Great Britain by Ipswich Book Co. Ltd., Ipswich, Suffolk

Contents

Foreword

The idea for this book developed out of our earlier work which looked more specifically at women in paid employment. That reinforced our belief that, although equality in the workplace is vital, it is only part of a much wider problem which must be addressed if women are to be equal participants both in and out of the working environment. The pursuit of equal rights at work is bedevilled by the inequalities that persist elsewhere, not least in the family, and by the contradictory objectives of legal rules which operate in other spheres, especially in relation to welfare benefits. Moreover, as lawyers, we were aware that there is a temptation in dealing with these rules to compartmentalise problems as belonging to one or other traditional legal categories, such as property law, employment law, welfare law or family law. As laws become more complex it is increasingly difficult to get a complete picture of the legal status and legal perception of women in the late twentieth century.

In our attempt to draw together an exploration of how the law deals with these fundamental issues, we leave ourselves open to a charge of sacrificing depth at the expense of breadth. The aim, however, is not to look at the technicalities of the law, but to examine its objectives and its consequences. We hope that by doing this, those who study in detail the intricacies of the different areas will be able to view more critically the underlying assumptions and aims of the law-makers and that those who are not lawyers may feel that we have helped to make the law more accessible and have answered some of their questions.

The law is stated as at 31 December 1994, though mention has been made of the 1995 White Paper, *Improving Child Support*, with its proposals to modify the Child Support Act 1991. We have been aware whilst writing of the rapidity and the extent of legislative and other changes. Of necessity, in drawing a line at a particular date, the result is a snapshot of the law. There is some room for optimism that some of the issues raised in the text may be tackled, but there is still a very long way to go and the criticisms we have made will, unfortunately, remain valid for some time to come. Drawing attention to the difficulties which women still face should not, however, be interpreted as a mere litany of complaints, nor should women be classed as victims by virtue of their inequalities. Quite apart from the fact that there are many successful women, progress for all women is more likely where we are able to identify obstacles and offer constructive remedies. In that spirit, we hope that this will be seen as positive criticism, rather than mere reproach.

We have drawn on the expertise and goodwill of many of our colleagues and are especially grateful for the support of those in the Feminist Legal Research Unit in the Faculty of Law, particularly Jo Bridgeman and Sue Millns, without whose expert guidance and patient explanations this book would never have been converted into camera-ready copy. Our thanks also go to Rachel Chapman, who prepared the index, case and statute lists *just* before Jacob was born. Our colleagues, Neville Harris, Christina Lyon, Debra Morris and Jean Warburton have willingly shared their knowledge of their particular areas of law and we are very grateful to them. Any errors or omissions are, of course, the responsibility of the authors.

Liverpool
January 1995

1   What It Is To Be Wealthy

A book which sets out to explore the access that women have to wealth must obviously address what it means to be wealthy. There is continuing debate about what it means to be poor and since women are disproportionately represented amongst the poorest in society[1] it is at least arguable that feminists would be better employed in dissecting the specific conditions and causes of women's poverty than in discussing the particular relationship that women have to wealth. On the other hand, an almost inevitable corollary of involuntary poverty is lack of power on both a personal and community level. To put it another way: wealth, however defined, equates with at least a degree of control over one's own existence. Wealth in this sense encompasses more than mere spending power, although disposable income, of course, forms part of the picture. Wealth - as the antithesis to poverty - can be simply "defined" as the gateway to independence. In this context independence should be understood as the conferring of the power to choose: how to live, where to live and with whom. It means not being involuntarily dependent on the state or another adult. In this sense it is not necessary to be *rich* to be wealthy, but it is an essential part of any definition of wealth that an individual is enabled to participate in meaningful ways in the society in which she exists. It is thus crucial to investigate the access which women at the end of the twentieth century have to wealth, because that allows for a judgment on how far they have travelled towards true independence and equality.

Despite significant progress towards equality, women generally still do not enjoy the same degree of independence and choice as men. With some exceptions, they do not wield the same degree of personal and political power. They lack, in other words, equal access to wealth. This book explores the ways in which laws and the legal system create and perpetuate these inequalities. It does so by examining the different areas of a woman's life in which the law - or the lack of it - may influence the creation and the distribution of wealth. It is not intended simply to prove that women are poor, though it will become apparent that for a significant number of women their lives are spent in what, by any definition, is poverty. Rather, it is an attempt to investigate the structures which have so far hindered the achievement of substantive equality for the majority of women. This includes women in work and at home, women in relationships and single women, mothers and childless women. Even women who consider themselves fortunate - perhaps in a well-paid job with a happy family life and a comfortable home - might be shocked to discover the precariousness of that situation in the face of some life event such as unemployment, divorce, bereavement, ill-health, domestic violence, bankruptcy - the list is depressing, but these occurrences are not unusual and are not limited to the feckless or the weak, no matter what some would have us believe. The single mother in bed and breakfast accommodation with her children living (or attempting to survive) on income support is one example of a woman who, lacking access to wealth, lacks independence and freedom of choice, but the middle-aged, middle-class woman who has been out of the job-market since her children were born and who discovers that her husband has left, together with his income and his pension, having remortgaged the family home, is another example of a woman who suffers - in different ways - from problems relating to the distribution and regulation of wealth.

Two such contrasting cases highlight the perennial problem in any discussion of wealth and poverty: they are experienced by different people in different ways and there is no universally accepted definition of either. Even the apparently simple statement that to be wealthy is to be free from economic dependence on others begs a number of questions, not least as to how any individual is to go about achieving the level of wealth necessary for that independence. The debate about the definition of poverty has often concentrated on the difference between absolute and relative poverty. The former focuses on what is needed as a minimum for the physiological survival of an individual: food, clothing and shelter. Only those who cannot provide these absolute basics of life are defined as poor, indicating that this is a measure of subsistence and not an indication as to whether an individual is able to live as a fully participating member of society. It is an approach which is favoured amongst those who wish to argue that there is no longer any poverty in the United Kingdom.[2] Those who tend to the relative approach acknowledge that there is a difference between the poverty experienced in an inner city or rural village in England and that suffered in the third world. The United Kingdom, despite the economic recession is, comparatively speaking, a rich society. That does not mean, however, that there is no poverty if that is defined as denial of access to the generally accepted standard of living in that society at that time. Poverty is on this view not simply about food and shelter but also about being able to take part in the normal activities of that community. That might involve visiting relatives, celebrating birthdays, playing sport, buying a friend a drink, watching television, or sending children on school trips. All of these are things which most people take for granted and without which they would consider themselves in some way deprived. It is pointless to argue that a television is a luxury which the poor can do without if the vast majority consider that it is as much a part of normal living as a bed and a cooker. Many would no longer consider a refrigerator and washing machine to be luxuries, although this might not have been the case too long ago.[3]

Such debates, though they may throw light on the depth and breadth of the social problems within society, do not address the issues which this book seeks to explore. It is not intended to be simply about poverty since not all women are poor. Instead it examines the contention that few women, even today, have the same access to wealth as do men. Further, an argument about where to draw the poverty line tends to concentrate on the living standards of the family unit and to ignore the kind of power inequality that exists within the home. As will be shown in Chapter 6, wealth is unevenly distributed within the household and a *woman* may lack wealth even where the family unit would appear to be well above any definition of poverty. The single mother may be immediately labelled as poor, whereas the deserted wife in her comfortable home may not be. Nevertheless, if the latter, unable to gain remunerative employment, faces an old-age without the benefit of a share of her husband's occupational pension, dependent on a state pension to which she has made no contributions, having lost what she thought was their home to the bank or building society, she may also be said to be lacking wealth: she no longer has ready access to the resources she once shared and becomes dependent on what the law will grant her in divorce proceedings or on the state.

It is hard for lawyers, who put their faith in the just ordering of society through the mechanism of laws implemented without bias, to acknowledge that those laws are failing women. In each section of this book there are examples of how the legal system has purported to legislate for equality while maintaining a profoundly unequal status quo. There are, admittedly, cases where the position of women has been protected or improved but this is within an unchanging framework which grants power and influence to those who hold the wealth. Obviously, not all men have equal access to this wealth. Men are homeless, unemployed, low paid and dependent on the state as well as women. But we are comparing the position of women in general with men in general and, generally speaking, women are over represented amongst those in our society who suffer disadvantages of one sort or another because, in being denied wealth, they do not wield equal power and influence. Thus, for example, despite laws which demand equal pay, women are not as well paid as men for the work they do outside the home. The 1994 New Earnings Survey (Part A) showed that in respect of average hourly earnings, women received only 79.5 pence for each pound earned by men. The figure is worse for average weekly earnings: the average for women of £261 was only 72 per cent of the male level of £362.[4]   Women tend to be clustered at the lower end of pay scales. Only 21 per cent of men earned less than £220 a week, while 47 per cent of women earned less than that. Conversely, under 6 per cent of women earned over £470 a week, while almost 20 per cent of men earned more than that figure.[5] Nor is this disparity confined to the United Kingdom. There is an even greater gap between the earnings of men and women in some other European states, the widest being in Luxembourg, where women manual workers earned only 65 per cent of men's pay.[6] The pattern is also repeated in the United States where Kessler-Harris found that in 1988, twenty five years after the Equal Pay Act became law, women employed full-time still earned less than 70 cents for every dollar earned by men in full-time employment.[7] Indeed, a review of the ratio of women's to men's earnings in manufacturing showed that in the sixteen countries considered, men earned more than women.[8] This simple and incontrovertible fact has enormous ramifications. It means that women are less able to invest in assets such as savings, pensions and property, which serve as protection in times of unemployment or in retirement. Women with young children, lacking adequate child care, are less likely to be in employment at all. The consequence of all this is that women are more likely to be dependent on a partner or on the state. In turn they are denied freedom of choice and an independent existence. At the start of this decade fewer than half a million men in the United Kingdom had independent incomes of less than £25 a week but the figure for women was over *4.6 million.* The average income for married people without children was shown to be nearly two and a half times higher for men than for women.[9] The low pay and poor employment prospects of many women result in their greater reliance on the benefits system. The more generous social security benefits tend to be those based on national insurance contributions and since women, more than men, find it difficult to maintain a sufficient record of contributions (because of breaks in employment, low pay, part-time work) they are more likely to claim the lower non-contributory and means-tested benefits. Even here, a woman who is living with a partner may well find that she has no right to claim in her own right, because of the way rules operate in treating a couple as one unit.

Responsibility for the day to day care of dependent children tends still to devolve mainly on women and this fact exacerbates their lack of wealth. This is particularly the case where the woman is a lone parent, and far more women than men find themselves in this position.[10] Lone mothers find it especially difficult to work outside the home and may thus be forced to rely on social security benefits. Even where a woman is married or co-habiting, her child care responsibilities will have considerable impact on her earning capacity measured over her working lifetime as compared with a man or a childless woman. Career breaks, switch to part-time employment or loss of seniority in the workplace hierarchy are all reflected in loss of earnings.[11] Apart from the financial costs, studies have found that women make personal sacrifices in order to feed and clothe their children.[12] They give up their social contacts and interests, not simply to make ends meet but because the enormous effort involved in living on the money available leaves little spare time. Living on low incomes is not only time consuming, it is also, ironically, expensive since those with only a little cash to last until the next benefit payment cannot, for example, afford to travel to the supermarket but must buy locally and less cheaply; since they cannot afford washing machines they must pay to use the launderette. Life is a constant struggle to balance the budget, so that a child who loses a coat at school creates a crisis. In these circumstances it is hardly surprising that women's health also suffers.[13] Women care not only for children but also for the sick, elderly or disabled. The more demanding the care required, the less likely is the carer to be working and most of those with such demands on their time are women.[14] Though care in the community is part of modern political dogma this is invisible work, by invisible people whose income and quality of life are adversely affected by the caring they provide. There is no spare cash, no spare time and no spare energy.

The precarious financial situation in which many women find themselves is made all the more striking when set against the increasing value of net wealth held by individuals in the UK which rose from £740 billion in 1981 to £2,300 billion in 1992.[15] Although it is hardly surprising that this wealth is not spread evenly amongst the population, the extent of the inequality is startling. The wealthiest 10 per cent own 50 per cent of marketable wealth, while the wealthiest 50 per cent own 92 per cent.[16] Moreover, the widening gulf between rich and poor was one of the hallmarks of the 80s:[17] since 1979 the richest 10 per cent have become 60 per cent richer and the poorest 20 per cent are no better off. The number living below the European poverty line (half average income) in this country has risen from 5 million in 1979 to 13.9 million - a quarter of the population - in 1991-2. Nearly a third of all children are said to live in poverty and since women tend to have sole or shared responsibility for dependent children this underlines women's presence amongst the poor. Indeed, the proportion of lone parents below the poverty line has risen in the same period from 19 to 59 per cent.[18]

Although figures suggest that "wealth" has increased, albeit unequally, this is only part of the story since it is also necessary to consider the amount of money that is available for spending, and which is referred to as disposable income. By and large this has been rising for the last twenty years or so and it is 80 per cent higher now than in 1971.[19] Statistics are, of course, a dangerous weapon and it is always possible to argue that another set of figures compiled in a different way or looking at different issues will suggest a quite different result. On the other hand, there are some obvious consequences even from complex figures. First, since the largest source of household income is derived from earnings from employment, it is clear that a woman's low pay will have an adverse impact on the amount of money she will have available to her independently and that women's wealth would be augmented by easier access to better paid jobs. Second, as the next most important source of income is social security benefits, the eligibility rules and level of payments are of particular significance to women, who are likely to be recipients of such benefits.[20]   Third, a good deal of the increase in marketable wealth noted above is tied up in houses - in 1992 a third of all personal wealth was in dwellings[21] - but this does not necessarily benefit women directly. A vital difference between owner-occupiers (even with mortgages) and tenants is that the property represents not only somewhere to live but also the largest financial asset. There has been a steady increase in the number of owner-occupiers which has been accompanied by a decrease in the numbers renting from local authorities, particularly during the 1980's with the sale of council houses.[22]   Irrespective of opinions on the desirability of a home-owning population and the depletion of public sector housing, it is significant in the context of women's wealth that, when tenure is broken down according to sex, it appears from the General Household Survey that, of those surveyed, 50 per cent of the men were owner-occupiers with mortgages, as compared with only 19 per cent of the women. Conversely, only 16 per cent of men surveyed were tenants of public sector housing, whereas 36 per cent of the women fell into that category.[23]

This brings the discussion back to the initial contention that wealth is best defined in terms of access to independence - the ability to live within one's community without being dependent on another person or institution. As Lewis and Piachaud illustrate in their essay "Women and poverty in the twentieth century"[24] women's dependency is not new and they have long been dependent on family, labour market and state. As they point out, these interlock in that a woman's participation in the labour market is often affected by her family status (the presence of dependent children or other dependent relatives), while dependence on social security reinforces her dependency within the family, since the system generally presumes that a woman within a family unit is dependent on her partner. Each aspect of a woman's existence serves to reinforce and validate these different dependencies. Women with children find it harder to take full-time work and thus accept lower status and lower paid part-time jobs. Employers see in women a cheap and disposable labour force and the work that women do, even full-time, in a labour market which stubbornly retains gender segregation attracts less favourable rates of pay, simply because it is classed as women's work. Women's lower wages mean they need to supplement their income either by relying on another wage earner, or on the state. Women who have had breaks for child care and are in low paid or temporary or casual work tend, however, not to have the complete contribution records which would bring them higher benefits. Of course, it is not simply the presence of children that affects women's access to wealth. Entry to well paid employment often depends on qualifications and training and it remains the case that men are more likely than women to hold qualifications and they are, at least for now, also more likely to be better qualified. The numbers of women entering higher education are, however, increasing. Lewis[25] records that the number of female first year university students more than doubled between 1965 and 1981 from 15,000 to 33,000. The corresponding figures for men were 38,000 and 50,000. These increased rates of female participation in higher education are reflected throughout Europe. Not surprisingly, those with higher qualifications tend to be higher paid but, significantly, women with the same level of qualifications as men earn less.[26] This may be attributed to the fact that women tend still not to opt for science and engineering subjects but to study social sciences or the arts, which lead, generally, to less well paid careers in the "caring" professions. Those women who do enter the professions seen traditionally as "male" having qualified, for example, as lawyers, doctors or accountants, do not necessarily compete on equal terms because of stereotypical perceptions about women's priorities which can mean that they find themselves on what is known in the USA as the "mommy track."

In many ways, it is clear that women are far freer than they have ever been. Marriage is no longer seen as an economic necessity and women are theoretically free to choose to support themselves and their children without the assistance of a man (though this will not meet with approval from politicians and those who support the traditional family). They are legally entitled to equal treatment at work and in public services. Few avenues are now closed to them simply because of their sex. But this kind of formal equality has no meaning at all if women are unable to enjoy the kind of substantive equality which is gained only through equal participation in society. It is meaningless to state that a woman may apply for a mortgage, join pension schemes, invest on the stock market and live as an "economic man" if the vast majority are unable to earn enough to make such choices realistic, but - even more importantly - it also wrong to aim for such an objective if most women find that their lives do not fit that pattern and their inclinations do not lead them in that direction. Women need access to wealth in ways which reflect the realities of their lives and take account of their needs. It is no use arguing for a model of equal access if that entails women foreswearing motherhood on the basis that dependent children are the root of their problems. It is pointless to argue simply for an increase in women's wages if the gendered nature of the labour market is not also addressed. Paying women the same as men for the same work is not sufficient if work done predominantly by women continues to be undervalued. This in turn raises the question of the education offered to girls and young women since women must be qualified for the jobs which bring greater respect and greater wages. Even then it is futile to argue for the greater participation of women in paid employment if that simply has the effect that all women carry the double burden of paid work outside and unpaid work inside the home.   The home remains the seat of some of the most serious, if hidden, inequalities. The unequal division of labour within the home attests to the tenacity of traditional views as to gender-roles but it also discloses the way in which women's contributions to the domestic economy are still viewed as secondary.

The life patterns which are currently typical of women still tend towards poverty rather than wealth. Although this is true for the majority of women, each will experience it differently depending on their particular situation - married or single, with or without children, responsible for family members who are unable to work or entirely free of such commitments. Women who conform most closely to the male stereotype are more likely to prosper, so that women who work in male dominated, higher paid jobs, who do not take lengthy breaks for child care, who pay into an occupational pension, who are free to move for promotion and training may well experience wealth in the same way as their male colleagues. There are, however, still far fewer women than men who fit this model and it is highly questionable whether the way forward for women is to force them into the male pattern in order to achieve equality. What women need is a rethinking of the distribution of wealth within the family and within the state to enable them to benefit in ways which are geared to *their* patterns of life. In his study of women's incomes[27] Webb concludes on a comparatively up-beat note, stating that the prospects for women's incomes during the 1990s are relatively bright but, crucially, he also comments that the pattern varies considerably between different groups of women.   Women's increased participation in the labour market means that statistically their access to independent income has improved - so much so, indeed, that whereas in 1971 only £1 in every £4 going into a private household went into the hands of a woman, that had risen to £1 in every £3 by 1991.[28] This is naturally encouraging, since independent income is the cornerstone of independent wealth. It is, however, important not to underestimate the continuing difficulties faced by women in gaining access to employment. Research repeatedly shows that the presence of young children hinders full-time employment and even if part-time employment were paid proportionately to full-time work (which it is not), it is by definition not as well-paid. Another hindrance to the employment of women is the increased unemployment amongst men. As will be seen in Chapter 4, the workings of the social security system have a dampening effect on the likelihood of an unemployed man's wife or partner seeking employment. A further factor which discourages employment amongst women is the role of carer which is increasingly being assumed by the community in the shift from state provision and by women within that community.

These restrictions on women's participation in paid employment are, however, as Webb points out, largely supply-side constraints, and not dependent on the demands of employers. In other words, participation rates for women with children and other dependents including those with unemployed partners could be improved if there was provision for child and elder care and if the benefits system were less punitive on a partner's income. Even these improvements would not affect all women, since those now of pensionable age are least likely to benefit from changes in the labour market. For the future, however, increasing access for women to independent income would also have advantages for pensioners since it would tend to improve not only their pension rights during retirement but also their chances of accumulating independent property rights during their working lives.

This book does not argue for a way forward in which self and selfishness dominate and in which women should cease to form relationships with men or to care for children and others. Arguments calling for economic and social independence do not eschew the notion of social responsibility, nor do they signal a rejection of the mutual support system which the family ideally provides. But there can be no equality amongst adult citizens whilst some are involuntarily dependent on others. The emancipation of women is incomplete while they do not enjoy the fruits of full citizenship. This book is not about poverty, nor is it about a world in which women will become more like men, or cease to like men. It is an examination of why, as we approach the twenty-first century, women are not men's economic equals. It is an exploration of the role that the law has to play in a world where women's wages are not equal; where women are not filling top jobs; where women are markedly poorer after divorce; where they do not benefit to the same extent as men from pension schemes; where facilities for child care are a low priority and where the move to community care is not backed by adequate support and funding. This is not a plea for women to be made rich but for women to be made independent actors in a fairer world.

The importance of law

It is plainly untrue and a disservice to numerous successful women to try to claim that all women are, by virtue of their sex, financially disadvantaged. Nevertheless, while some enjoy a standard of living higher than that of a great many men[29] many others are still economically dependent, and what needs to be explored is *why* women generally are at a disadvantage as compared with men. The disparity could be viewed from any one of a number of perspectives,[30] but the focus of this book is the extent to which the law contributes to the continuing economic imbalance between men and women and the degree to which it might be instrumental in correcting it. The whole problem of financial inequality between the sexes appears to some as a complex social phenomenon with the law playing, at most, a peripheral role. Law is often conceived of as a neutral force within society, reacting to events rather than shaping them. If this is so, it begs the question as to why so many women, both in the past and today, regard law as the key to securing change.[31]

Feminists are very aware of the power of the law, attributing to it a significant, if not necessarily positive, function within society. In *Feminism and the Power of Law*,[32] Smart acknowledges the potency of the law to define and exclude women's experiences. She counsels caution, advising women to "avoid the siren call of law"[33] and to resort instead to alternative strategies in order to further their cause. MacKinnon, for her part, in *Toward a Feminist Theory of the State*, accepts the need to recognise "the power of the state and the consciousness- and legitimacy-conferring power of law as political realities that women ignore at their peril."[34] At the very least, therefore, the law clearly "influences the world as well as responding to it."[35]

The argument advanced in *this* book is that the law has had a significant part to play in creating and promoting economic inequality between the sexes. To determine the extent of the law's influence, it is necessary to examine the current legal ordering of the relationship between women and wealth and to extrapolate from an analysis of individual rules the basis on which the law denies women access to wealth. To understand the present state of the law, however, it is important to appreciate how, historically, the law treated women, since the past still influences modern law. Chapter 2 looks in more detail at the making of the laws regulating women's access to wealth, but there are certain fundamental features of that history which inevitably influence the analysis in subsequent chapters.

First, the nature of the legal system itself has had an important influence on the way laws have developed. Crucially, until the beginning of this century, while male lawyers, judges and legislators determined the property rights of both women and men via legislation and litigation, women were excluded from policy and decision-making processes. Laws openly and systematically discriminated against women by denying them political rights, public office and access to public life except on the terms dictated by men. This clearly worked to men's advantage and effectively denied women any public persona. Hence it could be said of women that "... public functions they have none. In the camp, at the council board, on the bench, in the jury box there is no place for them."[36] By denying women direct access to the policy and decision-making processes men were free to shape laws and legal institutions in ways that satisfied their needs and reflected their lives. At the same time, women were legally defined according to men's perceptions of their role in society, rather than in ways which corresponded with women's aspirations. It is in this sense that feminists have argued that the law views women as men view women.[37] Men's domination of the law-making process from the eleventh to the twentieth century makes this inevitable. Nor can this domination be eradicated in a few decades of formal equality.

Men's control of the law did not extend to denying women access to the courts. Women could and did appear as litigants, though they enjoyed only a limited success in forcing a male judiciary to take account of female experiences. Any concessions they were able to extract, such as equity's concept of a married woman's separate estate, posed no fundamental threat to the status quo. The alternative strategy for women was to operate outside the law. If the law imposed disabilities on married women, the solution was for women to refuse to marry in order to avoid them.[38] Resort to extremes did not, however, solve the problem of women's exclusion from the law-making process. Indeed the campaign for female suffrage was an acknowledgement of how vital it is for women to participate in the political process. The irony is that women's success in securing equal political rights has not meant that women now play an equal part in the decision-making process. In both Parliament and the judiciary women remain under-represented with only 9 per cent of M.P.s and 4.6 per cent of judges.[39]

A further general point is that the acquisition and disposal of wealth whether by individuals, institutions or the state has always been the subject of regulation. The law is an essential aspect of that regulation though legally the term "wealth" is meaningless. In the eyes of the law the key term is property. This can take many forms - personal and real, tangible and intangible - and over the centuries new and more sophisticated forms, such as intellectual property, have developed in response to the increasing sophistication of society. Land and other tangible property, such as precious metals, have ceased to be the only basis for the accumulation of wealth by individuals. Today's aspiring millionaire may just as well aim to head a multinational company or a recently privatised public utility, with "perks" such as share options, as speculate in land. As Glendon points out in *The New Family and the New Property*,[40] for many individuals it is their employment or their entitlement to state benefits that constitute their claim to wealth in present-day society:

> In a seminal review article ... [Charles] Reich suggested in 1964 that, for most people, their employment or profession, and work-related benefits such as pensions, have come to be the principal forms of wealth, and that, for many others, claims against government are the main source of subsistence.[41]

Property in this less traditional sense is also legally regulated, but not in the ways and perhaps not to the extent associated with the "old property". The overall purpose of the law regulating "old property" is to determine who has control over it and can, therefore, legitimately deal with it or dispose of it. It specifies who can own property and whether there are any individuals or organisations who cannot. It identifies what interests may be created in property, since a piece of land, for example, may be owned by one individual, leased to another and be used as security for a loan from a third party. Finally, the law indicates what happens when some event befalls the owner of property; for example she dies, is declared bankrupt, divorces or lacks mental capacity.

Although employment, employment-related benefits and social security benefits are equally susceptible to legal regulation, the purpose of that regulation is rather different. It is not possible to acquire a job in the same manner in which one would a house. Employers hire and fire their workers and, by and large, employees cannot dictate where and for whom they will work. Employment law thus concentrates on regulating the relationship between two individuals, the employer and the employee.[42] The existence and extent of employment-related benefits are largely dependent on the employer. Employees cannot, for example, insist that their employer provide them with an occupational pension. In the case of social security benefits, the law again concentrates on regulating the relationship between the benefit-provider (the state) and the claimant, since the major purpose of the law is to determine who is entitled to benefits, and in what circumstances.

Whichever type of wealth is involved the practical consequences for women of that regulation were and still are far-reaching. Historically, the status accorded to women in the public sphere was determined by men so that it was perhaps inevitable that until comparatively recently women's access to wealth would be limited and priority would be given to men. Even so a balance had to be struck between preserving for men their priority in the public sphere, while at the same time allowing women sufficient access to wealth to ensure that they did not become a burden upon the public authorities. This was achieved by defining women's relationship with property primarily in terms of their relationships with men. A man had certain legal rights by virtue of the fact that he was a man, including the right to acquire and dispose of property. In contrast, the law did not so much concern itself with women, but with their status. Once a woman married, she lost her legal identity and with it her ability to deal as she wished with any property she owned. On marriage, control over his wife's property passed to her husband who was able in certain circumstances to dispose of it as he wished. There were ways of avoiding this assumption of control by the husband, such as the creation of a trust but even this device, though it prevented an unscrupulous husband from squandering his wife's fortune, did not necessarily place the control of her property in her hands. The inability of married women to deal directly with their own property was finally removed only with the passing of the Married Women's Property Acts[43] in the late nineteenth century.

Though a woman's loss of identity might seem to be a good reason for remaining single, there were financial pressures dictating otherwise and for many women marriage was more a question of necessity rather than choice. If a woman was from a wealthy family, she was expected to marry in order that her wealth could be used in forming alliances between her family and other wealthy families.[44] If, however, a woman was poorly provided for, then marriage was the way to ensure her future economic survival. On marriage a husband became responsible in law for his wife and his wife was regarded as dependent on him.[45] In the minds of some contemporary lawyers a married woman's loss of control over her financial affairs and her assumption of dependence on her husband was represented as being for her "protection and benefit."[46] It would, however, be more accurate to see marriage in the nature of an economic bargain sanctioned by law. The "price" extracted for a husband's domination and his wife's dependency was the state's expectation that a man would support his wife and children.[47]

The fact that married women could look to their husbands for financial support meant that when other forms of wealth began to develop in the nineteenth and twentieth century (and in the case of the Poor Law before that date) a woman's access to these "new" forms of property was restricted (whether she herself was married or single) by the concept of a wife's dependency on her husband. Even though legal regulation might focus on the relationship between employer-employee or benefit provider-recipient, it was still influenced by the same assumptions about the relative status of men and women which had informed its regulation of the old property. A woman was paid on the basis that she, unlike a man, did not have a family to support.[48] Social insurance systems were, in the main, inaccessible to women.[49] Women's desire to obtain greater access to the public sphere was rejected by the courts. The very fact that women had not sought entry to the universities or practised as lawyers or participated in public life to any great degree was translated by the courts into a legal prohibition on such activities.[50] The courts used the fact that a woman might marry and society's constant urging of this role upon her as factors disqualifying her legally and intellectually from pursuing other avenues. This too worked to women's financial disadvantage. Well-paid jobs in medicine and the law which relied on access to training or higher education were not available to them. Neither were they able to make their views heard directly in the decision-making process and thus secure laws that worked to women's advantage.

By the start of the twentieth century men's control of the machinery of law-making had allowed them to erect barriers which effectively restricted women's access to wealth. This had been achieved in a variety of ways, but primarily by the emphasis placed by the law on a married woman's dependency. When a woman had access to property, whether it was "old property" or "new property," the law gave her husband control over it. If she were propertyless, the Poor Law (the historical precursor of the welfare state) expected her husband to support her. The 1834 Report on the working of the Poor Law and the legislation which followed it, condemned and outlawed relief to able-bodied men. In so doing it embodied a particular assumption regarding the economic relationship between husband and wife:

The practice of the exclusion of able-bodied males, wives, and children from relief after 1834 thus followed the Malthusian assumption that the natural order of things required that the labourer should support himself, his spouse, and their children. Through the proscription of relief to this group, the poor law defines the family unit as a *natural* sphere of private economic responsibility which makes children and wives dependants of the male wage-labourer.[51]

Those women who, for whatever reason, had no man to support them had either to support themselves or look to the public authorities for help. In these circumstances also, men asserted their economic dominance, albeit less directly. If a woman earned her own living by entering paid employment she would find her earnings were adversely affected by her *potential* to marry. Her wages would be lower than those of a a male worker because he was assumed to need more as being, potentially, a "family breadwinner."[52] Her freedom to work when she liked, where she liked was also legally regulated in the interests of her future role as wife and mother.[53] If a single woman found herself without resources and turned to the public authorities for help, she might receive assistance provided her behaviour corresponded with that of a "respectable" woman:

> Through the poor law, the liberal state would assume responsibility for families on the condition they were fatherless or that the male breadwinner was infirm. Within the fatherless category, moreover, it is only widows and their children who are regularly included within out-relief while the disreputable single or separated mother is consigned to the less-eligible disciplinary regime of the workhouse.[54]

The power which the law gave to men was, inevitably, abused by some who, ignoring their supposed role as breadwinners, would squander their wives' income on their own pleasures. An all-male Parliament was induced to pass legislation giving married women the power "of acquiring, holding, and disposing by will or otherwise, of any real or personal property as her separate property, in the same manner as if she were a femme sole, without the intervention of any trustee."[55] The apparently radical philosophy behind such legislation, allowing a woman to maintain control of any property that she owned at the time of marriage or acquired subsequently, seems totally at odds with the idea of dependency that was so fundamental to the legal perception of marriage. Indeed, opponents of the legislation claimed that it would "make the woman, instead of a kind and loving wife, a domestic tyrant."[56] It is possible that Members were affected by the many pathetic tales of women stripped of their savings by errant husbands highlighted by the campaigners for legal reform:

A woman whose husband had failed in business set up a fashionable millinery establishment with the aid of friends. So successful was the venture that she made a considerable fortune and retired from business to live on the proceeds of her savings. Meanwhile her husband did not work, and she supported him. When he died, he left a will bequeathing her property to his illegitimate children, so that she was left penniless and had to become a milliner again.[57]

On the other hand, it is perhaps more likely that Parliament was persuaded less by sympathy than by the fact that the measure was not as radical as its opponents feared since it did little to advance the financial independence of women. It did not allow a woman a share as of right in her husband's property but merely permitted her to keep what was hers and did so by emphasising women's weakness and susceptibility. It did not address the argument that the care that women devoted to their husbands and their children entitled them to a share in family assets. This is not surprising, as the women who campaigned for the measure were responding to a particular problem. To them, the right of a wife to deal with her own property represented independence from the "slavery" of marriage; regrettably, it did not offer women financial independence, simply the freedom to deal with whatever resources to which they might have access.

For all their flaws, however, there is a sense in which the Married Women's Property Acts represent the start of a considerable process of legislative reform in response to women's changing position in society. Throughout the twentieth century increasing numbers of women have entered paid employment and more recently have continued to work after their marriage and after the birth of children. A consequence of this growing participation in the public sphere of work has been women's gradual acquisition of equal rights with men in the public sphere at least in a formal sense. Even though women are not rewarded equally for the work which they do, employment outside the home has given women a taste of financial independence and has thus challenged the notion of dependency that has become such a fundamental feature of the legal perception of the relationship between men and women.

Of equal significance for women's economic well-being has been the evolution in this century of the welfare state which, in theory, makes it possible for a woman to survive financially without having to turn to a man for support. Regrettably, the promise that the welfare state held out for women has not materialised. To a large extent, it has simply allowed women to substitute the tyranny of financial dependency on a man for dependency on the state, though many have seen this as a price they are willing to pay in order to escape an unsatisfactory relationship.

The law on trial

In arguing against dependency, this book is calling for the right of every woman, regardless of marital status, to participate in society as she would wish.   The achievement of this goal depends in some measure on recognising the part that law has played in perpetuating the financial inequality of women.   In order to understand the role of the law, subsequent chapters aim to avoid an over-concentration on the technical analysis of individual rules, which can result in no more than a list of the ways in which the law treats women unfairly.   On the other hand, there are equal dangers in treating the law as a single undifferentiated force which merely institutionalises the sexual power which men wield over women, and forces women to comply with male standards.[58] This neglects the diversity of legal rules and ignores the variety of pressures which have led to the present content of the modern law.   In steering a way between these two approaches, the aim has been to explore the practical consequences of rules which are created and enforced by a largely male legislature and judiciary.   This is not intended as a detailed handbook of the law, though it does focus on some of the specific ways in which women are failed by the laws regulating property, in the widest sense of that term.

When considering the extent of the inequality experienced by women, it quickly becomes apparent that while the law has to some extent been prepared (or forced) to accommodate changing perceptions of a woman, this legal redefinition is limited and has not been extended in any real sense to the family.   In particular, it has not eradicated the persistent and negative idea of a woman's dependency.   Although statistics show plainly that marriage or co-habitation may not last for life, the law is reluctant to relinquish the perception of a woman as existing within a life-long partnership in which she looks to her partner for support.   The law's attachment to this stereotype has ramifications in all spheres of a woman's life.   It affects not only women who are married or co-habiting but also single women: if women's pay, for example, is depressed by the persistent attitude that women's earnings are secondary to those of a male breadwinner, this has adverse consequences for all working women.

In assessing how far the law is instrumental in women's continuing inequality, there are three particularly pertinent questions.   First, does the law recognise the equal need of both men and women for equal access to property in the form of paid employment?   To do so, the law must be constructed by legislators so that it accommodates the different demands made upon women as compared with men.   In a number of European countries, for example, changes to the law have allowed greater access to paid employment for both sexes, by taking account of the demands that child care makes on women. The European Commission Childcare Network reported that a substantial number of EU countries - the United Kingdom being a notable exception - make provision for parental leave and some degree of publicly funded child care. The Nordic countries have one of the best developed systems of child care which emphasises the involvement of both parents in caring and Haavio-Mannila and Kauppinen's assessment of the welfare state in these countries concludes:

> The higher the proportion of GNP devoted to social security expenditure, the more equal the incomes of men and women in a country. Women's economic equality with men is both a cause and a consequence of the welfare state.[59]

Imposing obligations on employers and public authorities to provide for proper child care and to take account of family responsibilities is one example of how the law could improve access to employment for women. Since not all women, or men, would wish to relinquish care of their children, a parallel improvement would be to reward financially those who perform the caring tasks which are currently unpaid.

The second question concerns the legal structure of the welfare state. It is important to examine how far, if at all, the state's social insurance system takes account of women's life patterns and the responsibilities which they assume for others, their increased participation in the labour market, their dual role as workers and mothers, and their right to be treated as independent within a relationship. Thirdly and finally, there is the question of whether the laws governing marriage and co-habitation reflect on a formal level the equality which partners generally express and sometimes practise on a personal level. The answer to this requires an investigation into how the law deals with property accumulated during the relationship and in particular, given the distribution of property, what rights a woman may have to a share of that property both during the relationship, and when it ends whether by death or separation.

The intention, therefore, is to compare the way women are perceived, and thus regulated, by the law (and the law-makers) with women's actual lives and their current situation in society. If it should appear that the reality of women's lives is not reflected in the laws which regulate them, this would be a key factor in explaining women's financial inequality.

Notes

1. See especially Webb, S. (1993), 'Women's Incomes: Past, Present and Prospects', *Fiscal Studies*, vol. 14, no. 4, pp. 14-36.

2. For evidence to the contrary see, e.g., Oppenheim, C. (1993), *Poverty: The Facts*.

3. Mack, J. and Lansley, S. (1985), *Poor Britain*, (up-dated in the series *Breadline Britain -*

1990s, London Weekend Television, 1991). In 1972, for example, 66 per cent of households surveyed had a washing machine, but 88 per cent had one in 1992: (1994), *General Household Survey, 1992*.

4.   '1994 New Earnings Survey (NES) Part A' reported in (1994) *Equal Opportunities Review*, 58, p. 33.   Comparison of male and female earnings is difficult because of factors such as levels of qualifications, years spent in work, occupational segregation etc. Hourly rates at least allow for differences in patterns of working time. The figures quoted also hide differences between manual and non-manual workers: the latter earned only 68 per cent of male rates.

5.   Ibid.

6.   In Ireland the corresponding figure was 68 per cent. The narrowest gap was in Italy, where women manual workers earned almost 83 per cent of the wages of male colleagues: European Commission's Memorandum on Equal Pay for Work of Equal Value, cited in (1994), *Equal Opportunities Review*, 57, p. 3.

7.   Kessler-Harris, A. (1990), *A Woman's Wage: Historical Meanings and Social Consequences*, p. 3.

8.   Kahne, H. and Giele, J.Z. (1992), *Women's Work and Women's Lives: The Continuing Struggle Worldwide*.

9.   Esam, P. and Berthoud, R. (1992), *Independent Benefits for Men and Women: An enquiry into treating husbands and wives as separate units in the assessment of social security*.

10.   See the figures at p. 60 and at p. 110. See also, for a recent overview, Haskey, J. (1994), *Population Trends* 78, Winter, p. 5.

11.   Joshi, H. (1992), 'The Cost of Caring', in Glendinning C. and Millar, J. (eds), *Women and Poverty in Britain: the 1990s*.

12.   Kempson, E. et al (1994), *Hard Times: How poor families make ends meet*.

13.   For example, Millar, J. (1992), 'Lone mothers and poverty' in Glendinning, C. and Millar, J. (eds), *Women and Poverty in Britain: the 1990s*.

14.   See Chap. 4 and (1994) *Employment Gazette* 102, No. 9, LFS4. See also Parker, G. (1992), 'Counting Care: numbers and types of informal carers', in Twigg, J. (ed.), *Carers, Research and Practice*.

15.   (1994), *Social Trends* 24, HMSO, Table 5.22, p. 78.

16.   Ibid., Table 5.23, p. 78.

17.   (1994), *Households below Average Income: A Statistical Analysis 1979 to 1991-92*.

18.   Ibid.

19.   Op. cit., n. 15, Table 5.2. Low disposable income does not necessarily indicate poverty as families with middle incomes and large mortgages may have low disposable income but still have savings and consumer durables and may obtain credit on basis of their wealth: Townsend, P. and Gordon D. 'Let Them Eat Cake', *The new review, No 4*. This says nothing, however, about distribution within the household.

20.   Especially lone parents and pensioners: op. cit., n. 1, Table 2, at p. 19.

21.   Op. cit., n. 15, Table 5.22: figure refers to value net of mortgage debt. This has gone down

recently because of the fall in house prices.

22.   (1994), *General Household Survey, 1992*, Table 10.1, p. 132.

23.   Ibid., Table 10.8.

24.   In Glendinning, C. and Millar, J. (eds), (1992), *Women and Poverty in Britain: the 1990s*, p. 27.

25.   Lewis, J., (1992), *Women in Britain since 1945*. Evidence that girls do better in school than boys led the Secretary of State for Education to call for an examination of how the system is "failing" boys: *The Independent*, 10 November 1994.

26.   (1994), *General Household Survey, 1992*, Tables 8.2 and 8.6. Average gross weekly pay of female medical practitioners was £641 in April 1994 but comparable male doctors earned £147 more: '1994 New Earnings Survey (NES) Part A' reported in (1994) *Equal Opportunities Review*, 58, p. 33.

27.   Webb, op. cit., n. 1.

28.   Ibid.

29.   Hansard Society (1990), *The Report on Women at the Top*.

30.   Women's economic inequality could, for example, be explored in terms of Marxist or socialist-feminist economic theory. See Engels, F. *Origin of the Family, Private Property, and the State* described by Catherine MacKinnon as "the seminal Marxist attempt to understand and explain women's subordination," (1989), *Toward a Feminist Theory of the State*, p. 19.

31.   Campaigns for changes in the law have been a common feature of the women's movement from the nineteenth century onwards. Holcombe, L. (1983), *Wives and Property*, describes the struggle for the reform of laws relating to married women's property. The Equal Opportunities Commission is a contemporary example of a body that sees the law as capable of securing desirable changes for women.

32.   Smart, C. (1989).

33.   Ibid., p. 160.

34.   MacKinnon, op. cit., n. 30, p. xiii.

35.   O'Donovan, K. (1985), *Sexual Divisions in Law*, p. 19.

36.   Pollock, F. and Maitland, F.W. (1968), *History of English Law Before the Time of Edward 1*, Vol. 1, p. 485, quoted in Scutt, J.A. (1990), *Women and the Law*, p. 2.

37.   MacKinnon, op. cit., n. 30, Chap. 8.

38.   O'Donovan, op. cit., n. 35, pp. 42-50.

39.   There are no women judges in the House of Lords and only one in the Court of Appeal: (1994) 'Judged on Merit?' *Labour Research*, October, p. 10.

40.   Glendon, M.A. (1981).

41.   Ibid., p. 3.

42.   Only comparatively recently has the law recognised what might be described as an employee's proprietary right in her or his job: see e.g. redundancy pay provisions in Employment Protection (Consolidation) Act 1978.

43.   Married Women's Property Acts 1870, 1882.

44.   Stone, L. (1977), *The family, sex and marriage in England, 1500-1800*.

45.   Holcombe, op. cit., n. 31, Chap. 2.

46.   Blackstone (1765), *Commentaries on the Law of England*.

47.   The poor law authorities were always eager to secure the marriage of lone unmarried mothers as a way of removing the necessity to support them.

48.   Kessler-Harris, op. cit., n. 7, Chap. 1.

49.   Thane, P. (1982), *Foundations of the Welfare State*, pp. 28-30.

50.   *Bebb v Law Society* [1914] 1 Ch 287.

51.   Dean, M. (1991), *The Constitution of Poverty*, p. 171.

52.   Kessler-Harris, op. cit., n. 7.

53.   Mines Regulation Act 1842; Ten Hours Act 1844.

54.   Dean, op. cit., n. 51, p. 171.

55.   Married Women's Property Act 1882, section 1(1).

56.   Holcombe, op. cit., n. 31.

57.   Ibid., p. 66.

58.   MacKinnon, op. cit., n. 30.

59.   Haavio-Mannila, E. and Kauppinen, K. (1992), 'Women and the Welfare State in the Nordic Countries', in Kahne and Giele, op. cit., n. 8, p. 224, at p. 245.

2   The History of Women's Property

Women's relative lack of wealth is the product of circumstances which date back centuries and in which the law played a key role. Although an historical description of the laws and legal decisions which regulated women's access to wealth will almost inevitably fail to reflect the realities of life as lived then, it does help to explain how the present situation has been reached. The legal system has not always been the highly centralised bureaucracy that it is today, nor has there always been the sheer volume of legislation that now exists. Prior to the nineteenth century there was not simply one legal and judicial system but many. Canon or church law, common law, equity and local custom would each have its own relevance to a woman's life. The two legal systems to which reference will most frequently be made in the course of this chapter are common law and equity. These were of general application and hence their rules show how, generally, women were perceived. The diversity of rules also meant, however, that there was greater opportunity for local variations in practice to occur. Examples can be found of women playing a prominent role in the community and seemingly defying the common conception of women as "second class citizens."[1] These women were, nevertheless, exceptional and their numbers declined as the legal system became more centralised and its content more uniform throughout the country. Of course, the content of legal rules cannot necessarily be assumed to reflect the daily lives of all women at that time, but there is likely to be at least some relationship between the law and the circumstances of those whom it was intended to regulate. Moreover, historical examination of the law can elicit the policy and the preconceptions which lay behind it. The fact that, for example, women were as a matter of law excluded from public office, makes an important statement about how society then regarded women. As a matter of local custom or mere uncertainty about the law, some women may have been able to defy this ban but, whilst this may underline the irrationality of such a prohibition, it does not disturb the inference that can be drawn from the ban's very existence.

Though the volume of material[2] means that this chapter can consider only a small part of the available information, even a brief survey of the history of women's access to property provides valuable insights into modern inequalities. It was suggested in the previous chapter that a key to the current financial inequality between men and women might be found in the failure of the law adequately to redefine women's place in the family and the workplace so as to reflect the roles they now play in society. In exploring this proposition, it helps to appreciate how the law dealt with women in the period when their access to public life and to wealth was restricted. Since marriage has been central in establishing women's dependency, it is logical first to consider the legal regulation of marriage and, in particular, the effect which those laws had on the ownership of property.

Marriage

Prior to 1800

Under the common law, marriage had far-reaching consequences for women's access to wealth. A married woman's position in relation to the ownership of property was considerably inferior to that of a man, whether married or single, or that of a single woman, including divorced women and widows. In the period before 1800, a woman who married lost legal control of her property, which passed instead to her husband who acquired legal rights relating both to its use and disposition. In the case of land, which lawyers call real property, a husband gained possession of all his wife's freehold property[3] which she held at the time of the marriage or acquired during its duration. He was entitled to the income arising from such property, though he was unable to dispose of the land without his wife's consent. The law went to some lengths to try to ensure that any consent was freely given[4] but it must be a matter for conjecture how well a wife could resist her husband's threats or blandishments to consent to the sale of her land.

If his wife died a husband did not automatically inherit her freehold property since ownership passed by law to his wife's heirs - namely, her children or members of her family. The law stipulated that where there was more than one surviving child, the eldest surviving son would inherit. In the absence of a surviving son, any daughters would share the property equally between them. A married woman thus faced a double indignity: under the common law she lost control of her freehold property during her lifetime and in death she fared no better since she could not stipulate who would inherit it. The power to dispose of property by will was denied to women even though it was granted to men for the first time in 1540.[5] Instead, a married woman's property would pass automatically to a surviving male heir. Although a husband did not inherit, he was entitled by law to a right of curtesy, provided certain conditions had been satisfied.[6] This allowed him to remain in possession of his wife's real property for the remainder of his life (a life interest). Should a wife survive her husband, however, ownership of her real property reverted to her.

Beside having rights over his wife's real property, a husband also enjoyed rights over her personal property, which included any goods she might own, such as jewellery, and money. His control over this property was absolute and he was free to sell it, spend it or dispose of it in his will. In the nineteenth century when it became more common for women to work and earn wages, these rights over a wife's property were to prove particularly problematic. The only exceptions to the common law rule that a husband might use his wife's personal property as he thought fit related to her clothing and certain personal ornaments, known as paraphernalia, which were not regarded as part of her husband's estate and which reverted to her ownership on his death, provided that they had not been sold while he was alive.

Apart from real and personal property, Holcombe identifies two other forms of property that a wife might possess, namely, leasehold property[7] and choses in action.[8] The latter included items such as a debt owed under a contract. Leaseholds could be disposed of by a husband during his wife's lifetime, but on his death they reverted to her and he could not bequeath them in his will. Choses in action could not be sold by a husband and, if his wife survived him, they reverted to her ownership. If, however, they were converted into personal property - for example, if the debt due under a contract was paid - then they were treated in exactly the same way as any other item of personal property.

A wife's loss of control over her property was thus virtually complete. *Why* should the law choose so to disempower married women? The conventional explanation is that in medieval times personal property was of little significance whilst the ownership of land involved important obligations, including military and political duties. It was logical, therefore, to vest control of property, particularly real property, in a man as there would then be someone capable of discharging the obligations. This is Holcombe's view:

> The possession of real property, whether land held in exchange for service to the crown or that held in return for service to the lord of the manor, entailed obligations which a woman alone was considered unable to discharge. ... It was therefore natural that the common law should recognize a woman's husband as responsible in her stead for meeting the obligations imposed by landholder, and also natural that his responsibility carried with it rights - the right to assume sole management of her

property and the right to receive and use freely all rents and profits from it.[9]

This traditional explanation for a husband's extensive powers over his wife's property has, however, been challenged. It has been pointed out, for example, that it would have been feasible to provide for the discharge of obligations associated with ownership of real property without subordinating the rights of a wife to such a disadvantageous extent.[10] There must have been occasions when a man, either because of youth or advanced age or disability, would have been unable to fulfil his obligations, but that lack of capacity did not carry the same consequences. The credibility of the notion that women's unfavourable treatment rested *simply* on their inability to perform the feudal obligations then associated with property ownership also suffers when it is realised that other more recent legal systems adopted exactly the same strategy toward married women's property. In the United States of America, for example, which based its laws on the common law but never experienced feudalism, the Seneca Falls Declaration of 1848 listed women's loss of rights over property, "even to the wages she earns" as one of the injustices perpetrated by men toward women.[11] The same was true in other countries, such as Australia, where the common law was imported together with settlers from the United Kingdom.

Possibly the law was reflecting the nature of marriage rather than a woman's ability to discharge the obligations associated with the ownership of property. Marriage was conceived of as an institution whereby husband and wife became "one flesh" in the sight of God and of the law. The public embodiment of a married couple, however, was the husband, and for the duration of the marriage "the very being or legal existence of a woman is suspended ...".[12] Furthermore, the nature of marriage was then very different. Marriage today is a relationship entered by choice and which may be dissolved should the relationship break down. In the past, it was regarded as a business transaction negotiated between families, in which the couple had little or no say in the choice of partner, and dissolution of the marriage was well-nigh impossible. Stone traces various stages in family evolution during the period 1500 to 1800[13] and he describes how, at the beginning of that period, marriage was perceived:

> Marriage was not an intimate association based on personal choice. Among the upper and middling ranks it was primarily a means of tying together two kinship groups, of obtaining collective economic advantages and securing useful political alliances. Among peasants, artisans and labourers, it was an economic necessity for partnership and division of labour in the shop or in the fields. For both men and women it was the price of economic survival, while for the latter it was the only career

available.[14]

According to Stone the nature of the family gradually changed during that period: it became an increasingly private unit in which the husband exercised power over his wife and children, although the extent of that power did decline. Couples married the partners of their choice, and "their prime motives were now long-term personal affection rather than economic or status advantage for the lineage as a whole." [15]

Even though by 1800 couples might marry for love, throughout the period described by Stone it remained the case that an unmarried woman (and this would include a widow) would find it very difficult to support herself unless she had access to a private income. Work undertaken by women generally attracted rates of pay below those earned by men.[16] Middle or upper class women had few occupations open to them other than governess or companion. Not until the nineteenth century did opportunities for employment become more freely available to women generally, although lower down the social scale women might enter domestic service or work in the factories or on the farm. Whatever her occupation, a woman without a husband was vulnerable to poverty and marriage was the key to a more comfortable way of life.[17] Even at the beginning of the twentieth century, marriage among the working classes has been described as "not so much a matter of emotional and sexual intimacy as a contract between a husband who would bring home a wage and a wife who would manage household and children."[18] Contemporary comment indicates that working class women could not afford to remain single:

> Social investigators of the Edwardian period calculated that a single woman needed 14-16 shillings a week to subsist in 1906. The average wage of female textile workers was 15/5d and of women in non-textile industries, 12/11d.[19]

Women who did not marry were forced to look to the family rather than the outside world or the state for the means of support. Even though marriage placed a woman in a legally disadvantageous position, until the start of this century (and even beyond), it was an economic necessity for many women.

The economic significance of marriage was reinforced by the legal obligation imposed on a husband to maintain his wife. Should he fail to provide her with food or clothing then, by law, she was free to pledge her husband's credit for the necessities of life. This has been described as an "inevitable consequence of the doctrine of unity of legal personality; for the wife, lacking the capacity to hold property and to contract, could neither own even the bare necessities of life nor enter into a binding agreement to buy them."[20] In other words, a husband's common law duty to maintain developed at the same time as his common law right to control his wife's property. Should a husband predecease his wife, the common law entitled her to dower, a legal concept dating back to medieval times and entitling a wife to a life interest in one third of her dead husband's freehold property. This applied not only to the freehold property that a husband owned at the time of his death but also to any freehold property that he had owned during the course of the marriage. Dower was intended, in the words of a nineteenth century commentary on the law, "for the sustenance of the wife, and the nurture and education of the younger children."[21]   The fact that a wife was automatically entitled to a share of her husband's property indicates that it was expected that a wife would be supported by her husband, or rather his estate, even after his death. At a time when state pensions were unknown this was a way of ensuring that widows did not become burdens on the state, or rather the parish.   From the seventeenth century onwards a widow also received a share in her husband's personal estate, should he die intestate.[22] Such generosity on the part of the law seems less altruistic when it is recalled that ownership of his wife's personal property passed automatically to a husband on marriage. In many cases the law was probably doing no more than belatedly allowing a wife to regain control of what had previously been hers.

The manner in which the common law regulated the economic consequences of marriage from medieval times until the nineteenth century worked to the advantage of men while consigning women to the position of a dependant. During a marriage, a wife relied on her husband's goodwill to provide her with the necessities of life. Only a total failure to feed, clothe and house her could justify action on her part and that was limited to the pledging of his credit, if she could find anyone willing to supply goods in these circumstances.[23] A married woman's right to dower was also a mixed blessing. It contrasts with a husband's right to curtesy which gave him a life interest in *all* his wife's freehold property. Far from achieving economic parity between husband and wife, dower seemed principally to be designed to prevent widows becoming a charge on the public authorities.[24] An additional disadvantage was the fact that not all women could claim dower. First, the right existed only in relation to freehold property. If a husband did not own freehold land - and only the financially better-off would do so - a widow's right to dower was an empty one. Should a husband own copyhold land, that is land held according to the custom of a particular manor or locality, the custom of that place dictated whether there was a right to dower, or free bench as it was more correctly known, and the nature of that right.[25] There was in these cases the added problem that a husband might dispose of his copyhold land in the course of the marriage and if he did so, the right to dower would not arise. This contrasts with the position in relation to freehold property where the right still applied even if the land had been sold.[26] Finally, even where a widow was entitled to dower, it was not unknown for the heir to the property to deny her that right.[27]

Perhaps the most serious threat to a widow's right to dower came from schemes specifically devised to avoid conceding it to her. Some prospective husbands adopted the expedient of having property placed on trust for their benefit and, in such cases, the courts held that there could be no dower of the property in question.[28] Another means of evading dower was to enter into an agreement known as a jointure. This was seen as a substitute for dower and consisted of an agreement between husband and wife made either in anticipation of their marriage or after it had taken place. Under the terms of this agreement certain land would be held jointly by husband and wife, which might be disposed of during the course of the marriage only with the consent of both partners. On the death of either husband or wife, the surviving partner became the sole owner of the property in question. In this way a widow could be guaranteed an income after her husband's death. The value of the jointure varied but would apparently bear some relationship to the amount of property that the wife brought to the marriage.[29] In consideration of such an agreement, however, the Statute of Uses 1535 barred the wife's right to dower, provided the agreement had been concluded prior to the couple's marriage.[30] Where there was a post-nuptial settlement, then a wife could choose between jointure and dower.[31]

Contemporary opinion was that jointure offered advantages as compared with dower. The agreement between husband and wife came into operation immediately and would leave the surviving spouse as sole owner of the property in question. Since any arrangement would be negotiated between the bride's family and that of her prospective husband, this was viewed as a guarantee that a wife would be provided for fairly. Dower, on the other hand, "must be tarried for till the Husband be dead: It must be demanded, sometime sued for, sometime neither with suit or demand obtained."[32] Modern commentators, however, are less sanguine about the perceived advantages of jointure over dower. Staves, for example, draws attention to its negative aspects[33] which included the fact that there was no guarantee that the financial value of any jointure would be equivalent to any dower rights. The attempt made in the Statute of Uses to ensure that there was some degree of compatibility was, according to Staves, undermined by the courts. Jointures that terminated on a widow's remarriage or that were composed of property other than land were held to have successfully barred dower. Even if satisfactory jointure arrangements had been made, a widow might be forced to go to law in order to receive what was hers, particularly if another person held the title deeds to the land in question. Some women were also prepared to forgo their rights if this worked to the financial advantage of their children.

However inadequate, jointure was, at the very least, a substitute for dower rather than a complete evasion of the right. Like the right to dower, however, it was of use only if the prospective married couple had access to property. Jointures, dowers and settlements meant nothing to the many who had little wealth. Even so, the complex web of legal rights which regulated the property rights of wealthier married couples are a powerful indication as to the perceived nature of marriage. Although there was some legal "compensation" for a wife's loss of control of her common law property rights in the form of dower or jointure, the message conveyed by the law was one of women's inferiority to men. Moreover, the conception of what it meant to be a wife coloured the treatment of single women. It raised questions as to why women should be educated, trained for work and generally encouraged to play an active part in life when most women were destined to become legally dependent on their husbands. "In short, as feminists always argued, the law affecting married women was degrading to all women."[34]

In view of the financial uncertainty that marriage represented for women, legal expedients were developed to try to avoid the worst consequences. These devices derived not from the common law but from the courts of equity. Equity developed as a separate legal system which was designed to correct and right the injustices created by the inflexibility of the common law rules. In order to ensure that a husband did not simply use his wife's assets in whatever way he pleased, equity developed the concept of a wife's separate estate, described as "by far the most important contribution of equity to the law relating to a married woman's property."[35] The idea of a separate estate, which developed during the sixteenth century, involved the transfer of real or personal property to trustees for the separate use of a married woman. Once the trust had been created, equity recognised the right of the woman in question to deal with the property as she thought fit. A trust might be created by a bride-to-be's family or, if a widow was remarrying, she might create a trust in order to safeguard her position as well as that of any children from a previous marriage.

The creation of a wife's separate estate is regarded by some legal commentators as giving a married woman unprecedented freedom:

> Gradually, however, and quite apart from legislation, wives were placed by the courts of equity in an even more favourable position than men or unmarried women, a result that was due to the invention by the Court of Chancery of the doctrine of *equitable separate estate*.[36]

This is a somewhat exaggerated assessment of the benefits married women derived from property held on trust for their use. First, there was no guarantee that a woman would not be cajoled or threatened into surrendering such property to her husband. Secondly, any property dealt with in this manner was subject to a right of curtesy should a wife die without making a will, thus benefiting a husband.[37] This conflicted with the ruling, disadvantaging a wife, that there could be no dower of a trust.[38] Although the courts acknowledged this was anomalous, nothing tangible was done to correct it. Thirdly, a widow who created a trust before remarrying might discover that she had failed in her attempts to safeguard her position and that of her children. This would occur if she neglected to obtain her husband-to-be's consent to the trust, in which case her conduct would be regarded as fraudulent, in that it disappointed him of his expectations regarding his bride's property.

It is unclear what motivated the creation of a married woman's separate estate, since the device could be used for purposes other than maintaining a woman's financial independence. It enabled a woman's family to preserve their own interest in her property, rather than surrendering control of it to her husband and it could also be used as a means of ensuring that a woman did not have control over the property in question. To this end equity devised the "restraint upon anticipation," which effectively prevented a married woman from dealing with the property on trust as she wished, by denying her the power to dispose of anticipated income or the substance of the trust.

Post 1800

During the nineteenth century many of the legal incidents of marriage underwent change. The Dower Act 1833 abolished dower for all practical purposes by providing that a man could bar his wife's right to dower by disposing of the land during his lifetime or bequeathing it in his will.[39] With the virtual abolition of dower, a wife's automatic right to a share in her deceased husband's property disappeared. However unsatisfactory dower might have been, it did insist that a husband *had* to provide for his wife. The law now left a married man free to dispose of his property as he wished:

> By permitting a husband to extinguish his wife's right to dower, the Dower Act, 1833, abolished the last vestige of family provision in English law. After that there was nothing to stop a man (or a woman with respect to her separate property) from devising and bequeathing his whole estate to a charity or a complete stranger and leaving his widow and children penniless.[40]

Only if he died intestate would a defined share of his property pass automatically to his wife. Dower may have been intended to prevent widows becoming a burden on the public authorities, but it did nevertheless emphasise that a wife should not be left unprovided for and gave her some measure of financial independence.

The best known reform of the nineteenth century was the passing of the Married Women's Property Acts 1870 and 1882. Women mounted a sustained campaign for this legislation and succeeded only after many attempts.[41] The more important of these Acts, the Married Women's Property Act 1882, gave a married woman the freedom to acquire and dispose of real and personal property "as if she were a feme sole." No longer would her property pass automatically on marriage into the control of her husband: a married woman would now be free to deal with her property as she wished. There are various reasons why the campaign for reform proved successful when it did. The nineteenth century witnessed a gradual rise in the number of women, including married women, who engaged in paid employment. At the same time the public was disturbed by tales of husbands who deserted their wives only to reappear and seize the business assets or savings accumulated by the efforts of their wives. The nineteenth century was also the era of radical thinkers such as John Stuart Mill. Mill was an advocate of the freedom of the individual and argued convincingly for reform of the law on married women's property. Perhaps the most potent factor in favour of reform, however, was the reshaping of the judicial system which had taken place with the passing of the Judicature Act 1873. This Act had rationalised the court system in England and provided that in the event of a conflict between the common law and equity, equity was to prevail.[42] Equity had been responsible for the development of a wife's separate estate which had allowed married women some degree of autonomy over property. For many Members of Parliament, therefore, the Married Women's Property Act 1882 could be rationalised as a step in this process of fusion between the common law and equity rather than a concession to radical feminism, and Holcombe suggests that this is why the Lord Chancellor of the day, who had previously opposed reform, was willing to give it his support.[43]

The Married Women's Property Act 1882 was undoubtedly a milestone in the wider campaign for women's rights. It demonstrated that women were capable of mounting a sustained political campaign for law reform and paved the way for the struggle that was to come on women's suffrage. The Act was of benefit to wealthier women, in allowing them control of their own property though, in fact, most women with appreciable assets of their own could already enjoy this privilege by employing the equitable concept of a wife's separate estate. The Act also worked to the advantage of a woman married to a spendthrift or one deserted by her husband, as it protected her assets from his depredations. It was, however, a far from ideal measure and there were complaints at the time that the Act left many technical legal issues unresolved.[44] More important still was the philosophy behind the legislation.

Although the technical rules regulating the financial consequences of marriage were amended, the wider, continuing inequalities which women faced were not addressed. Allowing each partner to the marriage to deal with his or her assets as each saw fit was an incomplete reform, since women simply did not enjoy the same level of wealth as men. The access which women had to wealth was, with few exceptions, very restricted and meant, for most women, that they brought less to the marriage and accumulated less during it. Their wages were lower than those of men, certain types of employment were not available to them and their ability to take paid employment was severely curtailed by their family responsibilities. There was no acknowledgement by the law that a wife's contribution in remaining at home and caring for her family entitled her to a share in what her husband earned. As O'Donovan comments:

> This property regime of 'to each her own' focused on legal forms of subordination but leaves untouched questions of power and economic distribution within the family. Separate property is a realisation of formal equality but does not affect economic power within the conjugal relationship.[45]

Whilst the Married Women's Property Acts and subsequent legislation removed the most blatant formal examples of a married woman's subordinate status, the broader issues of women's dependence on men were left unaddressed. The earlier legal regime had denied married women independence and had thus subordinated them to their husbands: even after the reforms married women remained dependent. More was required than a change to to the laws regulating the distribution of property within marriage to alter this. As long as the law tolerated discrimination against women in the form of lower wages, inferior employment opportunities and in some cases automatic loss of employment on marriage, their dependency was a fact of life. Far from challenging it, the law was used to institutionalise this dependency and lend it respectability unless, as happened in the case of married women's property, women were prepared to mobilise in order to defeat such blatant discrimination.

This illustrates a simple and yet fundamental characteristic of the law. It is not merely a collection of rules which exist in a vacuum until a dispute or problem arises to which a legal solution is required. Rather, the law is a force within society which constantly shapes attitudes and behaviour. Hence the decision to change a single rule, as with married women's property, will have little impact if the legal system of which it is a part retains a different perspective on a woman's role within society and within marriage. Marriage remained, for women, a dependent relationship and the legal reforms for which women fought so hard failed to address this. Women's legal disabilities were removed but nothing was put in their place which would make marriage a more equitable relationship for women.

> The argument for greater regulation of the marital relationship is that the law, by laying down general principles, can influence attitudes and behaviour. By expressing in its content general community beliefs concerning interpersonal justice it exhorts spouses to behave with justice towards one another. Through regulation of matters such as marital property, finances, sexual conduct and behaviour, the law acknowledges

the special nature of the relationship and the value of sharing and equality. Without this legal recognition the individualistic path is clearly laid down.[46]

Since marriage could subject a woman to all manner of humiliations, not all of which were financial, many were eager to escape from the relationship. The conditions under which divorce was possible, together with its financial repercussions, provide further insights into the perception of marriage, as well as evidence as to the relative financial standing of men and women.

Divorce

Until the Matrimonial Causes Act 1857, marriage was to all intents and purposes an indissoluble union. The ecclesiastical courts might annul a marriage - that is, declare that it had never existed - or they could grant a divorce *a mensa et thoro*, which was the equivalent of a judicial separation. On the evidence of one party's adultery, cruelty or commission of an unnatural offence, the other was relieved of the duty to cohabit. This did not, however, end the marriage. A husband thus retained control over his wife's property though he would be expected to pay maintenance to his wife:

> The amount of alimony was set as a proportion of the parties' joint income if the wife had separate property in equity, or otherwise as a proportion of the husband's income, usually one-third, although it might be as much as one-half if his conduct had been especially bad or if the bulk of his fortune had come to him from his wife.[47]

There were, needless to say, problems associated with the payment of maintenance. There was no efficient procedure for the collection of arrears, payment ceased with the husband's death and a wife guilty of adultery received no financial support. A wife who obtained a divorce *a mensa et thoro* faced an uncertain financial future. The marriage was effectively, if not legally, at an end but her financial well-being depended on her husband's goodwill, which in these circumstances might be in short supply.

Prior to 1857, divorce by private Act of Parliament was the only means of dissolving, that is terminating, a marriage. The procedure required a married woman to prove that her husband had committed adultery and had aggravated his offence by incest, bigamy or the commission of an unnatural act. In contrast, a husband had merely to prove his wife's adultery. The costs, not to mention the standards of proof, associated with this process were enough to ensure that few married men and even fewer married women resorted to this procedure.[48] A Parliamentary divorce dissolved a marriage and a husband's rights in relation to his wife's property were thus terminated. The private Act of Parliament would normally make financial provision for her, even if she were the "guilty party." That financial provision was, however, unlikely to be excessively generous, in some cases representing no more than was required for a woman's survival. Its existence may well have represented the state's wish that a man who had been freed of his marriage should not also be freed of the financial burden of maintaining his former wife. The law prior to 1857 meant that dissolution of marriage was exceptional, but that it was easier for a man to obtain a divorce than it was for a woman. On those rare occasions when a divorce was granted there was no question of equal division of the couple's resources. Even though a wife was entitled to have enough to survive, "unwifely" conduct on her part could result in a financial penalty being imposed.

The rarity of divorce led to the "self-termination of marriage."[49] O'Donovan records instances of wife sales[50] and Stone suggests that desertion rather than divorce might have brought an end to some marriages:

> At the other end of the social scale, among the propertyless, there were also alternatives to death as a means of finally dissolving an unsatisfactory marriage. In a society without a national police force, it was all too easy simply to run away and never be heard of again. This must have been a not infrequent occurrence among the poor, to judge by the fact that deserted wives comprised over eight per cent of all the women aged between thirty-one and forty listed in the 1570 census of the indigent poor of the city of Norwich.[51]

Stone also suggests that bigamy was "both easy and common."[52]

The problem with these methods of "self-termination of marriage" was that, since no outside agency represented her interests, they could leave a wife destitute. Furthermore, there were men with property and business interests for whom desertion was not a viable proposition. In such circumstances, the couple might conclude a separate maintenance agreement. The purpose of such agreements was to allow the wife to be maintained whilst she and her husband lived apart. Staves comments that the courts were ambivalent in their attitude toward such agreements.[53] Their initial willingness to accept them was later undermined by arguments that they might be unfair to wives by failing to make proper provision for them or that they offered a way for a husband to defraud his creditors by settling property on his wife.[54] There may have also been the fear that such agreements tended to undermine the very institution of marriage and the power of the state. Eventually, the courts did acknowledge their validity provided they satisfied certain tests. Staves argues, however, that those tests were designed to impose restraints on women's freedom to act on their own behalf and to reassert their subordination to men.[55] For example, a separate maintenance agreement concluded by a husband with his wife would not be considered valid: instead trustees had to conclude the agreement on the wife's behalf. It is a matter for speculation whether or not such a condition prevented a wife being coerced into accepting an unsatisfactory agreement. There was no automatic guarantee that an agreement negotiated man to man would be more beneficial as far as women were concerned.

The Matrimonial Causes Act 1857 transferred jurisdiction over matrimonial matters from the ecclesiastical courts to a new Divorce and Matrimonial Causes Court which had the power to terminate a marriage. Whilst this strengthened the position of women by making divorce, that is the dissolution of marriage, a more accessible process, the rules governing that process discriminated against women. Although, for example, a husband was allowed to petition for divorce on the grounds of his wife's adultery, a wife could petition for divorce on grounds of her husband's adultery only if that were coupled with another offence such as incest or bigamy.[56] An adulterous wife was not barred from claiming maintenance under the Act but her "fault" was a factor to be taken into account.[57] In the eyes of those responsible for the 1857 Act, a woman could be expected to tolerate her husband's infidelity and much else beside before she could escape from an unhappy marriage, but a wife's infidelity gave a husband immediate cause for complaint since it could mean that his property would be inherited by a child who was not his. In other words the disparity in treatment derived from economic considerations.[58]

A number of very important principles were established by the 1857 Act, not the least being that divorce thereafter became a judicial process and marriage ceased to be seen, in law, as a union which to all intents and purposes was indissoluble except by death. On the other hand, whilst the legislation instilled the idea that spouses could escape from an unsatisfactory marriage, they could do so only at considerable personal cost, which for a woman might include losing custody of her children and social ruin. Indeed, the Act might be regarded more as a warning against the evils of adultery than an attempt to liberalise the laws regulating marriage.[59] Even the requirement for a husband to continue to support his ex-wife probably says less about a philosophy of divorce than about the desire of the state to prevent divorced wives becoming a financial burden on the state.

Since 1857 divorce has become, at least legally, a progressively easier process. Successive Acts have extended the grounds on which a divorce might be obtained and the forms of financial relief that might be granted to a wife, and indeed a husband, by the court. What has not changed, however, are the economic consequences for women. From its inception, divorce has been likely to have a more adverse effect on a woman's standard of living than that of a man. The task facing the divorce court was to determine the share of the husband's property which should be handed over to his wife and children and, in this context, the ideology of separate property introduced by the Married Women's Property Act 1882 worked against the interests of women. Opting for the doctrine of separate property rather than for a system of joint or community property meant that a wife was not automatically entitled to any share of her husband's resources, nor he of hers. In calculating what share would be proper for the divorced wife the courts could use her conduct during marriage, including her faithfulness or lack of it, as a factor. The fate of women on divorce served, in fact, to emphasise their dependency both within marriage and on its termination.

Single Women

As compared with a married woman, a single woman experienced few legal disabilities in dealing with property. She could acquire and dispose of property in the same way as a man might.[60] Until the twentieth century, of course, she had no say in shaping the legal regime that governed her, since the particular privilege of membership of the legislature or judiciary was reserved for men. For some women, the "civil death" represented by marriage was enough to persuade them to co-habit rather than marry in order to preserve their personal and financial autonomy. In spite of the *legal* advantages of being a single woman, however, the majority of women did marry since a husband was an economic necessity[61] and single women and in particular lone mothers were major recipients of poor law relief. The financial insecurity faced by single women resulted partly from the fact that the law (then as now) frequently treated a woman on the assumption that she would have a man on whom to depend and thus single women, more than single men, found that economic independence was a difficult goal. Inheritance, for example, was through the male line so that a daughter could well be overlooked. In defence of the rule which favoured the eldest son, it was said that women would have received their share of their father's estate on their marriage, since at that time they would have been given a dowry or a marriage settlement. This offered little consolation to an unmarried daughter. Even if a single woman tried to make her way in life by earning her own living she would find that she was less well placed to do so than a single man because she would find it harder to obtain employment capable of supporting her. Her wages would be lower than those of a man and less lucrative employment would be available to her. This was all in the expectation that at some stage in her life she would have a man on whom she could depend for financial support. The point is well illustrated by the laws which regulated wages and employment.

Wages

One of the reasons why women are not men's financial equals is attributable to the fact that, on average, they earn less than men. This is not a recent phenomenon but appears to have been the case since it became common to reward workers by the payment of wages. The setting of wage rates is not something about which English law makers have generally been enthusiastic. The British tradition has been, by and large, to adopt a non-interventionist approach and to leave it to negotiation between employers and employees or employers and the relevant trade unions. Quite clearly, this licence to negotiate can be abused by employers setting exceedingly low rates of pay or by employees demanding "excessive wages" at a time when labour is scare. Examples of legislation can be found, therefore, setting maximum or minimum rates of pay, though this is not as common an occurrence as it once was.[62] Apart from laws which directly affect levels of pay, legislation can also have an indirect effect on wage rates. Laws regulating the hours employees may work (perhaps for health and safety reasons) can cut pay by excluding overtime or premium payments for night or weekend work.[63] In the context of wages, therefore, the law is likely to exercise a considerable indirect influence on rates of pay depending on how the employer/employee relationship is regulated.

Legislation which has dealt directly with rates of pay has, in the past, quite openly condoned the payment of lower wages to women. In the fourteenth century a shortage of labour resulted in laws to control the rates of pay for agricultural workers[64] and these provide clear proof that women's rates of pay were lower than those of men. The Statute of Labourers 1388 states that a dairymaid, for example, was to receive 6 shillings a year, but a shepherd 10 shillings. This disparity could, of course, be attributed to the fact that men and women were not performing the same work, though both undoubtedly required certain skills and expertise on the part of those undertaking them. Atkins and Hoggett conclude, however, that the legislation "established a woman's rate regardless of occupation or degree of skill. The male rates, all higher, varied with skill. Although limited to agricultural work, this Act established the principle which affected all female wages thereafter."[65]

The idea that there was a woman's rate for a particular job persisted into the twentieth century. Even when men and women were performing the same work, women would be paid less than men. Lewis cites the 1909 example of the Trade Board for the tailoring industry setting an hourly rate of 3¼d for women and 6d for men.[66] A Trade Board (later a Wages Council) was an official body authorised by the Trade Boards Act 1909 to set legally enforceable minimum rates of pay in certain trades in order to protect the workforces in those trades and guarantee them a "living wage" in circumstances where they could not bargain effectively with the employer. For all the commendable motives behind the legislation, the Trade Boards accepted without question the notion of a "woman's rate" for a job which was markedly lower than the payment made to a man.[67]

It is not at all obvious *why* women should be paid lower rates than men, particularly if they were performing the same task as a man or one that was equally skilled. The law provides no clue to this, simply embodying what appears to be settled practice. One explanation might well be the assumption that a man would have to support a wife and family with his wage, whilst a woman would not. Certainly, trade unions actively campaigned for a family wage in the nineteenth and twentieth centuries, but women's lower rates of pay were already an established fact by this time. The pressure for a family wage, which attracted support from both men and women, seems to have been inspired by a desire to halt the employment of married women, rather than to establish appropriate rates of pay for the sexes. Married women's rightful place was seen as in the home attending to the needs of their husbands and children, whilst their presence in the workforce was believed to depress male wages.[68] Differential wage rates, however, became common at a time when married and single men were paid the same rate. According to Atkins and Hoggett, in order to survive, "married men were expected to augment their incomes with their wives' earnings from either home industry or work on the family smallholding."[69] Since a working woman might well be contributing to the family income rather than supporting herself, this might have been regarded as sufficient reason for paying her less than a man. Whatever the explanation for the disparity, it was accepted whenever the occasion arose for wages to be set by the law.

Another longstanding feature of women's work which has had a bearing on their rates of pay is the tendency, already touched upon, for them to perform different tasks from men. Bradley states that, although there were regional variations, by the nineteenth century certain agricultural tasks were commonly identified as women's work:

> In hop work, for example, men commonly set up the tall poles, while women tied the hops to them. It was considered 'that a man cannot get on' with what was described as an 'endless' fiddly job, while boys were not thought careful enough.[70]

She also refers to a phenomenon which still routinely occurs, namely that a task ordinarily performed by women may become a task performed by men if there is some technological innovation. Hence reaping, which she identifies as a job primarily carried out by women, was gradually transformed by technical advances, such as the introduction of the mechanical reaper, into a task for men.[71] The segregation of the sexes in the workplace clearly raises once again the question *why* it occurs. Various explanations have been offered, one being that men's dominance in the workplace simply reflects their dominance in the family unit. The control that men exercised when most work took place in the home was maintained when workplace and home separated.[72]   It is clear, however, that when a task was commonly performed by women the pay received for performing it would be lower than if it were performed by men. Cadbury, Matherson and Shann in their account published in 1906, *Women's Work and Wages*, relate what happened when women replaced men in the workplace:

> In the inquiry as to wages one of the outstanding facts elicited was, that whenever women had replaced men the former always received a much lower wage, and that this wage was not proportionate to the skill or intelligence required by the work but approximated to a certain fixed level - about 10s. to 12s. a week. The wage that the man previously received gave no criterion as to what the woman would get, though as a general statement, approximately correct, we may say that a woman would get from one-third to one-half the wages of a man.[73]

To this extent, therefore, job segregation is simply an aspect of the notion of a woman's rate for a job.

The role played by the law in relation to the whole question of job segregation seems peripheral. The idea that women would not be engaged in the same work as men seems to have been accepted as a fact of life and indeed as perfectly natural, if contemporary comments are any guide.[74]   The law simply acknowledged established practice when setting rates of pay. When presented, however, with the opportunity to affirm that employment should be open to both men and women the law makers persistently declined the invitation. In the nineteenth century women began to press for entry to the professions - in particular law and medicine. In the case of medicine this was an attempt to gain readmission to an occupation from which women had been excluded, having been assigned instead to the subsidiary role of doctor's helper, or nurse.[75]   During the course of protracted litigation to gain entry to university in order to train as doctors and to be admitted as solicitors the courts constantly denied women's claims. Relevant statutes which employed gender neutral terms such as "person" were interpreted so as not to include women. The judges justified this by regarding the absence of women in the profession as proof that they were disqualified from entering it. The possibility of women marrying was cited, in the case of entry to the legal profession, as an additional obstacle since married women were unable in certain circumstances to enter into binding contracts.[76]   Most damaging of all, however, was the attack made by some, though by no means all, members of the judiciary, on women's ability to engage in certain activities. Lord Neaves, for example, quoted women's inherent differences as one of his reasons for declaring as illegal Edinburgh University's decision to admit women students:

It is a belief, widely entertained, that there is a great difference in the mental constitution of the two sexes, just as there is their physical conformation. The powers and susceptibilities of women are as noble as those of men: but they are thought to be different and, in particular, it is considered that they have not the same power of intense labour as men are endowed with. If this be so, it must form a serious objection to uniting them under the same course of academical study.[77]

Apart from excluding women from well-paid professions the law was instrumental in regulating the employer-employee relationship in such a way as to adversely affect women's rates of pay. One of the best-known examples of legislation of this sort is that which commonly falls under the description of protective legislation. Beginning in the nineteenth century, a concerted public campaign resulted in a series of measures designed to limit the hours when children and women might work in factories. Of particular significance so far as pay is concerned, was women's exclusion from working at night, combined with restrictions on weekend working. When the legislation was passed the effect on women's pay may not have been particularly significant, and a 1906 account of the protective legislation certainly makes this claim.[78] Some women, however, were undeniably suspicious of the motives behind the legislation. The view was expressed in some quarters that "any special restrictions on women's work would handicap them in competition for a place in the industrial world, and that the men were fully aware of this probable result when they pressed for the limitation of the hours of women and young persons ...."[79] As working practices evolved and premium payments were made for night work and weekend work, or shift patterns included night shifts, this claim appeared to be justified, as women did suffer financially. The existence of the legislation made their employment in certain industries difficult and limited their potential to earn more than a basic wage:

> ... moreover, it [the legislation] acted to push women out of the best-paid factory jobs into the female ghettoes of sweatshops, laundries and domestic service where nobody seemed bothered about controlling hours and conditions.[80]

The other major criticism of this legislation is the negative picture which it projected of women, placing them in the same legislative category as children. Parliament made decisions concerning what was in their best interests, robbing women of the right to decide for themselves:

> The weight of the legislative evidence drawn from the nineteenth century constantly emphasises that women were to be treated differently from men

and were to be shielded from taking responsibility for themselves.[81]

The disappearance of this type of gender-based protective legislation does not necessarily eradicate the attitudes which are a product of its very existence. Modern health and safety legislation, which is the successor of the nineteenth century protective legislation, still operates to exclude women from the workplace when it perceives threats to a woman's well-being. If conditions in the workplace endanger her health, or more significantly her reproductive capacity, an employer may force a woman to quit her job. A woman worker is not permitted a choice, even though she may suffer financially as a consequence.[82]

Women and Poverty

The manner in which the poor are dealt with has always been of fundamental importance for women. For a variety of reasons, some of which have already been alluded to, women are more prone to find themselves in need than men. In the past women's restricted access to ownership of property, to paid employment and to the same levels of remuneration as men have made them particularly vulnerable when faced by events such as illness, the death or desertion of a partner, old age and unemployment. Low wages were a particular problem since the poorly paid might be unable to support themselves or their families. The history of how the needs of the poor were met has been the subject of considerable research but, although a great deal has been written on the poor in general, much less information is available on how poverty affected women in particular. Substantial numbers of women were forced to turn to those agencies charged with caring for the poor, but they tend not to figure prominently in commentary on the operation of the system as a whole.[83]

The notion that those in need should be able to look to the state for help is not new. As far back as the sixteenth century, legislation known collectively as the Poor Law, placed responsibility on the parishes to make provision for those without the resources to care for themselves. Even before that, a person in need had been able to appeal to agencies other than their immediate family. These included the Church, the monasteries and charitable foundations set up by the rich for the benefit of the poor. It was seen as the duty of Christians to help the poor "not wholly, and perhaps not even mainly, for the sake of those who were relieved, but for the salvation of the charitable"[84] which meant that little thought was given to whether the object of charity was a deserving recipient. Apart from the Church, the gilds of craftsmen in the towns helped those of their members in need, including their widows,[85] while for the rural poor the feudal manorial system was intended to take care of their needs. Finally, failing everything, the poor could turn to begging in order to survive.

By the end of the sixteenth century, however, the situation had changed dramatically. The gradual breakdown of the feudal system had provoked the emergence of a shifting population of individuals who worked for wages or made their living from begging. They were viewed with suspicion by central government, being seen as a source of unrest within the state. In addition, labour shortages caused by epidemics led to demands for higher wages. The dissolution of the monasteries also meant that previous arrangements to help the needy were no longer adequate. The legislature responded with measures such as the Statute of Labourers, which attempted to control wages and to direct the unemployed to take work on offer. The Statute also forbade the giving of charity on the ground that some were "rather willing to beg in idleness, than by labour to get their living."[86] Other laws distinguished between beggars capable of work and those described as impotent. The former were to be punished and sent back to the place where they were born, the implication being that they would then be expected to work for their living. In contrast, those incapable of earning their living were to be helped by the provision of relief. The desire to distinguish between the "deserving" and the "undeserving" failed, then as now, to acknowledge the fact that those who were capable of work might not be able to obtain it.

A final objective was to devise a system that would make general provision for the poor whether or not they were able-bodied, and this took the form of the Poor Law. The general scheme was that individuals within a parish would be taxed (the poor rate) and the money raised would be used for the relief of the poor. The legislation also contemplated that the able-bodied poor might be provided with some form of work and that living accommodation might be made available for the impotent poor. There was a great deal of local diversity surrounding the way these laws were applied. Some parishes, for example, provided accommodation for the poor and this gradually developed into the institution commonly known as the workhouse, the purpose of which varied in different places from caring for the sick to punishing beggars.

Debate over the appropriate use of workhouses highlighted the related dilemma of whether the poor should get indoor or outdoor relief. Clearly, if an individual was homeless or incapable of caring for herself then indoor relief in the workhouse might be the only option. The able-bodied individual without work or whose work did not pay enough to allow them to support a family posed a different problem. Offering indoor relief via the workhouse to such individuals might deter them from seeking relief, but also called for a complex system of administration. It was simpler to offer individuals relief (so-called outdoor relief) in their own homes. In the case of low wages, some parishes adopted what was known as the allowance or Speenhamland system whereby the parish supplemented low wages.

Whatever system of relief the parish adopted, it was clear that the fewer poor who lived there, the less provision it would have to make. The Act of Settlement 1662 allowed the justices to order the removal of people from one parish to another where they were last legally settled, if it appeared they might become a burden on their new parish. Amongst the many criticisms of this Act it was stated that it "virtually repealed the Poor Law, not only for the small group with no ascertainable settlement anywhere, but for any man as long as he was absent from his own parish."[87]

It was evident by the beginning of the nineteenth century that the administration of the Poor Law required considerable reform. In 1832 a Royal Commission for Inquiring into the Administration and Practical Operation of the Poor Laws was appointed. It unearthed considerable abuse and deficiencies in the system and made various recommendations for reform which were said to be animated by three guiding principles. The first demanded national uniformity so that the poor were treated the same wherever they might be and thus would not be tempted to move from one parish to another. The second guiding principle was that of "less eligibility" or in the words of the Commissioners: "his [that is the indigent's] situation on the whole shall not be made really or apparently so eligible as the situation of the independent labourer of the lowest class."[88]   Finally, the Commissioners commended the workhouse system in order to put their policy of less eligibility into practice. This meant that "all relief whatsoever to able-bodied persons or to their families, otherwise than in well regulated workhouses, ... shall be declared unlawful ...."[89]   As a result of the Poor Law Report, the Poor Law Amendment Act 1834 was passed, followed by further changes throughout the rest of the nineteenth century.

Related developments were taking place at the same time, including charitable initiatives responsible for the provision of low cost housing, for help in finding work and for the wholesale removal of families from town to country where work was available. Savings banks, friendly societies and trade unions were other nineteenth century institutions which played their part in helping workers to survive periods of need without having to resort to the workhouse. A weekly contribution to a friendly society, for example, would guarantee sickness benefit and medical treatment when a worker was ill. The nineteenth century also saw the increasing intervention of central government in everyday life. Legislation was approved on public health, education and working conditions in factories which had the indirect effect of making the situation of the poor slightly more tolerable and, in the case of education, began tackling a problem that the workhouse had never satisfactorily addressed. There was a dawning recognition that the general raising of standards of health and safety, hygiene and education might be a way of preventing poverty.

The start of the twentieth century was marked by increasing disillusionment with the operation of the Poor Law. Periods of high unemployment exposed the weaknesses of a system that rested on the assumption that work was available for those who wanted it. In 1905 a Royal Commission on the Poor Law was appointed and produced a report four years later revealing a difference of opinion between its members. The Majority Report favoured a reform of the Poor Law so that it could offer a programme of action to prevent poverty.[90] Measures were advocated, such as the setting up of employment exchanges and unemployment insurance, and the system was to be administered by public assistance authorities based in the counties or boroughs. The Minority Report favoured the abolition of the Poor Law and the tackling of the factors that cause poverty, such as old age and unemployment, at local government level.[91] Whilst there was quite a measure of common ground between the two Reports, the lack of a single solution meant that no immediate action was taken. Instead there was a steady stream of legislation which tackled specific instances of poverty. In 1908, for example, the Old Age Pensions Act was passed which gave persons over the age of seventy, whose income did not exceed a stated limit, a weekly pension, provided they were "deserving recipients" as defined by the Act. The National Insurance Act 1911 introduced health and unemployment insurance schemes which were to be financed by contributions from employer, employee and state. These and other measures had the effect of reducing the numbers seeking assistance under the Poor Law system and signalled its gradual dismantling. It was not until the National Assistance Act 1948, however, that the Poor Law finally came to an end.[92]

The Poor Law system regulated the treatment of those in need for over three hundred and fifty years and women were just as likely, if not more likely, to experience the system as men. A married woman whose husband was unemployed or too old or too sick to work would be forced to enter the workhouse with him, but would then be forcibly separated from him and any young children she might have. A woman with a young family whose husband was dead or had deserted her might also be forced to seek relief from the parish. This became more likely when one considers that as a matter of course women's wages were substantially less than those of men. A woman with a family to support was less well placed to cope than a man in the same situation. There is some evidence that lone mothers were more likely to receive outdoor relief than be forced to enter the workhouse. The Poor Law Report of 1834 mentions widows as being women who:

> ... in many places, receive what are called pensions, of from 1s to 3s a week on their own account, without any reference to their age or strength, or powers of obtaining an independent subsistence, but simply as widows. In such places, they receive an additional allowance if they have children.[93]

Unmarried mothers might also turn to the overseers of the poor for help and the

Poor Law Report implies that these women would also receive outdoor relief. Indeed, in tones that recall more recent condemnations of single parents, the Report deplores the generous treatment of such women, since it appears that the sum they receive for the upkeep of an illegitimate child exceeds that paid for a legitimate child: "to the woman, therefore, a single illegitimate child is seldom any expense, and two or three are a source of positive profit."[94]   The alleged father of an illegitimate child was supposed to contribute towards the child's support but the Report records the obstacles encountered in trying to ensure that such sums were paid. It also appears that parishes were keen to ensure that any unmarried woman who became pregnant did not become a burden on that parish unless she had a claim to be legally settled there. If she did not, the parish would prefer to incur the cost of removing the woman to the parish where she was regarded in law as settled.

When the Poor Law was amended in 1834 it is not immediately clear, according to commentators such as the Webbs, whether the harsh treatment that was to be meted out to the able-bodied poor, including the withdrawal of outdoor relief, was initially meant to include able-bodied women, such as widows, single mothers, married women who were not living with their husbands and single women without dependents.[95] If a woman was married and living with her husband, however, the treatment afforded him was the treatment she received. It also appears that in those parishes where outdoor relief was in principle forbidden, the exceptions that did exist allowed widows and wives living apart from their husbands the right to receive outdoor relief. Certainly the numbers of women falling within this category were high, particularly when their dependent children were taken into account. It is recorded that in 1858, 50,468 able-bodied widows, together with their 126,658 dependent children, were receiving outdoor relief. This amounted to 25 per cent of the total pauper population.[96]   To have forced all such women to enter the workhouse would clearly have been beyond the authorities' capacity to cope. An additional problem to which the authorities had no answer was the low wages received by lone women, always assuming there was work to be had. An able-bodied woman who worked, for example, as a seamstress would simply not have the earning power necessary to support her family. Women who were lone parents presented an intractable problem to the authorities. Prevailing attitudes meant, however, that the mother of an illegitimate child might be denied outdoor relief because of her conduct. In contrast, a widow or a deserted wife was regarded as being in need through no fault of her own and thus deserving of assistance.

Towards the end of the nineteenth century, the Webbs note an increasingly harsh policy towards women who found themselves in need, perhaps because they formed such a substantial proportion of those seeking relief.[97] Restrictions were imposed on outdoor relief for able-bodied single women, deserted wives and wives whose husbands were in prison or the armed forces.[98] It was also recommended that widows with a single child should not be given outdoor relief and that where a widow had more than one child the children should be admitted to the workhouse as opposed to granting outdoor relief. As a result of such policies the numbers of women claiming relief declined sharply.[99]

The fact that women were major recipients of Poor Law relief either in their own right or as wives, may be related to their inability to take advantage of other forms of help that developed in the nineteenth century. Very few friendly societies admitted both men and women as members.[100] Women, if working, were unlikely to be paid enough to afford the contribution and married men could not afford a contribution for both themselves and their wives. Women who did earn enough to belong to a friendly society were asked to contribute more than men because they were deemed to be less healthy. In addition, very few women were members of the trade unions which were another source of help when times were hard.

Women perhaps fared better from the introduction of central government schemes designed to address the problems of poverty. Schemes were introduced for the payment of old age pensions[101] and for sickness and unemployment benefit.[102] From the outset, sickness and unemployment benefits were contributory. Both schemes were open to men and to women but women's access to unemployment benefit was very limited since, in its early days, it covered those industries - building, shipbuilding and iron founding - which employed few women. In contrast, old age pensions were brought in as non-contributory benefits available to anyone who satisfied the conditions for payment. Because of the potential costs of such a scheme, the benefit was means-tested and was payable only to those whose annual income did not exceed a stipulated amount. Despite this, a major proportion of those over seventy were able to claim old age pensions[103] and they were of particular and significant benefit to women whose low incomes made them major beneficiaries. Another noticeable feature of old age pensions was that men and women were paid the same amount. Sickness and unemployment benefit, on the other hand, paid higher rates to men, though they were also expected to make higher contributions. This was presumably seen as justified by the higher rates of pay which men commanded at that time[104] and by the apparently unspoken assumption that, whether it was a question of wages or contributory benefits, women could survive on less than men.[105]

In the period between the First and Second World Wars, Britain suffered high levels of unemployment as a product of economic depression. The changes which were made to the social insurance system as a consequence of the economic crisis worked to the disadvantage of women. Reform was driven by two conflicting forces: on the one hand there was the need to make better social provision in order to prevent unrest and improve the quality of the workforce by raising standards of education and health. On the other hand, it was recognised that the better the benefits, the higher the costs that would be incurred. Apart from the fact that this left less capital available for investment, it was also argued that the availability of benefits made people less willing to work. Conscious efforts were made, therefore, to keep down the costs of benefits and women, especially married women, suffered at the hands of the cost-cutting programme. It may have been thought that women were better able to absorb these financial penalties on the basis that married women were supported by their husbands and single women needed less to live on, or it may be attributable to a belief that women were less likely to complain.

Measures taken to modify the system of unemployment benefit, which was the benefit most under pressure, show how women were marginalised within the developing system. Men were seen as the principal recipients of social insurance benefits and the system began more and more to reflect their concerns. To combat the rising numbers of unemployed, the Unemployment Insurance Act 1920 extended unemployment insurance to a greatly increased number of workers, though certain forms of employment - such as domestic service where there were large numbers of women workers - were still excluded. In 1921 the Unemployed Workers Dependents (Temporary Provisions) Act allowed a male contributor to claim additional payments should he have a dependent spouse and children. The same option was not open to female contributors. As the depression deepened, so-called extended benefit (later renamed transitional benefit) was introduced in the Unemployment Insurance Act 1922. Extended benefit was paid to those who had exhausted their unemployment insurance, the latter having always been intended as a short-term benefit. Although it was assumed that a man's wife and children were dependent upon him and he could thus claim the extended benefit automatically, a married woman could claim only if she could prove that her husband was in fact dependent upon her. Moreover, extended benefit was available only to those genuinely seeking whole-time employment but unable to obtain such employment. This test worked to the particular disadvantage of married women since it could be argued that their domestic responsibilities meant they were not available for employment. Another rule provided that if vacancies in domestic service were available, any woman who had previously undertaken such work would be refused benefit if she declined to accept such employment. Domestic work was generally regarded as suitable work for a woman claiming benefit[106] and the fact that it was outside the scope of the contributory social insurance system was an added advantage to a government seeking to make savings. More generally, it reinforced the divide between what was considered men's work and women's work. Finally, extended benefit was subject to a means-test which would, again, affect a married woman since her income was aggregated with that of her husband. The introduction of aggregation meant that, instead of each married person being treated as an independent entity, a married couple was treated as a unit. A married woman's financial dependency on her husband was thus reinforced and given statutory authority. The reforms in unemployment benefit between 1921 and 1934 effectively excluded more and more women from the contributory benefit system.

Married women were expected to rely on their husbands and, while the social insurance system was delivering that message, the personal taxation system was reinforcing it with devices such as the married man's allowance.[107] If women were employed, it was expected that they would work in jobs traditionally associated with women and they were discouraged from competing with men for "men's jobs."

During the period of economic crisis between the wars changes were also made to the system of sickness benefit and old age pensions. A Royal Commission investigated the state of the health insurance system in 1926[108] and, although changes were recommended, none was made largely on grounds of additional costs. Indeed, the government's wish to spend less rather than more led to reductions in the amount of sickness benefit paid to certain groups, including married women.[109] Rising costs also forced the government to reassess the system of non-contributory old age pensions and in 1925 the Old Age and Widows and Orphans Contributory Pensions Act introduced a contributory old age pension scheme. Those already contributing to the national health insurance scheme were required to pay an additional sum which would allow them to claim a pension at the age of 65 and the non-contributory pension at the age of 70. Both pensions would be available without a means-test. If the contributor were married his wife could claim a pension when she reached the age of 65 (later reduced to 60), provided her husband was already receiving a pension. The widow of an insured man was also entitled to a pension for herself and any dependent children. The non-contributory means-tested pension remained in existence but it was contemplated that it would gradually be replaced by the contributory pension.

The decision to make retirement pensions a contributory benefit is one that has had lasting consequences for women. Forcing married women to rely on their husbands' contribution records not only reinforced their dependency, it also produced one of the most glaring anomalies in the whole system of social insurance. Men received their retirement pension at the age of 65 and initially the same retirement age was adopted for women. Since many men married women younger than themselves, there were complaints that when these men retired they received no pension for their wives - who had not reached retirement age. The financial hardship which resulted was compounded by the fact that women over 60 found it difficult to obtain employment. The retirement age for women was therefore reduced to 60 and the ramifications are still being felt within the social security system.

Taking stock

If it is possible to summarise a woman's experience of wealth up to the Second World War, four factors seem to have predisposed women to experience relative poverty more frequently and more harshly than men. First, her lower earning power meant that a woman was less able to maintain herself, or any dependent family members. Marriage was a way of avoiding poverty, but the pursuit of a more tolerable life style required women to accept dependency on and subordination to their husbands. Second, her responsibilities in relation to child care, whilst rendering a woman less able to support herself, were not acknowledged as deserving some kind of recognition. When the most outrageous legal disabilities associated with marriage were removed, there was no effort legally to redefine the relationship to take account of the services which women performed and their changing expectations. Similarly, the emergent welfare state also failed to meet specifically female aspirations and to reward women for their caring responsibilities. Third, her susceptibility to finding herself unsupported as a widow, deserted wife or lone parent left a woman particularly vulnerable to poverty. If being able to depend on a man is the key to financial well-being, the lack of such support inevitably spells disaster. Fourth, her exclusion from private, and indeed public, schemes designed to alleviate poverty ensured that she would either have to rely on another person, most likely a man, who did have access to those schemes, or on whatever contingency arrangements the state made for those without resources of their own. Women were, by and large, denied the opportunity to make provision for themselves.

Notes

1. See for example (1981), *The Pastons*.
2. Staves, S. (1990), *Married Women's Separate Property in England 1660-1833*; Holcombe, L. (1983), *Wives and Property*; Bradley, H. (1989), *Men's Work, Women's Work*; Clark, A. (1992), *Working Life of Women in the Seventeenth Century*; Stone, L. (1990), *Road to Divorce*; Atkins, S. and Hoggett, B. (1984), *Women and the Law*; O'Donovan, K. (1985), *Sexual Divisions in Law*; Cioni, M.L. (1985), *Women and Law in Elizabethan England with Particular reference to the Court of Chancery*; Stone, L. (1977), *The Family, Sex and Marriage in England 1500-1800*; Webb, S.J. and B. (1910), *English Poor Law Policy*; Webb, S.J. and B. (1963), *English Poor Law History*.
3. Freehold property was land held in return for the performance of certain duties owed to the Crown. It later came to be regarded as any land held for a period of uncertain duration.
4. Holcombe, op. cit., n. 2, p. 20.
5. Statute of Wills 1540. Women had to wait until 1882. Husbands were not, however, permitted to dispose of a wife's real property by will.
6. This right, for example, depended on the birth of a child of the marriage who was born live and was capable of inheriting the lands. The subsequent death of the child did not affect the right of curtesy.

7. This is land held under the terms of a lease for a specified period of time. C.f. freehold land, n. 3.

8. This property took the form of claims against another individual which, once resolved, would be converted into tangible property such as money.

9. Holcombe, op. cit., n. 2, p. 20.

10. O'Donovan, op. cit., n. 2, p. 31.

11. Cary, E. and Peratis, K. (1977), *Women and the Law*, pp. 8-14.

12. Ibid., p. 12.

13. Stone L. (1977), *The Family, Sex and Marriage in England 1500-1800*.

14. Ibid., p. 5.

15. Ibid., p. 8.

16. See pp. 36-39.

17. Clark, A., op. cit., n. 2, p. xxxvii.

18. In Lewis, J. and Piachaud, D. (1992), 'Women and poverty in the twentieth century' in Glendinning, C., and Millar J. (eds), *Women and Poverty in Britain: the 1990s*, p. 31.

19. Ibid., p. 31.

20. Bromley, P.M. (1966), *Family Law*, p. 205.

21. Blackstone's *Commentaries on the Laws of England* (1765), Vol. 2, Part 1, p. 129.

22. Statutes of Distributions 1670, 1677 and 1685.

23. A wife could not take legal action in these circumstances since she and her husband were regarded by the law as a single entity and one partner could not sue another. See Bromley, op. cit., n. 20, p. 205.

24. Despite this widows were frequent recipients of Poor Law benefits. See n. 86 and n. 101.

25. Holcombe, op. cit., n. 2, pp. 20-22.

26. Ibid. There were, however, ways in which he might bar her right to dower of his freehold land.

27. Cioni, op. cit., n. 2, Chap. V discusses the legal remedies which might be available in such circumstances.

28. Holcombe, op. cit., n. 2, p. 43, Staves, op. cit., n. 2, Chap 2.

29. See the examples cited in Cioni, op. cit., n. 2, p. 196.

30. Bromley, op. cit., n. 20, p. 421.

31. Ibid.

32. Quoted in Cioni, op. cit., n.2, p. 197.

33. Staves, op. cit., n. 2, Chap 4.

34. Holcombe, op. cit., n. 2, p. 4.

35. Bromley, op. cit., n. 20, p. 424.

36. Burn E.H. (1994), *Cheshire and Burn's Modern Law of Real Property*, pp. 928-929.

37. Ibid., p. 242.

38. The reason given for not permitting dower of a trust was that to do so would disappoint the expectations of those who had created a trust in order to avoid dower.

39. Curtesy existed until Law of Property Act 1925.

40.   Bromley, op. cit., n. 20, p. 494.

41.   For a history of this campaign see Holcombe, op. cit., n. 2.

42.   Supreme Court of Judicature Act 1873 s. 25(11).

43.   Holcombe, op. cit., n. 2, p. 202.

44.   Ibid., pp. 219-230.

45.   O'Donovan, op. cit., n. 2, p. 56.

46.   Ibid., p. 182.

47.   Holcombe, op. cit., n.2, p. 95.

48.   Holcombe estimates the cost of a Parliamentary divorce to be between £600 and £800 in the 1850s. Holcombe, op. cit., n. 2, p. 96.

49.   O'Donovan, op. cit., n. 2, p. 51.

50.   Ibid., pp. 50-53.

51.   Stone, op. cit., n. 13, pp. 39-40.

52.   Ibid., p. 40.

53.   Staves, op. cit., n. 2, Chap 6.

54.   Ibid.

55.   Ibid.

56.   Vogel, U. (1992), 'Whose Property? The double standard of adultery in nineteenth-century law' in Smart, C. (ed.), *Regulating Womanhood* at p. 147.

57.   Matrimonial Causes Act 1857, s. 32.

58.   Vogel, op. cit., n. 56, p. 162.

59.   Ibid., p. 162.

60.   Atkins and Hoggett, op. cit., n. 2, p. 3.

61.   See pp. 26-27.

62.   For example, Statute of Labourers 1349 and the Trade Boards Act 1909.

63.   Factories Act 1961, s. 86 set maximum hours of work for women and s. 89 prohibited women from undertaking night work or Sunday work. O'Donovan, op. cit., n. 2, p. 163. This legislation has been repealed: Sex Discrimination Act 1986 and Employment Act 1989.

64.   Statutes of Labourers 1349, 1351, 1388.

65.   Op. cit., n. 2, p. 10.

66.   Lewis, J. (1984), *Women in England 1870-1950: Sexual Divisions and Social Change*, p. 163.

67.   Subsequently, Wages Councils set uni-sex rates and proved an impetus to equal pay in the industries covered: see p. 85.

68.   Lewis, op. cit., n. 66, p. 49.

69.   Atkins and Hoggett, op. cit., n. 2, p. 10.

70.   Bradley, op. cit., n. 2, pp. 82-83.

71.   Ibid., pp. 85-86.

72.   Lewis, op. cit., n. 66, p. 172.

73.   Cadbury, E., Matheson, M.C. and Shann, G. (1980), *Women's Work and Wages*, p. 119.

74.   Lewis, op. cit., n. 66, p. 162.

75. Bradley, op. cit., n. 2, Chap. 12.
76. *Bebb v Law Society* [1914] Ch 286, at pp. 297-299.
77. *Jex-Blake v Senatus of the University of Edinburgh* (1873) 11 McPherson 784, at p. 833.
78. Cadbury, et al, op. cit., n. 73, p. 41.
79. Ibid., pp. 24-25.
80. Bradley, op. cit. n. 2, p. 45.
81. Morris, A.E. and Nott, S.M. (1991), *Working Women and the Law: Equality and Discrimination in Theory and Practice*, p. 36.
82. Morris, A.E. and Nott, S.M. (1992), 'The Legal Response to Pregnancy', 12 *Legal Studies*, p. 54, and Morris, A.E. and Nott, S.M. (1995), 'The Law's Engagement with Pregnancy' in Millns, S. and Bridgeman, J.C. (eds), *Law and Body Politics*.
83. Snell, K.D.M. and Millar, J. (1987), 'Lone-parent Families and the Welfare State: past and present' in *Continuity and Change*, Vol. 2, p. 387.
84. Webb, S.J. and B. (1963), *English Poor Law History*, p. 1.
85. Ibid., p. 21.
86. Statute of Labourers 1349.
87. Poynter, J.R. (1969), *Society and Pauperism: English ideas on poor relief 1795-1834*, p. 4.
88. Checkland, E. and S.G. (1974), *Poor Law Report of 1834*, p. 335.
89. Ibid., p. 375.
90. Cmnd. 4499; Webb, S.J. and B. (1910), *English Poor Law Policy*, Chap. VI.
91. Ibid., Chap. VII.
92. S. 62 and Schedule 7.
93. Checkland, op. cit., n. 88, p. 114.
94. Ibid., p. 261. The idea also persists in some quarters that, by and large, poverty is avoidable and it is thus the fault of the poor if they are in need: see e.g. Minford, P. (1987), in Loney, M. (ed.), *The State or the Market*, at p. 81.
95. Webbs, op. cit., n. 90, p. 15.
96. Ibid., p. 103.
97. Ibid., p. 174.
98. Ibid., p. 176.
99. Ibid., p. 179.
100. Thane, P. (1982), *The Foundations of the Welfare State*, p. 29.
101. Old Age Pensions Act 1908.
102. National Insurance Act 1911.
103. An estimated sixty per cent of those individuals aged seventy or over were able to claim a retirement pension in 1912.
104. See pp. 36-38 for an account of the discrimination in the wages paid to women as compared with men. See also Chap. 3.
105. Either because women had a husband to support them or, if they were single, because they could manage with less money.
106. Lewis, (1984), op. cit., n. 66, pp. 189-190.

107.   Atkins and Hoggett, op. cit., n. 2, p. 164.
108.   Thane, op. cit., n. 100, p. 191.
109.   Ibid., p. 192.

3 Acquiring Wealth: Earning a Living

Waged Work

Wealth may be acquired in a variety of ways but, as seen in Chapter 1, for the majority of people today it is acquired, if at all, from waged work and its associated benefits, such as pensions.   The question "What do you do for a living?" is commonly heard even in times of high unemployment.   It assumes that to live we must work and that employment is the natural state of things.   Earning a living is central to the functioning of a capitalist society but it is not simply an economic transaction in which labour is exchanged for a wage.   First, the wage-work bargain between the employer and the individual worker directly affects not only that worker but also those who are dependent on him or her, most obviously in that the level of wages and the security of the job will have important consequences for the standard of living and stability of the whole family.   Second, employment is not only about material existence, it is about a complex range of social and cultural attitudes and beliefs, which become apparent when workers lose their jobs.   Although loss of income is the obvious and immediate consequence, there is also a perceived loss of status and identity.   Our place in society is moulded by our occupational existence and without a job - a position - we lose our place.   Unemployment is thus seen as a social evil, and those who are unemployed are pitied but also stigmatised as a "drain" on society.

The traditional stereotype of a worker is someone working around 40 hours a week,[1] perhaps plus overtime, on collectively agreed terms and conditions, for an indefinite number of years until retirement age.   It is into this context of waged work, with its attendant economic and social implications, that a woman's access to wealth in the form of employment must be placed.   Her access to waged work was affected in the past by certain key elements of which the first was the assumption that most women would, for much of their lives, rely on a man, normally their husbands, for financial support. Women would, therefore, undertake unpaid work in the home rather than paid employment outside it. Second, if a woman did enter the labour market, it was assumed that her wages did not have to equal those of a man since, if she were married, her wages would not be the sole source of income entering the home and, if she were single, she required only a minimum: "the pittance absolutely required for the sustenance of one human being."[2] Third, women who worked were segregated in jobs which were largely specific to women, and hence low paid. The gendered nature of the labour market favoured men who benefited financially as a result.

For centuries the subordination of women was supported by the law. It sanctioned their lower wages, barred them from some - usually well paid - forms of employment and did nothing to tackle sex discrimination. In its dealings with husbands and wives it emphasised a wife's financial dependency and made it exceedingly difficult for either partner, but especially the wife, to escape an unsatisfactory marriage. The law was complicit in stressing the importance of waged work for a man, but not a woman. A woman's contact with the labour market was assumed to be short term and not crucial to her financial well-being. Whether or not the law's view of women's, and indeed men's, lives ever accorded with reality, there have been significant changes since the Second World War. The idea of a steady nine to five job, or even regular shift work, was never in fact an adequate stereotype[3] but has become even less so in recent years. Part-time work, temporary work, individually negotiated contracts, self-employment, and flexible hours are all hallmarks of the new labour market, as is the marked increase in the incidence of women's participation in paid employment. The breakdown in the patterns of full-time, permanent employment, and the emergence of what is often referred to as employee flexibility, has not, however, been accompanied by improvements in workers' terms and conditions of employment. The flexibility tends to be for the benefit of the employer rather than the employee and expresses itself in lower wages, longer hours, fewer fringe benefits and the ability to lay workers off without having to pay compensation, rather than in flexible working hours, improved child care facilities, career breaks and parental leave.[4]

One of the most dramatic changes in the labour market has been women's increased participation in paid employment as more and more of them, single and married, work for longer periods of their lives. Male unemployment has increased as traditional industrial jobs have declined, while job opportunities for women have opened up, albeit largely in lower paid or part-time jobs. Even women who were not expecting to have to be financially independent are finding that, as more and more marriages end in divorce, they must assume financial responsibility for themselves and their children. With or without a partner, access to wealth via waged work has become a necessity for many women but is also seen as desirable and worthwhile to others. While it is clear from the statistics that many more women are working for longer periods, the figures must be examined more closely to discover who these women are, what kinds of jobs they are doing and what they are being paid for their efforts.

How many women work?

For the purposes of the next few sections of this chapter it is assumed that the phrase "women in employment" means those who are paid for the work they do, but it should be borne in mind that most women, whether or not they also have paid jobs, undertake unpaid labour in their own homes or the homes of family members. As mothers, "housewives" and carers, women fulfil a variety of functions which are currently not generally recognised as being work in the usual sense.[5]   Some women may also work within a family business and may or may not get paid a wage for doing so. Interestingly, other states within the European Union have recognised a special category of worker known as a "family worker" who is someone who helps another family member to run an agricultural or other business. This was not formerly the case in the United Kingdom, but unpaid family workers have been separately identified since 1992 and early indications are that women significantly outnumber men in this category. One survey found 124,000 women as compared with 55,000 men who could be described as family workers.[6] Women also outnumber men in a different category: those earning a living are far more likely than men to be employees rather than self-employed. The numbers of self-employed generally have been increasing and it has been suggested that self-employment may be particularly attractive to women with dependent children[7] but although the number of self-employed women has more than doubled since 1979 it is still well short of that for men. In 1994, for example, only about 7 per cent of women of working age in employment were self-employed (0.8 million) as compared with 17 per cent of men (2.3 million).[8] There may be a number of reasons for this marked difference including, for example, the fact that women, more than men, lack the mobility and flexibility which self-employment can entail. Alternatively, women may not, traditionally, have received the training and education which is particularly relevant to self-employment. It may also have something to do with the fact that starting a business requires capital or at least security for loans and investment by third parties. Part of the thesis of this book is that women are less likely than men to have access to such wealth.

Factors such as lack of flexibility and mobility may also help to account for the prevalence of women in a particularly disadvantaged sector of the workforce which has sometimes been overlooked, that of the homeworker. Since many homeworkers are, by definition, "hidden" within their own homes it has been difficult to assess their numbers and their conditions of working. Studies which have been done, however, suggest that the range of occupations undertaken either in the home or using it as a base are very varied and include manufacturing, computing, clerical work, selling, hairdressing, teaching and childminding.[9] The majority who work *in* the home, as opposed to operating from the home, and using it as a base, are women (the latter are mostly men).[10]   Although the increasing sophistication of information technology means that homeworkers may in the future be increasingly engaged in managerial, professional or technical occupations, there are still large numbers who are employed in manual work.   The traditional homeworker, assembling components, sewing garments or stuffing envelopes experiences in even greater measure some of the problems of part-time workers in relation to lack of employment security and protection.   They are unlikely to be the recipients of national insurance benefits, holiday or sick pay, their working patterns are unpredictable, they are unlikely to be organised into unions and their working conditions may be positively dangerous. Though the conditions of employment of many homeworkers may represent some of the worst experienced by working women, one view is that this is simply indicative of the plight of working women generally: "Homeworking is a particularly appalling example of women's position in the labour market, not a contrast to it."[11]

Statistics such as those on self-employment and homeworking are illuminating but should not be allowed to mask one essential fact: women - in or out of employment - are not an homogeneous group and different women within society experience employment and indeed other aspects of life differently.   This is especially true of the different ethnic groups found within Britain today. In relation to self-employment, for example, the figures vary significantly between ethnic groups: self-employment is commoner amongst both men and women in the Indian community, for example, while the numbers of Black women (defined as Afro-Caribbean and others) or Pakistani or Bangladeshi women who are self-employed is statistically insignificant. There is insufficient space within a work such as this to do full justice to the additional discrimination faced by women from ethnic minorities, who must deal not only with prejudice based on their sex but also on their colour or race.[12]   Some may also find independence that much harder to achieve because of the pressures that come from within their community and which militate against women seeking work outside the home. This would be true for example of some Muslim Asian women and could explain the absence of these women from the figures for the self-employed.[13] In the case of other groups, it is impossible to escape the conclusion that racism contributes to the concentration of Black women in lower status and lower paid jobs.[14]

Although participation rates differ amongst various sections of the community it is clear that, in general, female participation in the labour market has increased, and it is apparent across the European Union that attitudes to family life have also changed.   One survey found that only a minority (25 per cent) across the twelve member states said that the traditional pattern of male breadwinner with wife running the home corresponds to their idea of the family, while most support came for the family in which husband and wife have equally absorbing jobs, and household tasks and childcare are shared equally.[15] Looking more specifically at Britain, around one third of male and female respondents to the 1992/3 British Social Attitudes survey supported the traditional pattern of female homemaker and male breadwinner - a figure little changed over several years.[16] The strength of support varied, perhaps not too surprisingly, according to the age of the individual (the older, the more traditional) and also as to whether the individual was herself working or was a man in a household with a working partner.   Given these variations, however, the responses of men and women were surprisingly similar - except where both partners worked full-time in which case although 72 per cent of women rejected the traditional role, only 58 per cent of men did so, for reasons which can only be speculated upon.

Changing attitudes to gender roles are mirrored by the changing composition of the labour market.   Between 1979 and the early 1990s the number of women in employment in the United Kingdom increased by almost 20 per cent and by 1994 there were over 10 million women in employment making up nearly half of all employees.[17] Having established that almost half the workforce is female, the figures must be broken down further. For example, a Labour Force Survey showed that in the spring of 1993, 71 per cent of women of working age (16-59) were economically active (that is, in work or available for and seeking work). Of the remainder, classified as economically inactive, just over half still gave as their main reason that they were looking after the family or home[18] but the number of women who are economically inactive mainly for domestic reasons has declined significantly over the last decade.

Although the majority of women are thus "earning a living" from paid work, this must be further analysed in the context of the split between full- and part-time work.[19] The United Kingdom has one of the highest rates of part-time workers in the European Union.[20] In 1993, about a quarter of all workers in the United Kingdom were part-timers, and a very large percentage (about 87 per cent) were women.[21] Over 40 per cent of women employees work part-time.[22] The fact that so many part-timers are women and that so many women who work do so part-time has a number of consequences, and of particular importance in this context is that part-timers are usually viewed as second class workers. Employers have benefited from using part-timers in a number of ways: because many part-timers were not qualified for employment protection rights[23] they gave the employer scope for greater flexibility in meeting fluctuating demand, and their low pay may mean that no national insurance contributions are payable. All of these benefits obviously have corresponding disadvantages for the employee.

Traditionally, the large number of part-timers amongst the female workforce is explained by women's caring or domestic roles. Since it is still the case that women are expected to shoulder the main responsibility for looking after children (and the family generally), many will find that they cannot, even if they want to, work full-time.[24] Certainly this explanation is borne out by statistics. In member states of the European Union well over 90 per cent of fathers with children under 10 were economically active, while the percentage for mothers was only just over half (in the United Kingdom the figure was then 54 per cent).[25] Against all odds, however, mothers are returning to paid employment in increasing numbers. By 1994, 64 per cent of women with children under 16 were economically active and one in six employed women had children under 16.[26] Although these trends are highly significant, it remains the case that employment practices in the United Kingdom are not, in general, parent-friendly, and surveys still indicate that women with children are less likely to be in employment and very much less likely to be working full-time. The extent to which this is true depends on the age of the youngest child. A Labour Force Survey in 1993[27] found that where the youngest child was between 0 and 4 years, only 45 per cent of mothers were in employment, (about twice as many being in part-time as in full-time work). Almost all of the economically inactive in this group stated that they were looking after family or home. Where the youngest child was between 11 and 15, 75 per cent were in employment (41 per cent part-time, 34 per cent full-time). The presence of dependent children would appear to be a decisive factor in the decision to work part-time but it is interesting to note that even where there were no dependent children, although the employment activity rate was higher than for those with young children, a significant proportion still chose part-time work (nearly a quarter). The restrictions placed on women by children cannot therefore be the entire explanation for the prevalence of part-time working amongst female employees. This is important, since it suggests that the constraints which are placed on a woman's employment are not in fact confined to those years when she has dependent children but may prevail throughout her working life. One survey[28] set out to discover more about attitudes to work and found that, as the figures above suggest, the main reason for part-time working was to balance work with other responsibilities. However most respondents in the survey were classed as "voluntary" part-timers: they were said to have *chosen* to work those hours because of their child care or domestic responsibilities.[29] Of course, this too implies that female attitudes to work and home are extremely complex. Some of the respondents "choosing" to work part-time no longer had young children to care for, but nevertheless worked part-time because they were still looking after the family:

> I chose part-time. I have got a house to run and the meals to get ready for them all at night time and mine like the dinner on the table when they

come home... (sons) eighteen and twenty four and my husband... they all get home between five and six....[30]

Some of the women's partners obviously resented even part-time work and some had given up:

> I worked for an Estate Agent two years ago ... Saturday and Sunday morning ... 10 hours ... I don't think he (husband) wanted me to be a person of my own ... to go out and meet other people ... he likes me at home ... he would be quite jealous (of another job) ... I did feel guilty about leaving him for that 3 hours on a Sunday morning. But I had prepared the dinner and cooked the breakfast.[31]

Even among younger women traditional views about family responsibilities are still remarkably entrenched.[32] This affects the position and status of women in a society which, despite what some political groups aimed at "preserving" the family may say, does not tend to recognise childrearing and caring as "proper" jobs. In the context of wealth it can be seen that women who are the carers rather than the earners become the dispossessed.[33]

Particularly significant are the findings in the Survey on Part-timers on why the women chose to work at all. The disadvantages were numerous and obvious: those with children, for example faced horrendous problems of child care, especially in school holidays or when a child was ill. Most of the respondents said they felt guilty about combining work with their other responsibilities, continually feeling that one suffered at the expense of the other. Apart from having to juggle their two roles there are also problems concerning the work itself: part-time work tends to be in lower skilled jobs and because the pay is also low there are problems with tax and particularly with national insurance. No national insurance contributions are payable where earnings are below the lower earnings limit[34] but no contributions mean no benefits. In April 1993, 2.3 million women earned below the lower earnings limit and were thus excluded from the benefits system.[35]

And yet, despite the multifarious problems, these women still go out to work. Money is clearly an important motivating factor, though the extent to which this was true varied amongst the respondents and it is notable that many referred to the feeling of independence it gave. Other factors mentioned were the social contacts work engenders plus the mental stimulation and self-esteem. Some described part-time work as being the best of both worlds and it is true that other surveys have found higher levels of job satisfaction amongst part-timers.[36] This seems to derive not so much from the job as from the flexibility that part-time work offers. The part-time worker has at least some of the advantages of paid employment whilst retaining more time for herself. This raises interesting issues about the whole nature of work and the way it is currently structured. Whereas most working mothers in the United Kingdom still work part-time, most employed fathers (98 per cent) are in full-time employment. Moreover, these fathers not only work longer hours per week than do mothers who work full-time, but they also work longer hours than do fathers in any other member state of the European Union. In the United Kingdom, 36 per cent of fathers work more than 50 hours a week, whereas in all other member states apart from Ireland and Spain (27 and 21 per cent respectively), the figure is below 18 per cent.[37]   These figures illustrate the persistence in the United Kingdom, even in dual earner couples, of the traditional roles of men and women and they may also highlight the different ways that men and women perceive their working existence.[38] Last, but not least, they point to the unequal domestic burden carried by women in this country: if fathers are out working long hours it is the mother who will bear the principal responsibility for child care and household matters.

While the advantages of part-time work should not be ignored, some women would much prefer full-time employment which tends, currently, to bring higher status and better pay. The individuals in this category have not voluntarily chosen part-time employment. It may be that they do not want to work at all but need the money and find they cannot work full-time or cannot find a full-time job. Some may find a full-time job but cannot take it because they cannot afford to pay for child care out of their wages.   Among those who find it difficult to find employment to fit in with their other responsibilities, lone parents are a particularly notable example.

Although precise numbers vary from source to source, lone parents make up a significant proportion of those caring for children. One survey in 1990 found that there were in Great Britain over one million lone mothers and over 100,000 lone fathers with dependent children under the age of 19.[39] Lone mothers with children under 16 then constituted 15 per cent of mothers of working age and these women are in a particularly vulnerable situation in terms of acquiring financial support let alone the independence necessary to control their economic and personal lives. A particularly telling trend can be seen in the economic activity rates for lone mothers: in the same survey in 1990 only 49 per cent were in or seeking work, compared with 66 per cent of married mothers. As children got older, however, the activity rate for lone mothers increased more sharply than that for married mothers which would tend to indicate the additional problems that lone mothers face in terms of combining paid employment with caring for small children. Within the category, markedly the lowest participation rate was for single (as opposed to divorced or widowed) mothers. The employment and economic activity rates for lone mothers failed to increase during the 1980s, as compared to the significant increases in those rates for married mothers. These comparatively low participation rates and the reasons behind them are important because of the consequences that lack of access to employment has on the economic welfare of the woman and her family. Recent increases in the numbers of lone mothers mean that a higher proportion (nearly half) have a child under 5, which is always a factor mitigating against paid employment outside the home and is especially so for those without the support of a partner. But account must also be taken of the effects of the social security system[40] and the level of pay which the lone mother can earn. If earned income cancels out other benefits, or if child care is costing too high a proportion of the wages it is hardly surprising that these mothers do not work even if jobs are available. Differences between women from different groups are particularly apparent in the case of lone mothers. There are far more lone mothers amongst women of West Indian or Guyanese origin than there are amongst White women and there are fewer amongst women from the Indian, Pakistani and Bangladeshi communities.[41] The cultural or other reasons for these differences are probably less important in this context than the disadvantages which accompany the status of lone parent and which may well be exacerbated in the case of Black mothers.

The difficulties faced by lone mothers are simply one example of the factors which continue to militate against an even fuller participation by women in the labour market. In particular, the type of employment or the ability to accept employment at all are constrained by domestic and especially caring responsibilities. These are not the sole preserve of women, but they are affected by them to a far greater extent than are men. Whether it is a child or adult requiring care, women are more likely to take on the responsibility and to suffer the economic consequences. It has been estimated that mothers earn an average of 22 per cent less than non-mothers and that a woman's lifetime average income is reduced by having a family, whereas that of a man is increased.[42] Figures published in 1994 show that of the 728,000 carers of working age who would have liked regular work but were not looking for it because of care responsibilities, 94 per cent were women.[43] Of 684,000 women who would have liked to work, 56 per cent were caring for children below school age, and 6 per cent were caring for an adult dependent relative.[44] Women striving to assert a degree of financial independence may well be thwarted by the inability to combine the two roles of worker and carer. This could be remedied either by rewarding women for their caring role or, alternatively, by the state assuming more of the responsibility by improving facilities and support for carers. The Nordic countries are apparently proof that the greater the amount spent on social security, the more equal are the incomes of men and women,[45] which suggests that changes to the welfare state are as important as those relating to the relationship between employer and employee. Nevertheless, the regulation of that relationship is vital if women are to have improved access to the labour market. The European Union has recognised, at least in principle, that the pursuit of economic growth must be combined with attention to social policy and legislative measures on issues such as parental leave and part-time working have been actively promoted by the Commission. The lack of success in achieving their enactment may be attributable in part to the convoluted law-making processes within the Union, but also to consistent opposition to these measures on the part of the United Kingdom, which argues that they are too costly and threaten jobs. In the face of this opposition our European partners have decided to move ahead on their own - thus benefiting parents in the rest of the Union.

There is a final obstacle to women's fuller participation in paid employment which could prove resistant to change. It is the cultural or perhaps even psychological barrier which stands in the way of women's independence. There is little doubt that many women with families are ambivalent about paid employment: it brings independence and social contacts but it also makes their lives more complicated and troubles their consciences. Brannen and Moss remark that in dual earner households it was common for women to prioritise their husband's employment and they conclude that:

> The absence of ideologies which run counter to the breadwinner ideology cannot be explained by women's fear of poverty in the event of the break-up of their marriages since they were in full-time employment. Rather this absence may be explained at least in part, by a powerful ideology of marriage with its emphasis on marriage as a state of love, not conflict. A counter-ideology which emphasises women's economic power inside and outside marriage would need to make material exchanges part of the "effective bargain" of love.[46]

What work do women do?

As it was in the past, so today the labour market is gendered: there is women's work and there is men's work. There are, for example, three times more women than men in clerical and secretarial jobs, while, conversely, only about 12 per cent of employees in craft and related occupations are female. In manual occupations generally, men tend significantly to outnumber women particularly in skilled trades. On the other hand, women predominate in the service sector, including teaching and health associated professions (nurses, midwives and the like). In the latter, women outnumber men by about 7:1. The marked concentration of women in the service sector is further reflected by the high proportion of women workers in the public sector. This is important in the context of recent policies towards the public sector: pay rises have been restricted and the insistence on "contracting out" services to the private sector has led to redundancies or to worsening terms of employment.[47]

Even within those spheres where women predominate, jobs may still be segregated so that women tend to fill the lower grades. It remains the case, for example, that there are twice as many male managers and administrators as female.[48] In 1993, in teaching, women made up 80 per cent of primary school teachers but less than half of headteachers.[49] In secondary schools they comprised only 20 per cent of headteachers.[50] The same pattern is apparent in other professions and occupations. Moreover, the fact that women's jobs are segregated and that women tend, therefore to be working only with other women depresses women's wage rates. Even in the 1990s the majority of men and women report that they work in segregated occupations - 58 per cent of men and 54 per cent of women stated they worked only with their own sex. Part-timers are even more likely to be occupationally segregated: 59 per cent worked only with women.[51]

What do women earn?

Any examination of women's wages must start by noting that women still earn significantly less than men. This discrimination is not peculiar to the United Kingdom but is common in other developed countries, including the USA. Within the European Union the differences vary, the smallest gap being in Denmark where women earn 86 per cent of men's earnings and the widest in Luxembourg where they earn only 65 per cent.[52] The gap in the United Kingdom has been narrowing over several years but the 1994 New Earnings Survey (Part A) showed that in respect of average hourly earnings, women received only 79.5 pence for each pound earned by men.[53] The inequality is greater amongst non-manual workers where women earn less than 68 per cent of men's pay. Amongst the professions (for example medicine and law), women's average pay is less than that of male colleagues: in the case of solicitors, less than three quarters of the pay of their male counterparts.

The difference between the average wages of men and women are clear, but the reasons for the disparities are complex. On the face of it, there are some identifiable differences between the earning capacities of men and women which are readily attributable to factors which have already been highlighted. Traditionally, women have tended to have lower qualifications and to spend periods out of the job market. They also tend to work fewer hours,[54] and less of their pay is made up of overtime payments.[55] These differences may appear straightforward, but the reasons why women work fewer hours and are concentrated in certain jobs are themselves issues of gender. Some of the causes of this segregation and stereotyping are beyond the scope of this book[56] but it seems incontrovertible that some derive from gender discrimination prior to entry into the labour market. The type and content of the education which a woman receives, the perception of a woman's role within her family, the expectations she has of herself and which others have of her, pressures from peers are all relevant in shaping a woman's life. Once women are in work, however, further explanations need to be found for the lower rates of pay that attach to the work done by women and which represent discrimination working within the labour market. To say that women earn less than men because they are in lower status and lower paid jobs merely restates the problem. The real issue is to separate cause and effect: is the work women do less well paid because it is of intrinsically lower value, or is it perceived as being of lower value because it is work done by women?[57]

The complexities inherent in pay structures in the United Kingdom are well illustrated in a study commissioned by the Equal Opportunities Commission in 1990.[58] One of the conclusions was that pay structures and the differences between the pay and benefits received by men and women result from a myriad of different factors but, significantly, tradition is found to be perhaps the most important influence. This reflects the well documented fact that the laws which demand equal pay have had limited practical impact. The researchers conclude that there are a number of specific potential sources of inequality. In particular, pay structures themselves tend to be segregated by gender. One example given is that an organisation may have a managerial pay structure (dominated by men) and a clerical pay structure (dominated by women). As will be seen, when women try to use the law to claim equal pay, these separate and supposedly gender neutral schemes have created grave problems. Grading structures which cover mainly female employees tend, according to this study, to be shorter and within grading structures which cover men and women, women tend to be at the bottom. One important finding was that while the use of merit pay has increased, the ways that it is assessed and awarded are lacking in openness.

The fact that performance related pay appears to discriminate against women employees is reflected in another study which found that jobs where women predominated had lower average merit rises than those where men were in the majority. Merit pay is often used as a retention tool in jobs with high turnover and rewarding long service also favours men.[59] Further inequalities surface in the way in which pay is made up. Basic pay is for most employees the most important part of earnings but, for some classes of workers, additions to that are also significant. The Pay and Gender research found that where women predominate the pay structure is less likely to incorporate additional payments and that even where women are equally eligible, they do not receive as much as men. This is also true for part-time workers who, by and large, do not receive additional payments such as overtime and shift premia, though there is, theoretically, no reason why they should not, having worked their agreed hours.[60]

The picture that emerges from the statistics on women's employment is not a cheerful one either generally in the context of sex discrimination or more especially in the specific area of how women may acquire wealth and thus independence through waged work. Almost half the workforce is now female, and a very significant proportion of all women are economically active but many of these work part-time and women are paid, on average, 20 per cent less than men. It is true that the gap between women's and men's access to wealth in the form of paid employment is the result of complex social and political pressures which have been shaped over the centuries and as such could not be redressed instantaneously. Campaigns have been waged, however, from the nineteenth century onwards both in Europe and in the United States of America to secure equal pay for women. The length and ferocity of these campaigns have been compared with the struggle for women's suffrage but, for all that, the rewards which women have reaped from equal pay legislation, and from the anti-discrimination legislation in general, have not been as substantial or as swift as was hoped. Part of the problem lies in the very notion of equal pay, which by itself is a very narrow concept. At its simplest, it means only that men and women doing the same job should receive the same rate of pay. Since, however, the labour market is gendered and men and women are commonly not doing the same work, that simple idea is, obviously, inadequate. Recognising that the achievement of equal pay demands a rather wider approach, most developed countries, including the United Kingdom, have enacted, besides laws on pay, more general anti-discrimination legislation to address the issues of women's access to paid employment and their prospects for training and promotion once they are employed.

Perhaps, however, the most fundamental obstacle in the campaign for equal pay is that it demands rejection of the idea that women can be paid less because they are women and that, therefore, their work is worth less and their needs not so great. In the widest sense, equal pay requires that rates of pay must be set according to objective factors such as skill and responsibility, ignoring the sex of the person performing the job. This concept of equal pay, which concentrates on the value of the worker, is not easily embodied in legal rules which have to be applied in many different circumstances. In the United Kingdom the question of equal pay and the more general issues of sex discrimination were tackled in the Equal Pay Act 1970 and the Sex Discrimination Act 1975. The success, or lack of it, of these measures may be gauged by analysing the way in which the legislation has been used to address the problems identified in the preceding pages.

Equal Access

This chapter concentrates on what women earn from paid employment and how the law has attempted to achieve equal pay for men and women irrespective of their sex. It would be incomplete, however, without some reference to the laws aimed at ensuring that women have access to paid employment in the first place. The Sex

Discrimination Act 1975 governs matters of sex discrimination which arise outside the terms of a contract.[61] It covers many areas other than employment, including the provision of services such as mortgages, bank loans and education all of which are essential if women are to have equal access to wealth. In the context of this Chapter, however, the emphasis is on paid employment.

A woman in the job market may face discrimination at many stages and levels from recruitment, through to promotion, training and dismissal. The Sex Discrimination Act 1975 covers all of these through two basic mechanisms contained in section 1. The way the law is structured means that it is unlawful to discriminate against a woman in the circumstances listed in the Act, whether directly or indirectly. A woman suffers direct discrimination where an employer treats her less favourably than a man would have been treated. This covers the situation, for example, where a short list is drawn up which deliberately excludes women, or where a woman is not selected for a job because in the past it has always been work done by men.

The concept of indirect discrimination is aimed at outlawing more insidious forms of discrimination which may operate unconsciously, often at an institutional level. It occurs where a requirement or condition is applied equally to men and women, but which is such that disproportionately fewer women than men can comply and which is shown to be to the disadvantage of the woman complaining. A classic example of such discrimination would be where an employer, faced with the need to make a number of redundancies, decides that part-timers should be dismissed first regardless of their length of service, followed by full-timers on the basis of last in, first out. It is incontrovertible that more women than men work part-time and that they do so, by and large, because their domestic responsibilities, particularly caring for dependent children, make it impossible for them to work full-time. The employer in the example has imposed a condition: in order that length of service shall count, the employee must be full-time. Disproportionately fewer women than men can comply with this and the individual claimant should be able to show a detriment. Indeed, this has been done in at least one reported case.[62]

There is, however, another element to the concept of indirect discrimination. In relation to *direct* discrimination, the motive of the discriminator is irrelevant, so that even where an employer may have acted out of "good" motives to protect a woman from hard or dirty work, there will be unlawful discrimination.[63] With indirect discrimination, the employer is allowed a defence: the discrimination will not be unlawful if the employer can show that it is justifiable irrespective of sex.[64] In other words, if the employer can show that the discriminatory practice was adopted on grounds of cost or administrative efficiency and had nothing to do with the sex of the workers involved, the act will still be allowed. On this basis, in a case which involved the dismissal of part-timers before full-timers, it was held that the practice was not unlawful discrimination because of the marginal financial savings to the employer.[65] Confidence in the judiciary is not increased if it is also noted that in the same case the Employment Appeal Tribunal was not prepared to interfere with the finding of the Industrial Tribunal that it could no longer be assumed, without evidence, that more women than men had responsibility for child care to such an extent that it precluded full-time employment.

Such decisions underline the limits of the law: no matter what the intentions of the legislators, they can always be circumvented by the judges, whether deliberately or not. Nevertheless, since the Act came into effect there have been developments which have undoubtedly been to the advantage of working women. Some of these have been gradual or incremental, others more dramatic. Many have been influenced by European law in the form of the Equal Treatment Directive[66] which has been the impetus behind many of the most important decisions. Some improvements, however, are due simply to the gradual heightening of awareness caused by the law. For example, the legislation demands fairness in recruitment and there have been cases which have dealt with advertisements, interviews, and questions asked of candidates.[67] As a result, few large organisations would not now have codes of practice on selection procedures: the law has, if nothing else, acted to educate and indicate how things should be done. Of course, not all employers are so scrupulous. Neither can the law easily address the logically prior problem of how to ensure that women are qualified for the jobs on offer. Still, if employers are now more aware of what may and may not be done at the stage of recruitment, it could be said that the law has helped to achieve something.

There are two other examples of the law having played an important role in improving the situation of working women. The first concerns discrimination against working mothers and the other against pregnant workers. The battle in relation to the first was far less protracted than the second and is exemplified in the case of *Hurley v Mustoe*.[68] A woman with four young children had worked for several years as a waitress, child care being organised on a shift basis with her husband. She changed her job because the hours were more convenient but, once the owner of the restaurant realised that she had children, she was fired. His argument was that it was not sex discrimination since he would not employ anyone - male or female - who had children because he believed them to be unreliable. It was held that Mrs Hurley had been the victim of both direct and indirect discrimination. In relation to the former there was no evidence that the employer applied the "no children" rule to men and thus she had been treated less favourably than if she had been a man. Indirect discrimination occurred as the condition for employment (no children) could be complied with by fewer married than unmarried persons.[69] This was to their detriment since they lost the chance of employment and it would be unlawful if it could not be justified. There was no evidence produced that employees with children were unreliable and, in any event, reliability could be confirmed by the taking up of references so that there was no need to have a blanket exclusion of all parents. The effect of this decision is to give some protection to working mothers should they be refused employment simply because they have children, but of course it does nothing to make it easier for mothers to take up employment or to combine it with motherhood. A woman who is constantly taking time off to care for sick children or cope with school holidays may not be sacked for being a mother, but for absenteeism and if, hypothetically even, a man would be treated similarly, there is no *sex* discrimination.

The story in relation to pregnant workers shows the judges in a far less favourable light. The Sex Discrimination Act requires that like be compared with like so that a woman must be compared with a man in similar circumstances to assess whether there has been discrimination based on *sex* rather than on any other factor, such as qualifications or expertise. When a woman complained that she had been sexually discriminated against by being dismissed on disclosing that she was pregnant, the initial response of the courts was that this did not come within the Act at all because it was impossible to make a comparison. A pregnant woman was no longer simply a woman, but a woman with child and there was no male equivalent with whom to compare her.[70] Eventually, the fallacy of this argument was recognised, but only partially corrected. It was decided that the necessary comparison could be made between a pregnant woman and a sick man, since both would need time off work.[71] Not only did this ignore the fact that pregnant women are not ill, it also benefited the bad employer since, if a sick man would have been dismissed, it was not discriminatory to sack a pregnant woman.

Though the "sick man" comparison allowed a claim to be brought, it certainly did not guarantee a remedy for a dismissed pregnant worker. Far more likely to achieve a remedy is the argument that, logically, no comparison is called for in these cases: discriminating against women on grounds of pregnancy must, by definition, amount to *sex* discrimination, since only women can become pregnant. Although this view was upheld by the European Court[72] the English judges showed some reluctance to adopt that approach, requiring confirmation from the European Court.[73] The result, however, is that pregnant women are now protected from sex discrimination at work.[74]

Though the Sex Discrimination Act is not without flaws and though progress has been sporadic, the Act has improved women's access to paid employment. The protection which it offers to part-time workers, working mothers and pregnant employees is especially valuable since these workers are particularly vulnerable to discrimination, including dismissal. Part-timers are often viewed as expendable and as lacking in commitment to the job, while a pregnant worker may be thought to threaten the smooth running of the enterprise and as being expensive, especially if a replacement has to be employed. For such women the Sex Discrimination Act has been instrumental in ensuring that they can find and keep paid employment.

The Act has been markedly less successful in breaking down the segregation of the workforce and encouraging women into traditionally male areas. Segregation is a key factor in the campaign for equal pay, but seems largely untouched by the Sex Discrimination Act. Studies have shown that there are various ways in which anti-discrimination legislation is knowingly or unintentionally avoided. Jobs vacancies may be filled, for example, by word of mouth rather than by advertisement, thus allowing a perpetuation of an exclusively male, or indeed female workforce. Moreover, the Act does not require employers to counter segregation by recruiting specific quotas of women into trades or professions where they are poorly represented: positive discrimination is, indeed, unlawful. Nor does the legislation call for employers to adopt policies and working practices that make it more feasible for women to work or work full-time. Child care facilities at the place of employment would make a dramatic difference for many women, but it is not unlawfully discriminatory for an employer not to provide them, even though lack of them prevents women being employed there. Even where the Act does apply, its remedies are notoriously weak: if a woman is successful in establishing sex discrimination the principal remedy is compensation rather than an order that the employer should employ or re-employ her or should promote her.[75]

The undeniable limitations of the current legislation have led to allegations that it is fundamentally, rather than technically, flawed. The very basis of the Act, which requires like to be compared with like, calls for women to be treated in the same way as men and thus requires them to comply with male standards and male norms. Even the concept of indirect discrimination, regarded as having greater potential for change, may be seen as adopting a male perspective: a woman will prove indirect discrimination only when she demonstrates that the proportion of women who can comply with a requirement geared to the working patterns of men is significantly lower or, in other words, that women are unable to meet the male standard. Though the Sex Discrimination Act has helped women, it has not achieved the fundamental shifts in the composition of the workforce which are a condition precedent to the realisation of that most important goal - equal pay for men and women.[76]

Equal pay

Legislation on equal pay appeared in the United Kingdom in 1970 in the Equal Pay Act. It was another five years, however, before the law came into force, at the same time as the Sex Discrimination Act which was not passed until 1975. This five year delay was meant to give employers time to reform wage structures and it is true that there was a sharp rise in women's wages when expressed as a proportion of men's just after the law came into force but since then the rate of progress has slowed and it has been calculated that at the current pace it will take over 30 years for women to achieve equality.

The law on equal pay appears superficially to be relatively straightforward since the Act simply requires that in every contract of employment there should be implied an equality clause so that in respect of *all* contract terms (not just pay) men and women are treated equally. In order for the equality clause to operate, however, certain conditions must be fulfilled. If a woman wishes to claim equal pay with a man (or vice versa, as with pensions) she must base her claim on one of the grounds listed in the Act and she must be able to compare herself to a male "comparator." In other words, the Act does not operate as a universal social measure to reform wage rates and pay structures for workers generally in order to achieve what might be considered a fairer or more equitable distribution, it is simply a rather blunt instrument which women may use, within certain defined and narrow limits, to argue that they are entitled to equal pay with their male colleagues because the employer has taken their sex into account in setting wage rates. The Equal Pay Act is part of the laws aimed at eradicating sex discrimination, not a measure for wider social justice. It does not enable women to compare themselves with other women or men with other men. It does not entitle any group of workers to claim a remedy on the basis that their work is undervalued by society and is not adequately rewarded. It may be argued that, for example, a part-time nursing auxiliary worker in a NHS hospital is "worth" as much as a man in an industrial occupation but it is likely that his hourly rate of pay will be higher and there is no legal mechanism for challenging that.

Although the Equal Pay Act has been of limited success in equalising the pay of men and women, the years during which it has been on the statute books have seen improvements in women's pay. It cannot be said with any certainty that this is due to the law, but it is clear that some developments in this area have been due to the United Kingdom's membership of the European Community and the legal consequences of that. Unfortunately, it is also the impact of European law which has helped, if only indirectly, to make equal pay one of the most complex and most criticised parts of the laws affecting workers. The most important measures of European law in this context are Article 119 of the Treaty of Rome and the Equal Pay Directive (EC 75/117),[77] the former calling for equal pay for equal work for men and women and the latter explaining that this includes work which is of equal value. What follows will take account of both United Kingdom and European law and it will also be assumed that the claimant is female, as is usually the case.[78]

Complications start with the title of the Act which, since it covers all contractual terms of employment (entitlement to holidays, fringe benefits and so on) is somewhat misleading.[79] The cases concentrate on pay, however, and one of the most important developments in the decisions under both United Kingdom and European law has been the widening definition given to "pay." It has been held that pay includes concessionary travel facilities granted to retired workers,[80] sick pay,[81] redundancy pay[82] and, crucially, pensions. In a series of important, complex decisions the right to equal pay has been held to cover pension contributions, pension benefits, and access to pension schemes.[83]

The Act covers all employees and some categories of the self-employed but if a case is to proceed there must be one individual who is prepared to put her name to the claim and thus bring herself into dispute, potentially at least, with her employer. There is no possibility in English law of bringing what is known as a class action, on behalf of a class, or classes of worker, even though this is an area where it is highly likely that the outcome of the case is going to affect far more workers than just the claimant. In order to make a claim the individual must be able to point to an actual man in the same employment. This latter phrase, which has been the subject of judicial scrutiny, means that the claimant and comparator must have the same, or an associated, employer but they need not work at the same place provided the terms and conditions are "common" so that if they did work at the other's place of employment the terms of their contract would be the same as they are now.[84] This is especially important where the employer is a large organisation and groups of workers may be segregated not only occupationally but also geographically.[85] The drafting of the English Act calls for the claimant to be employed at the same time as her comparator, but European law, in the guise of Article 119, allows the claimant to compare herself with her predecessor.[86]

If the claimant can find a suitable comparator, she must then proceed on one of three grounds set out in section 1 of the Act. These are that she does like work, work rated as equivalent or work of equal value. The first of these is in some ways the least complex since it essentially involves the woman in showing that she and the man are doing the same job, even if they are labelled differently. Like work is work of the same or a broadly similar nature where any differences are not of practical importance. Tribunals have taken a fairly flexible attitude to this definition and it soon became clear, for example, that what mattered was *what* was done and not *when* it was done. It was held that night-shift workers doing the same job as day-shift workers should not be paid a higher basic rate; any differences would have to be justified as overtime or shift premia.[87] Of course, such a decision is of limited value unless women have equal access to the higher rates and it has already been noted that women do not earn the same proportion of their pay from overtime and shift premia as do men. Even where women are engaged in shift work it has been found that twice as many of them have to pay for child care as do working women generally which means that any higher rates paid for working unsocial hours are immediately reduced. Since women's earnings are generally lower than men's the costs of such child care form a higher proportion of their earnings.[88] The biggest drawback, however, to a woman claiming equal pay on the basis of like work is the obvious occupational segregation experienced by many women - there may not be a man doing the same work and if he is, the employer may have been wise enough to pay him the same rate as the woman.[89] Where men and women do the same work, it is also extremely likely that women are concentrated in lower grades and differences in qualification, responsibility, service and experience will prevent the work from being classed as "like work."

The other two grounds are theoretically more use in the face of a workforce organised in a gendered fashion. The first allows a claim where the work has been rated as equivalent which, according to section 1(5), means that the jobs have been given equal value, in terms of the demands on a worker under various headings (for instance effort, skill, decision). This entails carrying out an evaluation to grade the jobs according to such criteria and thus create a hierarchical wage structure. On the assumption that job evaluation is capable of being an entirely objective exercise, free of considerations of the sex of the workers concerned, this might be thought of as being the key to equal pay. It allows for comparisons across occupational boundaries and for the inclusion of a variety of criteria that take account of the abilities that are perceived to belong to the different sexes, for example, manual dexterity (often cited as a female attribute) as well as physical strength (seen usually as a male characteristic). It has not, however, proved to be the solution it might have been.

One of the principal limitations on the utility of this part of the Act is that it does not allow a woman to ask for a job evaluation, but depends on the employer having initiated or agreed to it. It was for this reason that the United Kingdom was found to be in breach of European law.[90] Moreover, the Act is of little use in deciding what constitutes a valid evaluation scheme (apart from saying that a sexually discriminatory scheme can be overridden if, but for the discrimination, the jobs would have been rated as equal) and it can be very difficult to identify the subtly discriminatory effects of some schemes. A scheme may look gender neutral on its face but it may still be the case that women are systematically coming out worse under it. This may be because certain attributes are not rewarded (say, communication skills) or it may be that attributes seen as "female" are not rewarded as highly (say, manual dexterity).[91] One presumably intractable problem with all evaluative schemes is that, whatever their complexity and despite their apparently scientific approach, they remain ultimately dependent on the judgment of those ascribing different values to different jobs or parts of jobs.

It is true that both the English courts and the European Court of Justice (ECJ) have denounced discriminatory evaluation schemes[92] but, to date, job evaluation as a way of achieving equal pay has not been a conspicuous success. One view of job evaluation is that "the procedure which produces any one judgment resembles more closely a lottery, dependent upon choices which lack rationale, than an objective assessment of worth."[93] The European Commission itself has recognised that, almost twenty years after the Equal Pay Directive, there has been, in its words, little effective progress on achieving equal pay. In June 1994 the Commission adopted a Memorandum on Equal Pay for Work of Equal Value[94] in the hope that it would help to make equal pay a reality rather than a mere legal right. The continuing disparity between the pay of men and women throughout the member states is attributed in the Memorandum largely to job segregation and to job classification systems which are often biased against women. It calls for the development of non-discriminatory evaluation schemes as an essential step towards the goal of equal pay.

As far as the United Kingdom is concerned some of the failure may be blamed on the way in which collective bargaining structures have developed. Job evaluation was traditionally a way of providing wage structures, not eradicating sex discrimination. It was seen as part of the British system of collective bargaining conducted by unions and employers free of intervention from the law. Traditionally also, trades unions were interested in protecting the wages and the wage differentials of their members and not, in most case, in sex equality. Trades unions are now, by and large, committed to equality for their members, and indeed play an important role in the area of equal pay for work of equal value, but for many years wage structures which unions and employers negotiated were blatantly, even if not intentionally, sexually discriminatory with women workers doing one set of jobs on one pay scale and men doing different jobs, and possibly members of a different union, on another. Women are still suffering from the historical effects of such bargaining and negotiating anomalies and this can be seen most clearly in the context of the employer's defence to a claim of equal pay.

As originally envisaged under the Equal Pay Act, job evaluation may not have made much difference to women's financial status but it is of even more importance since the Act was amended to take account of the decision of the ECJ which concluded that, since a woman could not insist on a job evaluation without the employer's consent, the United Kingdom was in breach of Article 119 and the Equal Pay Directive.[95] The equal value amendment[96] allows the claimant to argue that she is entitled to equal pay because she is doing work of equal value to that of her male comparator. By definition, a claim which involves equal value is going to be more complicated than one based on like work since, for a start, the equality or lack of it is not immediately apparent: an evaluation must be made of the two jobs and that requires an expert report. At this point the problems inherent in the evaluative process are compounded by the truly tortuous procedures laid down in the legislation which have attracted levels of judicial criticism rarely heard in public. In just one example, *British Coal Corporation* v *Smith*,[97] the President of the Employment Appeal Tribunal was driven to adverse comment in a case in which the first claims were submitted in 1985 and which was decided in the Employment Appeal Tribunal in 1993 but then went on to the Court of Appeal in 1994. Even then it was simply deciding whether the claim could be brought in the first place.

The first step in an equal value claim is when the industrial tribunal (the forum in which equal pay and other employment cases are heard) decides whether or not to ask for a report from an independent expert. The claimant may fail even at this early stage if the tribunal decides there are no reasonable grounds for deciding that the work is of equal value[98] or, alternatively, if there has already been an evaluation which gives the jobs a different value. Moreover, as it would be a waste of time and money to commission a report only to find that the employer can justify the pay difference, the Rules of Procedure for industrial tribunals allow the employer to ask that the tribunal hears his defence at the preliminary hearing.[99] If the tribunal does refer to the expert there are long delays while the report is prepared and when it is presented the tribunal is not bound to accept it, but if it does it will be taken into account in formulating the decision.[100]

These procedures are complex and time consuming and are not conducive to enforcement of the law or the widespread use of job evaluation as a method for equalising the pay of men and women. It is ironic, therefore, that the report Pay and Gender in Britain found that the use of job evaluation is spreading.[101]   The researchers comment:

> As employment structures in organisations become ever more complex, the need to create and control rational payment systems that reflect the emerging employment patterns and the organisation's employment policies has intensified. It is therefore not surprising that our findings suggest considerable growth in the use of job evaluation, which - on the face of it - can provide a logical framework for a payment structure.[102]

The reservation that evaluation leads to pay structures which are logical only "on the face of it" is borne out by the findings. If the schemes are to be useful in eradicating sexually based pay differences then it would seem sensible to have one scheme applying to all different groups of workers, but it was discovered that although this was the case in four out of ten organisations surveyed, others had more than one system, or had one scheme which was not applied to the whole workforce, or more than one scheme but again covering only parts of the workforce. This meant that about one third of the firms used different schemes for different groups, on the basis, largely, that this had always been the case. Significantly, "no respondent in organisations where more than two schemes were used seemed to see this as a potential problem in relation to equal value."[103] Moreover, along with the increasing use of job evaluation, the report found that firms were revising schemes or introducing new ones, but there was only one organisation in which equal pay was given as the main reason for this: "[a] number of our interviewees seemed either ignorant of the issues concerned or complacent about their implications for the companies in which they work."[104] Such findings merely reinforce the view that as a weapon in the armoury for achieving equal pay (which is simply one way of achieving something approaching equal status) job evaluation has not been a success. That is not to say, however, that it has been of no assistance at all.

Over the past few years trade unions have started to use the equal value provision as a means to negotiating better pay for their women members, on the basis that if improvements cannot be gained through voluntary means there is always the threat of litigation. The union can have ready a whole tranche of potential claims ready to submit to the tribunals if the employer does not come up with an acceptable formula. Indeed it is the bringing of these multiple claims that has contributed to the clogging up of the court proceedings. In the *British Coal* case, 1,286 canteen and cleaning workers submitted equal value claims comparing themselves to 150 male surface mineworkers or clerical workers.[105] Some trade unions now have very sizeable female membership[106] and it is these in particular who have taken advantage of the leverage provided by the law, albeit an unsatisfactory and unwieldy law. Even then, though the actual pay of women may improve, it does not necessarily alter the position of women workers in the general hierarchy of jobs, and even where the work is of equal value they may not take home anywhere near as much money as the men because of the impact of overtime and shift payments, which women on average are less able to benefit from, either because they are not in the jobs where these are available or because their domestic commitments militate against overtime or shift work.

Whereas the three grounds on which a woman may claim to have her pay brought into line with that of men have certain inherent deficiencies, these are only part of the problem. Assuming that she manages to show that she is doing like work, work rated as equivalent or work of equal value, there is no guarantee of equal pay. The legislation is aimed only at sex discrimination, not at wiping out all pay differentials and it thus open to the employer under the defence provided in section 1(3) to show that the difference in pay is not due to sex but to some other "material factor." There is some logic to this since most workers would accept that it is not wrong to pay more to someone with more experience, more responsibility, higher qualifications and so on. But even these apparently innocuous grounds for differentiating can work to the detriment of women. Women who spend time out of the labour market and then return part-time with increasing domestic responsibilities may find that their difficulties in building up experience or securing training opportunities mean in turn that they fail to achieve promotion and never graduate to the more responsible jobs. Those who work in predominantly female occupations may find themselves on different pay scales and in different bargaining structures from predominantly male jobs with correspondingly different gradings and promotion prospects - for example, a woman in a clerical job may find that there is no progression from that to an administrative or managerial post, while men on the shop floor may have a clearer career progression and an expectation of promotion. None of this would matter quite so much if the courts in the United Kingdom had shown themselves prepared to recognise the problems. Thus far, however, the most positive developments have been in the ECJ rather than in the English tribunals.

A good example is the case of the speech therapists, *Enderby* v *Frenchay Health Authority and Secretary of State for Health*[107] which began in 1985 and reached the ECJ in 1993. Enderby, a senior NHS speech therapist, claimed that her work was of equal value to that of male pharmacists and clinical psychologists, also employed by the NHS, whose salaries were higher by about 60 per cent. In the past, speech therapists have been regarded as medical auxiliaries and 99 per cent of them were women. Pharmacists and clinical psychologists were predominantly male and their salary scales were between £3,000 and £12,000 a year higher than their female colleagues. The case was rejected by English courts partly on the basis that, even if the work were of equal value, the employer could justify the differences in pay since they were attributable not to sex but to the different bargaining structures relevant to the different groups. Historically, speech therapists were covered by different negotiating structures, but according to the courts, there was nothing discriminatory within the structures themselves. The approach of the English courts was the object of sustained criticism not least because of the apparent inability to appreciate that the historical reasons themselves are likely to have been informed by sex discrimination and the value that is placed on what is seen as women's work.[108]

Enderby was referred to the ECJ, whose judges had previously shown themselves to be less blinkered in their approach to these systemic or institutionalised examples of bias. In a vitally important case, usually referred to as the *Danfoss* case,[109] the ECJ looked at pay scales which systematically resulted in disadvantage to women. The claim was initiated by a Danish trade union which complained that a pay system based on a collective agreement was biased against women. The employer paid the same basic pay to workers in the same grade, the grading having been decided on job classification, but within the grade additional pay was possible on the basis of what was termed employee flexibility, defined by reference to factors such as quality of work and responsibility and on the basis of training and seniority. The ECJ accepted that on the face of it the pay scale was gender-neutral, but held that if it did result in consistent disadvantage to women that had to be because it was discriminatory since it cannot be the case that work done by women will inevitably be of lower quality. A system based on merit which consistently fails to reward women must be flawed and is unlawful. Similarly, if flexibility is taken to mean the ability to adapt to variable schedules and sites, that too may *indirectly* discriminate against women as it is generally more difficult for women to organise their competing domestic duties to allow them that flexibility at work. Furthermore, quite apart from the fact that women were consistently at a disadvantage under the scheme, employees had no way of knowing which criteria were being applied to them or to what extent they were being used in the calculation of their pay. The Court was of the opinion that the scheme was not "transparent" and that where there is no transparency but the average pay of women in the pool is lower than that of men, it is for the employer to show that there is no sex bias in the scheme. Where the discrimination is indirect, the law allows the employer to seek to justify it on grounds that are untainted by sex and which relate to a real and objectively identifiable business need. So, for example, if the employer can show that a particular task requires certain training, it will not be discriminatory to reward that qualification. In *Danfoss* the ECJ held that seniority was an attribute which could be used without having to justify its use because it denoted experience but, in a later decision, the Court changed its mind and held that even in relation to rewards for long service there must be justification: women may be indirectly discriminated against because of their different work patterns.[110]

This background meant that it was always more likely that Enderby would succeed in Europe rather than in the national courts and this turned out to be the case. The ECJ held that where statistics show that there is an appreciable difference in pay between two jobs of equal value, one of which is done predominantly by women and the other by men, there is a *prima facie* case of sex discrimination and it is for the employer to show a justification independent of the sex of the workers. On the particular defence that the difference was explicable by the collective bargaining structure, the Court held that this was not enough of itself to justify the pay differentials.

Such decisions have, in theory, far-reaching consequences. The effects, however, do not necessarily percolate through to those who would benefit. Although, for example, *Danfoss* received a good deal of publicity, the *Pay and Gender* report[111] found that - along with increasing use of merit pay - there was an almost total ignorance about the case and its implications. This is particularly disturbing in the light of research which suggests that women are being discriminated against in such schemes. The Institute of Manpower Studies (commissioned by the EOC) found that many schemes were subjective, sexually stereotypical and led to lower pay rises for women. Jobs where women predominate also had lower average merit pay rises than those where men were in the majority.[112] If this shows nothing else, it is an illustration of the shortcomings of legislating for equality without wider social changes.

Women in the United Kingdom face the additional problem that the judges have not always seemed over-eager to apply the law in ways which would advance the position of women, sometimes seeming almost deliberately to ignore the mischief at which the Act was aimed. In *Calder* v *Rowntree Mackintosh Confectionery Ltd*[113] women were held to be doing work of equal value to male comparators but the employers argued that the difference was due to a payment made to the men for working rotating shifts (60 per cent on those shifts were men) while the women always worked a twilight shift (there were no men on the shift). At the same time, however, the employers conceded that there was in the extra pay an element to compensate for working unsocial hours which the women also worked. Nevertheless, the Court of Appeal held that despite the fact that some indeterminate part of the shift premium represented a premium for unsocial hours this did not prevent a finding that the shift premium was genuinely due to working rotating shifts. The Court was of the opinion that what the women were complaining of was unfairness and not sex discrimination - they seem to have failed to grasp the idea that unequal pay is an example of unfairness for which women are entitled to a legal remedy.

The decision in *Calder* pre-dates that of the ECJ in *Enderby* and it may be that in future United Kingdom tribunals will be more aware of the factors which lead to women's lower pay and more sympathetic to arguments that seek to address the problem. In *Enderby* it was not only the issue of bargaining structures that was before the Court since the employer had also argued that the pharmacists were easily employable in the private sector and thus market forces had affected their rates of pay. It had already been established by the House of Lords that market forces could justify indirect discrimination. In *Rainey* v *Greater Glasgow Health Board*[114] it was held that market conditions (inability to recruit on the NHS wages paid to the women) justified higher entry salaries to men from the private sector. The market conditions were held to be a material factor justifying a *temporarily* inflated salary. It was not that the women were under-valued, rather that the men were over-valued and were thus being paid above the rate for the job while the prevailing market conditions demanded that. It should be recalled, however, that in *Enderby* the difference in pay was as much as 60 per cent and the Industrial Tribunal had originally held that the employer could not explain the whole of that by market forces. The Employment Appeal Tribunal took the view that once market forces were found to have played *a* part, the employer was not required to prove that they justified the whole difference.[115] The ECJ came to a very important decision on this point holding that while market forces can be an objectively justifiable reason for pay differences, it is for the national court to decided whether and to what extent those justify the difference. In other words if the employer cannot show that the market explains the whole difference, it would, presumably be open to the Tribunal to award proportionate pay. At the time of writing, *Enderby* has not yet finished its long journey through the courts (it still has to be established that the work is of equal value) but the introduction of proportionality could have far-reaching consequences if it is taken up by the courts.

So far, however, cases decided post-*Enderby* do not indicate a radical re-thinking of the judicial approach in English tribunals. In *Yorkshire County Council* v *Ratcliffe*,[116] for example, the claims involved catering assistants (dinner ladies). Their rates of pay were originally set by reference to nationally negotiated local government collective agreements and they had been graded on an equal level with, for example, road sweepers and gardeners. After the introduction of compulsory competitive tendering, which allows private sector employers to bid for contracts to provide services previously supplied by local authorities, the Council discovered that it could not compete with outside firms and the women were dismissed and then re-employed on lower pay. They claimed equal pay with those with whom they had been equally graded (in other words their original rates).

Since the reason that the wages had been cut was to enable the Council to compete, the question was whether the need to compete with a commercial rival could amount to a material factor other than sex. The problem is, of course, that the catering assistants were doing the kind of jobs which have been traditionally seen as "women's work" and such work has been traditionally under-valued in the market. The Equal Pay Act represents the law's attempt to remedy that situation. The Industrial Tribunal found by a majority that the Council could not establish a defence since the need to reduce the women's pay in order to compete was tainted by sex. The Tribunal took note of the fact that the market was almost exclusively female: there were two men employed and 1,300 women. It further noted that the work was convenient to a female workforce from the point of view of hours and times worked. These were employees whose need for work which fitted in with domestic commitments would mean that they would continue to work even for lower wages. It was this that enabled competitors, who employed only women, to pay their workers rates lower than those which the Council had originally agreed. Even though the Council needed to reduce costs in order to win the contract and this could be said to be a material factor, it was one due to the difference in sex:

> ... arising out of the general perception in the United Kingdom, and certainly in North Yorkshire, that a woman should stay home to look after the children and if she wants to work it must fit in with that domestic duty; and a lack of facilities to enable her, easily, to do otherwise.[117]

When the case reached the Court of Appeal, however, the approach was different. That Court pointed out that the rates offered to men and women were the same - both by the Council and by the private sector competition. It was then held that the Council was not discriminating between men and women and the need to compete was unconnected with the difference of sex. This is a disappointing and short-sighted decision. The fact that the employer would have paid both men and women the same low rate of pay (about £3.00 an hour) is no answer at all to the proposition that the reason the rates were at that level is because of the under-valuing of work that is done predominantly by women. The presence of one or two men working alongside women does not alter that fact.[118] These women had been graded as equivalent to workers whose pay was now higher than theirs: unless that was wrong, they were now being paid below the rate for the job, which is the exact opposite of the situation in *Rainey*. The Court seems to have chosen to ignore the underlying discrimination that women face in the setting of wage rates. It is interesting that the Court of Appeal expressly states that it was "striking that the appellants should seek to establish their rights to equal pay even though, if they should succeed in doing so, they would find themselves redundant and unemployed."[119] Whilst it is not only women workers who find themselves being driven to accept worsening terms of employment by employers who argue that they cannot afford to pay more, it is "striking" that women are particularly vulnerable to this sort of pressure because of their need to find work that which fits in with their other responsibilities. Since they tend to lack flexibility in terms of hours, times and location the women end up paying for the privilege of being employed at all.

That kind of decision leads to the conclusion that the legislation is limited both in its scope and by the interpretation placed upon it. The prevalence of job segregation has diminished the usefulness of like work for claiming equal pay and the tortuous procedures involved in the equal value route amount almost to a denial of justice. Judges have compounded the difficulties by allowing the material factor defence to mask historical and institutionalised bias. Whilst these are serious shortcomings, it is possible to argue that the Act has also seen some real achievements for some sections of the female workforce and, in particular, part-timers.

Part-time workers remain a group who are generally disadvantaged in comparison with their full-time colleagues but in recent years a series of decisions largely, though not entirely from Europe, has gone some way to improving the conditions of part-timers. The first important step was to establish that paying part-timers lower rates than full-timers was capable of amounting to sex discrimination. As most part-timers are women, paying them less well immediately raises that suspicion but it had been suggested that the employer could argue that the difference was due to a material factor which had nothing to do with sex, namely the additional inconvenience and administrative costs of employing part-timers. Between them the ECJ and the Employment Appeal Tribunal laid this to rest, holding that the employer had to show an objectively justifiable economic reason for paying the (women) part-timers less than the (male) full-timers.[120] The ECJ which had been less decisive than the Employment Appeal Tribunal expressed itself more trenchantly in *Bilka-Kaufhaus GmbH* v *Weber von Hartz*[121] where it was held that in order to avoid a breach of Article 119 the employer must show that the differential rates disproportionately affecting more women than men "... correspond to a real need on the part of the undertaking, are appropriate with a view to achieving the objectives pursued and are necessary to that end ...".[122] The results of the application of this test may be seen in cases where it was held unlawful to disqualify part-timers from sickness benefits or from a redundancy scheme. The most recent cases to be referred to the ECJ are seeking rulings on whether it is unlawful indirect sex discrimination for a collective agreement to stipulate that part-timers will be paid overtime rates only when they have exceeded the basic *full-time* hours.[123] Whatever the ECJ decides in those cases the earlier decisions have helped to create a climate in which part-timers are not inevitably regarded as second class workers, but they do not, admittedly, raise the wages of the part-timers who tend anyway to be grouped in the lower paid occupations.

Part-timers in the United Kingdom have always suffered other disadvantages besides low wages, since the employment legislation which protects workers from unfair dismissal, entitles them to redundancy pay and maternity rights and a number of other rights, requires the worker to satisfy certain conditions, one of which relates to the number of hours that must be worked in any week. The basic rule has been that to qualify for protection the worker must work at least 16 hours a week for two years. Those who work for between 8 and 16 hours have had to work for five years in order to claim the same rights and those who work fewer than 8 hours have not qualified at all (all these qualifications derive from the Employment Protection (Consolidation) Act 1978). The developing case law on part-timers emanating from the ECJ caused many to think that the United Kingdom legislation was in breach of the law on the basis the qualifying conditions discriminated against part-timers and that this constituted indirect sex discrimination which was unlawful unless objectively justified. The Equal Opportunities Commission took up the claim and in 1994 won what must be described as an historic victory.[124] Not only did the House of Lords find in favour of the part-timers, but the Equal Opportunities Commission was itself allowed to bring the case, a development quite as important as the finding on discrimination.

The Commission was seeking judicial review, arguing that the legislation which laid down the qualifying thresholds was in breach of Article 119 and the Equal Treatment Directive in relation to both redundancy pay and unfair dismissal compensation. The case failed in its early stages, but when it reached the House of Lords it was held that the Commission was entitled to seek judicial review in pursuit of its statutory duty to work towards the elimination of discrimination and that it was open to an English court to declare that an Act of Parliament was inconsistent with European law. Furthermore, it was held that there was no justification for the qualifying thresholds. Where a discriminatory provision is contained in national legislation, it is for the state to justify it. Whilst the thresholds could be said to be necessary (to increase the amount of part-time work available) they could not be said to be objectively suitable and requisite for achieving that aim. The effects of this decision should not be underestimated. For the first time it means that all part-timers[125] will be able, potentially, to gain the same kind of employment rights as full-timers at least in relation to unfair dismissal and redundancy.[126] It also means that the Commission will be able to seek further clarification of areas of the law without there being the need for an individual to bring a test case.

Such decisions may cause those who question the utility of the law to grant it some credit. On the other hand, its successes, such as they are, have been relatively limited over the last twenty years and there remains the question of whether it would be better to turn to other means of achieving equality. The problem is that it is difficult to identify what those means might be. Support for the legal route to equality is found in an Equal Opportunities Commission report in which Rubery suggests that sex discrimination is so deeply rooted in the labour market that equal pay will never develop on its own out of the operation of a free market.[127] Although Rubery maintains that the costs of equalising pay are not such as would damage competitiveness, and that there would be real benefits, including reductions in poverty and an increase in the ability of families to choose more flexible work patterns, she also cites the factors which affect women's employment including job segregation, the undervaluing of women's work, the persistent belief that women work for "pin money" not to support families, and their lack of bargaining power. Her conclusion is that it is essential to maintain the equal value route to equal pay in order to "eliminate from the labour market the discrimination that is based on historically embedded views of women's position in society." Unfortunately, for every decision that advances the cause of equality in pay, another seems to hinder it. The law seems at best to be a flawed mechanism for achieving real progress. The Equal Opportunities Commission recognised this in so far as it submitted proposals to the government in 1988 and in 1990 for strengthening the law.[128] In 1993 these were, by and large, rejected[129] and the Equal Opportunities Commission referred a complaint to the European Commission alleging that the United Kingdom had failed properly to implement European law citing for example the complexity, delays and the unavailability of legal aid for those bringing claims.[130] It is clear that whether one turns to the law, to the market or to political campaigning, women have a long and uphill struggle before they obtain anything approaching equality in their wage packets.

Poor workers

Poverty, like wealth, is an elusive concept and some would have us believe that the poor - and certainly poor workers - are no longer with us.[131] Unfortunately, this is not the case, and although poverty affects both men and women, the latter figure disproportionately amongst poor workers since they are over-represented amongst the lower paid. One way of measuring poverty is to use the "decency threshold" set by the Council of Europe to assess whether states are complying with Article 4 of the European Social Chapter which calls for fair remuneration. Low pay is defined therein as being anything below 68 per cent of all full-timers' mean earnings which in 1994 would give just over £215 a week or £5.75 an hour.[132] The situation worsened for the low paid during the 1980s: in 1979, 28 per cent of full-time workers earned less than the decency threshold, by 1991 that had risen to 36 per cent (and just over half of female full-timers were low paid on this definition). In the same period the number of low paid part-timers rose by 36 per cent to over 70 per cent of all such workers (79 per cent of female part-timers were paid below the decency threshold).[133] In seeking to find an explanation for the steadily deteriorating rates of pay of lower paid workers it is necessary to remember the political background. During the 1980s the distribution of wealth became even more unequal - the poor became poorer but the rich became richer. This was partly due to changes in the tax and benefits systems, but was also in part traceable to the government's attitude to the mechanisms which had operated for many years to protect the poorest workers. In particular, in maintaining an attachment to non-intervention in the market, Conservative governments decreed that wages must be left to find their own levels, no matter how low, and this prompted the determination to abolish Wages Councils.

Wages Councils, then called Trade Boards, were established in 1909 to set legally enforceable minimum rates of pay in those trades where pay was exceptionally low - the so-called sweated trades. In introducing the legislation Winston Churchill said:

> It is a serious national evil that any class of His Majesty's subjects should receive less than a living wage for their utmost exertions. It was formerly supposed that the working of the laws of supply and demand would naturally regulate or eliminate that evil ... But where you have ... no organisation, no parity of bargaining, the good employer is undercut by the bad and the bad employer is undercut by the worst...[134]

The Trade Boards, which later developed into the Wages Councils, were envisaged as a temporary substitute for collective bargaining in trades where workers were not unionised or for some other reason found it difficult to bargain effectively with the employer. The idea was that once a minimum living wage had been imposed on the employer, with the threat of criminal sanctions for non-compliance, voluntary collective bargaining could develop and eventually the Wages Council in that trade would become otiose. In neither respect was the system an unqualified success: wage levels set by the Councils remained very low relative to other workers and unions did not find it easy to organise in the trades covered by the scheme. Nevertheless, for the workers covered by the Councils the system did offer at least some protection.

Prior to 1986 Wages Councils could set not only minimum wages, at different levels for categories of worker, but also other terms and conditions, such as holidays and holiday pay. The government began its attack on the system by asserting that Councils interfered with the freedom of employers to offer and job-seekers to accept jobs at wages which would otherwise be acceptable: workers were pricing themselves out of jobs by wishing to adhere to minimum wage levels. Of course, it was obvious from the start that women would be disproportionately and adversely affected by the disappearance of the Councils: the government, however, was sanguine stating, for example, that "the low paid are mainly young with no family responsibilities, or married women bringing a second income into the home."[135]   Plans to abolish the Councils in 1985 met a hostile response from a range of interests including both the trade unions and the CBI and the Wages Act of 1986 simply restricted their powers. By that stage there were 26 Councils still in existence and the amendments to the law made it necessary for the United Kingdom to denounce the International Labour Organisation Convention 26 (Minimum Wage Fixing Machinery Convention, 1928). The Act removed all workers under the age of 21 from the system[136] and provided that the Councils could no longer deal with terms other than wage rates and were restricted to setting only one rate for all workers. The enforcement mechanism remained the same: breach of the law was a criminal offence and so failure to pay the minimum rate, keep records or inform workers (including homeworkers) of the minimum rates could be met with a prosecution which could lead not only to a fine but also an order to pay arrears of wages for up to two years. In the civil courts an affected worker could claim up to six years back-payment. The Wages Act was policed by the Wages Inspectorate but the restrictions in the powers of the Councils was matched by swingeing cuts in the Inspectorate (just prior to abolition there were only 55 Inspectors as compared to 177 in 1979). These Inspectors were responsible for nearly 400,000 establishments and over two million workers.   Perhaps not surprisingly the level of non-compliance was extremely high: in 1991 in the North West region (which included part of Wales) over 1,000 firms were found to be underpaying and one was prosecuted.[137]   These were only the firms detected in underpayment: many more were uninspected. Even after 1986 the government were not satisfied and from time to time gave notice that there was no long term future for the Wages Councils until in November 1992 abolition was announced, the Prime Minister stating that:

> These days Wages Councils are an anachronism. They no longer have a useful role. They were set up in 1909 and they are not relevant to 1992.[138]

The Councils were abolished by section 35 of the Trade Union Reform and Employment Rights Act 1993.

Given their limited success it might be asked whether abolition is really so serious, but this ignores the extreme vulnerability of the workers who were covered. At the time abolition was announced the system covered nearly two and a half million workers of whom nearly two million were women. The sectors covered included retail and catering, hairdressing and clothing manufacture and minimum rates payable ranged from £2.59 to £3.10 an hour (as compared with the decency threshold which was then £5.15). Levels of pay were thus already very low, and workers were often casual, part-time or temporary. Without even the protection of the Wages Councils it was predicted that their rates of pay were likely to fall even further. This was borne out by experience: in 1994 a survey found that one third of jobs formerly covered by the Councils were paying less than the rate the Councils would have set.[139]

The disappearance of the Councils also adversely effects the equality of women's pay with their male colleagues: in Wages Council industries the gap between male and female rates was actually lower than in industry generally.[140] The statutory minimum was an impetus to equal pay: once the equal pay legislation was in force Councils had to set a uni-sex rate and especially since 1986, when only one rate could be set, this created a push towards equality (subject to the usual differences in relation to men's greater overtime and shift payments). The positive aspects of the Councils were recognised not only by the Equal Opportunities Commission in its response to the government's plans on abolition but also by trade unions such as the GMB and the TGWU. The unions noted that the government appeared to be justifying abolition by saying that many workers covered were part-timers, bringing a second income into the home. As the GMB pointed out in its response, "this is tantamount to saying that it is okay to abolish wages councils because most of the workers covered are women," while the TGWU pointed out that wages should reflect the demands of the job and should not in any way be related to the family circumstances of the worker.[141]

The abolition of the Wages Councils was preceded by opposition from many quarters but this time - further away from a general election - the government stuck to its views that the Councils were interfering with the availability of jobs and that if employers were free to offer wages even lower than the minimum wage levels there would be more jobs available. The premise was challenged not only by unions, church and voluntary organisations but also by some employers who realised that, as Churchill commented over 80 years ago, undercutting by bad employers is to the benefit of nobody and simply helps to create the dependency culture so disliked by governments, since the payment of wages below subsistence levels merely places additional burdens on the social security system.[142] These arise partly from the payment of family credit to low paid workers with families but, as is discussed in Chapter 4, because of the inter-relationship between benefits and wages, there is little or no incentive for those who are unemployed and on income support to accept a job with very low wages. Despite the arguments in favour of their retention the Wages Councils vanished, leaving the United Kingdom as the only member of the European Union which has no mechanisms for protecting workers against very low pay. Seven states within the Union have a statutory minimum wage system ranging from 42 per cent of average manual industrial wages in Spain to 69 per cent in France.[143] The reversion to nineteenth century conditions by the government in the United Kingdom will have inevitable effects on poor workers who, as has been seen, are largely women.

Wages for housework?

The mixed feelings many women have about accepting paid employment outside their homes stem inevitably from a number of complicated motives, many of them involving guilt about the neglect of family and home. One aspect of the difficulties faced by women cannot, however, be avoided: working women, with very few exceptions, actually have two jobs, but for only one of them do they receive any wages. It is not just the work done for the family which is unrewarded in any monetary sense: women are volunteer workers in schools, hospitals, charities, churches and numerous other organisations. None of this work is rewarded (at least not in this life, unless by mention in the honours list) and it is even more "invisible" than the other, paid work which women do. Researchers for the Legal and General Insurance company calculated that a housewife spends around 70 hours a week on domestic duties but that a wife with a part-time job still works an average of 59 hours a week at home. Women working full-time work longer hours at home than they do at work. The rates needed to employ someone to do what women do unpaid (nanny, cook, shopper, cleaner, gardener, driver, seamstress, laundress, and so on) were calculated to be a basic £349 per week - or where there is a child under the age of one, £457 per week.[144] Some estimates put the value of this work even higher, but does it really mean anything? The wages which women would be paid for this work would have to come from money raised by the state and it is difficult to see a government already looking for ways to restrict the welfare system introducing these level of payments. In a period of unemployment with most growth coming in part-time female employment, there is not even the incentive to get women back into the home - women are not taking jobs from men, they are doing the jobs which men have not traditionally done for wages men would not traditionally accept. There is, however, an argument that whilst women may never actually be paid these sort of sums by a grateful nation, it is vital to raise awareness of the work which is done and thereby change perceptions of the status of women. It is also important that these contributions are recognised in any discussion of the welfare benefits system or child maintenance.

  For two decades or more groups such as the International Wages for Housework Campaign have been fighting for recognition of and reward for women's unwaged work and they have had some success in getting these issues on to the international agenda. Figures issued by the United Nations indicate that, for example, women do two thirds of the world's work but receive only 5 per cent of the income. The US Department of Commerce has estimated the value of housework in the US at $1,461 billion a year. At the 1985 UN Decade for Women Conference it was agreed that:

> The remunerated and, in particular, the unremunerated contributions of women to all aspects and sectors of development should be recognized, and appropriate efforts should be made to measure and reflect these contributions in national accounts and economic statistics and in the gross national product. Concrete steps should be taken to quantify the unremunerated contribution of women to agriculture, food production, reproduction and household activities.[145]

The gross national product (GNP) or gross domestic product (GDP) is the total value of goods and services produced, but includes only those goods and services exchanged for money, thus overlooking women's unwaged work which has been estimated as producing as much as 50 per cent of the GNP. International campaigns for the implementation of this resolution have been matched by those on a European level. A Report was produced for the Women's Rights Committee of the European Parliament calling for member governments to count women's unwaged work in their GNP, for independent social security and pension rights for housewives and for an allowance for those raising small children whether or not they go out to work.[146] In the United Kingdom there has not so far been any sign that the government intends to implement the UN resolution or in any other ways to move towards any financial rewards for the currently unpaid work of women.[147]

Although a magazine survey in 1988 found 87 per cent in favour of greater recognition of domestic work by the government, the question of its remuneration raises strong feelings amongst feminists. Does it simply add to stereotypical perceptions of what women do (and are fit to do) and thereby negate the struggles that have gone on in the workplace, or is it a vital way of making society aware of the value of the work done by women, not least in producing and rearing the next generation of workers?

Earning a living

The question posed in the opening chapter of this book was whether the law takes account of the equal need of men and women for access to wealth in the form of paid employment, since wages are a prime source of wealth. In theory, the law has acknowledged the need, and indeed the wish, of women to work by outlawing workplace discrimination against them. In practice, the anti-discrimination legislation pays lip-service to this need, but fails to provide the legal support which would enable women to compete in the labour market on equal terms with men. The law is inherently complex and is over-reliant on action by an individual, rather than a class or group of workers. It has had little effect on the gendered nature of the labour market, nor on the assumption that work done predominantly by women is worth less than that done by men. The Sex Discrimination Act signals to working women that they may complain only if their treatment does not match the male standard which is at the heart of the legislation. They may not ask the law to give them any recognition of their special or different needs (except for the nine months of pregnancy and its immediate aftermath). The Equal Pay Act is not sufficiently radical to challenge the fundamental problem that women's work has always been seen as secondary and as worth less than men's work. The judges have been unable or unwilling to question the workings of a capitalist system which puts profit above fairness and which thus allows the continuing underpayment of women where there is an apparently gender-neutral commercial reason - such as competition.

These laws are, despite their apparent aims, blind to the very factors that prevent women earning a "living wage." There is little recognition of the forces which uniquely affect women's work patterns. Whilst the concept of indirect discrimination, for example, may give welcome support to part-timers, there is no effort to counter the pressures which compel part-time working or force women to withdraw entirely from the labour market. Some states and the European Union have acknowledged that these pressures must be addressed by programmes of social policy, but this approach has been rejected by the United Kingdom which has, by and large, adopted measures only when forced to do so as a consequence of membership of the European Union. Consequent upon the law's shortcomings, women are generally less able to accumulate wealth through employment. Women who conform most closely to the male pattern may not be affected, provided they are not ghetto-ised in low paid women's work, but for those who struggle with low pay, the demands of a family, and the insecurity of part-time work, the outlook is bleak and has been exacerbated by the gradual dismantling of the very basic system of wage regulation which existed in the United Kingdom. As more and more European states accept the logic of a minimum wage the United Kingdom has pursued the path of deregulation. Whatever reasons lie behind such a step, it has undoubtedly prejudiced the financial standing of women, as they were much more likely than men to be employed in the industries affected by the legislation.

Since many of the structural factors which prevent women competing with men in the workplace are related to women's caring responsibilities, a "grateful nation" might be expected to have found some way of rewarding their dedication. This could be achieved in a variety of ways from tax breaks to social security payments. A more radical solution would be to pay women wages for housework, the very idea of which is generally met with incomprehension or amusement. Whilst a woman is expected to perform these tasks, her contribution in doing so is undervalued to the point where the notion of rewarding her financially is seen as nonsense. Though there may be little or no prospect of wages for housework, the low regard in which women's caring functions are held has a practical impact, since it means that when a woman performs similar functions as an employee, she is unlikely to be well-rewarded for doing so.

As Lewis concludes[148] the legal regulation of women's access to paid employment does not permit the majority of them to enjoy financial independence and she must be correct in her assertion that many will need to depend on the state or on a partner. Women may not be stigmatised for this[149] and indeed may even be encouraged to stay at home, and be told that their domestic role is valuable work, but the status accorded them does not bear this out and the resulting attitudes are profoundly damaging to the idea of women acquiring control over their lives. The next chapter considers whether the laws which deal with state benefits allow for women's economic independence by this alternative route.

Notes

1. The UK opposed a European Community proposal for a working week of no more than 48 hours. Including paid and unpaid overtime, 3.3 million employees in Great Britain usually worked over 48 hours a week in autumn 1992: that is 15 per cent of all employees. The British average for men was 43 hours and for women was 40 hours: (1993) *Employment Gazette* 101 (No. 4), p. 113.

2. Mill, J.S., quoted in Kessler-Harris, A. (1990), *A Woman's Wage*, at p. 10.

3. Sections of the labour force were always subject to spells of unemployment or short-time working: see e.g. Szyszczak E. (1990), *Partial Unemployment: The Regulation of Short Time Working in Britain.*

4. The Institute of Management and Manpower found that 60 per cent of employers surveyed thought that at least 25 per cent of employees will be "complementary" to the "core" workforce by 1998: cited in (1994) *Labour Research* Vol. 83, No. 10. Flexibility for *employers* is increased, for example, by the switch to annual hours in which employees are contracted to work a specified number of hours over 12 months thus allowing hours to be varied week by week: 'Annual Hours', *Incomes Data Study* No 544.

5. See pp. 86-87 on wages for housework.

6. (1993) *Employment Gazette* 101 (No. 5), Table 2, p. L3.

7. (1992), British Social Attitudes, 9th Report, 1992/3 (Eds Jowell, R., Brook, L., Prior, G., Taylor, B.), at p. 90.

8. (1994) *Employment Gazette* 102 (No. 7), LFS1.

9. See e.g. Allen, S. and Wolkowitz, C. (1987), *Homeworking: Myths and Realities*; Hakim, C.

(1987), *Home-Based Work in Britain*, Department of Employment Research Paper No 60.

10.   (1994) *Employment Gazette* 102 (No. 6), LFS4, Table 1.

11.   Allen et al. (1987), op. cit., n. 9, p. 85. Local studies on homeworkers have found extremely low rates of pay, one in 1988 finding rates as low as 10 pence an hour: cited in Pearson, P. and Quiney, M. (1992), *Poor Britain: Poverty, inequality and low pay in the nineties*, p. 7.

12.   Differences between ethnic groups are apparent throughout the labour market: Sly, F., 'Ethnic groups and the labour market', (1994) *Employment Gazette* 102 (No. 5), 147.

13.   Conversely, such women are found amongst homeworkers.

14.   See especially Cook, J. and Watt, S. (1992), 'Racism, women and poverty' in Glendinning, C. and Millar, J. (eds), *Women and Poverty in Britain: the 1990s*.

15.   Kiernan, K., 'The roles of men and women in tomorrow's Europe', (1992) *Employment Gazette* 100 (No. 10), 491, at p. 495.

16.   British Social Attitudes 1992/3, op. cit., n. 7, p. 97.

17.   See (1994) *Employment Gazette* 102 (No 7), LFS2. Figures vary according to source and the method of calculation.

18.   Sly, F., 'Women in the labour market', (1993) *Employment Gazette* 101 (No. 11), 483, at p. 494.

19.   There is no universally accepted definition of part-time working. Many surveys rely on the respondents' own assessments rather than any set limit. Part-time work is defined by the Department of Employment as under 30 hours a week, while for the employment legislation it has been anything under 16 hours a week.

20.   Parliamentary answer in the House of Commons, February 4, 1994, reported in (1994) *Employment Gazette* 102 (No. 3), 75. See also Sly, F., (1993) op. cit., n. 18.

21.   Sly (1993), op. cit., n. 18, p. 487.

22.   Ibid. See also (1994) *Employment Gazette* 102 (No. 10), LFS2.

23.   Part-timers will, in future, benefit from the decision in *Equal Opportunities Commission v Secretary of State for Employment* [1994] 1 All ER 910, see p. 80.

24.   Not all may want to: when there are children under school age one in three women under the age of 35 think that women should stay at home. The proportion rises with age. British Social Attitudes 9th Report 1992/3, op. cit., n. 7, p. 100.

25.   Women and Men in Britain 1992, EOC, p. 21: three out of the four countries with the highest activity rates for mothers with children under 10 (Denmark, Belgium, France) also provide the most publicly funded childcare for children up to school age.

26.   Sly, F., 'Mothers in the Labour Market', (1994) *Employment Gazette* 102 (No. 11), p. 403.

27.   Sly (1993), op cit., n. 18, p. 496. See also Sly (1994), op cit., n. 26: figures for economic activity amongst mothers in all groups continued to rise.

28.   Watson, G. and Fothergill, B., 'Part-time employment and attitudes to part-time work', (1993) *Employment Gazette* 101 (No. 5), 213.

29.   In one survey 81 per cent of women working part-time said they did not want full-time work: (1994) *Employment Gazette* 102 (No. 7), LFS7. This begs the question why: if it was because they were *unable* to work full-time, there is little element of choice.

30.   Op. cit., n. 28, p. 215.

31.   Ibid., p. 218.

32.   See especially British Social Attitudes 9th Report, 1992/3, op. cit., n. 7, pp 97-106.

33.   And see pp 86-87: wages for housework.

34.   £57 a week in 1994-5.

35.   Parliamentary answer cited in (1994*) Employment Gazette* 102, (No. 3). It was estimated that 75 per cent were married women, 20 per cent were single women and 5 per cent were lone parents. See also op. cit., n. 28, p. 219.

36.   For example, Witherspoon S. and Taylor B. (1990), *British Social Attitudes 1989 Survey: A Report for the Employment Department*. 91 per cent of part-time employees were satisfied with their jobs. Also (1982) *OPCS General Household Survey 1980*.

37.   Harrop, A. and Moss, P. (1994) *Employment Gazette* 102 (No. 10), p. 343, at p. 351.

38.   Given a completely free choice eight out of ten women and four out of ten men would prefer not to have to work full-time when their children were young: (1990) Eurobarometer Survey, Commission of the European Communities, op. cit., n. 15.

39.   These and following figures are taken from Bartholomew, R. et al., 'Lone parents and the labour market: evidence from the labour force survey', (1992), *Employment Gazette* 100 (No. 11), 559. See also Sly, F. 'Mothers in the Labour Market', (1994) *Employment Gazette* 102 (No. 11) p. 403; Haskey, J. (1994) *Population Trends* 78, Winter, p. 5.

40.   See pp. 115, 117. The child care allowance for those on family credit is some recognition that costs of child care can be a disincentive to paid employment. Proposed changes to benefits paid to the unemployed may also ameliorate the problem of income cancelling out benefit: see Chaps. 5 and 7.

41.   See Bartholomew et al., op.cit., n. 39, at p. 563.

42.   *Women working for less: a longitudinal analysis of the family gap*, London School of Economics, 1993.

43.   (1994) *Employment Gazette* 102 (No. 9), LFS4.

44.   Ibid. Proportions vary significantly with the age of the individuals. Of the 44,000 men who were carers, 31 per cent were looking after a dependent adult relative.

45.   Kahne, H. and Giele, J. (1992), 'Women and the Welfare State in the Nordic Countries', in *Women's Work and Women's Lives: The Continuing Struggle Worldwide*.

46.   Brannen, J. and Moss P. (1991), *Managing Dual Earner Households after Maternity Leave*, p. 89.

47.   'Public service, private hardship', *The New Review*, April/May 1994. See also *Yorkshire County Council v Ratcliffe* [1994] IRLR 342, p. 77.

48.   Sly (1993), op. cit., n. 18. The UK has the largest number of women in the service sector in the Community: *Women and Men in Britain 1992*, EOC, p. 27.

49.   *Women and Men in Britain 1993*, EOC, p. 29.

50.   Ibid.

51.   British Social Attitudes 9th Report 1992/3, op. cit., n. 7, pp. 94-95.

52.   Kiernan (1992), op. cit., n. 15, at p. 494.

53.   '1994 New Earnings Survey (NES)', (1994) *Equal Opportunities Review* 58, p. 33. See also Chap. 1.

54.   Even women working full-time work on average 5 fewer hours a week than men: (1994) *Employment Gazette* 102 (No. 1), LFS7.

55.   For manual workers, about a quarter of a man's wage is made up of overtime, incentive pay and shift premia, compared with 15 per cent for a woman: see 'Patterns of pay: results from the 1993 New Earnings Survey', (1993) *Employment Gazette* 101 (No. 11) 515. See also, adding to these findings, *Pay and Gender in Britain: A Research Report for the EOC from the Industrial Relations Services*, (1991).

56.   See, e.g., Yeandle, S. (1984), *Women's Working Lives: Patterns and Strategies*; Martin, J. and Roberts, C. (1984), *Women and Employment: A Lifetime Perspective*; Dex S. (1987), *Women's Occupational Mobility*.

57.   Most part-time employees are women. Their average hourly earnings are significantly lower than those of both male and female full-timers.

58.   *Pay and Gender in Britain: A Research Report for the EOC from the Industrial Relations Services*, (1991).

59.   (1993) *Merit pay, performance appraisal and attitudes to women's work*.

60.   The ECJ has been asked to rule whether this is indirect discrimination: see (1993) *Equal Opportunities Review* 49, p. 33.

61.   It applies equally to women and men and in certain circumstances to married couples: ss. 1-3.

62.   *Clarke v Eley (IMI) Kynoch Ltd* [1982] IRLR 482.

63.   *James v Eastleigh Borough Council* [1990] ICR 554; *Greig v Community Industry* [1979] ICR 356.

64.   *Home Office v Holmes* [1984] ICR 678. C.f. *Greater Glasgow Health Board v Carey* [1987] IRLR 484.

65.   *Kidd v DRG (UK) Ltd* [1985] IRLR 190.

66.   EC Council Directive 76/207.

67.   See e.g. *Cardiff Women's Aid v Hartup* [1994] IRLR 390.

68.   [1981] IRLR 208.

69.   See s. 3, Sex Discrimination Act 1975.

70.   *Turley v Allders Department Stores Ltd* [1980] ICR 66.

71.   *Hayes v Malleable Working Men's Club and Institute* [1985] ICR 703.

72.   *Dekker v Stichting Vormingscentrum voor Jonge Volwassen (VJV-Centrum)* [1991] IRLR 27.

73.   *Webb v Emo Air Cargo (UK) Ltd (Case C-32/93)* [1994] 2 All ER 115 and see Morris, A. E. and Nott, S.M. (1992), 'The Legal Response to Pregnancy', 12 *Legal Studies* 54; Morris, A. E. and Nott, S.M. (1995), 'The Law's Engagement with Pregnancy' in Millns S. and Bridgeman, J. (eds), *Body Politics*.

74.   See especially Council Directive 92/85 on the introduction of measures to encourage improvements in the health and safety at work of pregnant workers and those who have recently given birth or are breastfeeding, and the maternity rights scheme in the Employment

Protection (Consolidation) Act 1978, amended by the Trade Union Reform and Employment Rights Act 1993: see pp. 153-155.

75.   Compensation may, however, be substantial: the previous upper limit on the compensation (£10,000) was removed as a result of *Marshall v Southampton and South-west Hampshire Area Health Authority (No 2)* [1993] IRLR 445 and Sex Discrimination and Equal Pay (Remedies) Regulations 1993, S.I. 1993 No. 2798. Unintentional indirect discrimination attracts no compensation.

76.   A crucial flaw is lack of a class action: an individual woman must be determined enough to take a case to the tribunal: Morris, A.E. and Nott, S.M. (1991), *Working Women and The Law: Equality and Discrimination in Theory and Practice*, Chap. 8. Proposals by the EOC to introduce such actions have been rejected by the government, see below, n. 127.

77.   See also Equal Treatment Directive 76/207; Social Security Directive 79/7; Social Security Directive 86/378 and see Chap. 5.

78.   For a detailed account of the laws on equal pay see *Harvey on Industrial Relations and Employment Law*, Vol. 2.

79.   Article 119 is restricted to pay, but not to rights arising under the contract.

80.   *Garland v British Rail Engineering Ltd* [1983] 2 AC 751.

81.   *Rinner-Kühn v FWW Spezial Gebaudereinigung GmbH & Co* 171/88 [1989] IRLR 493 ECJ.

82.   Both statutory and contractual: *Barber v Guardian Royal Exchange Assurance Group* 262/88 [1990] ICR 616; *McKechnie v UBM Building Supplies (Southern) Ltd* [1991] IRLR 283.

83.   *Worringham and Humphreys v Lloyds Bank Ltd* 69/80 [1981] ICR 558; *Bilka-Kaufhaus v Weber von Hartz* 170/84 [1987] ICR 110; *Barber v Guardian Royal Exchange Assurance Group* 268/88 [1990] ICR 616. For a fuller discussion, see Chap. 5.

84.   *Leverton v Clwyd County Council* [1989] ICR 33 HL, further refined by the Court of Appeal in *British Coal Corporation v Smith* [1994] IRLR 342.

85.   As in *Leverton*, above, where a nursery nurse employed in a school compared herself to clerical officers employed at council offices.

86.   *Macarthys Ltd v Smith* 129/79 [1980] ICR 672 ECJ.

87.   *Dugdale v Kraft Foods Ltd* [1977] ICR 48. Also *Capper Pass Ltd v Lawton* [1977] ICR 83; *Coomes (Holdings) Ltd v Shields* [1978] ICR 1159. Compare *Calder v Rowntree Mackintosh Confectionery Ltd* [1993] IRLR 212, below n. 113.

88.   Research by the Daycare Trust, cited in *Labour Research*, September 1994, p. 5.

89.   As in *Pickstone v Freemans plc* [1988] ICR 697.

90.   *EC Commission v United Kingdom of Great Britain and Northern Ireland* 61/81 [1982] ICR 578.

91.   For examples see 'Making the invisible visible: rewarding women's work', (1992) *Equal Opportunities Review* 45, p. 23 which cites as matters frequently overlooked or ignored writing correspondence for others, establishing and maintaining filing systems, training new staff, concentrating for long periods at computer terminals and work benches, representing the organisation through dealings with the public, dealing with upset or irate people,

cleaning.

92. *Bromley v H & J Quick Ltd* [1988] ICR 623; *Rummler v Dato-Druck GmbH* 237/85 [1987] ICR 774 ECJ. See also the effects of merit pay systems, n. 112 and the *Danfoss* Case, below n. 109.

93. Plumer, A-M. (1992), *Equal Value judgments: objective assessment or lottery.*

94. COM (94)(6).

95. *EC Commission v United Kingdom of Great Britain and Northern Ireland* 61/81 [1982] ICR 578.

96. The Equal Pay (Amendment) Regulations 1983, S.I. 1983 No. 1794. See also Equal Pay Act 1970, s. 1(2)(c).

97. [1993] IRLR 308, at p. 310. Court of Appeal: [1994] IRLR 342.

98. There are proposals to abolish this: (1994) *Equal Opportunities Review* 55, p. 3.

99. Industrial Tribunals (Rules of Procedure) Regulations 1985, S.I. 1985, No. 16, (as amended), Schedule 2, Rule 8(2E)

100. The claim in *Pickstone v Freemans plc* [1988] ICR 697 began in 1984. In 1988 the House of Lords decided that she could bring an equal value claim even though a man was doing like work. In 1993, an Industrial Tribunal rejected the finding of the expert that the work was not of equal value, and the employer appealed to the Employment Appeal Tribunal.

101. (1991), *Pay and Gender in Britain: A Research Report for the EOC from the Industrial Relations Services.*

102. Ibid., p. 27.

103. Ibid., p. 32.

104. Ibid., p. 33.

105. In 1986, of 1,481 equal value applications, just over 1,000 involved British Coal. In 1992 there were 470 claims, of which 122 were against North Yorkshire County Council: 'Equal value update' (1993) *Equal Opportunities Review* 51, p 11.

106. Trade union membership has been decreasing due almost entirely to falls in male membership, while female membership has increased. Unions with a majority of women members include NALGO, NUPE, COHSE (now UNISON), USDAW, NUT and the Royal College of Nursing: see Bird et al, 'Membership of trade unions', (1993) *Employment Gazette* 101 (No. 5), p. 189 and 'Women in the unions', (1993) *Equal Opportunities Review* 48, p. 34.

107. [1992] IRLR 15, Court of Appeal, Case 127/92 [1993] IRLR 591, ECJ.

108. Also *Reed Packaging Ltd v Boozer* [1988] ICR 391, where the £17 a week difference was held lawful because she was on the staff pay scale and he was on the hourly paid scale. Compare *Barber v NCR (Manufacturing) Ltd (No 2)* [1993] IRLR 95 where the Scottish EAT stated that collective bargaining is the historical process by which the difference has been arrived at, not an "objective factor which justified, or even supported, the result which had been produced."

109. *Handels-og Kontorfunktionaerernes Forbund I Danmark v Dansk Arbejdsgiverforening (acting for Danfoss)* 109/88 [1989] ECR 3199.

110. *Kowalska v Freie und Hansestadt Hamburg* 33/89 [1990] IRLR 447 ECJ

111. (1991), *Pay and Gender in Britain: A Research Report for the EOC from the Industrial Relations Services.*

112. (1993), *Merit pay, performance appraisal and attitudes to women's work.*

113. [1993] IRLR 212

114. [1987] ICR 129

115. [1991] IRLR 44

116. [1994] IRLR 342 (decided with the *British Coal* case).

117. Ibid., at p. 351.

118. Compare *Pickstone v Freemans plc*, n. 89.

119. [1994] IRLR 342 at p. 363.

120. *Jenkins v Kingsgate Clothing Productions Ltd (No 2)* [1981] ICR 715 (EAT), [1981] ICR 592 (ECJ).

121. [1987] ICR 110.

122. Ibid., at p. 126.

123. (1993) *Equal Opportunities Review* 49, p. 33.

124. *R v Secretary of State for Employment ex parte Equal Opportunities Commission* [1994] 1 All ER 910.

125. The House of Lords declined to hold that unfair dismissal compensation was within Art. 119, but held that it came under the Equal Treatment Directive. This allows public, but not private sector workers to bring a claim, as the Directive cannot be relied on directly by those in the private sector. The Employment Appeal Tribunal subsequently held such compensation to be pay: *Mediguard Services Ltd v Thame* [1994] IRLR 504.

126. This may lead to reform in relation to other rights governed by thresholds, for example the right to return to work after the longer period of maternity leave governed by Employment Protection (Consolidation) Act 1978, s. 39.

127. Rubery, J. (1992), *The economics of equal value.*

128. *Equal Treatment for Men and Women - strengthening the Acts* and *Equal Pay for Men and Women - strengthening the Acts*, EOC, 1988 and 1990: see (1988) *Equal Opportunities Review* 11 and (1990) *Equal Opportunities Review* 35.

129. See (1993) *Equal Opportunities Review* 52, p. 35.

130. (1993) *Equal Opportunities Review* 52, p. 20.

131. See Chap. 4

132. Compare, for example, the Low Pay Unit's measure which is two-thirds median male earnings which, in 1994, gave £203.07 per week or £5.75 an hour. The 'European Poverty Line' is half of national average income. The Institute of Fiscal Studies have estimated that in 1994 11.4 million people in Britain were below this level.

133. Pearson, P. and Quiney, M. (1992), *Poor Britain: Poverty, inequality and low pay in the nineties*, pp. 4-5.

134. Hansard, 28 April 1909, vol. 4, col. 388.

135. (1983) *Who Needs the Wages Councils?* at p. 11.

136. On the low wages of young workers see: 'Taking the Bloom off Youth', (1992) *New Review*

of the Low Pay Unit No. 15, p. 13.

137. Pearson, P. (1993), *More Crime and Still No Punishment, Wages Councils and illegal underpayments*, at p. 6.

138. Hansard, 5 November 1992, col. 407.

139. Reported in *The Independent*, 30 August 1994.

140. See *New Earnings Survey*, 1993: women's gross weekly earnings were 75 per cent of men's and their gross hourly earnings were 83 per cent of men's (compared with 71.5 and 79 per cent outside the Councils).

141. Responses cited in Bryson, A. (1989), *Undervalued, underpaid and undercut: The Future of the Wages Councils.*

142. It also tends to *reduce* the number of available jobs as consumption decreases due to low pay: Bryson, A. (1992), *The New Review of the Low Pay Unit*, No. 16.

143. 'Minimum Wage: How Europe Copes', (1994) *Labour Research*, Vol. 83, No. 10, p. 15.

144. Reported in *The Independent*, 3 February 1993.

145. *Forward Looking Strategies for the Advancement of Women*, para. 120, ratified by UN General Assembly in 1985.

146. There have been similar moves in the USA, e.g. a Bill which attempted to include the value of housework in the GNP (Unremunerated Work Act 1993).

147. In 1989, a private member's Bill, Counting Women's Unremunerated Work, which sought to implement the 1985 UN Resolution, failed.

148. Lewis, J. (1992), *Women in Britain since 1945*, p. 3.

149. Compare the 'idle' unemployed man who might be unable to find work. Compare also the tolerance of the non-working wife with the odium heaped upon single mothers. At the same time women may feel guilty that they do not work (the 'only a housewife' syndrome): see e.g. Watson, G. and Fothergill, B., 'Part-time employment and attitudes to part-time work' (1993) *Employment Gazette* 101 (No. 5), p. 213 at p. 216.

4 Redistributing Wealth: Taxes and Benefits

"The redistribution of wealth" is a phrase redolent with the kind of political overtones which colour and alter its meaning according to one's particular views. In the present context, however, it should be taken to denote, at its simplest, requiring those who have resources to help support those who do not, by means of redistributing those resources from the richer to the poorer. In this sense it refers to the processes or mechanisms through which a society seeks to protect its needy, its weak or its disadvantaged. The concept of redistribution is fraught with difficulties of both a political and terminological nature. In attempting to find a way through this, the focus of this chapter will be on the women who are, for whatever reasons, the recipients of (or at least the claimants on) what historically was thought of as charity but is now known as the welfare state. In the course of this exploration it should be borne in mind that the purpose of this chapter is not to prove that women are inevitably and by reason of their gender poor, although they are now acknowledged to be especially vulnerable to poverty.[1] Wealth is here defined as having power over one's own existence and having the resources to ensure personal control over one's life. That must be the first step to anything approaching substantive as opposed to mere formal equality. Of the three main routes to wealth which have been identified - paid employment, social security and the family[2] - social security may not be the one in which gender inequalities are immediately obvious. It cannot be said that women do not have access to social security since they make up a large proportion of claimants, but that does not mean that the system is best meeting their needs. For women who are unable to work, or who earn very low wages, support from outside the home becomes an important factor in achieving access to wealth and thus to independence. The dependence experienced by women is especially visible and significant where they lack sufficient income. In Chapter 3 it was shown how women are relegated to a secondary role in the labour market and how this is used to justify their low pay and poor conditions of employment. It is equally clear where women are not in paid employment that their access to benefits is hampered by the notion that they are of secondary importance because of their assumed dependence on a man.

Fundamental issues such as the undervaluing of women's skills, the gendered nature of the work place and the demands made on women by their caring responsibilities have been so inadequately addressed in the United Kingdom that the inevitable consequence is that many women find themselves at some time without sufficient resources to meet the demands of everyday life. Living as a full member of the community depends on more than just money, but it is an important key:

> To keep out of poverty, [people] must have an income which enables them to participate in the life of the community. They must be able, for example, to keep themselves reasonably well fed, and well enough dressed to maintain their self-respect and to attend interviews for jobs with confidence. Their homes must be reasonably warm; their children should not feel ashamed by the quality of their clothing; the family must be able to visit relatives, and give them something on their birthdays and at Christmas time; they must be able to read newspapers, and retain their television sets and their membership of trade unions and churches. And they must be able to live in such a way which ensures, so far as is possible, that public officials, doctors, teachers, landlords and others treat them with the courtesy due to every member of the community.[3]

Lack of resources may, of course, result from a variety of causes. A woman may be unable to work because of illness, disability or old age or she may lose her job and be unable to find another. A single woman may not be able to earn enough to support herself - or her children, if she has any. A married or cohabiting woman may find herself in need because of the low wages she and her partner earn or because one or both is out of work. Even if her partner is earning an adequate wage, she may not benefit if he does not share his earnings with her. Deprivation derives from a complex pattern of cause and effect, and decisions made as to who should be assisted and in what circumstances are absolutely crucial to women. This is not because men are immune to poverty, but because women are more likely to find themselves in the particularly vulnerable groups such as single parents.

No matter what the details of any benefit scheme might be, there are some general underlying principles. The state must first decide how it will raise the revenue necessary to meet the costs of a social security scheme. Second, it must be decided what should be the purpose of a system of social security. Redistribution may be acceptable only within limits, so that whilst some might argue for a generous and generally available level of benefit (perhaps dependent on falling within a particular category, such as lone parents) others prefer to see a safety net approach, setting an absolute minimum below which the poorest will not be allowed to fall. The first idea tends to assume that some will always be poor or at least that some conditions predispose towards poverty. In granting assistance to all within the category the scheme is not necessarily progressive since some of those benefiting may be better off than some of those contributing. Attempts to avoid this may lead to the benefit being kept at an inadequate level for everyone (a classic example is child benefit). On the other hand, such schemes avoid the stigma that attaches to the second, safety net idea. This targets the poor, but brands them as dependent, with the result that the benefits are likely to be minimal and the effect on the recipients likely to be negative. Finally, it must be decided whether benefits should be contributory or means-tested. Both types have disadvantages for women: the first because women may not accumulate the necessary contributions and the second because they are assessed with reference to the income of the family unit and take no account of the fact that there may be an inequitable sharing of the main earner's income: a woman denied money by her partner does not because of that qualify for assistance.

Laying the foundations of the welfare state

The origins of the modern welfare state can be traced to the Beveridge Report in 1942.[4] The philosophy underlying this was that benefit in return for contributions is a better way of providing for the needy, rather than free allowances from the state. A scheme based on contributions from earned income inevitably excludes sections of the population who, for whatever reason, are not able to work and it was clear that there would have to be another layer of provision, which did not depend on contributions, to protect those who could not provide for themselves. Beveridge recognised the need for such a safety net operating in parallel with the contributory insurance scheme, but it was to be less respectable, more like the old poor laws: "... it must be felt to be something less desirable than insurance benefit: otherwise the insured persons get nothing for their contributions. Assistance therefore will be given always subject to proof of needs and examination of means."[5]

Beveridge's original emphasis on contributory benefits was significant, since many women were never able to take advantage of these in their own right. As will be seen in Chapter 5, although a single woman in employment was expected to make contributions and could then claim benefits, Beveridge believed that most married women would not work and, accordingly, their access to benefits depended largely on their husbands' contribution records. A husband paid his contributions from his earned income and any benefits he received made provision, in theory, for his wife and children by including a dependant's allowance. The result of this scheme was that few women had the contributions necessary to allow them to claim benefits on their own behalf.

Beveridge believed that his system of contributory benefits would dramatically reduce the numbers having to rely on means-tested benefits. As is now apparent, this has not been the case. Contrary to what Beveridge expected, increasing numbers have been forced to turn to means-tested benefits which are payable only by way of a safety net when resources fall below a certain level. The means-test is thus central to these benefits and it focuses on the financial situation of the claimant. If, however, the individual claimant is married or cohabiting, the principle of aggregation comes into play and the resources of the couple are assessed, rather than just those of the claimant. The idea that means-tested benefits might be concentrated on the individual rather than the "family unit" has rarely been considered as an option and, when it has, it has been rejected:

> ... benefit is paid for the claimant, his spouse and their dependent children, if they are living with him. This reflects the assumptions of the overwhelming majority of people in Britain. To change to a system where adults were means-tested individually would mean giving benefit to the wives of well-paid men without regard to their husband's earnings. It would bring a great increase in the cost and the extent of means-testing and the means-test would become more intrusive ... .[6]

Such automatic rejection of an individual's right to benefit ignores the fact that for women the consequences of aggregation are considerable. The principle of aggregation does not make explicit women's dependent status, as did the rules in relation to contributory benefits for married women, but its practical effects are similar. A woman who finds a part-time job may discover that her additional wages mean her partner is no longer eligible for means-tested benefits and as a consequence she may decide not to work. In such cases, aggregation is a disincentive to paid employment and a barrier to a woman's financial independence. Even though the family may be better off on benefit, if that benefit is claimed by and paid to her partner, a woman can find herself entirely dependent on him.

Means-tested benefits do, however, have a positive side. They mean that, in theory, a woman with no partner, with or without children, can survive on her own, without depending on a man and, in this sense, marriage ceases to be an economic necessity for women. Whilst some deplore this route to independence on the basis that it contributes to the undermining of the family, feminists have pointed out that it is merely the substitution of state patriarchy for a male patriarchy. The state (which could anyway be seen as male) is as likely to try to regulate women's behaviour as are men. There is also the practical problem that means-tested benefits are generally so ungenerous as to make a truly independent existence most unlikely.

Nevertheless, the fact that such benefits are available does offer the theoretical prospect that women can achieve economic survival without a man to depend on.

The personal taxation system

A system which aims to support those with inadequate financial resources of their own demands adequate funding as well as a mechanism for collection and distribution. The pool out of which payments can be made or services paid for is regulated by the Government and filled both from taxes, channelled into the Exchequer, and from social security (or national insurance) contributions, paid into the National Insurance Fund. In the case of means-tested benefits it is the tax system which must bear the burden. The level at which tax rates are set is obviously crucial from the point of view of generating sufficient income to pay for those benefits, but equally important is the way the tax system operates and the policies which inform it. By exempting some expenditure and by granting tax allowances, the state can encourage certain forms of behaviour, for example, by giving tax incentives to invest money in savings. Adjustments to tax rates and allowances in the personal taxation system influence the income of the employed worker just as the benefits system impacts on the lives of the unemployed or the poorest workers. Whilst it could be said that the benefits system subsidises the poor, so the tax system can cushion the situation of the better off. One important difference, however, is that there is no stigma attached to the beneficiaries of tax relief while the same cannot be said for the recipients of means-tested benefits. Women are well represented amongst claimants on the social security system, but their increased participation in paid employment means that they also make up a sizeable proportion of tax payers, and for these women the tax system can have a crucial effect on their financial well-being.

The British scheme of personal taxation is based on a system of tax bands graduated according to income and personal allowances which are used to reduce the income on which tax is payable. While these are of benefit to the lower paid, the overall effect is not markedly progressive since the lower rates and the allowances are available to all, with the higher tax rates applying only to income over certain levels, and the allowances being of greater benefit to the higher paid. Redistribution through taxation has actually declined markedly over the years with more wage earners becoming subject to tax at lower levels of income and fewer being taxed at the higher rates. In 1988, when the highest tax rate was reduced to 40 per cent it was a change of obvious and immediate advantage to the more highly paid. It has been calculated that between 1979 and 1991 tax cuts totalling almost £29 billion were made, of which about one-third benefited the top 1.4 per cent of tax payers with incomes over £50,000 while about one-fifty-seventh went to the bottom 13 per cent of tax payers. The decrease in the weekly tax paid by these two groups was, on average, £421 for the first group and £2.50 for the second.[7] This does not suggest a particularly progressive tax system. The figures should, moreover, be looked at in the context of women's earned income: there is little likelihood of many women benefiting from the changes. Moreover, despite the cuts which were applied to income tax, the overall tax burden has actually increased due to increases in national insurance and VAT. Any increase in the rate of national insurance contributions can easily wipe out gains from income tax cuts: within just six years (1979 to 1985) the level of contribution rose from 6.5 to 9 per cent and since then has risen to 10 per cent. Indirect taxation represented by VAT is especially important to those on low incomes because although it is a spending tax and supposedly placed only on items which individuals can choose to do without, it is a disproportionate burden on the poor since it is levied irrespective of ability to pay and takes a relatively higher proportion of lower incomes. When VAT was placed on heating fuels, it met with opposition not only because it taxed a necessity, but also because it is the poorest and the most vulnerable who are the worst affected.

Current direct tax arrangements are supposed to assist the lowest paid through the variable rates of tax depending on income. In the tax year beginning in 1994 the lower rate of tax was set at 20 per cent on taxable income (income left *after* deducting allowances) of up to £3,000. Above that level the basic rate was 25 per cent on taxable income up to £23,700 and the single higher rate was 40 per cent on income over that figure. Of course, while this may give some help to the very low paid, and may take some out of income tax liability altogether, it is of assistance also to higher earners. More importantly, the recent practice of not always increasing allowances each year is regressive: more earners at the lower end of the wages scale are brought into the tax system and again the poorest are the hardest hit.[8]

A hallmark of the present tax system is the continuing, though rapidly declining, special treatment of married couples. In 1990 there was a significant, though far from radical, change in the way married women are treated under the tax system. Women's social and legal position when income tax was introduced in 1799 renders it unsurprising that a husband was responsible for her income tax since the rules of the common law dictated that, on marriage, a wife's property automatically came under the control of her husband.[9] It is more surprising, however, that for the purposes of taxation this was still the position in 1990. The relevant piece of legislation, the Income and Corporation Taxes Act 1970, provided that during any year in which a married woman was living with her husband her taxable income was to be deemed to be his income and not her income. Quite apart from the fact that this meant that a married woman lacked all privacy in relation to her income (since her husband was the tax payer he had to fill the income tax return and have details of her earnings), it perpetuated in a very concrete fashion the legal, financial and social dependency of a wife.[10] It may certainly have discouraged married women from seeking work: as her earned income would be added to that of her husband it could, in some cases, have taken the couple into one of the higher rated tax bands. From 1971 onwards it was possible for a married couple to choose to be taxed separately, but this would normally be done only where each was relatively highly paid since it would reduce the allowance available to the husband by replacing his married man's allowance with a single person's allowance. It was also the case that even where there was separate taxation, the husband was responsible for completing the tax return. Reform of the system took a long time finally to reach the statute books, not least because of the problems engendered by the existence of the married man's allowance.

Allowances are linked not to income but to personal circumstances, so that a single person under the age of 65 is allowed to earn £3,445 before paying any tax (£3,525 in 1995-6). If that person falls into certain other categories, including that of a lone parent with responsibility for a child living with them, she is entitled also to an additional personal allowance of £1,720.[11] Prior to the 1990 reforms, a married man had an allowance which was significantly higher than that of a single person[12] and this applied whether or not his wife was also earning. If she was in paid employment, she had an allowance of her own equivalent to the single person allowance. Many who were in favour of reform wanted to see the abolition of the married man's allowance, and at least some of the reasons for this were to achieve equality between the sexes. The move towards abolition became linked, however, with the idea of transferable allowances under which everyone would have their own tax allowance, whether or not in paid employment. A married couple would be able to transfer the allowance from one to another, so that a wife with no earned income could transfer her allowance to her husband, thus reducing his tax bill. This was to recognise that within a marriage one partner might from time to time be dependent on the other, but made no judgment as to which partner it would be at any given time. The proposals met with opposition from a number of quarters and for a variety of reasons, not the least among them being the difficulty which a wife might find in reclaiming her allowance from her husband, since to do so would adversely affect his net pay. More pertinently in the context of this chapter, it was pointed out that tinkering around with the system in this way has little redistributive effect: it is hardly going to help those with the lowest earnings who pay less tax, and it was thus an inefficient targeting measure, especially since in most cases any extra money was going into the husband's pay packet and not directly (or even at all) to the wife.

The new system which was introduced in 1990 was a compromise and calls itself "independent taxation." The independence refers to the fact that a husband and wife are now taxed and assessed separately. The married man's allowance has disappeared but has been replaced by the married couple's allowance. Every tax payer, married or single has the same basic personal allowance. A married couple, however, has an additional allowance of £1,720 which, in the first instance, is awarded to the *husband*.[13] If he has insufficient income to use up the whole allowance, he may ask for the surplus to be transferred to his wife, or a husband and wife together may ask for the whole amount of the allowance to be transferred to her (if, for example, she is earning and he is not). It is also provided that a wife acting alone may request half of the allowance to be transferred to her, though whether a wife would be willing to insist on this in the face of spousal opposition is another matter. Neither party may transfer their personal allowance. As a means of empowering women through access to resources, the effects of this change are minimal and it fails utterly as a means of redistribution. Where the husband is the only earner he will still get his personal allowance and the married couple's allowance which is effectively the same as the previous married man's allowance. Any changes are theoretically of most use to higher earners: since each now has a separate tax band, couples who might have been in the higher bands when income was aggregated may not be caught separately. Those couples who, pre-1990, were highly paid enough to have made separate taxation worthwhile even though it meant giving up the married man's allowance, will now have separate taxation *and* the married couple's allowance and may be better off (though the value of the married couple's allowance is declining). For non-working wives or those on very low incomes it makes very little difference.

The reforms do not help to target resources at those who need them but they do continue to favour marriage over any other family arrangements. The increasing numbers of cohabiting couples who choose not to marry begs the question as to the reasons behind this adherence to tradition.[14] A noticeable thread running through the rhetoric of the Conservative governments in the 1980s and 1990s has been the support for "the family" so this lingering financial bolstering of the married state is perhaps unsurprising. On the other hand, such support is matched by the desire to control public spending and means that policy does not always match rhetoric. The married couple's allowance has not been increased over recent years, so that its real value is declining. While it is true that none of the allowances has kept pace with inflation, it appears that the married couple's allowance is actually being phased out: although previously, high earners were benefiting from tax relief on the allowance at 40 per cent, this was first restricted to the basic rate of 25 per cent, then, as from 1994, it was lowered to 20 per cent and as from 1995 it is only 15 per cent which would seem to indicate abolition by stages. If allowances do not match inflation the tax payer ends up paying more tax, and one may speculate as to whether the freeze on the allowance is simply another way of increasing revenue rather than having any other hidden agenda. In the light of changing patterns of women's employment and the numbers of unmarried couples it is certainly becoming more difficult to justify the married couple's allowance. Naturally, it could be defended as an acknowledgement of the cost of caring for children and this is generally accepted as a legitimate focus for the targeting of public finances. But the argument is difficult to sustain in the case of the married couple's allowance given the Conservative government's fondness for targeting. For a start it is not dependent on the presence of children, nor even of a non-working wife. Secondly, there is no guarantee that the notional money realised by the allowance will ever be seen by the wife and children. As was pointed out at the time reforms were being considered, a serious intention to target the persons in need would be better met by a real increase in the rates of child benefit which is a non-contributory benefit payable in most cases to the mother and which depends on the presence of dependent children.

It is possible to use a slightly less blunt instrument than the married couple's allowance if there is a real desire to target families through the tax system and it was once the case that there were child tax allowances which were graduated according to the numbers and ages of children in the family. These were again payable to the main earner and were again more beneficial (relatively speaking) to earners in the higher tax bands (which were then much higher) because they reduced the amount of income on which tax was payable. These allowances were phased out as child benefit came in but in any event they suffered from all the usual drawbacks of such mechanisms: they were not progressive as between rich and poor and since the allowance was operated through the PAYE system, it would benefit the principal wage earner, which would be the father rather than the mother in most instances. There remains a vestige of targeting through the tax system in the additional personal allowance, payable to any lone parent who has a child living with him or her during any part of the year. It is equivalent to the married couple's allowance, and may be shared by the parents if the child is spending time with both. Although usually thought of as extra help for lone parents, it is also available to a *father* who is living with his child and his wife, where the latter is totally incapacitated because of illness or disability.[15] It is not, however, available to a mother in a similar situation, thus providing another example of the persistent stereotyping of the male and female roles. Being simply another example of tax relief the allowance is no more progressive than any other and there seems little doubt that the best way of helping those with children is the simple method of child benefit, which must, however, be paid at realistic levels.

Although the tax system has little to offer those caring for children, there is an important tax relief available to property owners, which has proved extremely valuable to middle income, owner-occupiers in the past. Mortgage interest tax relief has increased in importance as the numbers buying their own homes have escalated, though its days would now seem to be numbered. A mortgage or other loan used to buy the principal home attracts tax relief for the interest paid on the first £30,000 of the loan.[16] Prior to 1988, co-habitees were each allowed to claim the relief on their joint mortgage - one example of the tax system favouring the unmarried rather than the married - but this "discrimination" was cited as a reason for changing the system so that relief now attaches to the property rather than the person (even though of course, not all those who buy property together are "couples"). Tax relief on mortgages is clearly not redistributive since owner-occupiers tend on average to be better off than those in the rented sector and its greatest value has been to those on middle and higher incomes. Neither is it means-tested nor dependent on family status though of course, as with most tax reliefs, the principal beneficiary tends to be the main earner. From time to time proposals are made to reform or abolish this form of tax relief. To the extent that the qualifying limit has stayed at £30,000 since 1982 it might be argued that government has preferred simply to see it wither away. This process was augmented by the rule that relief was limited to the standard 25 per cent rate of tax so that those on higher incomes, while still benefiting no longer received relief at the higher 40 per cent rate. In 1994 the rate was reduced to 20 per cent and is to be 15 per cent from 1995. Again, as with the married couple's allowance it would seem that it is simply a matter of time before it disappears.

A tax relief which many *women* would welcome would be that related to the costs of child care. Brannen and Moss[17] discovered that in the majority of cases the costs of child care were met from the woman's earnings, since it was her "choice" to return to work. For some women the costs are so high that it is not worthwhile for them to work and they might benefit from tax relief. It is argued, however, that such a scheme would favour only those women who are already better off - on the basis that the wealthier the tax payer the more the tax relief is worth. An alternative to tax relief would be a substantial up-rating of child benefit which would help all women with children and those wishing to work could use the increased benefit to defray some of the costs of child care.

As it is currently structured the taxation system seems to favour those in well-paid employment. Independent taxation and the ability to apportion certain allowances, including mortgage relief and the married couple's allowance, mean that, in theory, women working in well-paid jobs are likely to benefit as much as similarly situated men. In reality, this may not be so. In dual-earner households, a man is likely to earn more than his partner: Esam and Berthoud estimated that among women in employment, only one in eight had an income higher than her husband in 1990-91 and this figure included women whose husbands were unemployed.[18] In such circumstances it is likely to make more sense to transfer allowances to the higher earner, particularly if this avoids liability for higher rate tax. There may also be problems in relation to mortgage relief: if the house which is being purchased happens to be in the sole name of the husband, rather than in joint ownership, he is helped by the tax system to acquire, to the exclusion of his wife, what is probably the most valuable asset in the marriage.

The benefits system

A common complaint about the social security system in the UK is its horrendous complexity deriving from the number and the technicality of its regulations. It is not necessary to describe all the detailed regulations which apply to contributions and benefits[19] but it is important to examine the nature of the benefits which are most commonly sought by women and to ask whether they are really meeting the needs of those they are meant to help. There are no straightforward ways of classifying benefits because many of them overlap and can be claimed in combination, but there are some broad categories which will be used here.[20]

Contributory (or insurance) benefits
These rely on the contributions made by the individual through the national insurance system. Eligibility is dependent on having made sufficient contributions within the stipulated period of a level which satisfies the regulations. The most obvious benefits in this category include the state retirement pension and unemployment benefit. The problems faced by women in respect of these are linked to their work patterns, their levels of earnings and their status (married or unmarried). Some of the contributory benefits are dealt with in Chapter 5 within the discussion of provision for financial security.

Means-tested (income related) benefits
Whereas contributory benefits depend on what the potential beneficiary has paid, in this second category eligibility depends on what the potential recipient has by way of resources (both income and capital). These do not simply apply to the unemployed or the elderly or the sick but may be far more generally directed at the poor depending from time to time on how they might be defined according to the means-test. Benefits in this category are those which are perhaps most accurately described as the safety net. They include income support, family credit and housing benefit.

Non-contributory and non-means-tested benefits
This category depends neither on what has been paid, nor on the resources available. In some cases the only requirement is status: child benefit is payable to any person (normally the mother) having responsibility for a child under the specified age. This could be described as a universal benefit, not because everyone receives it but because it is aimed at *all* children, irrespective of the wealth or poverty of those caring for them. Other non-contributory benefits are dependent

not simply on status but also on need. This applies in particular to benefits linked to disability, where the disabled claimant might have to prove a particular level of disability. Similarly, the invalid care allowance, which is payable to carers, may be claimed only where the person being cared for is so severely disabled as to meet the qualifying criteria for other disablement benefits.[21]

None of the benefits dealt with in this chapter is dependent on the contribution record of the claimant. Two issues arise: first, exactly when these payments may be claimed which thus focuses on the criteria for eligibility; and second, what the benefits are supposed to achieve - whether they are simply aimed at ameliorating disadvantage by providing some form of financial assistance or whether they may have other functions, for example acting as an incentive to find work or punishing those judged to have caused their own difficulties, for example by reducing the benefits of those who are "voluntarily unemployed." Because these benefits are not "earned" they highlight problems alluded to earlier in that those which are means-tested retain for some the stigma of poor relief and, where there is no means-test, it is alleged that those who do not need the payments are benefiting at the expense of others, one often cited example being child benefit. Tax payers are defined as the givers, those on benefits as the takers or indeed as the welfare "scroungers." These are the "undeserving poor" who need to be spurred into working by deductions from benefits and stringent means-testing (as compared to the rich who need to be spurred into working harder by being given greater tax relief).

There is no immutable rule that lays down that means-tested benefits must fulfil the function of a safety net. Nevertheless, those benefits which do depend on means have, in Britain, tended to be associated with the very poorest claimants. Perhaps because of this and the intrusive nature of means-testing there is little doubt that such benefits tend to get a bad press. In theory, however, not everything about them is bad and indeed, judged from the perspective of shifting resources to women, they should have certain advantages. The most obvious is that they allow for a significant degree of targeting so that those most in need in a specific area (say those caring for children) can be helped more directly. Moreover, they are redistributive since only those who satisfy the means-test (that is lack of means) will qualify for them. Whether or not these objectives are met depends in turn on the way the system operates. One of the problems implicit in regarding benefits as a safety net is that by and large the level of assistance will be set fairly low, otherwise there will be a disincentive effect. Hand in hand with this goes the poverty trap: once the minimum level has been set, anyone rising above it will, logically, cease to be eligible for help. At best, if benefit is lost pound for pound, this would be a reason to wonder if it were worthwhile working, but it may well be the case that every pound earned from employment occasions a greater loss in terms of benefits, (especially because of the loss of "passported" benefits such as free school meals which are available only in tandem with certain other benefits) which is a positive incentive not to work. The amount of redistribution achieved depends to some extent on the take-up rate of the benefit and this tends to be lower for means-tested benefits than for others. There are many reasons for this, not least those connected with the claimant's own perceptions of accepting "charity" or facing unhelpful bureaucracy and this is always assuming the benefit is known to exist and to be available.[22] The means-tested or income related benefits dealt with here are the principal examples of safety-netting: income support, family credit, housing benefit and grants or loans from the social fund.[23]

Who claims means-tested benefits?
Income support and family credit were introduced by the Social Security Act 1986[24] with the intention of guaranteeing a subsistence income which may or may not include housing costs, depending on whether the claimant is in rented accommodation, in which case housing benefit must be claimed. Income support is payable either to individuals or to families where there is no income from employment, while family credit is available to families where there is an earner, but income falls below specified limits. It should be borne in mind that these are not earnings replacement schemes which may operate where lack of resources is the result of some temporary set-back (short term illness or unemployment) but are benefits paid to those who may face long-term disadvantage and the daily reality of battling with poverty. Those who rely on income support and family credit are not deciding whether they can afford a holiday but whether there is enough money to buy food, clothes *and* pay the gas bill. These benefits, theoretically, mark the line between being poor and being destitute and it is therefore instructive to examine the number and type of recipients. Beveridge's vision was, after all, that such benefits were to be merely residual, catching only those who had not made the requisite insurance contributions. The extent of the failure of this plan is indicated by the fact that by late 1992 there were five and a half million recipients of income support and 460,000 families in receipt of family credit.[25] In attempting to decide whether the situation of women is different from that of men - and whether in this context they are more dependent on the state and thus less able to lead independent lives it is helpful to look more closely at the type of claimants to see if any patterns emerge.

The Department of Social Security categorises recipients of income support as those aged 60 and over, the disabled, lone parents, unemployed and other. The statistics thus produced are notoriously misleading, not least because of the "invisibility" of many women within them, especially in relation to unemployment.[26] In terms of the bare numbers of recipients according to sex, (and irrespective of status) there is a difference: in 1992 there were 2.35 million men receiving income support and 2.73 million women.[27] These figures must, however, be read with caution since they are influenced by various competing factors. Because of the way figures are compiled there is, for example, an under-estimate of the number of women who are unemployed. On the other hand, the figures are influenced by the longevity of women: there are significantly more female than male pensioners receiving benefit.[28] A particularly important influence, however, is the rule that where there is a couple only one partner may claim income support although the income of both is aggregated. This has a number of consequences, and in particular, because income support cannot be claimed where one partner is in full-time employment, women whose partners are in work are ineligible on grounds of status even though they may be in need. There is, however, one category where the bare statistics may be of some help in shedding light on the situation of women within the system. The figures for lone parents are not affected by longevity or the vagaries of the unemployment statistics (although this does not mean that they are entirely accurate). In 1992, according to the Department of Social Security, there were 985,000 one parent families in receipt of income support, of whom only 52,000 were headed by a man. Since single (that is unmarried) mothers are often blamed for being, amongst other things, a disproportionate burden on the state, it is interesting to note that in the 933,000 families headed by women, more women were divorced, widowed or separated than were single parents.[29] The predominance of women as the heads of lone parent families is repeated in the figures for family credit. In January 1993 there were 272,000 couples in receipt of family credit and in nearly 184,000 of those the main earner was male. Conversely in 197,000 lone parent families, the main earner was female in 190,000 of those families.[30]

The incidence of poverty amongst lone parents and in particular lone mothers is well documented.[31] Lone parents are concentrated in the lower reaches of income distribution and there is a widening gap between two parent and lone parent families. Within the lone parent category, lone mothers tend to be worse off than lone fathers, a consequence of the different patterns of lone fatherhood and of men's greater earning power.[32] There is nothing new about the poverty experienced by lone mothers[33] though in the past it was more likely to occur through the death of a partner rather than through divorce or conception outside marriage.[34] Nor is their dependence on the state a recent phenomenon: Snell and Millar found that this has always been the case.[35] More recently it was found that about 85 per cent of lone mothers had spent some time on income support and of those still on benefit, half had been receiving it for over two and a half years.[36] Dependence on income support brings with it a variety of other problems, principally how to survive from week to week on such a low income. It is true that for some women it may be their first taste of a *regular* income, but the pressures of trying to budget for the costs of living take a toll in terms of physical and emotional health.[37] This is compounded by the housing problems which lone mothers also face with a much larger proportion living in rented accommodation or sharing with other family members. The difficulties experienced by lone mothers are myriad and a life which is dependent on state benefits is far from ideal. Nevertheless, despite the serious problems, some of these women felt that there were advantages to being a lone parent, the most important of these being the independence they experienced: almost half wanted to remain by themselves in the near future rather than re-marry or cohabit.[38] Taken with the findings as to why women work and how they feel when they lose their jobs, this is compelling evidence of the need that women have for access to resources to control their own lives both financially and in a wider sense.[39]

The evidence of poverty amongst lone mothers may show no more than what has already been noted more generally in Chapter 3: women are amongst the lowest paid workers, the presence of dependent children acts as a constraint on earning capacity and it is predominantly women (whatever the type of family) who have responsibility for child care. This means that those who are unable to earn are forced to seek help elsewhere - in this case from the social security system. What the figures do not show, however, is whether or not the system operates in such a way that it is adequate to meet the needs of those forced to rely on it.

Income Support

Income support is in general payable only to a person over the age of 18[40] whose resources do not exceed a certain level, termed the applicable amounts. As might be expected from the rationale of this benefit, it is not normally available to anyone in full-time employment, nor may it be claimed by someone whose *partner* is in full-time work. The definition of full-time work is, however, anything above 16 hours a week: above that, entitlement to income support is lost (though in appropriate cases family credit may be payable). The limit used to be 24 hours a week and the move to the lower figure is likely to discourage many women from taking up part-time work. The low pay which such work tends to attract means that when expenses for travelling and especially any child care costs are taken into account, it is simply not worth working. There is, moreover, a general rule that a claimant for income support must be available for employment in a way similar to that for claimants of unemployment benefit.[41] There are exceptions, however, and since these include those with caring responsibilities[42] they are especially important for women who make up a large proportions of carers.

Unlike family credit, income support may be paid to individuals as well as to families but, importantly for women, within any family unit only one person may claim. For these purposes, a family may be a married couple or unmarried couple living together as husband and wife, together with any children and young persons. This is important not only for deciding on the level of need and thus of benefit (two single people are generally more favourably treated than a couple) but also for assessing the extent to which resources should be taken into account to reduce that benefit. The issue of whether one partner should be assumed or made to rely financially on the other is often raised in the context of cohabiting couples[43] but it is also significant for married couples. If the benefit payable to the claiming partner is reduced on the assumption that the income of the other is available for both this raises important questions about the management and sharing of finances within the family unit[44] especially since it is clear that the partner with the greatest resources will normally be male. The aggregation of resources also has consequences on the employment prospects for the non-claiming partner since her employment will adversely affect the level of or even eligibility for the benefit. It is not unusual for the partners of unemployed men to give up their work, particularly where his unemployment is lengthy. In one survey it was found that three-quarters of the sample who were available for work said they were deterred from working because it would not be financially worthwhile when their husbands were unemployed.[45]

The level of benefit paid out in income support depends on a complicated network of rules and regulations which are aimed at arriving at an amount which is calculated to cover the claimant's needs.[46] To put it at its simplest, the amount payable is that which is needed to bring the claimant's resources up to her applicable amount. This is personal to each claimant and it is made up of personal allowances, premiums and housing costs. Any relevant income of the claimant is then subtracted from the resulting total to arrive at the benefit. The use of a formula in assessing benefit levels presupposes a prior decision as to what is reasonable for someone to live on - and what therefore life involves for someone at the bottom of the income scale.[47] Personal allowances are meant to reflect day to day expenses depending on the status of the claimant. They are to cover all normal expenses including food, clothing, fuel, travel and, supposedly, the kind of amenities that everyone expects to be able to enjoy in the late twentieth century. The actual amount of the allowance varies according to age and whether or not the claimant is part of a couple. The age bands are under 18 (with different categories within the band), 18 to 24 and 25 and above. There are further variations according to whether the claimant is single or part of a couple and in the latter case on the ages of the partners within the couple.[48] A personal allowance will take account of any dependent children (aged up to 16) or young persons (aged from 16 to 19 who are in full time education) for whom the claimant or claimant's partner has responsibility. Again the amount of allowance depends on age bands, this time applicable to the child: under 11, 11-15, 16-17 and 18 and over. Once the personal allowance has been worked out it may be possible to add an appropriate premium which is intended to reflect the differing needs which the particular circumstances of the individual or family may create: one obvious example might be where there is a severely disabled person in the family, necessitating additional fuel for heating and washing, or special dietary needs. These premiums are broadly payable in respect of children, disability and age. Thus there is a family premium payable to any family where there is a child, though it is only payable once, regardless of the number of children. There is a lone parent premium payable to a single parent (or person responsible for the child) while the child is a dependant, again payable only in respect of one child. In certain circumstances there are premiums for disability where there is a disabled child, or where the claimant is disabled or where there is a carer in receipt of invalid care allowance. Finally there is a premium for pensioners.[49]

The final component in calculating the benefit relates to housing costs though as a general rule these are covered not by income support but by housing benefit, administered by local authorities and available in appropriate cases to anyone paying rent. Only housing costs not covered by housing benefit are relevant in assessing income support and in general this means mortgage payments.[50] A claimant who lives in property on which there is a mortgage will be able to ask for help with the repayments of mortgage interest, (not capital repayments) if she can show that she is responsible for the payments[51] and that they relate to her home.[52] To counter suggestions that paying a mortgage in full was likely to act as a disincentive to work, and that it would benefit the unemployed unfairly, special conditions apply so that only 50 per cent of the mortgage interest repayments are met for the first 16 weeks of income support: this can be very hard for women who may have taken over payments following the departure of a partner. The rule was meant to act as an incentive for applicants quickly to find themselves paid employment but since after the 16 weeks the applicant is able to claim not only 100 per cent of interest payments for the future, but also the additional interest payable on the arrears of interest accumulated during the period, it is questionable if it serves any real purpose other than making life difficult during those four months. Despite the difficulties claimants already faced, it was announced in the November 1994 Budget Speech that existing mortgage payers who found themselves on income support would not qualify for *any* help with repayments during the first two months, followed by payment of half the interest for the next four months. Those taking out mortgages after October 1995, will not qualify for any help for nine months.[53] Such restrictions make it even more important for a claimant to find work, but it should be further noted that, should a woman find herself a job, her earnings may worsen her position in relation to housing costs, as losing entitlement to income support prevents *any* help with mortgage liabilities, and as an owner-occupier she is ineligible for housing benefit. She may find, therefore, that she is worse off than when she was claiming benefits. This epitomises the enormous leap that someone has to make between dependence on benefits and financial independence. A final calculation which can work to the detriment of the householder is that in calculating the amount of income support payable, housing costs are reduced by the amounts which are paid or which are *deemed* to be paid by non-dependants, that is people living in the house but not part of the family for the purposes of income support, for example adult sons and daughters. These deductions are made regardless of whether the individual is in fact making any contribution to household expenses.

Once the aggregated elements have been used to arrive at the applicable amount, the rate of benefit is calculated by deducting from the applicable amount any resources which the claimant has. These include both income and capital, subject, under the rules, to what are called disregards. Only where the claimant is entirely destitute will the benefit be the whole of the applicable amount. It may seem logical to make deductions in respect of resources since the benefit is meant to provide a safety net for those without means, not to bolster someone's standard of living. This raises the question, however, of why only some income or capital is taken into account, while some is simply disregarded. The answer lies, of course, in the persistent belief that those on benefit require incentives, and that thrift and work must be encouraged, if need be by allowing some to benefit from the full rates even though they have some savings or some earnings. There is thus a delicate formula to be worked out: saving can be encouraged by disregarding a certain level of capital but set too high a level and the benefit is paid to those who do not really need it; set it too low and there is no point in saving. There is a similar dilemma with earnings - allowing people to work to improve their living standards is to be encouraged, but it is important to avoid the situation where, because of their earnings, they cease to be eligible for benefit, but having lost benefit are worse off working. All of this is compounded in the case of a couple since resources are treated as common to the unit and not as particular to the individual. This is of little use to a woman who does not in fact have equal access, but who is discouraged from seeking financial independence by the effect this will have on the family income. Needless to say, the rules governing disregards are complex and subject to change and only some of the most important points will be outlined here.

Perhaps one of the most crucial points about the effect that income has on the level of benefit is that if the claimant is part of a couple, the partner's income (which must only be from part-time work) is treated as belonging equally to that claimant - this is irrespective of what may actually happen within the household. The amount of earnings disregarded depends on the circumstances of the claimant. The basic level is £5, and where both partners are earning each may claim that as a disregard.[54] A higher level of disregard applies to certain categories of claimant where presumably it is felt that it is not going to operate as a disincentive to work because full-time work would be impracticable. Thus for example a lone parent who qualifies for the lone parent premium is entitled to a £15 disregard[55] and other categories include some pensioners and couples who are long term claimants of income support. Only one £15 disregard may be claimed even if a claimant comes within more than one category. Apart from earnings from part-time employment, all other income, including from other benefits must be examined to decide whether it is to be taken into account in full or in part. The principal national insurance benefits such as pensions, unemployment benefit and disability benefits are counted in full as is child benefit. A few benefits are partially disregarded and some are entirely ignored especially those connected with disabilities. This interplay between the different types of benefits arises since, although in theory the contributory benefits are supposed to represent the more generous and "respectable" side of the welfare system, the level at which they are payable means that those in receipt of them may well have to turn to means-tested benefits in order to survive.

The advent of the Child Support Agency has focused attention on another extremely important source of income taken into account in full, namely maintenance payments. The DSS operates the notion of the "liable relative" under which certain persons, if they have the means, are expected to maintain others, rather than have them dependent on the state. These include husbands, wives, ex-spouses, and parents of someone under 19. Thus, where a parent leaves a partner with a child to support, he is expected to provide for the child and where appropriate for the person caring for the child. One survey discovered, however, that whereas only 29 per cent of lone parents received maintenance from former partners, this fell to just 13 per cent of single mothers.[56] If the carer is a claimant she *must* apply for maintenance and the amount is used to reduce benefits even though this ignores the fact that maintenance payments may be irregular or non-existent. The issues raised by maintenance and financial provision after divorce are detailed in Chapter 7 but it should be borne in mind that the interaction of maintenance payments and state benefits can be crucial: maintenance payments which take the claimant just above income support levels mean that she loses the passported benefits which go with income support such as free school meals. This assumes that there is no difficulty about claiming and receiving maintenance. A deserted mother who refuses to co-operate with the Child Support Agency in seeking maintenance from her ex-partner will find that her benefits will be reduced unless she can convince them that she has good cause not to identify her partner and pursue him for payments. If she does apply for maintenance there is no guarantee that the payments will be regular or reliable. The problems caused by this in terms of practical financial hardship are obvious and it seems equally clear that although the Agency was set up by a government committed to the idea of combating the so-called dependency culture, the effect is merely to shift dependency from the state to the absent father. Whatever might be the moral or social justifications for seeking to make men shoulder their responsibilities for their children, any development which entails, directly or indirectly a reinforcement of women's dependency on men is a retrograde step. Women need greater access to paid employment and affordable child care rather than a system which condemns them to long term unemployment and dependency.

When all the calculations have been done (after taking into account also the amount of capital assets owned by the claimant or her partner) the level of benefit can be worked out. Taking as an example a single mother aged 26, living in rented accommodation with two children under 11, the 1994 benefit levels would have given her £45.70 a week as her personal allowance, personal allowances for the children of £15.65 each, a family premium of £10.05, and a lone parent premium of £5.10 making a total of £92.15 a week.[57] She would be entitled to child benefit but, as income, it would be deducted from her income support and thus cancelled out. She would also qualify for housing benefit. These figures should be seen in the light of the fact that in 1994 the average gross weekly wage of a male manual worker was just over £280. The Child Poverty Action Group estimated that in 1993 almost 3 million children living on benefits were surviving on levels 25 per cent below that needed for "basic sustenance."[58]

The most striking features of income support are the complexity of the rules governing its availability and the low levels at which the benefit is set. It would seem that those receiving the benefit would enjoy a higher standard of living if they could engage in paid employment. The rules, however, appear calculated to ensure that for many this is not a realistic possibility and this is especially so for women whose employment is less likely to be sufficiently well paid to justify the switch from benefits to wages. All mothers face additional problems in relation to the costs of child care, since that alone can so reduce wages that employment ceases to be a viable choice. In an attempt to ameliorate this particular problem, regulations came into force in 1994[59] which allow working parents who are claiming certain benefits (including family credit and housing benefit) to have the costs of child care for a child up to the age of 11 deducted from their earnings before those earnings are taken into account. The maximum that may be deducted in respect of child care for any one family is £40 a week. This is supposed to encourage people with children back to work, especially lone parents. What the regulations do not do, of course, is tackle the paucity of provision of adequate child care, nor do they recognise the real costs of child care, which for many, particularly those with more than one child, will exceed the £40 limit. The regulations are restricted to children under 11, even though working parents will find it difficult to arrange free after school care for young teenagers.

Despite this gesture in the direction of easing the situation of working parents, it is still the case that the scheme for income support does not assist women to become financially independent. It remains true, as Maclean observed, that:

> In the UK, benefits keep women who live alone with children out of employment unless they can earn enough in one leap into the labour market to compensate for the lost cash benefit plus all the other fringe benefits which accompany it such as free school meals, help with housing, and so on.[60]

Even where a woman is part of a couple claiming income support, the rules on aggregation may discourage her from taking waged work. Another large group of women claiming income support are those past retirement age and they find themselves having to claim because their access to well paid jobs and their consequent ability to provide for their long term financial security were never adequate.

Family credit

Whereas one of the eligibility conditions for income support is that the claimant is *not* in full-time work, the second means-tested non-contributory benefit, family credit, is designed to top-up the wages of low paid workers with children. It was noted in Chapter 3 that with the abolition of Wages Councils, Britain has finally rid itself of even the vestiges of any system of minimum wage regulation. The work ethic and the system of work incentives inherent in social security payments do not extend to ensuring that the worker receives a living wage for herself and her family: workers must work for whatever the market decrees is the wage for the job and if that is too low to live on, it is not the function of the state to make the employer pay more: to do so would interfere with the market. On the other hand, if families cannot survive on their earned income this would be an incentive not to work but to rely entirely on state benefits. One compromise is to boost the wages earned to take account of the extra expenses incurred by raising a family.[61] This could be done through the tax system, and indeed there were child allowances for some time, but it has been decided to achieve the supplementation of incomes through the social security system in the guise of family credit (though as a non-contributory benefit it is financed through general taxation).

In order to qualify for family credit the claimant or her partner must be in full-time work (an average of 16 hours a week, which may be done in more than one job, but only by one of the partners), there must be at least one dependent child, or a young person under 19 in full-time education, and the income from the work must be below a certain level. Calculation of family credit involves working out the maximum credit for the family, taking account of the number and ages of the children, then comparing income with the applicable amount, which in 1994 was £71.70. If income is below that, full family credit is payable. If it is more, the maximum credit is reduced by 70 per cent of the difference between income and £71.70. Maximum family credit is made up of one adult credit (whether the claimant is single or not) plus a credit for each child, the amount of which will depend on the child's age, the bands being the same as for income support.[62] In calculating income, the claimant must take into account net earnings plus most other forms of income,[63] including that of a partner, which yet again serves as a disincentive to women taking paid employment. A nod in the direction of dealing with disincentives is apparent, however, in the decision to introduce the so-called child care allowance. Anyone on family credit who needs to pay for child care is allowed to deduct up to £40 per week from earnings before the earnings reduce the benefit.[64] In announcing this, the Chancellor of the Exchequer referred specifically to the costs of child care as being a disincentive to lone parents and married mothers seeking work, but there was no indication that the Government is intending to tackle either the shortage or the cost of such child care. Awards of family credit are made for a fixed period of 26 weeks and entitlement carries with it a passport to other benefits including free NHS prescriptions, dental treatment and eye tests, but not free school meals. Unlike income support, where either partner in a couple may claim, a claim for family credit must be made by the woman, unless the Secretary of State decides it is reasonable for her partner to claim. Both parties must, however, sign the claim form.

One of the most serious criticisms of family credit as an instrument for combating family poverty has been the disappointingly low take-up rate. A study in 1993[65] estimated that it reaches only 64 per cent of those entitled to it, making it the least effective benefit in reaching its target. It was found that those who did receive the benefit were on average £23 a week better off than they would have been on income support (for lone parents this rose to £30 a week). The highest take up rates were among lone parents and council tenants while those losing out tended to be white collar families buying their own homes. This may result from a dislike of being dependent on benefits or may quite simply be due to ignorance of its availability.

Social Fund

It is inevitable that if income support and family credit are designed to maintain merely a minimum level of standard of living there are going to be times when the basic benefits are not enough. There might be a crisis such as a flooded bedroom or a kitchen going up in flames, at which point the person concerned simply cannot find the funds to replace the bed or the cooker, let alone repair any damage and replace curtains, carpets and clothing. Such sudden and heavy expenses cannot be encompassed within the limits of the normal expenditure of income support nor indeed could they in relation to its forerunner, supplementary benefit. One of the many criticisms made of that previous system was in relation to the practice that had grown up of dealing with exceptional or emergency needs through single payments, which in the case of the so-called urgent needs payments could be made to both claimants and non-claimants. The rules relating to both types of payments were highly complex and the payments themselves had grown to such a level that they were seen as an undue burden on the cost of the system as a whole. This was the background to the setting up of the Social Fund.

The system of single payments was governed by extremely detailed regulations laying down the circumstances in which the payments could and could not be made.[66] Payments were proscribed not only in relation to expenses which it was argued could be met from elsewhere (say from local authority grants) but also in relation to things which, as a matter of policy, it was decided should not be provided out of public funds - presumably on the basis that the poor either did not need them or did not deserve them. These included telephone charges, the cost of renting and licensing a television or radio and, of course, holidays. Whereas there may well be some willing to argue that, even in the 1980s, the poor had no right to such amenities unless they could pay for them out of ordinary benefits, it is interesting to speculate how many would also agree that a list drawn up to reflect essential items of furniture for someone on benefit moving into their own home in the 1980s should not include a refrigerator. The rules surrounding the implementation of the single payments system were infamous in their complexity and apparent illogicality. The way in which they were applied was similarly incomprehensible, sometimes to the point of absurdity. To give just one such example: a claimant had, after a long spell of unemployment, acquired a part-time job for which he required safety clothing and in respect of which he asked for a payment. Such claims were decided by adjudication officers, with a right of appeal to a Social Security Appeal Tribunal. From there the claimant could appeal to a social security commissioner whose decisions had the force of law. Both the adjudication officer and the appeal tribunal while accepting the clothing was needed to protect the claimant's health, refused a single payment on the basis that the only regulation under which he fell required that the payment was the *only means* by which the risk to health could be prevented and he could avoid the risk by leaving the job. The only redeeming feature in this case was that the commissioner reversed the decision.[67] Clothing generally did not come within the system for single payments after 1980 when it was provided that replacement costs for clothing that had simply worn out through normal wear and tear should not be covered - they were provided for in the normal rates of supplementary benefit. Only in special cases, for example if there was a serious risk to health, could clothing grants be made. The likelihood of this happening is perhaps indicated by the decision of an adjudication officer that a child was not entitled to a pair of shoes because she had three pairs of socks which, worn together, would be a suitable alternative to shoes.[68]

There was, clearly, a good deal wrong with this system and the cuts that were imposed on it during the 1980s meant that the difficulties which claimants experienced in gaining access to single payments were compounded by a reduction in what was available. For example, a young, unemployed, single, pregnant woman would have found in April 1987 as the Social Fund reforms began to take effect that, if eligible, she would have been awarded a maternity grant of £80 (now up to £100). That £80 was to meet the costs associated with a new baby, despite the fact that even the most cautious estimates at the time put those costs at £275.[69] Assuming that this young mother, who was going to have problems buying the essentials for her baby, also needed furniture for any accommodation she might have, she would have found in April 1987 that items including furniture and carpets (plus a variety of other items) were no longer considered essentials. A grant *could* be made subject to stringent qualifying conditions, but only by way of lump sum payment (£75) regardless of the cost.

Apart from the fact that the system of single payments was riddled with inconsistencies and complexities, it was costing a great deal of money. Naturally, one reason for the escalating costs was the depth of poverty that the system had to deal with. The system was degrading to those using it and patchy in what it achieved. Changes aimed at tightening up access had not worked so a larger scale reform was attempted in the shape of the Social Fund. There are a number of ways in which the Fund differs from the pre-existing system and explain why it met with a more or less universally hostile reception. The first important difference is that while the single payment system responded to needs as they arose (and thus had spiralling costs), the Fund has a fixed budget: that budget determines the needs that can be met in any one year. Secondly, the idea of grants has been largely abandoned in favour of repayable loans, the repayments for which are taken out of weekly benefits. The final crucial difference relates to the way the Fund is administered. Whereas the previous system had been at the mercy of officers interpreting fixed regulations, the new one is at the even more unpredictable mercy of the officers' discretion. Although the regulations were complex, they conferred certain *rights* (however meagre). Now, though the poor may apply for help, the decision is wholly in the hands of the Social Fund officers. In the light of this it was probably inevitable that the right of appeal was abolished: a disappointed applicant may simply ask for a review of the decision within the department concerned, although there is in theory the possibility of judicial review by the courts - a complicated and lengthy process. As with other welfare benefits, the Social Fund is of particular relevance to women, not because of their sex, per se, (though maternity grants are obviously sex-linked) but because women are so well-represented amongst the poorest in society. It is instructive to examine the workings of the Fund if only to see how those poor are treated.

The Social Fund is not in fact entirely discretionary but has two quite distinct aspects: the first is the non-discretionary or regulated Social Fund, so called because payments are based entirely on regulations which lay down the purposes for which and the circumstances in which entitlement arises. Under these regulations payments are made in respect of three things: maternity expenses, funeral expenses and cold weather payments. In the first case a payment of up to £100 may be made to help with the expenses of a new baby provided the claimant or partner are in receipt of other benefits, for example income support. Capital over £500 is taken into account to reduce the payment pound for pound but the payment is in effect a grant and is not repayable. In 1992-3 there were 228,000 such payments.[70] Funeral payments, intended to cover the cost of a basic funeral, averaged £791 in 1992-3[71] which serves as an interesting comparison of the costs of birth and death. Help with funeral costs is available only to those in receipt of other benefits and is repayable out of any estate left by the deceased. Cold weather payments are dependent on there being a spell of cold weather which satisfies regulations in which case those on income support with a pensioner or disability premium or with a child under 5 automatically receive a payment in respect of the period (set at £8.50 from November 1995).

The regulated part of the Fund bears some of the hallmarks of the previous system and is subject to similar drawbacks but it is the discretionary aspect of the Social Fund which has excited the greatest disapproval ever since it was first proposed. The Social Fund budget is decided annually by the Secretary of State with Treasury approval. Under the terms of the Social Security Administration Act 1992, allocations from this national budget are then made to local offices who thus have their own budgets which must not be exceeded. Decisions may rest on a discretion but the officers have plenty of advice as to how to operate. The Act gives the Secretary of State power to issue directions which are binding on the Social Fund officers making the decisions. The Secretary of State also issues guidance which is published together with the legally binding directions in the Social Fund Guide. The guidance explains the directions but is not itself legally binding. Local offices will also have guidance notes for use in that area. In managing the budget officers must approach claims in terms of priorities and the guidance indicates that priority depends on the individual and the particular circumstances.

Discretionary payments come in a number of guises: budgeting loans, crisis loans and community care grants. The last of these is linked to the policy of getting people back "into the community" and out of institutional or residential care. Eligibility for the community care grant is restricted to those on income support but the grants made are not repayable. In 1992-3, 322,000 grants were made and averaged £280.[72] They are meant to assist vulnerable people to exist within the community, giving special attention to certain groups including the elderly, disabled, victims of drug abuse, families under stress and young people leaving local authority care. The grant is said to be intended to help in re-establishment or remaining in the community or to relieve exceptional pressure on families (couples or single parents with at least one child). This might occur in the case of marriage breakdown or where there is a severely disabled child. The grants can cover the cost of furniture and other household items and also clothing if the person claiming can show she has very few clothes. Although this is not classed as a loan - an obvious advantage - the other two types of grants are each repayable.

Budgeting loans are intended for those who have been on income support for at least 26 weeks to deal with large, intermittent expenses. The grant is repayable on the basis that while income support is supposedly sufficient for meeting all needs, those on low incomes will sometimes find it necessary to have help in budgeting for unexpected or heavy expenditure and so much of what would have been met with a single, non-repayable grant is now dealt with by means of a loan. The Fund officers decide whether the item requested is high, medium or low priority. High priority items include essential furniture and bedding and non-mains fuel costs while clothes are medium priority. Personal circumstances may alter priorities: a washing machine may be high priority for the elderly and housebound but not for a young person. The maximum that can be lent according to the directions is £1,000 though in 1992-3 the average award was £217.[73] One of the most controversial aspects of these loans is that the amount of either budgeting or crisis loans may not exceed any sum which the applicant is likely to be able to repay so that the loan will be only as much as the officer considers is likely to be repaid. The Alice in Wonderland logic of this leads inexorably to the conclusion that those most in need and thus least likely to be able to repay are those who are least likely to obtain a loan.

Whereas budgeting loans are available only to existing claimants, though for a range of purposes, crisis loans are available generally (subject to specific exclusions) but only for special problems. The rules refer to an emergency or disaster where the loan is the only means of preventing serious damage or serious risk to health and safety. Crisis loans are generally to be regarded as high priority (for obvious reasons) but even so must come within the budget. In 1992-3 the average award was £65. With all Social Fund payments the Social Fund officer must have regard not only to matters such as the nature of the need, any resources of the applicant and the likelihood of repayment, but also the possibility that the need may be met elsewhere. This means that the applicant may be referred to other agencies such as charities. Officers are advised, however, that they should not routinely refer applicants to employers, relatives or friends unless there is reason to believe an offer of help will be forthcoming.[74] In other words the Social Fund is to be a means of absolute last resort - those in such dire need that they are forced to approach it should first have to consider begging and borrowing elsewhere.

Since most of the payments from the Fund are loans, they must be repaid and in the case of those on benefits this means through deductions which may be up to 15 per cent of the applicable amount. Debtors are supposed to repay within the shortest possible period and normally within eighteen months. Bearing in mind that the loan is made in the first place because of extreme need and that the levels of benefit are far from generous (if they were the need would not be so extreme), making deductions from benefits may well begin an ever worsening situation for the poorest claimants. There is plenty of evidence that debt is an ever present problem for those dependent on social security benefits and since the Social Fund is so rigidly structured and less than generous in its payments, claimants are tempted to turn to more expensive and sometimes unregulated sources.[75]

Housing benefit

Many of those who turn to the Social Fund do so because of the need for furniture or other household items: this presupposes somewhere to put them. Housing benefit is the means-tested benefit which is meant to help with the cost of accommodation. Adequate housing is a central concern for any programme of social welfare but there are conflicting views on how best the problem should be addressed.[76] Not only must there be enough suitable accommodation for those who require it, but the cost must be such that those in need can take advantage of it. In Britain during the twentieth century there has been a steady move from renting to buying property. When most people lived in rented accommodation there was a system of rent control which meant that the law intervened in the market to keep rents at a level which was affordable. There are still some lingering remnants of rent control[77] but the private rented sector is now very small as compared with owner-occupation and local authority housing, while even the latter has decreased with tenants' "right to buy." The number of homes in the private rented sector fell by 1.3 million between 1979 and 1987 while the number of houses owned by local authorities decreased by 1.5 million (from 6.9 million) in the period 1979 to 1990.[78] The early 1990s saw some disillusionment with the ideal of home ownership but there is still a good deal of attachment to it: two-thirds of tenants would prefer to own their home.[79] Those who are most dependent on the private rented sector and council housing are lower income households and women in particular. This is borne out time and again by surveys which find that households headed by women are heavily dependent on the rented sector. In one such study it was found that lone mothers are much more likely than married mothers to be living in rented rather than owner-occupied accommodation (33 per cent as compared to 77 per cent) and in the case of unemployed lone mothers, three out of four lived in local authority housing.[80]

The current methods used by government to assist with the costs of housing operate through the tax system, as mortgage interest tax relief and through the means-tested housing benefit administered by the local authorities. The cost of tax relief on mortgages increased tenfold between 1961 and 1991 by which time it cost the government £8.3 billion, though it fell significantly subsequently with the fall in interest rates and the end of higher rate relief.[81] Housing benefit, which was paid to over 4 million recipients cost slightly over £3.5 billion in 1992-93.[82]

Mortgage tax relief is clearly not a progressive redistributive measure, but housing benefit, on the other hand, *is* intended to achieve those objectives by assisting with the housing costs of those whose income is so low that the market costs of accommodation are prohibitive.[83] It first appeared in the Social Security and Housing Benefit Act 1982 as an attempt to simplify existing arrangements and has never been free from criticism. One attempt at simplification was to unify, without incurring any cost, the two types of means-tested benefits then available to tenants to help with housing. There were complications because local authorities were responsible for rent rebates while the DSS was responsible for supplementary benefits and it was notoriously difficult to assess who was eligible for what and whether an individual would be better off claiming one rather than the other. Another attempt at simplification was to transfer the administration of the scheme from the DSS to local authorities. The result on both scores was, to put it mildly, a failure. For a start, local authorities were overwhelmed by the changeover and the system began to creak alarmingly. Perhaps more importantly, the unification of the two schemes did not work and for various reasons the new scheme was perceived to be unfair. Those on supplementary benefit did better than those who were not even though the latter may have had incomes which were no higher. An additional and very complicated benefit was introduced to deal with those on the margins of supplementary benefits and the idea of a simplified scheme began to look unattainable.

Further reforms were demanded and appeared in the Social Security Act 1986. By this stage, however, the government had decided it wished to save a considerable amount of money on housing benefit and it was also proposed that there should be further harmonisation as between various means-tested schemes. Thus, for example, the rules for income support (above) were to be used in relation to entitlement for housing benefit. One effect was that for the first time housing benefit would take account of the householder's capital. The proposed capital limit over which no benefit was payable was set so low that a politically unacceptable number of households would have lost entitlement to housing benefit and the limit was raised at the last minute. Other criticisms were ignored, however, and in particular it was provided that everyone, including those on income support, should be liable for 20 per cent of their rates (pre-community charge tax and council tax). Opposition was such that in the end the government was forced to concede that those on income support would be compensated by increasing their benefit by an amount which would be equivalent to the rates contribution.[84] Yet another criticism of the scheme is the so-called taper: where the claimant is in receipt of income above the applicable amount the benefit is tapered to reflect that. Rather than losing benefit pound for pound, which would be a disincentive, a percentage taper is applied. In 1982 the taper was 23 per cent - for every pound of extra income the claimant would lose 23 pence: by 1993 that taper stood at 65 per cent.

Given that the scheme of housing benefit remains complex, it is nevertheless helpful to look at some of its basic principles. Eligibility depends on the claimant being legally liable to pay rent in respect of her home whether that is public or private sector housing. If a woman is part of a couple, it may be her partner whose name appears as the tenant but if he should cease to pay and she takes over payment she will be entitled to claim the benefit. Needless to say, couples are treated as a single benefit unit. The amount of benefit depends on three factors: rent, income and the applicable amount. Eligible rent is the amount that can be met by housing benefit so, for example, water rates are excluded, as are mortgage payments.[85] Income is assessed largely in the same way as for income support, the general rule being that all income of the claimant and her partner is taken into account, including capital over a certain level. Earnings are deemed to include some benefits such as statutory sick pay and maternity pay but some income is wholly or partially disregarded, depending on the claimant's circumstances.[86] The applicable amount is a personal allowance which depends on family circumstances, plus premiums for disability, pensioners, lone parents, disabled children and carers and is assessed in the same way as for income support. For those on income support, who qualify automatically for housing benefit, the amount of benefit is simply 100 per cent of eligible rent, less deductions for any non-dependants. For a claimant not on income support, the amount depends on whether income is less than the applicable amount (in which case the calculation is the same as for someone on income support) or over that amount in which case housing benefit will be 100 per cent of eligible rent, less any deductions for non-dependants, less 65 per cent of net income above the applicable amount. One important difference between housing benefit and income support calculations is that the lone parent premium is higher for housing benefit than it is for income support, presumably because the housing costs of a single parent are not that different from those of two parents, whereas the same cannot be said in relation to food and clothing.

Housing benefit is an integral part of the safety-netting approach to social welfare and the contribution it makes to that welfare should not be ignored, but it suffers nevertheless from similar drawbacks to income support: apart from its reliance on the family unit in a way which is disadvantageous to many women, the policies behind it have ignored both the changing shape of the property market and changing family structures. The very fact that homelessness has become such a problem in recent years is an indication, if one were needed, that all is not well with housing policies in Britain.[87]

Non-contributory benefits

If the means-tested benefits are failing women, is it possible that the non-contributory ones are doing any better? These are not dependent on resources and include benefits payable in respect of disability such as disability living allowance, and in respect of caring such as invalid care allowance and child benefit. The financial problems associated with disability are numerous and well-documented[88] but the focus here is on child benefit and invalid care allowance, as examples which are particularly relevant to women.

Child benefit, like family credit, is an explicit acknowledgment of the additional costs of bringing up a family. The cost of dependent children is high, not only in real terms in respect of food, clothes and fuel, but also because of the restrictions which the presence of the children tend to place on the carer's earning capacity. The figures for lone parents illustrate that the vast majority of those caring alone for children are women, but it is also the case that in couples the principal responsibility for child care still falls largely on the mother. As long ago as 1924 Eleanor Rathbone argued for the "endowment of motherhood." She was of the opinion that caring for children was a responsible job rather than a private undertaking for which women should be rewarded by society. When Beveridge recommended the payment of family allowances to mothers this looked to be a first step toward achieving that goal. Unfortunately this proved not to be the case. Payments of this nature were regarded as for the benefit of the child rather than as an acknowledgement of the importance of mothering skills. Moreover, although it might be thought that benefits aimed at assisting with the expenses involved in rearing children would be most logically targeted at the child's mother, this was not the case. Until 1980[89] allowances came in two forms: one payable through the tax system and the other through the social security system. The child tax allowance benefited the better off more than it did the poor and the father rather than the mother. The social security family allowance was in contrast payable to the mother, but it was not payable in respect of a first child and the rates were far from generous. Moreover, the rates were increased infrequently so that the real value to the mother fell during the 1950s and 1960s.

In 1975 the Labour Government replaced the existing system with child benefit which was to be a benefit payable to everyone with responsibility for a child, regardless of their income and, in deciding entitlement to the benefit, where a couple was living together priority was given to the mother. At first sight this seems to be a sensible and efficient method of recognising the costs of a family *and* of targeting the benefit where it is most needed and likely to fulfil its purpose. Looked at more closely, this may not be the case. First and foremost the level of child benefit is almost universally acknowledged to be woefully inadequate. The 1994 level is £10.20 a week for the first child and £8.25 for the second and subsequent children (£10.40 and £8.45 in 1995). In a now infamous undertaking the Conservative Government promised in 1980 to up-rate child benefit in line with inflation, but this has quite obviously not been done. Not only were the increases in the mid-1980s below inflation levels but in 1988 there was no increase at all. The Government's explanation is that the policy is now to target benefits more efficiently at those who really need help. This reflects a widely held belief that child benefit, being a non-contributory, non-means-tested benefit, is going to families who do not need it. The picture is painted of the middle class wife using her child benefit for extras ranging from exotic holidays to bottles of gin, but this sort of ill-informed criticism is seriously to misunderstand the purpose of the benefit.

Everyone, rich or poor, faces additional costs in bringing up children and if as a

society we value its continuing existence and the well-being of the next generation
there are compelling arguments for saying that those engaged in nurturing that new
generation ("the workers of tomorrow") deserve recognition and assistance. Child
benefit can thus be argued to have more functions than the simple alleviation of
poverty. Indeed, in that role it is a singular failure. Not only are the rates low, but
those on income support do not gain by it since the child benefit counts as income
to reduce the income support (though it is not taxable). Neither can it be said to be
redistributive in that the rich are helping the poor since its structure means that it is
the childless who are assisting those with children. In so far as the benefit is paid to
the mother it is a welcome recognition of the realities of child care within families
and that includes the better off. To say that the middle class mother does not need
child benefit assumes that she is an equal beneficiary of her husband's income or
that her own income equals his. Neither of these assumptions is necessarily true
and in many cases it is patently not the case that she is as well off as her husband,
nor that she has access to the income she needs. Though she benefits indirectly
from a higher standard of living, she may yet lack real independence. Child benefit
is in many ways an unhappy compromise: it does not reflect the true costs of
families, but it does acknowledge that it is proper to use general taxation to assist
families; it does not distinguish between rich and poor, but it does direct income
from men to women. In fact, the criticism that child benefit is badly targeted is not
necessarily accurate as it appears that 92 per cent of child benefit goes to middle
and low income families (incomes less than £300 a week after housing costs).[90] Of
course, if that is the only independent income a woman has, she still has a long way
to go, although Pahl found that for many women the low level of the benefit was
outweighed by the fact that it belonged to *her*.[91]

The structure of child benefit is relatively uncomplicated (indeed in comparison
to other benefits it is positively straightforward) and perhaps because of this and the
lack of means-testing, the take up rate is high. The law provides that a person
responsible for a child shall be entitled to the benefit and a child is defined as being
under 16 or, in certain cases, generally connected with education and training, under
18 or 19.[92] In order to claim, the person responsible must be able to show that the
child is living with him (sic) *or* that he is contributing to the cost of maintaining the
child at a rate which is at least that of child benefit. The first of these conditions has
priority over the second so that if the child is living with his mother while the father
is making maintenance payments, the mother will still be the one to claim benefit.
Since more than one person may fulfil the eligibility conditions for child benefit,
there are rules laying down the priority of claimants and these stipulate, for
example, that where a married couple is living together priority goes to the wife
rather than husband, and to the mother where parents are unmarried but living
together.

Child benefit may bring with it entitlement to a further benefit of special interest to women namely one parent benefit. Provided the claimant is entitled to child benefit for a child living with her and she is not living with her husband or with anyone else as her husband she may claim an extra £6.15 (to rise to £6.30 in 1995) a week in relation to her eldest qualifying child. It is not taxable but it is taken into account for income support and it cannot be claimed in tandem with certain other benefits. This is a recognition of the additional needs of lone parents and if it is compared with the usual rate of child benefit it can be seen that whilst not generous in its own right it compares very favourably (at over 50 per cent of the eldest child rate).

Another non-contributory benefit considered to be of interest to women is invalid care allowance. To say that this is of particular relevance to women is to run the risk of being accused of sex stereotyping: of assuming that women are the carers in society. The intention is not to make this assumption but to recognise that it is often the woman in the family who does fulfil that role, whether it falls to her as wife, daughter, daughter-in-law, mother, sister or friend. Indeed, so entrenched is this idea of the female carer that until 1986 this allowance was not available to married and cohabiting women, and change came not as the result of the enlightenment of those responsible for deciding on the categories of persons eligible but because of a decision of the ECJ that the position in Britain contravened EC Directive 79/7.[93] The debate about the provision of care services and their financing has come to prominence with the development of the philosophy of care in the community which to all intents and purposes means shifting the responsibility for care from statutory service providers to individuals linked to the dependant by family, friendship or proximity. Care is needed by a variety of people at various levels at different times in their lives: a new born baby needs constant care while someone who is sick may need less care and for a shorter period. Often, however, when talking of the need for a long-term commitment to care, the paradigm is the severely disabled or infirm person who is going to need a high degree of care for an indefinite period. In these cases it is still women who tend to shoulder the major responsibilities. At first sight, surveys which have investigated the sharing of care as between men and women have found high numbers of male carers, but differences become apparent when the degree and type of care and the amount of time given over to caring are compared.[94] Figures from 1993[95] suggest that in Great Britain at that time there were 728,000 people of working age who would have liked regular work, but were not seeking employment because they had to look after the family or the home. Women formed 94 per cent of the group and, of those, over half were caring for children below school age, 30 per cent for older children and 6 per cent for an adult dependent relative. There were 44,000 men within the group, of whom almost a third were caring for an adult dependent relative.[96] There are many reasons why women should find themselves the carers within our community, and these are very pertinent to the question of women's independence and the question of substantive equality.[97] Because so much care is given within the family and within the private sphere of the household, the role fulfilled by women remains hidden and unrewarded in ways similar to the unpaid work carried out by "housewives." However, caring has attracted the attention of those interested in costing out what the work involves and what it costs those who are responsible. Some of the costs are obvious: women who take on caring responsibilities find their opportunities to take paid work severely restricted so that they either have to give up employment altogether or accept part-time, lower paid jobs, and this has consequential effects on their own prospects for financial security in old age. Even when the caring ceases, because it may have involved absence from the labour market for prolonged periods, there is no guarantee that the carer will be equipped to rejoin the labour market. Some costs are less apparent: caring involves expenses which are often met by carers out of their own income or benefits because the disabled or infirm individual simply does not have enough income of their own. This may relate to items purchased to ease the burden of care, such as labour saving devices, or may cover the comfort and needs of the person cared for, such as heating and clothing. It is patently clear that while the emotional rewards of caring should not be ignored, it carries a heavy cost which is emotional, physical and most definitely, financial.

The invalid care allowance is a benefit aimed at meeting some of these financial costs. It is paid to a person under pensionable age[98] not earning more than £50 a week or in full-time education who cares for a severely disabled person[99] for at least 35 hours a week. The carer will receive £34.50 a week (£35.30 from 1995) with some additions for dependants.[100] This payment, which is taxable, is supposedly a recognition of the adverse effects on earning capacity that full-time care represents (and Class 1 contributions are credited under the scheme) but the level is hardly a realistic replacement for earnings, even from part-time work, particularly given the amount the state is being saved by having someone cared for in their own home. Furthermore it is significantly affected by rules on overlapping benefits so that, for example, if a married man in receipt of invalidity pension is cared for by his wife and she claims invalid care allowance, he loses his right to claim an additional payment for his wife which may mean a greater loss for him, since the increase of invalidity pension in respect of a wife is *not* taxable. Further, if a carer receives the invalidity care allowance, the person cared for cannot claim the severe disability premium under the rules on income support and housing benefit. Means-tested benefits payable to the carer are reduced by the amount of invalid care allowance. All of this may mean that a decision is taken not to claim the benefit because of the effects elsewhere. In turn, the carer's independence is jeopardised and she may become dependent on the person being cared for. It has been calculated that the allowance is received by less than one-tenth of all carers who provide the requisite amount of care.[101]

Fundamentally, the invalid care allowance is an ungenerous and fundamentally dependency-inducing payment. At a level even lower than income support payments it does not begin to reflect the real costs of care. It predisposes to dependency through the rules surrounding its payment and the poverty which it induces. A woman who gives up her employment to care for an elderly relative will find herself increasingly having to rely on the income from other members of the family (husband, sibling, child) or even, especially in the case of single women, on the person being cared for. It is a prime example of how women are failed by the social security system in that their contributions are under-valued, their access to benefits is problematic and their dependency is assumed and encouraged. Furthermore, the women who struggle to survive on the woefully inadequate levels of welfare benefits grudgingly handed out by a government which castigates recipients as scroungers, face additional problems in dealing with the system which is supposedly there to help the beneficiaries.

Claiming benefits

There is much to be said about the day to day operation of the system which seeks in name to protect the most vulnerable in our society and not enough space here to do it justice. Both the tax and social security systems are put in place by law and regulated by law. Not only does the law lay down rates of tax and levels of benefit, but it also provides for what is to happen when an individual is aggrieved by a tax assessment or refused a benefit or when someone evades tax or wrongly claims benefits. It is a fundamental principle of any legal system that there should be "natural justice" which simply means that everyone is entitled to a fair hearing before an impartial judge. One of the most noticeable features over recent years in the United Kingdom in the regulation of social security has been the increasing use of delegated legislation and discretionary powers. When an Act of Parliament is passed it has long been common for it to set out in fairly general terms what the law is and to provide that a Minister or Secretary of State should have the power to make detailed regulations which will put flesh on the bones of the statute. The advantage of this method of law making is that the Act itself need not be overlong and unwieldy and regulations are more easily amended to meet changing circumstances. However, these regulations do not have to be debated in the same way as would a Bill and many important changes to rights can slip through almost unnoticed.

The use of technical and complex regulations together with discretionary powers make it difficult for the average claimant to find out what they are entitled to (although entitlement is hardly the accurate term where awards are discretionary). Legal advice is not, however, necessarily easy to find in this area and not likely to become any more available as lawyers find the squeeze on legal aid makes such work less lucrative and thus less attractive. Social welfare law has never made up a large proportion of the average solicitor's case load[102] though advice has been available from law centres (where they exist) and increasingly from Citizens Advice Bureaux and other advice centres. The lack of advice may be crucial: studies have shown that representation in tribunals makes a real difference to the outcome and there is a real need to strengthen the availability of free advice and representation.

For individuals who are refused benefits or are receiving less than they believe is their entitlement, there *may* be an appeals process.[103] An aggrieved applicant may either appeal to a social security appeal tribunal or ask for the decision to be reviewed. The latter is an internal procedure and the decision which is being challenged may be reviewed by the official who originally made it. Baldwin, Wikeley and Young comment that the discretion of social security tribunals has declined considerably with recent changes to the system.[104] In many cases the tribunal is simply applying inflexible rules and applicants thus stand little chance of altering a decision. In the case of some benefits there is no appeals procedure at all. Decisions on payments from the Social Fund are at the discretion of the Social Fund officer and the most a disappointed applicant can hope for is an internal review. Housing benefit is also outside any formal appeals system and contested decisions are merely subject to internal review. Apart from the apparent lack of fairness which this can create, it also means that decisions will be made which are, almost inevitably, at least inconsistent and at worst wrong.

Prolonged periods on benefits can induce a degree of fatalism and acceptance. In *Punishing the Poor*,[105] a chapter entitled "A Poor Service for Poor People" details the quality of service provided to claimants and reveals an appalling catalogue of inaccuracies, delays, queues, lack of privacy and lack of facilities for those waiting, often with small children, for hours in benefit offices. These facts help to explain the low take-up rates for many benefits: not only are claimants unaware of what they have been able to claim, the thought of having to suffer ordeal by the DSS is simply too overwhelming. Claimants are made to feel second class citizens - the stigma of the old Poor Laws in a modern guise.

Indeed, so much does society dislike and distrust social security claimants that, despite the fact that many do not receive what is their due, it remains the case that enormous efforts are put into catching those who defraud the system. It is entirely proper that government should act to prevent such fraud, as it is proper that tax evasion should also be punished but a comparison of the two is illuminating. In *Rich Law, Poor Law*,[106] Cook studied differing responses to tax and supplementary benefit fraud. She found differences not only in the perpetrators and in their motives but also in the investigation and prosecution of suspects and offenders. Women, for example, figured more prominently in social security fraud and Cook argues that this is as a result of the DSS using the family as its key assessment unit. One type of fraud linked to social circumstances may arise where a woman whose family needs extra cash alleges that her partner has left her in order to qualify for support as a lone parent, though this could now mean she would have to deal with the Child Support Agency. Another and more complex case arises where a woman lives with a man, and they are treated by the DSS as husband and wife. Because of the rules, she is then assumed to be financially dependent on him and if, for example, she claims income support while he is working she will be committing an offence. This is so even if her partner is in fact giving her and her children no financial support at all. Cook suggests that such cases often do not arise out of greed, but of necessity and also points out that this kind of fraud, based on what the state predicates as "normal" family life, is used to justify a policing of an individual's private life of a particularly intrusive and unpleasant nature. Those who defraud the state through the welfare system are castigated as scroungers and worse, and the explanation which is often given - that it is poverty which causes the offences - is overlooked in the zeal of those determined to punish the "undeserving poor."

Tax fraud, on the other hand, is seen as stemming from a range of motives which centre around a belief (shared by some politicians) that tax is an evil imposition which stifles enterprise and makes it difficult to provide incentives. It is also sometimes alleged that everyone does it, thus diminishing its importance, and stressing the ingenuity of the offender, although the suggestion that fraud is widespread in the benefits system induces rage rather than resignation. When it comes to prosecuting and punishing those guilty of fraud, Cook again found differences, reflected both in the way people are dealt with (benefit fraudsters are, for example, more likely to face criminal proceedings) and in the way the offenders are viewed. Not only does this mean that the tax fraudster may be seen as someone standing up to the over-powerful Revenue, and the benefit fraudster as being a lazy, good-for nothing enemy of the tax payer, it is also the case that the courts are more ready to take into account that a tax fraudster is punished by loss of reputation whereas the poor, by virtue of their poverty, are assumed to have little in the way of reputation to lose.

Surviving adversity

It was not the aim of this chapter to argue that all women are poor, but an examination of the operation of the systems which purport to redistribute wealth within society reveals the particular vulnerability of women to poverty. This is an inexorable result of women's inequality which in turn stems from the perception of women as secondary, not only in the public world of paid labour, but also in the private sphere of the family. This is made manifest by the State's use of mechanisms which assume and then enforce women's dependence on men. A desire to improve the position of women and make them "wealthier" does not have to espouse radical redistribution, and in so far as some policy-makers view "egalitarian" as a term of disapprobation it would be futile to argue for this. Nevertheless, it is neither unwise nor unreasonable to wish for the achievement of a greater degree of equality which raises standards generally, reduces the gap between the rich and the poor and eliminates deprivation. It is most unlikely that such arguments would find favour with any government facing recession and the need to reduce public expenditure, but the British population are not necessarily of the same mind. In 1991 only 3 per cent of those surveyed wished to see tax and spending cuts, while 65 per cent favoured an increase in taxes and social spending.[107] Of course, for many that social spending means more on health and education rather than on benefits for the poor, but even here there is evidence that increased spending would find some support. Over half of respondents thought the government should spend more on welfare benefits even if the results were higher taxes.[108] This is especially true in relation to pensions and child benefit: in relation to benefits such as unemployment benefit the survey reveals that there remains within the British psyche a well-developed notion of the deserving and undeserving poor. Whatever the views of the citizen, recent government policy has been to stress the need to reduce spending on the welfare state for the good of those who rely on it: redistribution must be limited in order to provide an incentive for people to provide for themselves. There is an inescapable irony in any plan to reduce dependency on the state while concurrently increasing the dependency of women on men: a dependency culture is bad only if it means dependence on the state.

Recent policies have favoured "trickle down" over simple redistribution, that is, the idea that greater economic growth in the country as a whole will trickle down to assist even those at the bottom and to this end tax cuts for the rich were to provide incentives and promote the creation of wealth. It is undoubtedly true that the rich have got richer, as it is also true that the gap between rich and poor has widened. Central to many of the problems highlighted in this chapter is that the social security system in Britain is aimed at supporting those who have fallen to the bottom of the pile, by giving them just enough to survive. What it does not do is to address the wider inequalities which have put them there in the first place. Women make up an uncomfortably large proportion of those at the bottom and find it almost impossible to rise from that level. It is not enough to have a system which purports to stave off destitution without also having policies which are aimed at creating wealth - in its widest sense - and this would require a markedly more interventionist approach into the means of production and labour, for example by introducing a minimum wage and providing a range of social services which support those unable to work and enable those who can to pursue paid employment. Failing that, it would be a start to redefine the basis on which benefits are assessed and move away from the patriarchal notion of family, which for many women today does not reflect their day to day life.

Notes

1.   See e.g. Millar, J. and Glendinning, C., 'Gender and poverty', (1989) 18 *Journal of Social Policy*, pp. 363-81. Also Glendinning, C., and Millar, J. (1992), *Women and Poverty in Britain in the 1990s*; Glendinning, C. (1987), in Walker and Walker (eds), *The Growing Divide*.

2.   Millar, J., and Glendinning, C. (1989), 'Gender and poverty,' op. cit., n. 1.

3.   *Annual Report of the Supplementary Benefits Commission*, 1978, para. 1.4, Cmnd 7725.

4.   Beveridge, W. (1942), *Social Insurance and Allied Services*, Cmnd 6404, and see p. 140 et seq. There were earlier moves towards the introduction of certain benefits: see p. 43, pp. 45-47.

5.   Beveridge, op. cit., n. 4, p. 141.

6.   Supplementary Benefits Commission (1979), *Response of the Supplementary Benefits Commission to Social Assistance*, HMSO, quoted in Esam, P. and Berthoud, R. (1992), *Independent Benefits for Men and Women: An enquiry into treating husbands and wives as separate units in the assessment of social security*, p. 4.

7.   Pearson et al. (1992), *Poor Britain: Poverty, inequality and low pay in the nineties*, p. 2.

8.   In the November 1994 Budget changes were announced for the tax year 1995-6: the 20 per cent tax band is raised to £3,200 (after allowances), which is a rise above the rate of inflation; the next band is raised to £24,300. Tax rates are unchanged.

9.   See pp. 22-29.

10.   From 1914 onwards it was possible for a married person to elect for separate assessment which guaranteed some privacy but did not alter the amount of tax payable.

11.   This figure remains in 1995-6. Moreover, the rate of relief on the additional personal allowance has been reduced to 20 per cent, and falls to 15 per cent in 1995.

12.   In 1989-90, the levels were £4,375 for a married man and £2,785 for a single person.

13.   It is not available to unmarried cohabiting couples no matter how long the relationship or that the woman is wholly supported by the man: *Rignell v Andrews* [1991] 1 FLR 332.

14.   The number of couples cohabiting has risen dramatically: see p. 176.

15.   Income and Corporation Taxes Act 1988, s. 259(1)(c).

16.   If the mortgage is in joint names, the relief may be shared; if in one name, it goes to that person only. There is no capital gains tax on principal residence: this cost the Treasury £7 billion in 1989-90: Land, H. (1992), 'Whatever Happened to the Social Wage?' in Glendinning, C. and Millar, J. (eds), *Women and Poverty in Britain: the 1990s*, at p. 58.

17.   Brannen, J. and Moss P. (1991), *Managing Mothers: Dual Earner Households after Maternity Leave*.

18.   Esam and Berthaud, op. cit., n. 6, p. 10.

19.   See for details CPAG Handbooks: *Rights guide to non-means tested benefits*, *National Welfare Benefits Handbook* (published annually) and Ogus, A.I. and Barendt, E.M. (1988),

The Law of Social Security, (3rd ed.) plus Supplements.

20. Although social security now depends generally on the distribution of cash payments, redistribution could occur through the provision of free services or goods, e.g. school meals, school transport, health care (including prescriptions) and education. For arguments against benefits in kind see Spicker, P. (1993), *Poverty and Social Security*, pp. 95-98.

21. Eligibility conditions are considerably more complex than this summary suggests: see, for example, the CPAG Handbooks referred to above, n. 19.

22. See Spicker, P. (1993), *Poverty and Social Security*, pp. 139-142; Callender, C. (1992), 'Redundancy, unemployment and poverty' in Glendinning, C. and Millar, J. (eds), *Women and Poverty in Britain: the 1990s*.

23. Also council tax benefit and disability working allowance which are not dealt with here. For details see *National Welfare Benefits Handbook*, CPAG.

24. The schemes came into operation in April 1988. For the background to the measures see Ogus, A.I. and Barendt, E.M. (1988), *The Law of Social Security*, Chaps 11 and 12.

25. *Department of Social Security Statistics 1993*, Tables A2.01 and A1.01.

26. For example, figures for claimants differ significantly from figures for availability for work, a fact linked to the failure of many women to qualify for unemployment benefit and see pp. 151-152. See also Callender, op. cit., n. 22.

27. Op. cit., n. 25, Tables A2.10 and A2.12.

28. See Chap. 5 for a discussion of pensions.

29. Op. cit., n. 25, Table A2.14. The total for divorced, widowed and separated mothers on income support was 482,000 and 448,000 for single mothers.

30. Op. cit., n. 25, Table A1.02.

31. E.g. Central Statistical Office's *Family Expenditure Surveys*; DSS, *Households below Average Income*; Bradshaw, J. and Millar, J. (1991), *Lone Parent Families in the UK*, Department of Social Security Research Report, No. 6; also Millar, J. (1992), 'Lone mothers and poverty' in Glendinning, C. and Millar, J. (eds), *Women and Poverty in Britain: the 1990s*; Oppenheim, C. (1993), *Poverty: The Facts*.

32. Lone fathers tend to be older and to have older children. But see Harrop, A. and Moss P., 'Working Parents: trends in the 1980s', (1994) *Employment Gazette* 102 (No. 10), p. 343: lone fathers are three times more likely to be unemployed than fathers living with partners.

33. E.g. Rowntree, B.S. (1902), *Poverty: A Study of Town Life*; Snell, K.D.M. and Millar, J. (1987), 'Lone parents, families and the Welfare State: past and present', *Continuity and Change*, Vol. 2, p. 387.

34. See pp. 43-44.

35. Snell et al., op. cit., n. 33.

36. Bradshaw et al., op. cit., n. 31.

37. See e.g. Graham, H. (1992), in Glendinning, C. and Millar, J. (eds), *Women and Poverty in Britain: the 1990s*.

38. Millar, J. (1992), 'Lone Mothers and Poverty', op. cit., n. 31.

39. Compare the Child Support Act 1991 which aims to lessen a woman's dependence on the

state by shifting that to dependence on a man: see p. 247 et seq.

40.   Pre-1988 claimants had to be at least 16. Since 1988 those over 16 and under 18 must satisfy special conditions or show special hardship: Social Security Act 1986, s. 20(4A). One exception to the general rule is single parents. On young people and the social security system see Harris, N. (1989), *Social Security for Young People*.

41.   Under rules on the 'voluntarily unemployed' income support is reduced by up to 40% for up to 26 weeks. In cases where the claimant is judged unavailable for work, no income support is payable: see, inter alia, Income Support (General) Regulations 1987, S.I. 1987, No. 1967, and Social Security Act 1986, s. 20(3)(d).

42.   For example single parents, or carers of disabled people. Also, those over 60 or within ten years of pensionable age who have been unemployed for the last ten years, during which they have not been required to be available for work, which would include older women with grown up children.

43.   See Chap. 6 on family finances, and on legal and other issues of cohabitation: Parry, M.L. (1993), *The Law Relating to Cohabitation*; Priest, J. (1993), *Families Outside Marriage*.

44.   See Chap. 6.

45.   Mclaughlin, E., Millar, J., Cooke, K. (1989), *Work and Welfare Benefits*, Chap. 3. More generally, it is significant that couples surveyed accepted the secondary nature of the wife's earnings: her earning role was seen as additional not central. See also Sly, F., 'Mothers in the labour market', (1994) *Employment Gazette* 102 (No. 11), p. 403.

46.   See generally Social Security Act 1986 and the Income Support (General) Regulations 1987, S.I. 1987, No. 1967. For guidance generally see *National Welfare Benefits Handbook*, CPAG.

47.   See especially Andrews, K. and Jacobs, J. (1990), *Punishing the Poor*, Chap. 8.

48.   The age of 25 is relevant only for single, childless claimants who are assumed to have fewer expenses. For couples the important age is 18. Lone parents under 18 may claim, the level depending on whether they live with their parents.

49.   Depending on age and whether part of a couple. There is an ordinary premium payable from 60-74, an enhanced rate from 75-79 and a 'higher pensioner premium' for over 80's.

50.   Income Support (General) Regulations 1987, S.I. 1987, No. 1967, Sched. 3. Housing costs in relation to water rates and council tax are not taken into account.

51.   Including where the person legally liable has stopped paying, but his *partner* continues to pay.

52.   Generally costs for only one house may be claimed but there are exceptions for example where the former home was left for fear of violence.

53.   It was also announced that the limit for payments was to be cut from £125,000 to £120,000 and that interest would be payable at a standard rate. Borrowers were warned to take out private insurance cover (which presupposes the means to do so).

54.   In the case of housing benefit, £5 is disregarded for a single claimant, £10 for a couple, whether or not both are working: Housing Benefit (General) Regulations 1987, S.I. 1987, No. 1971, Sched. 3.

55.   Lone parents who are claiming housing benefit but not in receipt of income support are entitled to a £25 disregard: Housing Benefit (General) Regulations 1987, S.I. 1987, No. 1971, Sched. 3 para 4.

56.   Bradshaw, J. and Millar, J. (1991), *Lone Parent Families in the UK*.

57.   The 1995 levels are respectively: £46.55; £15.95 (for each child under 11); £10.25 and £5.20 making £93.70.

58.   *The Independent*, 5 November 1994. See also: Pearson et al., *Poor Britain: Poverty, inequality and low pay in the nineties*; Landsdown, G. (1994), 'Respecting the rights of children', *Poverty* 86, pp. 9-11.

59.   The Income-related Benefits Schemes (Miscellaneous Amendments) (No. 4) Regulations 1994, S.I. 1994, No. 1924. See also (1994) *Journal of Social Security Law* No.1, p. 6.

60.   Maclean, M. (1991), *Surviving Divorce*, pp. 113-114.

61.   Compare the Speenhamland system of Poor Law Relief: see p. 41.

62.   1994 credits: adult, £44.30; child under 11, £11.20; 11-15, £18.55; 16-17, £23.05; 18, £32.20. For 1995 the figures are: £35.15; £11.40; £18.90; £23.50; £32.80.

63.   Certain benefits such as child benefit and housing benefit are ignored in the calculation under rules similar to those applying to income support. See generally Family Credit (General) Regulations 1987, S.I. 1987, No. 1973.

64.   Above, n. 59.

65.   Marsh, A., and McKay, S. (1993), *Families, Work and Benefits*.

66.   Supplementary Benefit (Single Payment) Regulations 1981, S.I. 1981, No. 1528.

67.   Case R(SB) 4/86 cited in Andrews and Jacobs, above n. 47.

68.   See Cohen, R. and Tarpey, M. (1988) (eds), *Single Payments: The Disappearing Safety Net*, cited in Andrews and Jacobs, above n. 47.

69.   Before April 1987 the maternity grant for those on benefits was significantly higher.

70.   *Department of Social Security Statistics 1993*, Table A 5.01.

71.   Ibid, Table A5.02. There were 62,000 awards.

72.   Ibid, Table A5.03. There were well over one million applications.

73.   Ibid, Table A5.04. 55 per cent of cases that were subject to decisions were successful.

74.   *Social Fund Guide*, para. 4127.

75.   See pp. 193-196. See also Kempson, E., Bryson, A. and Rowlingson, K. (1994), *Hard Times: How poor families make ends meet*.

76.   Consider e.g. the debates on the sale of council houses, and regulation versus deregulation of the private rented sector. See Johnson, N. (1990), *Reconstructing the Welfare State: A Decade of Change*, Chap. 6.

77.   Housing Act 1988, but protection for tenants against high rents is much diminished. The average private sector rent rose by 44% between 1989 and 1991: 'Are fair rents losing their appeal?,' *The Independent*, 14 October 1993.

78.   Land, H. (1992), 'Whatever happened to the Social Wage?' in Glendinning, C. and Millar, J. (eds), *Women and Poverty in Britain: the 1990s*. By the end of 1992, more than 2 million public sector tenants in Great Britain had applied to buy their own homes and nearly 70 per

cent had purchased. The numbers are now decreasing: (1994), *Central Statistical Office's Social Trends 24*, Table 8.4.

79.   Jowell et al., (1992) *British Social Attitudes, 9th Report.*

80.   Bartholomew, R., Hibbett, A. and Sidaway, J., 'Lone parents and the labour market: evidence from the Labour Force Survey', (1992) *Employment Gazette*, 100 (No. 11), 559-578, at p. 570 and Table 10.

81.   (1994), *Social Trends 24*, Table 8.23.

82.   Ibid., Table 5.9 and see also Andrews and Jacobs, op.cit., n.47, at p. 35; Land, H, op. cit., n. 78.

83.   Also council tax benefit which will not be dealt with. With rules similar to housing benefit, it works as a rebate on the liability to pay.

84.   Whether or not this was achieved has been challenged: see Andrews and Jacobs, op. cit. n. 47, pp. 30-32.

85.   From 1995, local authorities will not be fully reimbursed for the costs of housing benefit if they pay benefits for tenants which are significantly above the average for that area and type of housing. This is to encourage private landlords to set rents at reasonable levels - rent controls having been previously abolished by the government.

86.   E.g. lone parents receiving housing benefit but not income support have £25 earnings disregarded.

87.   Although the Homeless Persons Act 1988 tightened the meaning of "unintentionally homeless," in 1989 126,680 were accepted as homeless: 1991 *Annual Report of the Department of the Environment*, Cmnd 1508. Women, children and young people are particularly affected by homelessness.

88.   See for example, Alcock, P. (1993), *Understanding Poverty*, Chap. 11 and references therein.

89.   Child benefit appeared in the Child Benefit Act 1975 but became payable only in 1977 and the tax allowances were then phased out.

90.   Figures for 1990-91, income adjusted for family size: *Family Expenditure Survey*, House of Commons, Hansard, 20 July 1993, col. 203, cited in (1994) *Poverty* 86, p. 15.

91.   Pahl, J. (1989), *Money and Marriage*, p. 158 and see also Chap. 6.

92.   The age of 19 seems arbitrary since many students are in full-time education beyond that age.

93.   *Drake v Chief Adjudication Officer* 150/85 [1986] 3 All ER 65. The Directive requires equal treatment for men and women and covers benefits provided under statutory schemes in relation to unemployment, sickness, invalidity, old age: see pp. 148-150.

94.   For example, older men tend to be caring for their wives. See Glendinning, C. (1992), '"Community care:" The financial consequences for women' in Glendinning, C. and Millar, J. (eds), Women and Poverty in Britain: the 1990s.

95.   (1994) *Employment Gazette* 102 (No. 9), LFS4.

96.   These figures refer only to those of working age: there will be many elderly people of both sexes caring for relatives.

97.   Glendinning (1992), op cit., n. 94. The stereotyping of women as carers is discussed in Finch, J. and Groves, D. (eds), (1983), A Labour of Love: Women, Work and Caring.

98.   Social Security Act 1975, s. 27(1): 60 for women, 65 for men, but in *Secretary of State for Social Security v Thomas* Case C-328/91 [1993] IRLR 292, the ECJ held that denying invalid care allowance to women over 60 contravenes EC Directive 79/7. See also pp. 147-149.

99.   Who must themselves be receiving either the highest or middle rates of the care component of disability living allowance, attendance allowance or constant attendance allowance in respect of war or industrial disablement. Effectively, the carer does not have an independent right to this benefit but must qualify through someone else's claim.

100.   See generally Social Security Contributions and Benefits Act 1992, s. 70 and Sched. 4.

101.   McLaughlin, E. (1991), *Social Security and Community Care: The case of the invalid care allowance.*

102.   See e.g. (1992), *A Strategy for Justice: Publicly Funded Legal Services in the 1990s.*

103.   See CPAG Handbooks for details of the processes.

104.   Baldwin, J., Wikeley, N. and Young, R. (1992), *Judging Social Security: the adjudication of claims for benefit in Britain.*

105.   Op. cit., n. 82.

106.   (1988), *Rich Law, Poor Law: Differential Response to Tax and Supplementary Benefit Fraud.*

107.   Jowell et al. (1992), *British Social Attitudes: 9th Report,* pp. 41-43.

108.   Ibid.

5   Financial Security

Poverty may strike at any stage of life, but the threat is particularly acute if someone is unable to work as, for most people, the key to wealth is access to paid employment. Unless steps have been taken to guard against unemployment and its results, financial security is inevitably threatened by the loss of an income. There are of course other events, most notably marriage, the birth of children, divorce or the death of a partner, which can also have major effects on personal finances, but it is in relation to the ability to support oneself and one's family through waged work, that there is a requirement to "insure against" the consequences which flow from lack of paid employment.

A fundamental feature of private, voluntary insurance is that the insured pays a premium to the insurer based upon risk. Anyone applying, for example, for life insurance must answer detailed questions as to her status, health and habits, on the basis of which the insurers will decide whether or not to accept the risk, and if so at what level the premium should be set. A bad risk may be unable to get any insurance cover or may have to pay way above the average rates. The advantage of such a personalised scheme is that although it is costly to run and expensive for the insured, the benefits paid out can be significant. When the state initiated its own national insurance scheme to protect workers against events such as unemployment, it abandoned some of those principles that are an essential feature of private insurance schemes. Risk pays no part in the assessment of contribution levels: workers in industries prone to unemployment pay the same as those on the same wage in secure employment, meaning that there are some contributors who effectively subsidise others. The ideas of insurance have not, however, been completely abandoned. Insurance implies an element of self-help, of thriftiness and concern for one's future welfare. The national insurance system works on the basis that in order to obtain benefits an individual must contribute to the scheme. This reflects the belief that "benefit in return for contributions" is a better way to protect the needy than handing out free allowances from the state.[1]

A scheme based on benefits in return for contributions immediately bars certain individuals from participating. Those outside the labour market have no direct personal access to the scheme and even those who have worked but whose contribution records are patchy because of career breaks or low earnings may find that they have insufficient contributions to entitle them to benefits. An adequate contribution record is an essential feature of a contributory national insurance scheme and, since this is a goal which women have more difficulty than men in achieving, it is a fundamental obstacle to women's financial independence. When a woman is sick or unemployed or reaches retirement, she may find that her contributions do not entitle her to a sufficient level of benefit, in which case she is faced with a choice: she can turn either to another person for support, probably her partner, or she can look to the state for help in the shape of means-tested benefits.

National insurance benefits

The laws which govern a state's welfare system are based on certain assumptions about what it is appropriate to offer in the way of benefits and these assumptions are themselves inspired by views on how individuals should behave. A gap can easily develop between the assumptions behind the laws which regulate social insurance and the reality of people's lives. Reform becomes necessary but, given the long-term nature of many of the objectives of a social insurance system, changes may take a considerable time to make themselves felt. Women's role in society has altered dramatically during this century and an analysis of the laws governing social security benefits must consider whether those laws adequately reflect that change. It is essential to investigate the extent to which the state's social insurance system has been restructured to take account of women's current life patterns and the responsibilities they assume for others, their increased participation in the labour market, their dual role as workers and mothers, and their right to be treated as independent within a relationship.[2]

The major social insurance benefits, old age pensions, sickness and unemployment benefit, all date back to the start of the century. The foundations of the present welfare state are seen as originating with the production by Sir William Beveridge of his report *Social Insurance and Allied Services*.[3] This proposed the establishment of a comprehensive system of state social insurance though the state scheme was not seen as excluding self-help on the part of the individual:

> The State in organising security should not stifle incentive, opportunity, responsibility: in establishing a national minimum it should leave room

and encouragement for voluntary action by each individual to provide more than that minimum for himself and his family.[4]

The Report recommended that those of working age, including the self-employed, should contribute to the system, as should employers and the state. This would then entitle the contributor to a range of benefits as of right (not necessarily identical for each class of contributor) including unemployment and sickness benefit, as well as a pension on retirement. There would be a flat rate of contribution (lower for women than for men) and contributions would not be graduated to take account of an individual's earnings. This meant that those who earned low wages, and women formed a substantial number within this group, would have to surrender a greater proportion of their earnings as compared with the higher paid. It was contemplated that the benefits paid would be the minimum necessary to guarantee the bare essentials. No account would be taken of regional variations in the cost of living.

It was clear that the fact that access to the proposed national insurance system was based on ability to contribute would pose problems for women and Beveridge acknowledged this. Married women were singled out for special treatment. Those who did not work were to gain access to benefits not directly but by relying on their husbands' contribution records. Payments to a married man would contain an allowance in respect of his dependent wife, though there was no arrangement for her to receive the money directly. Married women who worked were to be given a choice. They might pay lower national insurance contributions but, if they chose this option, they surrendered their entitlement to claim benefit in their own right and would in future have to depend on their husbands' contribution records in order to obtain access to social security benefits. If a married woman decided to pay a full contribution, she was able to claim benefit independently of her husband, although that benefit was paid at a lower rate than that for a single woman.

It has been said of Beveridge that he "had long been concerned to give recognition to the particular problems of women and to give women an equal footing in social provision."[5] The measures which he proposed in order to give women this "equal footing" had the practical effect, however, of encouraging them to perform their traditional role of unpaid worker in the home. In particular, by permitting married women to "opt out" of the social security system, Beveridge provided them with a positive incentive *not* to make provision for their future financial security. Where he did try to give some recognition to the particular problems faced by women some of his proposals were abandoned or watered down because of the opposition they attracted or their potential costs. These included help with domestic work when a wife was ill and required hospital treatment, as well as allowances for deserted or divorced wives.[6] Other proposals seen as helpful to women were, however, subsequently acted upon. These were associated with women's caring responsibilities within the family and included suggestions for the payment of maternity grants and maternity benefit as well as a system of family allowances.

Following the publication of the Beveridge Report, legislation was passed to give effect to the Report's major recommendations and a new Ministry was set up to administer the social insurance system.[7] The post-war government rationalised the system of national insurance contributions and benefits in the National Insurance Act 1946. There were three classes of contributor: the employed, the self-employed and unemployed persons. Each class would pay a flat rate contribution, which was lower for any women in that particular class, and in return contributors would be entitled to a prescribed list of benefits. The list was most extensive for employed persons and included unemployment benefit, sickness benefit, pension and certain maternity and widow's allowances. Employers and the state would also contribute to the national insurance fund which would pay benefits at the level of subsistence as advocated by Beveridge.

The post-war national insurance system in some ways represents a lost opportunity for women. The Beveridge Report and subsequent legislation assumed that most women would marry and that once they were married they would not work. Husband and wife were - in the words of Beveridge - to be regarded as a team. The husband would pay national insurance contributions and, when necessary, receive benefit including payments for the support of his wife and children. Women were labelled as dependent on men and the national insurance system was thus geared to the needs of men in the expectation that women would withdraw from the labour force at various times during their working lives. Even then, this assumption was not based on reality as is evidenced in the census findings for this period which show that women consistently accounted for almost 30 per cent of the labour force.[8] That figure itself ignores the rise in participation rates that occurred in the course of the First and Second World Wars. The national insurance system's insistence on treating husband and wife as a single unit contrasted sharply with other situations in which partners to a marriage were treated as independent[9] and most importantly, conspired to produce a national insurance system that marginalised women. Not only were women encouraged not to provide for their future, but, unless she was a claimant in her own right, a woman's husband would receive any payments on her behalf and there was no guarantee that some or any of the money would reach his wife. Once contributory benefits were exhausted, a husband also controlled his wife's access to means-tested benefits which were, and still are, assessed on the basis of family income, since the costs of doing otherwise are regarded as prohibitive.[10] The national insurance system as devised by Beveridge was designed for men, and women were viewed simply as the potential wives of those men rather than direct participants within the system.

It is, of course, easy to criticise Beveridge retrospectively, and there was a section of contemporary opinion which believed that his attitude toward women was not totally unhelpful. Whilst his Report did stress a woman's traditional role as wife and mother, it also conceded that the state should be prepared to reward her for performing those tasks. Women were not totally excluded from the national insurance system, and their access was based in part on Beveridge's acknowledgement of the importance of the unpaid work that they performed in the home. Family allowances and maternity benefits also reflected a willingness to recognize the importance of those unpaid caring responsibilities undertaken by women. Unfortunately, this germ of an idea that the caring tasks performed primarily but not exclusively by women should be rewarded has never been substantially developed in the United Kingdom.

The post-war welfare state which was greeted with so much optimism soon began to display the weaknesses of some of the assumptions underlying its establishment. As Ogus and Barendt point out, Beveridge had envisaged the scheme as one where a flat rate contribution would provide a flat rate benefit. Whereas other European countries opted for an earnings-related system, citizens in the United Kingdom were given the option of supplementing state benefits by contributing to private insurance schemes.[11] This placed a disproportionate burden on those earning low wages who surrendered a higher proportion of their earnings in contributions to the state scheme and were, therefore, ill-placed to supplement that scheme from other sources. Both men and women felt the effects of this flaw in Beveridge's "grand design" but there was little or nothing that women could do to combat the disadvantage they suffered. If a woman fitted the Beveridge stereotype of the non-working wife, her fate was inextricably linked to that of her husband. His ability and willingness to supplement state benefits sealed his wife's fate during periods when he was unable to work. Single women and those married women who paid a full national insurance contribution had more control over their financial affairs but, since a woman's earning power was substantially less than that of a man, they were among those least well-placed to supplement the state scheme.

The present national insurance system

The national insurance system as originally conceived by Beveridge has undergone a variety of changes which have been inspired by very different and often contradictory motives. First, the need to improve the efficiency of the system has been recognized. Second, succeeding governments have felt it necessary to modify the system in order to make it more politically compatible with their own and their supporters' opinions. Finally, the sex discrimination which was an integral feature of the original system has ceased to be acceptable and steps have been taken to achieve equal treatment of the sexes. The system has therefore been modified, but it has never been the subject of a through-going overhaul designed to expose and re-evaluate the very principles on which it rests. As a consequence, the present system represents a hotch-potch of old beliefs and current values which add up to a very unsatisfactory amalgam.

Operational changes

One of the major changes to the manner in which the national insurance system operates has been the move from flat-rate contributions to ones that are linked to earnings. In addition married women are no longer permitted to opt out of making contributions. Instead they are expected to contribute to the scheme at the same rates as any other worker and as a consequence have access to the full range of national insurance benefits. Under the scheme as instituted in the Social Security Act 1975 there are four[12] classes of contribution: earnings related Class 1 contributions paid by employed earners and their employers; flat-rate Class 2 contributions paid by the self-employed; flat-rate Class 3 contributions voluntarily paid by employees or those not in work, and Class 4 contributions paid on profits by some self-employed persons. These contributions are used to finance the social security benefits which depend on contribution records but they are also used for other purposes.[13] The regulations relating to the assessment of contributions are complex but it is possible to give an outline of the more important rules.

Although the number of self-employed women is increasing[14] the majority of those who earn do so as employees within the category of Class 1 earnings-related contributions. There are two elements: payments by employees (primary contributions) and payments by their employers (secondary contributions). The money is deducted at source along with PAYE income tax. The decision as to whether there is liability to pay such contributions is crucial since without them or without enough of them the worker is not entitled to any of the associated contributory benefits, such as unemployment benefit. One of the hurdles that women in particular may face is to establish that they are employees in the legal sense. The definition of an employee unfortunately remains elusive and becomes no clearer as the forms of atypical employment increase.[15] An employee is said to be someone who works under a contract of service, whereas a self-employed person works under a contract for services, but it must then be decided what are the essential characteristics which distinguish a contract of service. Sometimes the status of the worker is obvious but it is precisely in those areas where women tend to predominate that problems have arisen. This is true in relation to homeworkers,[16] casual workers[17] and temporary workers.[18]

Even if it is established that the worker is an employee and potentially liable for Class 1 primary contributions, there is another hurdle: whether or not earnings during the relevant period were at or above the current "lower earnings limit" (£57 a week in 1994-5). Contributions are paid with reference to the tax year and in each year lower and upper earnings limits are prescribed. Those who earn below the lower limit are exempt from contributions which means that the lowest paid neither contribute nor benefit. From 1989,[19] once an employee has reached the lower earnings limit, she pays a reduced contribution on all earnings up to and including that limit.[20] For earnings between the lower limit and upper limit (£430 a week in 1994-5), the employee pays a standard rate, depending on whether the employment is contracted-out of SERPS, the state scheme's earnings-related pension.[21] The contracted-out standard rate payable by the employee is 8.2 per cent, while for non-contracted out employments the rate is 10 per cent.[22] The amount of earnings on which the contributions are made is called the earnings factor and is used to assess entitlement.

Anyone now who comes within the scope of primary Class 1 contributions is treated in the same way, male or female, married or unmarried. Until 5 April 1977 married women could choose to make reduced Class 1 contributions, but as patterns of employment changed and married women became an increasingly significant part of the workforce, reforms were instituted and the option to pay reduced contributions was abolished in the Social Security Act 1975, although it was provided that those already paying the reduced rates should be able to continue to do so unless one of a number of specific events, such as divorce, ended their eligibility.

Class 2 contributions are payable by the self-employed at a flat-rate (£5.65 a week in 1994-5) but married women with reduced liability do not pay them.[23] Class 3 contributions are flat-rate and voluntary and are paid to help someone qualify for certain benefits[24] if Class 1 or 2 contributions are insufficient in any tax year.[25] Class 4 contributions are payable by the self-employed on profits or gains between certain sums which are chargeable to income tax under Schedule D[26] but payment confers no entitlement to benefits. In certain circumstances liability to pay may arise under more than one Class, in which case special rules apply.[27]

While the decision to relate national insurance contributions to earnings undoubtedly makes the system more equitable, it also results in the exclusion of some women from the system. Anyone whose earnings fall below the lower earnings limit is not required to contribute but neither can she claim benefits. The lower earnings limit is likely to affect far more women than men because far greater numbers of women than men work part-time and hence earn weekly amounts that are below the lower earnings level.[28] Such low earners cannot, therefore, plan for their future financial security and in times of need they must either rely on someone else to support them or apply for means-tested benefits. The upper earnings limit represents a ceiling on contributions and even if an individual earns £1000 per week contributions are due only on £430. This "bonus" to the highly paid is likely to be enjoyed by fewer women than men, given that women's average wage rates lag behind those of men.[29]

Since contributions are now more closely related to earnings it might seem logical to expect the same to be true of benefits but this is not the case. Whether or not benefits should be earnings-related raises the question of what can legitimately be expected of the state. When someone loses a job or becomes too ill to work the demands made in the shape of rent, food, clothing, mortgage repayments or fuel costs do not cease. In these circumstances should the state be prepared to pay a rate of benefit that reflects previous earnings (perhaps for a limited period) in order to enable these costs to be met? Alternatively, should it adopt the Beveridge philosophy of flat rate benefits and expect individuals to make their own plans to deal with emergencies such as unemployment? Adopting the latter approach requires a further decision on how to deal with those who are either unwilling or unable to make their own arrangements when they find themselves in need.

The national insurance system has used both approaches, the choice largely depending on the political views of the party in power. In the 1960s, for example, a Labour administration introduced various forms of earnings-related contributory benefit and although the Conservative administration has retained this option, it has done so reluctantly and only in the case of retirement pensions. Earnings-related supplements to the short-term benefits for sickness and unemployment were introduced in 1966 but abandoned in 1982 by the Thatcher administration. The state earnings-related pension scheme (SERPS) was established in 1975 but concerns voiced over its rising costs led to proposals for its abolition.[30] In the event SERPS was reprieved, though entitlements under the scheme were substantially reduced.

Although flat rate benefits might not be ideal, there are ways to ensure that they offer some degree of financial security. Even Beveridge conceded that such benefits should offer a minimum level of subsistence. At present, however, this is hardly the case. The Child Poverty Action Group highlighted the extent to which the value of benefits had been eroded between 1979 and 1992 by taking the example of a man claiming unemployment benefit with a non-earning wife and two children:

> The 1979 benefits totalled £47.20 a week, including a £12 earnings-related supplement. Uprated in line with prices, the 1992 equivalent would have been £127.70; in line with average earnings, £166.55. But the 1992 benefits amounted to only £87.15; and that is without taking into account the fact that, since 1982, unemployment benefit has been taxable.[31]

Both men and women are affected by the failure to relate contributory benefits to earnings or to uprate flat rate benefits in line with prices or average earnings. The national insurance system's persistent attachment to the traditional notion of the family, where the man works and has access to full-time, long-term employment while the woman takes primary responsibility for care within the family has exacerbated those problems for women. More and more women, married and single, work either full or part-time. Marriages break down more frequently; couples choose to cohabit rather than marry. Periods of high unemployment occur at regular intervals. Society has changed but the contributory benefit system has not changed with it. Fewer women wish to be reliant on their husbands for financial support but flat rate benefits no longer guarantee a sufficient level of income and are particularly prone to attack either in the name of political dogma or in times of financial stringency.

The ease with which one can make private arrangements then becomes crucial. One of the commonest ways of securing higher benefits is through an employer's occupational scheme but these also may be problematic for women.[32] Those who, for whatever reason, have not supplemented contributory benefits must rely on the state's means-tested benefits to make up any difference between what they are paid by way of the contributory benefits and what it actually costs them to live. One fundamental difference between non-means-tested and means-tested benefits is that the former are available to anyone who has made the relevant contributions, whilst the latter depend on the resources of the family as a whole. A married or cohabiting woman may have no access to means-tested benefits, especially, though not exclusively, where her partner is in work.

Sex discrimination

At all stages in its development it has been a feature of the national insurance system that it did not treat men and women equally. Membership of the European Union has forced the United Kingdom to tackle this issue and to take somewhat reluctant steps to eradicate discrimination. At the European level, two Directives have been agreed, one dealing with statutory, and the other with occupational social security schemes, whilst a third Directive is planned.[33] Directive 79/7, "on the progressive implementation of equal treatment for men and women in matters of social security," requires Member States to implement the principle of equal treatment in relation to statutory (as opposed to occupational) social security schemes. Article 4(1) provides that:

> there shall be no discrimination whatsoever on grounds of sex either directly, or indirectly by reference in particular to marital or family status, in particular as concerns:
> the scope of the schemes and the conditions of access thereto,
> the obligation to contribute and the calculation of contributions,
> the calculation of benefits including increases due in respect of a spouse

and for dependents

and

the conditions governing the duration and retention of entitlement to benefits.

This measure has successfully dealt with clear and specific examples of sex discrimination such as the United Kingdom's refusal to allow married women living with their husbands to claim invalid care allowance in cases where a married man would have been entitled to it.[34] More questionable is its success in tackling the stereotypical view of men and women's roles within society upon which so much social security legislation is based. In *Teuling v Bedrijfsvereniging voor de Chemische Industrie*[35] the ECJ was given the opportunity to question some of these gender stereotypes. Steps had been taken by the Netherlands government to implement Directive 79/7 and as a result certain sickness and invalidity benefits which had previously guaranteed the recipient the equivalent of the statutory minimum wage ceased to do so. Instead, benefit at that level was available only to those recipients with a dependent spouse and children. This was done in order to bring this particular benefit into line with other social security benefits but, as a result, women who had previously received the equivalent of the statutory minimum wage suffered a reduction in benefits since, in many instances, their spouses were working and could not be described as dependent. The European Court of Justice was asked to rule whether this practice constituted indirect discrimination contrary to the Social Security Directive, as far fewer women than men could claim the supplement. The European Court, although it acknowledged that considerably fewer women than men could claim, held that the practice could be justified:

> ... if supplements to a minimum social security benefit are intended, where beneficiaries have no income from work, to prevent the benefit from falling below the minimum subsistence level for persons who, by virtue of the fact that they have a dependent spouse or children, bear heavier burdens than single persons, such supplements may be justified under the Directive.[36]

It appears that the outlawing of indirect discrimination in the Social Security Directive has a limited potential for removing those features of state social security systems that are not overtly discriminatory but still prejudice women. Provided the state can justify its actions by arguing that they are necessary to maintain minimum standards of subsistence, this would seem to be sufficient.[37] Ellis does suggest that the *Teuling* decision "offers some, albeit limited, scope for argument to litigants in future cases; if it can be demonstrated that the payment of higher benefit levels to claimants with dependents is not an *effective* means of making provision for those dependents, because the payments are not passed on to them, then the *de facto* discrimination against women would not, seemingly be justified."[38]

Directive 79/7 is further limited in its usefulness by the long list of issues excluded from its scope. Article 7, for example, mentions five exclusions including the determination of pensionable age, the advantages given to those who have brought up children when claiming benefits and the granting of certain benefits to dependent wives. These and other exclusions in the Directive permit women, especially married women, to be treated in a distinctive and some might even argue a preferential manner. Women are allowed to claim their pensions earlier than men and are allowed access to benefits in circumstances when a man might not qualify. Yet these exceptions emphasise the "maleness" of the current structure of the state social security system, based as it is on male work patterns and a perception of women as wives and mothers rather than workers with the right to ensure their future financial security.[39]

Directive 79/7 does contemplate that at a future date some, if not all, of these exceptions to the principle of equal treatment must be eliminated.[40] One of the most glaring is the difference in state pensionable age.[41] Men in the United Kingdom are currently eligible for a state retirement pension when they are 65, women when they are 60.[42] This contrasts with occupational pensions where the principle of equal treatment in respect of pensionable age already applies.[43] After much debate, the decision has been taken to equalise the state pensionable age at 65 for men and women.[44] It is contemplated, however, that so fundamental a change will have to be phased in over a considerable period of time.[45]

The attempt to rid the social security system of sex discrimination may offer some gains to women, but it is a double edged sword which may also lose them the preferential treatment which they have sometimes received. The contributory benefit system has been geared to traditional ideas of men's patterns of life and work. Women received special treatment because their participation in the workforce was seen as temporary and as something that would be relinquished in favour of their responsibilities in the home. This no longer describes the reality of women's lives and stresses women's dependency on men in a way that is no longer accurate or acceptable, although it remains true that women's working lives are different from those of men. A contributory benefits system that simply demands that women be treated in exactly the same way as men is not the solution. To allow women to provide against their own unemployment, the system has to acknowledge these differences and take account of them. In this particular context, the mere elimination of discrimination may not provide a complete answer.

Political changes

Many of the recent changes made to the social security system have been inspired by political dogma. The major political parties each have a separate agenda for how best to organise the welfare state. Because the Conservative government has been in power for fifteen years, its views have had a considerable impact on the national insurance system and in particular on the manner in which specific benefits are structured. This is very obvious when one considers the changes made to two major contributory benefits - unemployment benefit and state retirement pension. The other political force which has had a significant effect on the system is the European Union. This can be seen in the context of pensions and maternity pay. It is also apparent that the government in the United Kingdom has not always agreed with the political views expressed within the European Union.

Unemployment benefit Unemployment benefit is a contributory benefit with rigorous qualifying conditions. A claimant must demonstrate that she has paid contributions of at least twenty-five times the lower earnings limit in one of the two years preceding unemployment. In addition, she will be required to show that in the two years preceding unemployment, contributions have been paid of at least fifty times the lower earnings limit. Consequently, many will fail to qualify, including those who earn less than the lower earnings limit - perhaps because they are engaged in part-time employment. Clearly, these qualifying conditions are likely to prejudice more women than men because they are seemingly geared to allow only those who have previously been in full-time and long term employment to claim. This is confirmed by the fact that in 1990, for example, 68 per cent of claimants of unemployment benefit were male.[46]

Even if a woman can satisfy the qualifying conditions, she will not automatically receive benefit. She will then have to satisfy the official dealing with her case that she is capable of work, available for work and actively seeking employment. Once again, these conditions of entitlement may mean that a disproportionate number of women may be prevented from claiming unemployment benefit. Proving availability for work can be particularly problematic for those women who have young children or are caring for someone such as an elderly relative, since it involves being able to accept an offer of employment at once. Women in this position may find that they have to satisfy the Employment Service that they have suitable care arrangements in place, otherwise they may be refused benefit. Having responsibility for the care of young children may also mean that a woman is forced to restrict the times when and the places where she willing to work. Setting such conditions can be regarded as making oneself unavailable for work if they significantly restrict the chances of obtaining employment. She must then convince the Employment Service that, even with these conditions in place, she still has a reasonable chance of obtaining work, or face the loss of benefit. The same considerations may also arise when a woman has to show that she is actively seeking work which she may be required to do from time to time in order to retain benefit. An unemployed person is expected to apply for jobs, contact potential employers and visit Jobcentres. A woman who is caring for another on a day-to-day basis may not find this particularly easy, but her lack of "effort" can be used to withdraw benefit.

Apart from the complex conditions governing the availability of unemployment benefit, the rates at which it is paid are very low. A claimant is entitled to a flat rate payment which is payable for a maximum period of twelve months and is taxable. If that claimant has a dependent husband or wife, they may seek a dependant's allowance for that person provided that they are either residing with them or contributing to their maintenance at a rate that is equal to or greater than the allowance. If, however, the claimant's spouse is working and is earning more than the increase that would be payable then no dependant's allowance will be available. Unemployment benefit includes no allowances for children. If, therefore, a claimant has children to support, or indeed simply cannot survive on the unemployment benefit she is paid, she can seek additional help in the form of income support which is a means-tested benefit.[47]

The rules governing the rate at which unemployment benefit is paid mean that a claimant, together with the claimant's family, may have to think very carefully about the best strategy to adopt. If a man is claiming unemployment benefit, it may be more advantageous for his partner to cease work, if she is working, and for the whole family to claim income support, which will include the payment of certain housing costs, than for her to continue in work if her job is low paid. If it is a woman who loses her job then, if her partner is working, she will be unlikely to receive more than the flat rate benefit. To be in receipt of such a low payment may mean that she will find it very hard to find new employment if that requires money for travel, new clothes, or other expenditure.

A study undertaken by the European Commission showed that the United Kingdom had the lowest rates of benefits in the European Union. In the majority of European Union countries, unemployment benefit is earnings-related. In Denmark, for example, it is set at 90 per cent of earnings, whilst in Germany it is 68 per cent of net earnings. In these countries unemployment benefit also tends to be paid for longer periods than is the case in the United Kingdom. Here, low rates of benefit result, it appears, from the desire to cut the social security budget and in that respect at least the United Kingdom has been successful. It is the only country in the Union where expenditure on unemployment benefit has fallen in the period 1980-1992.

This desire to "save" and also, perhaps, to make life sufficiently unpleasant for the unemployed to spur them into finding work has inspired the latest changes to unemployment benefit. In its White Paper, *Jobseeker's Allowance*,[48] the government has announced plans to replace unemployment benefit with this new allowance, the purpose of which is to emphasise to the unemployed that they qualify for benefit by virtue of trying to find work rather than simply being out of work. Individuals will qualify for the contributory jobseeker's allowance by satisfying the current national insurance conditions for unemployment benefit. The allowance, however, will be payable only for six months as opposed to the present twelve months, and there will be no dependant's allowance. As a consequence, the family of an unemployed person will have to rely on means-tested benefits. The rate at which the jobseeker's allowance will be paid is on a par with income support. Many claimants, for example young persons, will thus experience a fall in their benefit rate.

For those who exhaust their six month contributory jobseeker's allowance, or who never qualified for it in the first place, there is a means-tested jobseeker's allowance which is similar in many respects to income support. The allowance is not, for example, payable if the claimant has capital of more than £8,000. It consists of three components: a personal allowance with additions for dependants and children; premiums for such things as disability, and mortgage interest payments. These changes are very unlikely to work to women's advantage. If a woman becomes unemployed and qualifies for the *contributory* jobseeker's allowance, she loses since her benefit lasts only six months. Her chances of qualifying for *means-tested* jobseeker's allowance may rest on whether or not her partner is in full-time work, and if he is, she is unlikely to qualify unless his earnings are very low. If it is her partner who is unemployed, and she does not work, she must turn to means-tested benefits. If she is employed, she and her partner may have to decide whether it is more advantageous for her to give up her job and for them to rely on means-tested benefits.[49]

Another notable feature of this new arrangement concerns the undertakings which the unemployed must give in order to obtain benefit. They will be expected to sign an agreement detailing the steps they will need to take in order to gain employment. The Employment Service will also be able to direct claimants to undertake certain activities, such as training, in order to improve their prospects of gaining work. Failure to cooperate could result in a loss of benefit to the individual concerned. It must be of a matter of concern to women whether this determination on government's part to make the unemployed prove their credentials as jobseekers will be compatible with women's caring responsibilities. The White Paper does make the point that caring responsibilities can be a valid reason for declining a job offer or restricting the hours when an individual is available for work, but it remains to be seen how this will operate in practice and whether women will be discouraged from claiming this particular benefit. It is beyond doubt that these proposed changes to the law will not make the position any simpler. Although the declared purpose of the reform is allegedly to encourage people to take employment, the way in which this benefit is structured seems designed to force individuals into dependency on the state. One week someone may be earning £200 per week and the next week she will be forced to survive on benefit, without any intermediate stage designed to cushion the blow of unemployment. In these circumstances it appears more tempting to maximise the benefits available, including housing and passport benefits. Women could be forced to sacrifice the financial independence they may have obtained through paid employment, because of the way the social security system still directs its help to the family unit rather than to the individual.

Maternity benefits On the basis that pregnancy and the birth of a child have an impact on a woman's ability to work, it is logical to include these as a "risk" in a system of social insurance, and maternity benefits were a feature of Beveridge's national insurance system. He recommended the payment of two benefits in respect of pregnancy: maternity grant and maternity benefit.[50] Maternity grants were paid to all women and were meant to go some way to covering the costs of having a child. It was not necessary for a woman to have made national insurance contributions in order to claim this grant, since she could rely either on her own or on her husband's contribution record.[51] Maternity allowance, however, was to be available only to those women who were employed and had themselves made the appropriate number of national insurance contributions, provided they gave up work during the period immediately before and after the birth of their child.[52] The benefit was payable for thirteen weeks and at a level that compared very favourably with other national insurance benefits.[53]

The post-war maternity benefits system demonstrates that if it was guilty of adopting a stereotypical view of women as wives and mothers, it was at least committed to acknowledging the importance of that role. The maternity grant was a benefit that recognised the important task undertaken by mothers and although it did not meet the full costs of having a child, it at least made some contribution toward them. Maternity allowance, even though available only to women who worked, was set at a level that was substantially higher than that of other flat rate benefits. Such generosity toward women who had recently given birth contrasts sharply with the current system of maternity benefits, which is complex and penny-pinching. The system has undergone considerable restructuring but still remains one of the least generous in the European Union.[54] Maternity grants were an effective and simple way of directing some money to the majority of new mothers, but their value was allowed to fall and they were abolished in 1986[55] except for mothers receiving certain means-tested benefits, who may be entitled to a grant of £100. The Government argued that, rather than paying a universal grant, it would make more sense to direct resources to those who had most need of them.[56] Those above that level of need were expected to make their own provision for the impending birth of a child.

For working women there are now two maternity benefits available: statutory maternity pay (SMP) and maternity allowance. Both benefit schemes have been amended in order to comply with the Pregnant Workers Directive 92/85.[57] This deals with various aspects of the treatment of pregnant workers, not simply maternity pay[58] but, on that subject, it provides that a pregnant worker is entitled to be paid for fourteen weeks[59] an allowance "at least equivalent to that which the worker concerned would receive in the event of a break in her activities on grounds connected with her state of health."[60] If, however, when the Directive was adopted Member States were making payments to pregnant workers in excess of the amounts payable in respect of sick leave, they are not allowed to reduce the level of payments.[61] The new arrangements introduced in the United Kingdom in order to comply with this Directive[62] require a pregnant worker to satisfy various conditions if she is to claim either SMP or maternity allowance. To qualify for SMP a pregnant worker must have been continuously employed in the same job for twenty-six weeks by the beginning of the fifteenth week before the expected week of childbirth. In addition, her average weekly earnings must exceed the lower earnings threshold for national insurance purposes. If she satisfies these conditions, a pregnant worker is entitled to eighteen weeks SMP. For the first six weeks she will receive 90 per cent of her earnings, and then £52.50 per week for the remaining twelve weeks.[63] A worker who does not qualify for SMP may be able to claim maternity allowance. To do so she must have made at least twenty-six weeks of national insurance contributions in the sixty-six weeks before her baby is due. For workers in employment who can satisfy these conditions, maternity allowance is paid at the rate of £52.50 a week for eighteen weeks. Pregnant workers who are out of work or are self-employed are entitled to £44.55 per week for eighteen weeks.

Though this latest scheme is far from generous, it represents an improvement on previous arrangements, not least because the relaxation in the conditions governing eligibility will mean more women will be entitled to maternity benefits than in the past.[64] A considerable number of women will, however, continue to receive no maternity benefit during their maternity leave. This applies in particular to those women whose earnings are below the lower earnings threshold.[65] Beveridge's principle that all women - whether or not they worked - were entitled to some payment to help with the costs associated with having a child is thus abandoned. SMP and maternity allowance are most unlikely to compensate women for the shortfall in earnings that many will suffer on maternity leave. The haphazard nature of the reforms, brought in reluctantly to meet the requirements of the Directive, is exemplified by the anomaly that the payment period for benefits continues beyond the period of maternity leave (eighteen rather than fourteen weeks).

The limited gains secured for pregnant workers by Directive 92/85 highlight the difficulties faced by the European Union when it attempts to promote social legislation among Member States. Drafting a Directive which will command the necessary support requires compromise and the legislation which results represents the lowest common denominator on which Member States can agree. As originally drafted by the Commission, for example, the Pregnant Workers Directive called for pregnant workers to be paid the equivalent of their salaries. Objections (especially by the United Kingdom) and delay eventually forced a retreat which results in considerable loss for women.

The deficiencies in the statutory scheme of maternity benefits are underlined by the disparity that has developed between pregnant workers who are entitled only to the statutory benefits and those whose employers offer more generous occupational schemes. Some employers now have maternity schemes far superior to the statutory minima and which offer payments more closely related to earnings. This is perfectly legitimate, and is to be welcomed, but it helps only those women fortunate enough to be employed by such firms. The idea that the law should provide for a basic floor of rights, on which collective bargaining should then improve, looks unconvincing in times of high unemployment when there is a pool of readily available labour and when employers are already bemoaning the cost of employing women of child bearing age. Discrepancies in the financial circumstances of pregnant women also exacerbate the problems in arguing for payment of a universal maternity benefit, as in the case of the maternity grant. Why, it is argued, should women who earn substantial salaries be entitled to that kind of windfall? This ignores the original intention behind the grants which was not to reward an individual woman but to act as society's recognition of the considerable financial and emotional burden of motherhood.

Pensions The basic state retirement pension, which in 1994 is £56.10 for a single person, can be claimed by women at the age of 60 and by men at 65. Retirement pensions are, clearly, long-term benefits, since a person may expect to live an average of another ten to twenty years after retirement age. If all that person has to survive on is the basic state pension, it is almost inevitable that she will have to resort to means-tested benefits. By insisting, therefore, that an individual has to contribute toward an earnings-related pension, whether it is a state or occupational pension, the chances of their enjoying financial security in old-age is enhanced. SERPS is the state's earnings-related pension scheme and is there to ensure that workers who have no access to an occupational pension scheme can, and indeed must, contribute (via an additional deduction from their wages) to an earnings-related scheme. SERPS, in common with occupational pension schemes, works on the basis that individuals have to contribute for a considerable period of time in order to extract the maximum benefit from the scheme and women's patterns of employment may militate against this. Another crucial factor is earnings: as a general rule, the higher a person's earnings, the greater the amount they can accrue in pension. Women's generally lower earnings means that their ability to provide for retirement via SERPS is diminished.

1.1 *SERPS* When first introduced, SERPS did take account of some of the difficulties women experienced in trying to secure an adequate retirement pension.[66] Originally, individuals were allowed to select the twenty best years of their working lives - meaning the twenty years in which their earnings were highest - on which to base the pension. These years did not have to be consecutive years nor did they have to be the final twenty years of a working life. This allowed women who might have enjoyed quite substantial earnings at the start and end of their careers to count those years rather than other periods when they might have worked part-time. The scheme also offered an indirect benefit to some women in that it entitled the widow of a pension holder to inherit the whole of her partner's pension, so her standard of living did not drop dramatically on her partner's death.[67] The level of additional pension that could be secured by contributing to SERPS, whilst not over-generous, did provide a useful supplement to the basic state pension. In rough terms, since the method of calculating the pension to be paid was very complex, a full additional pension entitled a person to twenty five per cent of their average earnings up to a stated ceiling.

The fate of SERPS was put in the balance, however, by proposals to phase it out because of its high potential costs.[68] In the light of adverse reaction, it was decided to modify the scheme, rather than end it. Changes were therefore introduced in the Social Security Act 1986 which will affect all those retiring from the year 2000 onwards. From that date, any additional pension is to be calculated on the basis of a lifetime's earnings rather than the best twenty years. Realising that this would adversely affect certain groups, in particular married women, lone mothers and carers, some effort has been made to safeguard their position. Years spent out of work because of the need to care for children or the disabled will "not be counted in the working lifetime over which earnings are averaged."[69] An individual must, however, work for at least twenty years in order to secure a full additional pension. The percentage of average earnings that any additional pension represents has been cut from 25 per cent to 20 per cent. In addition, the proportion of an additional pension that a partner may in future inherit has been cut to one half as opposed to the full pension.[70]

At its inception SERPS had a great many positive features and, in particular, it tried to tackle the poverty that many face on retirement by giving employees access to an earnings-related pension scheme. A fundamental problem, however, is that SERPS is not financed in the same way as occupational pension schemes. The money paid into an occupational scheme is invested to produce sufficient returns to satisfy the demands on the scheme. The money paid into SERPS was simply absorbed into the government budget. Claims to pensions were accumulating, but the money to satisfy them had to come from general taxes. The government view was that this drain on future resources could not be sustained and it reasoned that the only way to reduce costs was to cut benefits. The way in which this has been done will be to the disadvantage of women: the years when they are caring for children can still be excluded from the calculation of any additional pension, but only if they give up work completely. Many women choose to work part-time when their children are young rather than cease work completely and the result will be that the years of low part-time earnings may be taken into account when calculating any additional pension. Even women who remain in full-time work for the major part of their career will, in general, receive lower pensions than their male counterparts because of women's lower earnings as compared with men.

1.2 *Basic state retirement pension* Apart from the problems they experience with SERPS, women also face greater difficulties in building up a contribution record that guarantees them a basic state pension. A claimant for the basic state pension must satisfy two contribution conditions. The first requires the claimant to have paid in any one tax year contributions on earnings that exceed the lower earnings limit for that year. The second contribution condition is based on an individual's working life. This can begin with the tax year in which a person reaches sixteen years of age and ends when she or he attains pensionable age, which is currently 60 for a woman and 65 for a man. The working life between these ages is calculated and, depending on its length, the so-called requisite number of years is calculated.[71] In order to satisfy this second condition a claimant must have paid or been credited with contributions on earnings that exceed the lower earnings limit for each of the requisite number of years.

A benefit based on working life is very likely to penalise women as they are still more likely than men to take career breaks and to work part-time. Both women and men are also vulnerable to periods of unemployment or sickness during which they may not make any relevant contributions, but the national insurance system will credit a contributor with contributions in certain circumstances, including illness and unemployment. Home responsibility protection may be of particular help to women though it can be claimed by either men or women. It was introduced in April 1978 and helps those who are caring either for a child or an invalid.[72] If a woman in this position is unable to make national insurance contributions, she can deduct any year of home responsibilities protection from the number of years for which she has to satisfy the contribution conditions.

Another way in which someone can ensure access to the basic state retirement pension is by relying on a partner's contribution record as opposed to their own.

This option is open to either sex, provided they are married, divorced or widowed. It may well be of use to women since someone whose contribution record is insufficient to claim the basic state retirement pension can rely on her husband's contribution record to claim what is known as a Category B retirement pension. The rate at which this is paid is lower than the basic state retirement pension - £33.70 as opposed to £56.10 in 1994. In order to claim a Category B pension, however, the husband or wife on whose contribution record the other partner is relying, must be entitled to the basic state retirement pension. As a result, a wife who does not herself have an adequate contribution record, may reach 60 (pensionable age) but not be able to claim a Category B pension because her husband, who is also 60, is not yet entitled to his basic state retirement pension.

2.1 *Pensionable age*   Since 1940 women have been able to draw their state retirement pension at 60, whilst men have had to wait an additional five years. This inequality arose out of the traditional pattern of men marrying women younger than themselves.   At that time, many married women would not undertake paid employment and would have to rely on their husbands in order to obtain a pension. It became commonplace, therefore, for a man who retired at 65 to receive a pension for himself but nothing for his wife, since she had not yet reached the age of 65. By allowing a woman to claim a pension at 60 this particular problem was overcome. The government proposed in *Equality in State Pension Age*[73] to equalise state pensionable age and is in the process of making the necessary legislative changes. The equalised state pensionable age will be 65, despite calls to choose 60 or 63 as the appropriate age.   The reasons given for this decision are linked to the costs which would fall on industry, in terms of increased national insurance contributions, if pensionable age were lowered.   Within the European Union, other Member States such as Germany, Portugal and Italy are said to be raising pensionable age to 65 rather than lowering it, and the government fears a loss of international competitiveness if the United Kingdom were to ignore the trend. It is also argued that in future a growing retired population will be looking to shrinking workforce to finance pensions. Hence another step that will increase social security costs, such as lowering pensionable age, is not considered wise.

This fundamental change to the law will not be introduced overnight.   The government proposes to phase in its plans beginning in the year 2010, which will give individuals adequate time to adjust to the change. All women who were born before April 1950 will receive their state pension at 60. Women born from April 1955 onwards will have to wait until they are 65. Women born between these two dates will have to work for an additional month for every month that their birthday falls after April 1950.   Hence a woman born in April 1951 will have to wait until she is 61 years and one month to claim her state retirement pension.

The government believes that the time is right for this change because circumstances which in the past have meant that women failed to qualify for a state retirement pension, have themselves changed. Many women currently retiring opted to pay the married woman's national insurance contribution which rendered them ineligible to claim benefits in their own right. Married women, with the exception of those who were already paying this reduced contribution, have been unable to take advantage of this option since 1977. The situation of women who take breaks from employment to care for their families is, in the government's view, adequately catered for by home responsibilities protection (HSP) which reduces the number of contribution years needed to qualify for a full pension for those able to claim it. The government concludes that "by 2010 almost all women will retire with a basic pension entitlement in their own right; and many of them will receive the full basic pension."[74]   On this basis, the change is presented as timely and without prejudice to women. Further, the equalising of state retirement age will be accompanied by related changes which, it is claimed, should make it even easier for women to obtain a state retirement pension. HSP will be improved and, in addition, women will be able to claim autocredits. These have been available only to men between the ages of 60 and 64 who are not paying national insurance contributions and serve to safeguard their entitlement to a state retirement pension. The same provision will eventually be made for women.

Although these law reforms are presented as not harmful to women, it seems likely that an appreciable number will fail to qualify for a full basic pension when pensionable age is equalised. This is because many women, rather than taking a complete break from employment when their children are young, opt for part-time employment. As a consequence they cannot take advantage of HSP but, should their earnings fall below the minimum level for national insurance contributions, they will not be accumulating contributions toward a basic retirement pension.

Occupational Benefits

The benefits available via the national insurance system are unlikely by themselves to guarantee financial security where someone is not working. National insurance benefits may need to be supplemented and this can be done through an occupational benefit scheme. The notion that an employer should provide employees with benefits when they are unable to work because of old age or ill-health is not new. In the nineteenth century it was not unknown for employers to grant long-standing employees ex gratia payments when they were no longer able to work. At the same time formal occupational pension schemes were established both by large private sector companies and within the public sector.[75] As Groves points out, the pattern for occupational pensions was set at a time when the majority of workers were men and hence they reflect male working patterns and aspirations.[76] A woman was expected to marry and become dependent on her husband and, in time, on her husband's pension scheme for support. Indeed, because of this, many employers operated a marriage bar which stipulated that once a woman married she must resign from her job and any pension rights she had accrued were lost.[77] Apart from the essentially male ethos that surrounded occupational pension schemes, there was no law which obliged employers to provide them and many chose not to do so. In such circumstances employees might make their own private arrangements and would look to organisations such as friendly societies, trade unions and private insurance companies for help. These bodies had a predominantly male membership and were not easily accessible to female employees.[78]

This background is important in assessing the present system of occupational benefits: women had little part to play in shaping the schemes, they were denied access to them and, even when they were free to join, they may have found the contributions required too heavy in view of their lower earning power. Women were marginalised just as much by occupational social security systems as they were by the state scheme. The twentieth century has seen women gaining greater access to occupational benefit schemes partly through their sheer weight of numbers. As more and more women work and do so for the greater part of their lives, it becomes increasingly illogical to exclude them from such schemes, where they are available. Allowing women access, however, did not necessarily guarantee that they would be treated in the same way as men and given the same benefits. Occupational benefit schemes consciously discriminated against women and this was particularly true of occupational pensions. Were a male employee to die, his wife would be entitled to a widow's pension, since it was automatically assumed that she was a dependent. In contrast, few schemes would automatically pay a widower's pension but would insist instead on proof of a man's dependency on his wife. The benefits paid to a woman under the terms of an occupational pension might well be less than those paid to a man even though each had contributed the same amount to the scheme. This was justified on actuarial grounds. Women, it was argued, survived longer than men, and this had to be taken into account in calculating the benefits they received. It was also not unusual for the age at which women were allowed to join occupational pension schemes to be set higher than that for men. Employers using such a device presumably hoped that female employees would leave to start a family before they reached the relevant age. Many occupational schemes were closed to part-time workers and, since the numbers of women who work part-time are substantially greater than the numbers of men, such an exclusion had a disproportionate effect on women.[79] Finally, the age at which an occupational pension was paid in general reflected the age at which men and women became entitled to the basic state retirement pension. Once pensionable age was reached - at 60 for a woman and 65 for a man - employees were expected to retire. It might be argued that women's lower retirement and pensionable age was an example of discrimination in their favour, yet forcing women to retire at 60 denied them the opportunity to accrue additional pension rights at the end of a working life in order to compensate for any earlier career breaks.

Discrimination against women thus meant that they were unable to benefit from occupational schemes to the same degree as men. The last twenty years have seen steps towards the elimination of this discrimination, with the European Union and the European Court of Justice taking a leading role. Ironically, despite all the efforts, women do not appear to have made any appreciable gains. On the one hand, the concepts of direct and indirect discrimination in the context of occupational benefits have produced some unusual results, as will be apparent from the analysis of the relevant case law which follows. In addition, although the ECJ has been keen to tackle discrimination, the Member States have shown less enthusiasm in addressing the structural problems which make it so hard for women to participate fully in the labour market and hence enjoy the full range of occupational benefits. The United Kingdom in particular has used its ability to opt out of the Social Chapter to evade measures in relation to parental leave and part-time workers. In other contexts, use has been made of so-called soft law, that is, measures that are not binding on Member States, to deal with issues that are of significance to women. As a result, Member States are not *obliged* to take positive steps to achieve the objectives, as they would be if the requirements were contained in a measure such as a regulation.

Occupational pensions

The discrimination experienced by women who were members of occupational pension schemes could well have been dealt with in Sex Discrimination Act 1975. Matters relating to death or retirement were, however, specifically excluded from the remit of that legislation.[80] This issue, it was said, required separate treatment but the legislation that followed, the Social Security Pensions Act 1975, did little to eradicate discrimination, simply requiring that men and women be given equal access to a scheme. In reality this does no more than ensure that membership of the scheme is open to both men and women "on terms which are the same as to the age and length of service needed for becoming a member and as to whether membership is voluntary or obligatory."[81] In confining itself to the issue of access, the 1975 legislation did nothing to tackle unequal benefits, indirect discrimination or unequal pensionable ages.[82] Women, therefore, continued to be discriminated against in occupational pension schemes. Discrimination in this context is particularly invidious. Pension schemes are long-term commitments based on a lifetime's work. A decision to eradicate discrimination will not bear fruit immediately but will take decades for its full effect to be felt. The decision to defer this process, which is what the Social Security Pensions Act 1975 represents, will be felt for many years by thousands of women in a very concrete form. They will either have no occupational pension when they retire or the pension they are paid will have had its value reduced by discrimination experienced ten, twenty or thirty years before their retirement.

The United Kingdom's half-hearted attempts to abolish sex discrimination in occupational pension schemes, led individuals to look to Europe to provide a remedy. Article 119 of the Treaty of Rome states that men and women should receive equal pay for equal work. For the purposes of Article 119 "pay" is defined as including "the ordinary basic or minimum wage or salary and any other consideration, whether in cash or in kind, which the worker receives, directly or indirectly, in respect of his employment from his employer." In view of this extended definition of pay, it was argued that the benefits which accrue from an occupational pension scheme are deferred pay and therefore included within the scope of Article 119. This interpretation was disputed by the United Kingdom because of a mechanism in the British system known as "contracting out." Workers have no choice over whether to make national insurance contributions: once a worker earns over the lower earnings level, she must contribute. Her contributions may then entitle her to a basic state retirement pension as well as an earnings-related pension. Contracting-out allows an employee to contribute to an occupational scheme, as an alternative to SERPS. Provided certain conditions are satisfied, the occupational scheme substitutes for SERPS and a worker's national insurance contributions are reduced. The United Kingdom argued, therefore, that contracted-out occupational pensions were not a form of deferred pay: the basic state retirement pension and SERPS are clearly social security benefits and as such are not affected by Article 119; since occupational pension schemes substitute for SERPS, it was thus claimed that they too were outside the scope of Article 119.

The European Court of Justice (ECJ) rejected this argument in relation to all occupational pension schemes. It was settled in *Barber v Guardian Royal Exchange Assurance Group*[83] that occupational pension schemes do constitute pay within the meaning of Article 119. This finding has extremely important consequences. First, it means that the principle of equal treatment applies to such schemes and any discrimination, either direct or indirect, will be unlawful. This applies as much to the benefit of men as to women: many occupational pension schemes use the age at which a state retirement pension is paid as their pensionable age and it has been common practice for a woman to receive her occupational pension five years before a man. The ECJ has held that it is contrary to Article 119 if an occupational pension scheme allows women access to a pension at a different age from men. As a consequence of this ruling, many occupational pension schemes in the United Kingdom were in breach of Article 119 and had been for a very considerable period. In order to contain the impact of their decision the ECJ ruled that "the direct effect of art 119 of the Treaty may not be relied on in order to claim entitlement to a pension with effect from a date prior to that of this judgment [17 May 1990], except in the case of workers or those claiming under them who have before that date initiated legal proceedings or raised an equivalent claim under the applicable national law."[84]

The attempt by the ECJ to define precisely the effect of the *Barber* decision in order to achieve clarity, produced exactly the opposite result. A whole range of possible interpretations was placed on the Court's statement. The broadest of these was that equal treatment was required in relation to any *benefit* payable after 17 May 1990. This sparked off a great deal of protest from Member States, including the United Kingdom, based on the huge potential costs of such a broad interpretation which, it was feared, would jeopardise the finances of many pension funds. After a period of uncertainty, there was clarification as to the time from which men and women must receive equal treatment in respect of occupational pensions.[85] Article 119 may be relied upon "for the purpose of claiming equal treatment in the matter of occupational pensions, only in relation to benefits payable *in respect of periods of employment subsequent to 17 May 1990.*" This is subject to an exception in respect of any workers who initiated legal action on this issue before 17 May 1990.[86]

Requiring equal treatment in respect of pensionable age has had unlooked for consequences so far as women are concerned. It is arguable that women's lower pensionable age was a rare instance where women were gaining at the expense of men. The majority of occupational pension schemes have decided to interpret the demand for equal treatment as requiring them to treat women in the future as men have been treated in the past, and not vice versa. In other words, benefits have been levelled down rather than up. According to the 1992 annual survey of occupational pension schemes, 59 per cent of those who have equalised pension ages have done so at 65 and only 28 per cent have decided to equalise at 60. Many schemes which have raised their pension age still permit retirement at 60, but in some cases those choosing to exercise this option will find their benefits sharply reduced.[87] Doubts have been expressed over the legality of firms levelling down benefits but the ECJ has ruled that this practice is legitimate.[88] The ECJ's decision that an occupational pension is pay and subject to the principle of equal treatment has, therefore, produced few of the advantages that might have been hoped for when the ruling was first made. Men have not been allowed to share the advantages of women's lower pensionable age, rather many women are being required to work an extra five years before they can claim their full occupational pension. As a result, those women who wish to retire at 60 and until quite recently believed that they would then receive a certain level of pension, are being given a choice of either retiring at 60 on a reduced pension or working five extra years.

The ECJ has also ruled that other features of occupational pension schemes, which seemed contrary to the principle of equal treatment, are in fact legitimate. Indeed, it appears that having determined that occupational pensions represented "pay," the ECJ has felt it wise to limit the consequences of that decision. Part of the reason for this may be the costs involved if occupational pensions had to adhere strictly to this principle. One instance of the ECJ declining to apply the principle of equal treatment, apparently by way of damage limitation, arose in relation to the actuarial factors used in many occupational pension schemes and which differ according to sex. The aim of a funded defined benefit pension scheme is to accumulate a fund that will be capable of meeting specific benefits promised to employees. The contribution which an employer has to make to such a fund, in order to ensure that it is adequate, is calculated according to actuarial factors based on sex. Women are presumed to have a longer average life expectancy than men. An employer will, therefore, make larger contributions in respect of a female employee, as it is assumed that she will make greater demands on the pension fund. If an employee wishes to transfer accrued pension rights from one scheme to another or to convert part of their pension into a cash sum, a male employee will be offered less than a female employee, on the basis that what he is surrendering or transferring is based in part on his employer's contributions, which in their turn reflect actuarial considerations based on sex. The ECJ has held that employers' contributions to such schemes do not constitute pay within the meaning of Article 119 and therefore the funding arrangements of individual occupational pension schemes are outside the scope of the Article.[89] Inequalities that arise as a consequence of those funding arrangements are also outside the scope of the principle of equal treatment of men and women.

This produces a very complex situation in relation to the extent to which the principle of equal treatment affects the financing and payment of occupational pensions. For example, if an employer's contributions to a pension fund can in certain circumstances vary according to the sex of the employee, can the same be true of an employee's contribution? The answer seems to depend very much upon the way in which the scheme is structured. An employer cannot use the fact that he has one occupational pension scheme for his male employees and a separate scheme for his female employees to justify paying his male employees more than his female employees. This is the case even though the additional sum paid to a male employee goes straight into their occupational pension scheme. Such a practice has been held to breach the equal pay principle of Article 119.[90] An employer is, however, justified in deducting a sum from a male employee's salary to provide a fund for widows' pensions, even though a similar deduction is not made from a female employee's salary to provide a fund for widowers' pensions.[91] The inconsistency this causes in male and female net, as opposed to gross, salaries is not a breach of Article 119.

Even if the *funding* arrangements of an occupational pension scheme can still take the sex of the potential beneficiary into account, it seems that both sexes must receive the same pension at the same age. The pensions paid by some occupational pension schemes take account of any basic state retirement pension that the individual receives. Until an employee reaches state pensionable age, he or she may receive from the employer a bridging pension which either ceases or is reduced once the basic state pension becomes payable. In the case of women, any bridging pension they are entitled to claim will currently cease when they reach 60, but a male employee will continue to draw a bridging pension until he is 65. This practice was challenged on the ground that it infringed the principle of equal pay in Article 119, but the ECJ disagreed. The purpose of reducing the bridging pension was to produce substantive equality between men and women and ensure that both were receiving an equivalent pension between the ages of 60 and 65.[92]

The web of legal regulation which derives from these decisions from the ECJ, is extremely complicated, but it tends to the conclusion that, after some promising starts, the principle of equal treatment has done little in the area of occupational pensions to encourage financial independence. Many women will find themselves in a worse position because they will have to work longer for their occupational pension. The ECJ also seems clear that Article 119 does not require an employer to organise an occupational pension scheme in such a manner as to take into account the particular difficulties which those with family responsibilities may face in meeting the conditions for entitlement to such a pension.[93] The ECJ's willingness to apply the concept of indirect discrimination in the context of Article 119 has its limitations. As has been demonstrated, occupational pensions work best for those who are able to work full-time for long, uninterrupted periods. Arguably, fewer women than men are capable of maintaining such a work pattern and hence occupational pension schemes, by definition, tend to discriminate against women. The European Court appears to be saying that, although Article 119 can be used to guarantee women equal treatment in relation to this particular form of pay, it cannot be used to ensure that the pension scheme takes account of their special needs.

There have, however, been notable achievements. Not all working women were allowed to join an occupational pension scheme and this was particularly true of part-time employees. In a welcome decision, the ECJ ruled that it is contrary to Article 119 to refuse part-time workers access to an occupational pension scheme unless their exclusion "is based on objectively justified factors which are unrelated to any discrimination based on sex."[94] Article 119 encompasses the notion of direct and indirect discrimination: the application of a condition by an employer demanding that employees work so many hours per week or full-time for so many years before they are allowed access to an occupational pension scheme penalises part-time workers and hence disproportionately affects women, since so many more women than men work part-time. In the case of indirect discrimination, the employer can attempt to justify the discrimination but the ECJ has stressed the importance of proportionality in assessing justifiability. In other words, what the employer has done must meet a need of the enterprise and be both necessary and suitable for answering that need.[95] If an employer argues that part-timers are excluded from a pension scheme in order to encourage more workers to work full-time, then a court might be expected to ask whether this was an appropriate way of achieving this objective.[96]

Although a part-time employee must still prove in any given case that her exclusion from her employer's occupational pension scheme constitutes sex discrimination, this ruling from the ECJ does seem to encourage greater financial independence by allowing women access to occupational pension schemes. In particular, the ECJ has stated that any part-time employee who has been subjected to discrimination can back-date her membership either to the date she joined the firm in question or 1976. In reality, however, far fewer part-time employees may gain from this judgment than would initially appear to be the case. First, a part-time employee has to prove discrimination and the United Kingdom courts are not always whole-hearted in their application of ECJ rulings. In a different context the Employment Appeal Tribunal held that pension payments made under the Local Government Superannuation Scheme are social security payments as opposed to occupational pension payments.[97] This decision has been described as a "misguided approach to construing decisions of the European Court of Justice"[98] but there is no guarantee that a similarly misguided approach will not be adopted in relation to part-time workers. Even if a part-time employee is given access to her employer's scheme, much will depend on the type of scheme it is. In the case of a contributory scheme, in order to benefit from a pension, a part-time employee would have to make the appropriate back-dated contributions which could amount to several thousands of pounds. Only if the scheme is non-contributory would a part-time employee automatically gain. Perhaps the real significance of the ECJ's decision is its clear message that part-time employees should not routinely be excluded from occupational benefit schemes.

Many of the problems experienced in relation to occupational pension schemes have their origins in the fact that women are entitled to claim their state retirement pension five years earlier than men. The age at which social security benefits are payable is outside the scope of Article 119 but many employers have chosen in the past to base the age when an occupational pension became payable on the ages already chosen by the state. They also expected their employees to retire at those ages. It is at least clear now that employers must use the same pensionable ages for men and women in relation to any occupational pension scheme and they must also use the same retirement age for both sexes. To force a woman to retire at an earlier age than a man is sex discrimination.[99]

Much that is helpful to women has been decided by the ECJ, but the decisions do nothing to attack the inherent unfairness to women in occupational pension schemes. The cases do not insist that schemes take account of the career breaks that many women take in order to care for children or other dependents. They do not ensure that occupational pension schemes work as well for part-time workers as they do for full-time workers. They simply emphasise that men and women must receive equal treatment. If that equal treatment is geared to male rather than female lifestyles, women will find it exceedingly difficult to use occupational pension schemes to ensure their financial well-being.

Occupational social security schemes

Intervention by the ECJ may not have entirely solved the problem of occupational pensions, but it has at least focused attention on the issue. Women who do work full-time for the whole or the greater part of their lives, and there are increasing numbers of these, are as a matter of law guaranteed equal treatment. Indeed, the Court has seized the initiative from the politicians who were making much slower progress towards the goal of equal treatment. Proof of this is to be found in relation to Directive 86/378, "on the implementation of the principle of equal treatment for men and women in occupational social security schemes" which is thus wider than occupational pensions alone. Occupational social security schemes are defined as schemes which provide protection against sickness, invalidity, old age, industrial accidents, occupational diseases and unemployment. The purpose of the Directive is to guarantee equal treatment in respect of entry into such schemes, the benefits accruing under such schemes and departure from such schemes. A major criticism of the Directive is that it lists numerous exceptions to this general principle. For example, it does not require the equalisation of pensionable ages or survivors' benefits. In addition, it allows the continuing use of actuarial tables which are based on sex in order to calculate benefits.

The United Kingdom implemented Directive 86/378 in the Social Security Act 1989, but this ran into difficulties when some of the exceptions listed in Directive 86/378 were held to be contrary to Article 119 in so far as they relate to occupational pension schemes. The most notable example is pensionable age. In view of the confusion over Directive 86/378, the United Kingdom postponed the coming into force of those sections of the Social Security Act 1989 which were intended to implement the Directive. The interpretation given to Article 119 by the ECJ in many ways appears to have overtaken the UK legislation and raises questions about the legitimacy of some of the exclusions it contains. Employees can use Article 119 in order to insist on equal treatment and the ECJ has held, for example, that an employer's sick pay scheme falls within the scope of Article 119.[100]   More importantly still, the Court has held that discrimination in occupational social security schemes, which has been inspired by national legislation, can be challenged using Article 119.[101] An occupational sick pay scheme which on the authority of national law excluded employees whose working week did not exceed ten hours was indirectly discriminatory, since far fewer women than men could comply with that condition. Since the scheme was based on national legislation, it was for the *state* and not the employer to try objectively to justify its behaviour on grounds other than those of sex.

The principle of equal treatment has thus had an impact on occupational social security schemes and the ECJ's commitment to the principle has secured change. Unfortunately, as employers react to rulings from the Court and to Directives from the Council, the state of confusion surrounding the whole topic of occupational social security benefits grows. This confusion is compounded by the fact that the changes made to ensure equal treatment are not necessarily the changes that will guarantee the greatest number of women financial security when they find themselves unable to work.

Personal provision

State and occupational social security schemes are designed primarily to offer financial security to employees. The self-employed are expected in the main to assume responsibility for their own future financial security.[102] Those who, as a matter of law, are considered self-employed may include some very vulnerable groups such as homeworkers. Since the self-employed are expected to make their own social security arrangements, they have been offered incentives, such as tax relief, if they make payments into private insurance schemes.[103] Plainly, a scheme which leaves it to the individual whether to provide for their future makes two major assumptions: that he or she will have both the will and the resources to make that provision. If either is lacking, that person may be forced to rely on means-tested benefits at times of financial crisis.

The notion that an individual should be allowed to make private arrangements for the future and not rely on the state or an employer has been extended in recent years. Successive Conservative administrations, worried by the numbers relying on SERPS for an earnings related pension, took various steps to try to reduce reliance on the state scheme. These included providing financial incentives for individuals to contract out of SERPS as well as occupational pension schemes, and to make personal pension arrangements.

There is, however, a problem with personal pension schemes since there is an element of risk associated with their operation. A fund is accumulated based on payments made by the individual from earnings as well as a national insurance rebate from the government. The fund is then invested and, depending on the skill with which that is done, a capital sum is built up from which an annuity will be purchased on retirement. As a report commissioned by the Equal Opportunities Commission points out, personal pensions with their high administration fees, their insistence that contributions must be made from earnings and the uncertainty surrounding the benefits they may produce are not in general a good choice for women.[104] Occupational pensions and SERPS may well offer greater advantages to women, since what is on offer in terms of a pension is normally clear at the outset.

A secure future?

The fact that virtually all women work at some stage in their lives means that most women will have contact with the state's or an employer's social security scheme. Crucially, such schemes may not work as well for women as they do for men. Beveridge's assumption that most women would marry, and that married women would not work but would choose instead to depend on their husbands for support was proved wrong, if indeed it was a justifiable belief at the time. Women are increasingly aware of the need to make their own arrangements for their future financial security. As increasing numbers of marriages end in divorce, women realise that they cannot assume that they will have access to their husbands' occupational or state earnings-related pensions when they retire.

It is also clear that, because of the efforts of the European Union and the ECJ, contributory schemes are being forced to accord men and women equal treatment. Those women who can match men's working patterns and level of earnings are perfectly capable of providing for their future financial security. Against these very positive developments must be set the fact that for some women, including those with low earnings, those who work part-time and those who take long career breaks, the system fails. The one exception is the basic state retirement pension which has the flexibility to take account of women's working patterns, but is a low flat-rate benefit. Without access to adequate earnings-related social security a woman is likely to be forced to depend on the state or her partner if she is to survive when she finds herself unable to work.

Notes

1.   This was the philosophy of Sir William Beveridge in *Social Insurance and Allied Services*, (1942) Cmnd 6404, and still forms the principle behind the present-day National Insurance system.

2.   See pp. 45-47.

3.   (1942) Cmnd 6404.

4.   Ibid., p. 7.

5.   Thane, P. (1982), *The Foundations of the Welfare State*, p. 249.

6.   Beveridge, op. cit., n. 1 paras 344, 347. The payment of an allowance to a divorced wife would, however, depend on her not being to blame for the failure of the marriage.

7.   Ministry of National Insurance Act 1944

8.   Lewis, J. (1984), *Women in England 1870-1950: Sexual Divisions and Social Change*, p. 147.

9.   Under the Married Women's Property Act 1882, for example. See pp. 29-31.

10.   Esam, P. and Berthoud, R. (1991), *Independent Benefits for Men and Women*.

11.   Ogus, A.I. and Barendt, E.M. (1988), *The Law of Social Security*, p. 23.

12.   Social Security Contributions and Benefits Act 1992 added Class 1A contributions payable by employers in certain cases where the employee has the use of a company car. They confer no entitlement to benefits.

13.   In particular, allocations are made from this fund to the National Health Service.

14.   See p. 55.

15.   See e.g. Leighton, P. (1986), 'Marginal Workers' in Lewis, R. (ed.), *Labour Law in Britain*, p. 503.

16.   *Mailway (Southern) Ltd v Willsher* [1978] ICR 511, compare *Airfix Footwear v Cope* [1978] ICR 1210.

17.   *O'Kelly v Trusthouse Forte plc* [1983] ICR 728, which graphically illustrates the conditions under which the catering trade operates. O'Kelly was male, but there are large numbers of women in the industry.

18.   *Market Investigations Ltd v Minister of Social Security* [1968] 3 All ER 732

19.   See generally Social Security Act 1989 which introduced important changes into the contribution system.

20.   Prior to 1989, there had been a system of graduated contributions according to earnings. The employer's secondary contributions remain graduated.

21.   See p.157.

22.   Social Security Act 1989, s. 1.

23.   Social Security Contributions and Benefits Act 1992, s. 11. If earnings are expected to be below a certain level an exemption certificate may be applied for.

24.   Widow's benefit and retirement pensions.

25.   Social Security Contributions and Benefits Act 1992, s. 13. £5.55 a week in 1994-5.

26.   Ibid., s. 15.

27.   See e.g. Social Security (Contributions) Regulations 1979, S.I. 1979 No. 591, as amended.

28.   See p. 59.

29.   See p. 63.

30.   Ogus and Barendt, op. cit., n. 12, p. 18.

31.   Poynter, R. and Martin, C. (1993), *Rights Guide to non-means-tested benefits*, p. xii.

32.   See p. 162 et seq.

33.   Directive 79/7 (statutory social security schemes), Directive 86/378 (occupational social security schemes. For progress on a third Directive which would demand equal treatment in

relation to those matters not dealt with in the earlier Directives see Commission of the European Communities (1992), *Completing the Internal Market*, p. 170.

34.　*Drake v Chief Adjudication Officer* 150/85 [1986] 3 All ER 65.

35.　30/85 (1987) ECR 2497.

36.　Ibid., p. 2520-1.

37.　Ellis, E. (1991), *European Community Sex Equality Law*, p. 192.

38.　Ibid., p. 192.

39.　Prechal, S. and Burrows, N. (1990), *Gender Discrimination Law of the European Community*, p. 181.

40.　Article 7(2).

41.　The Commission has proposed a third social security directive which will do just this. See Ellis, op. cit., n. 37, p. 203.

42.　For normal retirement ages under social security systems in Europe and the United States see Foster, H. (ed.) (1994), *Employee Benefits in Europe and the USA*.

43.　See p. 163.

44.　(1993), *Equality in State Pension Age*, Cmnd 2420, see p. 158. Legislation to implement this change was announced in the Queen's Speech in 1994.

45.　It is contemplated that changes will be phased in from 2010 onwards.

46.　Lister, R. (1992), *Women's Economic Dependency and Social Security*.

47.　See p. 111.

48.　(1994) Cmnd 2687.

49.　The new proposals contain measures aimed at encouraging part-time work by both claimant and partner, and at easing the shift from benefits to wages.

50.　Beveridge, op. cit., n. 1, para 341.

51.　National Insurance Act 1946, s. 14.

52.　Ibid., s. 15.

53.　At a rate of 36 shillings a week. This compares with the weekly rate for unemployment benefit which was 26 shillings for a single person over the age of 18, or for a married man.

54.　According to the Equal Opportunities Commission. See (1993) *Equal Opportunities Review*, 52, p. 5.

55.　Social Security Act 1986, s. 38.

56.　(1985), *Reform of Social Security*, Vol. 2, Cmnd 9518, p. 52.

57.　Council Directive (EEC) 92/85 on the introduction of measures to encourage improvements in the safety and health at work of pregnant workers and workers who have recently given birth or are breast-feeding.

58.　The Directive is concerned with the health and safety of pregnant workers and those who have recently given birth. Maternity pay is germane to this issue since it should encourage women not to risk their health by, for example, returning to work too soon after the birth of a child.

59.　Directive 92/85, article 8.

60.　Ibid., article 11(3).

61.   Ibid., article 1(3).
62.   Social Security Terms and Conditions of Employment: The Maternity Allowance and Statutory Maternity Pay Regulations 1994, S.I. 1994 No. 1230; The Social Security Maternity Benefits and Statutory Sick Pay (Amendment) Regulations 1994, S.I. 1994 No. 1367.
63.   £52.50 is equivalent to Statutory Sick Pay.
64.   Previously, to qualify for SMP at a rate equivalent to 90 per cent of her earnings a pregnant worker had to work full-time for the same employer for two years or part-time for five years.
65.   See p. 59.
66.   Walker, A. (1992), 'The poor relation: poverty among older women' in Glendinning, C. and Millar, J. (eds), *Women and Poverty in Britain the 1990s*, 176, at p. 188.
67.   Similar arrangements also applied to widowers.
68.   (1985), *Reform of social security*, Vols. 1 and 2 Cmnds 9517 and 9518.
69.   (1985), *Reform of social security, Programme for Action*, Cmnd 9691, p. 13.
70.   Social Security Act 1986, s. 19.
71.   This is their actual working life minus a set number of years (1-5 years) depending on length of actual working life.
72.   Social Security Act 1975, Schedule 3.
73.   (1993) Cmnd 2420.
74.   Ibid., para 1.3
75.   Hannah, L. (1986), *Inventing Retirement: the development of occupational pensions in Britain*, p. 10; Groves, D. (1992), 'Occupational Pension Provision and Women's Poverty in Old Age' in Glendinning, C. and Millar, J. (eds), *Women and Poverty in Britain the 1990s*, at p. 194.
76.   See above, n. 75, Groves.
77.   Creighton, W.B. (1979), *Working Women and the Law*.
78.   Thane, op. cit., n. 5, pp. 29-30.
79.   For a full account of the problems experienced by women with occupational pension schemes see Nobles, R. (1993), *Pensions, Employment and the Law*, pp. 197-198.
80.   S. 6.
81.   S. 53(2). Exceptions could be made to this general rule. See Occupational Pension Schemes (Equal Access to Membership) Regulations 1976, S.I. 1976 No. 142.
82.   Nobles, op. cit., n. 79, p. 199.
83.   Case 262/88 [1990] 2 All ER 660.
84.   Ibid., p. 704.
85.   *Ten Oever v Stichting Bedrijfspensioenfonds Voor Het GlazenWassers En Schoonmaakbedrijf* Case 109/91 [1993] IRLR 601 at p. 603. See also the 'Barber Protocol' which was annexed to the Treaty on European Union.
86.   Ibid., p. 603. Authors' italics.
87.   (1993) *Equal Opportunities Review*, 49, p. 3.
88.   *Smith and others v Avdel Systems Ltd* Case 408/92 [1994] IRLR 602.

89.   *Neath v Hugh Steeper Ltd* Case 152/91 [1994] IRLR 91. The reasoning in this case was confirmed in *Coloroll Pension Trustees Ltd v Russell and others* Case 200/91 [1994] IRLR 586.

90.   *Worringham v Lloyds Bank Ltd* Case 69/80 [1981] ECR 767.

91.   *Newstead v Department of Transport* Case 192/85 [1987] ECR 4753.

92.   *Roberts v Birds Eye Walls Ltd* Case C-132/91 [1994] IRLR 29.

93.   *Bilka-Kaufhaus GmbH v Weber Von Hartz* Case 170/84 [1986] ECR 1607, [1987] ICR 110.

94.   Ibid. See also *Vroege v NCIV Instituut Voor Volkshuisvesting BV* Case 57/93 [1994] IRLR 651 and *Fisscher v Voorhuis Hengelo BV* Case 128/93 [1994] IRLR 662.

95.   *Bilka-Kaufhaus GmbH v Weber Von Hartz* Case 170/84 [1986] ECR 1607, [1987] ICR 110.

96.   Compare the House of Lords decision in *R v Secretary of State ex parte EOC* [1994] 1 All ER 910, and see p. 81.

97.   *Griffin v London Pension Fund Authority* [1993] IRLR 248, and see (1993) *Equal Opportunities Review*, 50, p. 41.

98.   Ibid., *Equal Opportunities Review*.

99.   *Marshall v Southampton and South-West Hants Area Health Authority* Case 152/84 [1986] ECR 723. As a result of this decision, the Sex Discrimination Act 1986, s.3 requires men and women to have the same retirement age.

100.   *Rinner-Kühn v FWW Spezial-Gebaudereinigung GmbH* Case 171/88 [1989] IRLR 493.

101.   Ibid.

102.   The self-employed are required to pay national insurance contributions and can claim certain benefits such as sickness benefit and the basic state retirement pension, but not unemployment benefit.

103.   Finance Act 1956.

104.   Davies, B. and Ward, S. (1992), *Women and Personal Pensions*.

6 Wealth Within the Family

The rules which discriminated against women acquiring and owning property are long gone and, on a formal level, a woman has as much right as a man to earn a wage, claim from the state and own property.[1] Formal equality is not sufficient, however, unless in practice women's access to wealth is also free from constraint. The complexities and inadequacies of the benefits system together with women's lower earning power have an inevitable effect on their ability to acquire property. Moreover, the disadvantages suffered by women in the "public" sphere of work and welfare are reflected in the "private" area of the family. Where a woman is living with a man, whether as wife or cohabitee, the relationship between them raises complicated questions relating to the ownership of, or control over wealth *within* the family unit. Although a single woman may not have much in the way of resources - especially if she has dependent children - she does at least has control over her income and her property.[2] Some of the issues relating to wealth within the family are of particular significance when a relationship breaks down or a partner dies[3] but cohabitation, with or without a marriage certificate, raises important issues of power within the family. Where that power lies is evidenced, at least partly, by who has control over the family's wealth.

Because this chapter is concerned with the management of wealth within the family, and looks at the ownership of property (in particular the family home) and the control of income, some consideration must be given to a definition of the "family." The fact that those who talk about "the family" in various contexts often have very different views as to what it should represent is an indication that it is doubtful that there can ever be a universally accepted definition and it is certainly not a legal term of art in the same way as, say, "public limited company." For present purposes, however, it means two persons of opposite sex, who may or may not be married, living together as husband and wife, in a social unit, with responsibility for any dependent children. This description noticeably excludes lone parents with dependent children of whom there are significant numbers. Whereas, in general terms, a parent and her or his dependent children are undoubtedly a family, the focus in this chapter is the relationship between men and women within the home.[4]

Though the definition which is adopted for the purposes of this chapter does not depend on whether the parties are married, it remains the case that in law the status afforded by marriage may be crucial in deciding rights to income and property. Increasing numbers of couples live together in quasi-marital relationships (usually referred to as cohabitation), and the trend can be seen in figures produced by the Office of Population Censuses and Surveys: between 1971 and 1991, the number of marriages fell by over a fifth.[5] The decline in the numbers getting married was matched by an increase in the number of babies born to unmarried women but, although the proportion of births outside marriage in 1992 was one in three, many of these seemed to occur in continuing relationships to the extent that over three quarters were registered by both parents.[6]

The changing attitudes evidenced by such findings raise the question as to whether marriage continues to deserve its special treatment or whether, as some have argued, it has been or should be subordinated to a more important status such as that of cohabitation or parenthood. In relation to the former, the trend to date has been rather to assimilate cohabitation to marriage so that in some respects the two relationships are almost interchangeable. Such moves may, as we shall see, serve to increase the protection of a financially weaker party, who will more often be the woman, but there are those who argue that a couple who have deliberately chosen not to marry should not have imposed upon them the very trappings of the relationship which they have rejected. This leads to the argument that if marriage is becoming redundant (at least in the legal sense) and if relationships of all types are breaking down more frequently, it is better to base legal regulation of the family on the fact of parenthood (which is permanent) rather than cohabitation, with or without marriage (which is often temporary). Focusing on parenthood might have the advantage of encouraging greater recognition of the importance of this role, but by itself this would hardly combat the problems of dependency which tend to afflict those who assume the full-time care of children. Laws are never static and there is no doubt that shifts in the way people choose to organise their lives have prompted and will continue to prompt changes in family and property law in order to reflect the different needs and expectations of the individuals concerned, but the judges who are bound by earlier decisions tend in any event to be innately conservative and the law is not necessarily able to keep pace with social trends. Cohabitees in particular may find that the law does not always recognise their status, sometimes treating them as quasi-spouses and sometimes simply as two people who happen to be sharing a home. In any event, the law provides only part of the picture. It does not deal with all aspects of family life and there is much that remains outside the legal domain. This chapter will therefore examine the law as it applies to the married and unmarried family, concentrating in particular on how it affects the status of the female partner, but there will also be discussion of areas where the law has, as yet, much less to say.

For centuries there has been extensive legal regulation of all manner of rights relating to the ownership and transfer of different kinds of property and this is no less true in the context of family wealth. Most of the law applicable to property within the family relates to the setting up and the dissolution of family relationships. As might be expected, the law has traditionally been concerned primarily with the adjustments required when two individuals "contract" a marriage and with what happens to those arrangements should that marriage end by death or divorce, though more recently the law has extended its reach to certain aspects of the creation and breakdown of cohabitation arrangements. When it comes, however, to what happens during the currency of such relationships, the law is markedly absent, graphically illustrating what has been termed the public-private divide or the dichotomy between two distinct social spheres: on the one hand, the public world of the state and the market and, on the other, the private realm of the family. The boundary between the two is allegedly marked, indeed partially constructed by, the limits of the law, so that the public is subject to legal regulation while the private supposedly is not.[7] From this is developed the premise that since the unregulated, private world of the family is traditionally associated with women (the home makers and child rearers) and the public with men (the rulers and providers), this divide is the root cause of inequalities between the sexes.[8] In the words of O'Donovan, the belief has been encouraged that home is "a private place, a refuge from society, where relationships can flourish untrammelled by public interference"[9] but, as she goes on to argue, the reluctance to regulate what happens within the privacy of the household simply ignores and by ignoring perpetuates the inequalities which exist within that home. Any attempt to conceptualise the family as entirely private or to categorise its functioning as unregulated quickly runs into difficulties. There are areas where legal regulation is both common and extensive, divorce and the welfare of children being two obvious examples, and there is no avoiding the fact that even if law is absent, there are often other regulatory influences at work, including the education and health services. Nevertheless, the idea remains that within a liberal society there are areas of life which are properly exempt from the interference of the state, and that these include not only the thoughts and opinions of an individual, but also how the individual organises his or her life[10] and thus the view persists that it is not the place of the law to inquire into or to dictate what goes on within the family. So, although the law once decreed that the wife's property passed on marriage to the husband,[11] beyond that it was largely for the couple to sort out their own financial affairs. This would not have meant a life of hardship for all women, but it undoubtedly meant an existence whose hallmark was total dependence on a husband. The Married Women's Property Act 1882 freed married women to the extent that it gave them, in law, the same rights as men and unmarried women over their property and income but it takes more than an Act of Parliament to alter the balance of power between the sexes. This quickly becomes apparent when considering wealth within the family.

Once the unit is created and while it remains in existence the law shows little interest in who owns what and where control lies. In the case of a couple whose marriage breaks down, the law's interest is immediately reawakened and complex rules come into play to assess how property should be divided and children maintained, often regardless of the wishes of the individuals. At that stage the law shows no reluctance at all to intervene in the "private" affairs of the protagonists. In other words the law's reluctance to impose itself when partners are living in (relative) harmony contrasts sharply with its readiness - some might even say its eagerness - to dictate what should happen when a marriage fails. It might well be argued that if the law were to take a more interventionist role initially, there would not be so much to argue about subsequently. The absence of regulation within the relationship may be especially significant for cohabiting couples as the courts have limited powers of property adjustment when such a relationship breaks down.[12] Ironically, however, it is the fact that the courts lack powers of property adjustment at the end of cohabitation which may allow the parties a freedom and certainty that a married couple does not have. It is possible for a couple to express the financial - and other - aspects of their relationship in a contract drawn up at the start of the marriage or cohabitation.   Such agreements by cohabitees are theoretically enforceable, including those which set out to govern what is to happen in the event of a separation. So, although on one level the financially weaker cohabitee is more vulnerable than a wife, she has the opportunity to take positive steps to protect herself. Such an opportunity is meaningless, of course, unless she is aware of it and is well advised - neither awareness nor advice is likely in most cases. Married couples, however, are very unlikely to find such agreements are legally enforceable as the courts jealously guard their wide discretion as to the distribution of property on divorce.[13]

Express agreements are not, in any event, necessarily the answer to every problem. Quite apart from various issues of a technical nature (are they sufficiently certain, was there consideration) the very idea of contract being used in this way begs a number of questions. First, it is assumed when a contract is entered that each party is a free agent able to bargain effectively and equally on their own behalf. Because in many areas of modern life this is obviously not the case, statute has stepped in to impose obligations and restrictions on the stronger party. Terms are implied into agreements between an individual consumer and a business concern which apply irrespective of the parties' wishes and which seek to protect the individual, whose bargaining power is so much less than that of the business. It cannot be said that in a close relationship the parties are always going to be equal: would it therefore be necessary to have statutory safeguards and what form could these take? If terms were to be implied by statute or by judges in the same way as in consumer law, parties to a cohabitation agreement could find their wishes overruled by the law's view of what should happen, thus negating freedom of contract. It is already the case that a parent with parental responsibility cannot simply agree to transfer that to another and maintenance agreements relating to children are open to review by an outside agency. Further, an agreement which favours one party rather than another could be open to challenge on the ground of undue influence and this possibility would detract from the contract's finality, raising doubts as to whether it was really safe to rely on it. Finally, this would be, at least potentially, a very long term contract and it is entirely possible that the circumstances of the parties would change over the years: the contract might well need reviewing from time to time. This is not a fatal flaw - wills have to be altered with the birth of children and the death of spouses and partners - but it does underline the difficulties inherent in trying to govern something as protean and unpredictable as an emotional relationship by a device as legalistic as a contract. This does not mean that it cannot be done or should not be attempted, but if the purpose is to protect the position of women as the (generally) more vulnerable partner, it is not the whole solution.[14]

The laws which do exist to regulate wealth within continuing relationships can be roughly divided into those which deal generally with ownership of and rights over property and those concerned with the day to day finances and the maintenance of the family, or in other words the use and control of money, whether that be earned income or capital. Exploration of these two very general categories must be located within the framework of English family and property law which has chosen to treat the married (and indeed the unmarried) couple as two individuals within the unit bringing separate and identifiable wealth to that unit. This is crucial for women during and especially after the relationship, since it will normally be her partner who has the greater earning power, if indeed she earns at all, and he will thus have contributed a greater share of the family wealth. The legal regime which calls for an individualistic treatment of family wealth and which will often work to the disadvantage of the economically weaker party was, ironically, probably influenced in its inception by ideas of equality. The common law prior to the Married Women's Property Act 1882 had operated on the basis that the unity of spouses created by marriage[15] legitimised the treatment of the wife's property and earnings as effectively under the ownership and control of her husband. Equity had endeavoured to mitigate the rigidity and harshness of the common law by creating for the wife a separate equitable estate (although this was to benefit a wealthy family rather than the wife) and it was the idea of a *separate* estate which is the basis of the 1882 reforms. This was seen as achieving equal treatment as between husbands and wives, since each was accorded the same rights over the property they owned, but this principle took no account of the inequalities inherent in the relationship between husband and wife. Since, in most cases, it is the husband who would have the greater income and would thus be contributing more to family finances, he would appear to be in a stronger position in relation to the acquisition of property, and the law has struggled to synchronise the theory of independent property rights with the practical results of women's dependence within the household economy.

That there are other ways of approaching this question is shown by the adoption in many countries of the idea of community of property operating on the basis that husband and wife have equal and reciprocal shares in property belonging to each. Logic would suggest that such sharing is a more likely route to equality as between the parties but the ideas have not met with universal approval.[16] Some of the criticism is technical in nature and relates to the actual mechanics of community property schemes,[17] some is based more on a philosophical objection to the subordination of the individual to the couple, especially at a time when many marriages turn out to be merely temporary arrangements. There have been suggestions for reform of English law and a move away from the current separate treatment of the parties but proposals have not met with success. One suggestion was that certain assets including the home and pooled income should be jointly owned during marriage and that on its termination there would then be an equal division, subject to provision for children.[18] Such schemes, however, often allow for the exemption of certain property and for contracting out which militates against certainty and uniformity. For the moment it would seem that English law is wedded to the idea that the two parties to a relationship are better treated as individuals rather than constituent parts of a couple. In this the law does not seem to reflect either the practice or the beliefs of many couples, since research has indicated that amongst owner-occupiers the majority own their homes in joint names and even where this was not the case, the home was thought of as joint property. At first sight it might be thought to be of little consequence that the law is at variance with the reality of modern relationships: while the marriage or cohabitation subsists the law is unimportant and problems created if the relationship ends can be dealt with then by specific rules derived from legislation or case law - or even by judicial discretion. But this piecemeal approach to family regulation which is principally concerned with occupation of the matrimonial home and financial provision for children after separation or divorce, effectively denies the opportunity to tackle the wider issues of the distribution of power within the family. This is especially apparent when attention is focused on the dearth of legislation over the ownership of income and property during the relationship. Men and women may believe that they should be joint and equal owners of the economic assets of their relationship but these beliefs are not necessarily reflected in the law. English law has chosen to make men and women equal by treating them as individuals who must prove their individual entitlement to property. By and large, however, women are not equal to men when it comes to the acquisition and ownership of wealth, and it is possible that the imposition of equality, rather than benefiting women serves merely to highlight the inequalities inherent within the family and within society. Whether or not that is the case is one of the themes of this chapter.

Income

Lawyers define property as something which may be bought, sold or otherwise disposed of and they divide it into real and personal property. The latter includes material possessions such as consumer goods, financial assets such as shares and also money. For most families the acquisition of personal property depends on the income entering the household, and that is where the focus lies here. As it happens, the absence of law from the regulation of wealth within a family is particularly marked in relation to the distribution and control of household income, but the indifference exhibited by the legislators to the potential impoverishment experienced by women within the private realm of home has not prevented research into income management in the family. This has illustrated very clearly that the curtain drawn across domestic financial arrangements hides a substantial degree of inequality. Inevitably, the law is not entirely absent and there are some few basic legal rules applying to family finances. Thus, where money is earned it belongs, in law, to the person earning it; where things are bought during a marriage or cohabitation they belong to the person who provided the money.[19] It is apparent that these rules favour the party with the greater earning power since he or more rarely she has the better opportunity to acquire wealth and property. These rules may be avoided if the parties actually set out to do so, but most couples probably would not think of it, or if alerted to the consequences one of them might not wish it. There are, however, certain circumstances in which the general rules do not apply including housekeeping allowances, pooled income and the right to maintenance.

For women who do not have paid employment (or any other sort of income) the housekeeping money which is paid over to them by a husband or partner might well be their sole source of money. Those who have children will also receive child benefit but this is set at a very low level and is certainly not enough by itself to feed and clothe a family. As far as the common law was concerned, housekeeping money provided by a husband and anything purchased with it remained his, regardless of the fact that it had been given to the wife and even if by careful budgeting she managed to save something from it for her own purposes.[20] The position was altered by the Married Women's Property Act 1964 which provides that, subject to any contrary agreement being shown, money derived from an allowance made by the husband for the expenses of the home or similar purposes, or anything bought with such money is to be treated as belonging jointly to the husband and wife. There are a number of problems with this seemingly straightforward provision, most obviously the fact that it applies only to money given by a husband to his wife and not the other way around. Nor does the Act apply to cohabitees: in their case the right to the money transferred for housekeeping purposes will depend on what was intended, which would require a court to investigate whether there was an express agreement or if not (as is probable) did they, for example, have a joint bank account, or was any surplus treated as belonging to the recipient?[21] From time to time proposals are made to alter the 1964 Act, usually to extend the notion of joint ownership[22] which would, in theory, have some advantages, particularly if ownership were not to depend on who provided the money for a particular purchase, thus benefiting the non-earning spouse. On the other hand, reforms in this area of the law may not have any practical effect since such laws usually require the parties to have reached some prior agreement, which in turn depends on whether they knew of their rights and directed their minds to the question. Furthermore, if reforms were limited to married couples, a good number of women would be no better off than they are now under the common law.

Linked with the provision of housekeeping money is the question of joint accounts. Where parties pool their income and have joint bank or other accounts, the money in the account belongs to them equally, regardless of who contributed what and this applies to both married and cohabiting couples.[23] Such rules are well suited to the dual-earner couple and acknowledge the intention of the parties to share rather than focusing on their (unequal) earning power. The judicial attitude to this may be seen in *Jones* v *Maynard* where it was held that the "... idea that years afterwards the contents of the pool can be dissected by taking an elaborate account as to how much was paid in by the husband or the wife is quite inconsistent with the original fundamental idea of a joint purse or common pool."[24] Although the money in the account is shared by the parties equally, there is still a presumption that anything bought out of the account belongs only to the purchaser and where the purchase is of a personal nature, say clothes, that would be very difficult to rebut. In other cases, such as the purchase of furniture or investments, it may be that it can be shown that it was intended to benefit both and it will then, and only then, constitute joint property.[25]

Joint accounts are not confined to couples where both are earning, and it is not uncommon to have such an arrangement where only one of the parties is contributing. This might arise where a dual-earner couple with a joint account to which they both contributed loses an income when one ceases employment on the birth of a child and in such cases the legal results are less certain. Although the money and items purchased with it may well be owned jointly, this depends on what was intended so that unless evidence could be found to indicate an intention to create a shared fund, it is possible that the money would be held to belong entirely to the contributor. If, for example, a husband is the sole earner, but he finds it difficult to get to the bank and so opens a joint account purely for convenience (to enable his wife to pay bills and draw money) the money and items bought with it will belong to him.[26] In technical terms, where there is only one income going into a joint account the law assumes that there is a "resulting trust" in favour of the contributor, although the courts will look for evidence that there was an intention to benefit the other partner and if it is possible to find such evidence, joint ownership will be allowed.[27] In practical terms, however, the non-contributing party cannot rely on being automatically entitled to half or even a proportion of the fund and her position is thereby weakened. If she knew enough about the law she would be advised to spell out in writing that the account was intended as a common pool but, needless to say, this degree of foresight is rare.

Joint accounts are seen by many couples as an indication of trust and commitment and are thus an unexceptional part of a happy relationship. They have many practical advantages for a partner who is not earning or earning less, but they do also have a significant drawback should the relationship break down. Where both parties are contributors to the account, each would be entitled to a half share, unless they had previously stipulated the extent of their separate shares. Even if only one has contributed, the non-earner may be entitled to a share if there is evidence to that effect. While the account is open, however, either party to a joint account has access to the funds and could use the account for his or her own benefit even to the extent of spending all the money. Joint accounts are thus particularly vulnerable in the last stages of a relationship where it is open to one party to withdraw all the funds prior to a separation.

If women earned as much as men and if all women worked many of the rules outlined above would be less important, but since women do not generally earn as much as men and as many may spend some time out of paid employment the lack of certainty which surrounds a wife's legal right to share in her husband's income means that her situation may be precarious and the cohabitee's even more so. Given this vulnerability the third set of legal rules becomes important and these are concerned not with access to income but with maintenance. Although this is something usually associated with the breakdown of a relationship there are other circumstances in which it may arise and it is helpful to put this into its historical context. The common law regarded a husband as obliged to maintain his wife which meant no more than a duty to provide shelter, food and clothes. This obligation was a corollary to the law's insistence that a wife's property and income belonged to the husband: without the duty to maintain, a husband could leave his wife destitute. It was logical to ask the husband to provide for his wife, and equally logical that the obligation should not be reciprocal and that it should not apply to unmarried couples. In fact the husband's duty to maintain his wife was of little practical value, as during the marriage it amounted to no more than the right of a wife to pledge her husband's credit to buy what the law described as necessaries (provided she could find a trader willing to supply her on the promise that her husband would pay) and the husband could in any event revoke this agency. The first legislative moves towards providing an enforceable right to maintenance applied only to the breakdown of a relationship and not until 1925 could a court order a husband to pay maintenance to a wife still living with him.[28]

The law now provides in the Domestic Proceedings and Magistrates Courts Act 1978 that if either a husband or a wife fails to provide reasonable maintenance for the other the court may order payments to be made. Crucially, however, although the parties may be living together when the order is made, it will lapse if they are still together six months later. In other words, this is not really an example of legal intervention in the management of family wealth. It presupposes that a spouse forced to resort to court for maintenance is probably contemplating separation and consequently it is of limited use for a wife who simply wishes to gain access to her husband's income. Even if she were to use the Act, she would be granted only a six month period of grace during which time she would have to decide whether or not to continue in the relationship. To this extent it underlines the failure of the law to tackle the problems of inequality of income within the family. There is no other legal mechanism which would enable the wife to enforce a right to an allowance from her husband. In the case of cohabitees, they do not even have the protection of the 1978 Act since there is no obligation to maintain.[29]

At this point those who are sceptical of the value of the law in achieving equality for women might ask whether the policy of non-intervention adopted by the law to the management of money within the family is such a bad thing. After all, it might be argued that the rules on joint accounts and housekeeping allowances only matter either when something has gone wrong and the parties are sorting out their affairs in the wake of a separation or if one of the parties has died and there are problems with the estate. This argument is echoed in the words of one commentator who states: "There is little point nowadays in spouses litigating over their strict property rights *inter se*. In a happy marriage it does not matter (except to creditors, executors and the Inland Revenue) who owns what."[30] From the point of view of a practising lawyer, he may well be right, but this discounts what the law represents and the role it can play in shaping attitudes. If the law were to state that partners to a relationship have equal rights to the income coming into the home, it is highly unlikely that many couples would be driven to litigation during their relationship but the law would have articulated a particular view as to how things should work and what the expectation is, very much in the same way as the Sex Discrimination Act lays down what are expected standards within its remit (which does not mean it is always followed). The law would have indicated that, even within the private world of the family, women are entitled to a share of the family wealth, such as it might be. The fact that the law does not do that may be interpreted to mean that women are expected to continue their dependent existence, reliant on the good will of their partner. This raises the question of what really happens in practice.

There are a number of studies which have concentrated on discovering how families organise the management of money and among them is the valuable work done by Pahl, on whose research the following discussion draws.[31] Although she points out that her study was a small sample, she also comments that the couples surveyed were reasonably similar to the larger population of married couples with dependent children and thus could be reasonably supposed to be representative of how married couples in general allocate their money. She set out to discover how finances were arranged and what might be deduced from that as to power sharing within marriage. Interest in this subject derived from her realisation that women who had left their violent husbands for life in a refuge actually said they were better off on basic social security benefits than they had been even in family homes which might, objectively, have been categorised as well off.[32] Pahl noted that treating the household as an economic unit disguises the poverty of individuals within the unit: family income may be above the poverty line but that does not mean that everyone in the family benefits equally from the money coming in. Indeed, it has been suggested that there is a useful distinction to be drawn between the "household income" and the "domestic income" where the former is the total amount of money received by members of the household and the latter is total available for spending on the collective needs of the household, such as food, fuel and accommodation.[33] Traditional economic theory does not distinguish between the people who make up the household and the household itself, hence what Pahl refers to as the "black box, within which the transfer of resources between earners and spenders has been rendered invisible."[34]

When examining distribution of wealth in the family it is helpful to distinguish between earning, controlling, managing and consuming since these may involve different individuals at different times and change according to the pattern of management adopted. In a family with a working husband and a non-working wife, if he were to give her an allowance out of which she is expected to budget for all household expenses, not only does he earn, he also controls allocation and distribution, while she manages, in so far as she puts into operation the decisions made by the controller.[35] Where both partners work and pool their income, control and management may be shared. In fact, Pahl categorised the management of family finances into four groups: whole wage, allowance, pooling and independent management. Which of these is adopted depends on a complex array of factors ranging from the practical to the ideological but each has, in its different way, something to say about power and dependence within the average relationship. The whole wage system, which tends to occur in poorer families, involves one partner, usually the wife, in managing all the household income after the husband has handed over his whole wage packet, though Pahl includes in this system instances where the husband may retain a small amount of money for his personal use and it might be argued that those cases should really be included as a variant of the second, allowance system. Under that arrangement the principal earner, usually the man, hands over a set amount each week or month out of which the wife-manager must buy certain items such as food and clothes. The money which is kept back is used for areas of expenditure which are seen as belonging to the husband - say fuel bills or the car and of course his personal consumption, if any. Under the pooling or joint management system, as its name suggests, both may contribute and both have access to the pool although each may be responsible for different outgoings. The system of independent management is marked by the fact that neither has access to the other's income and each is responsible for specified areas of expenditure - mortgage, fuel, food and so on. By definition this would require a two-earner family and, depending on the precise arrangements, one where the wife is earning sufficient to meet at least some share of the costs. Such completely independent systems were less common but are on the increase, and are especially prevalent amongst cohabiting couples who may not have made a permanent commitment or a long term financial investment, or amongst young professionals with no children. Closer investigation of each of these systems reveals where the balance of power lies though it is also necessary to add in the different perceptions which individuals have of their own contributions to the family wealth and to ask, for example, whether the fact of a woman earning alters the power structure, or whether there are other factors which perpetuate a culture of dependency.[36]

In a whole wage structure, Pahl found that a wife takes on responsibility for family expenditure and where she is also earning she simply adds her wages to her husband's. Such an arrangement is commonest in poorer households and is especially common where the only income is that from social security benefits. This points to an interesting phenomenon of an apparent shift of responsibility from the husband in high income families (see below) to the wife in low income families. The reasons put forward for this are equally revealing since they underline the generally dependent and secondary nature of women within the family. First, when there is very little money coming in, a higher proportion of it must be spent on essentials such as food and fuel[37] and these are matters traditionally seen as falling within the domestic sphere which is controlled by the wife. Similarly, there is less likely to be any need to make decisions about high cost items such as a new car, which might otherwise have been within the province of the husband. It is also true that management of money in these circumstances is no easy task. The constant need to account for every penny requires close attention to detail and creates an ever present anxiety. It is the wife who is "saddled with the burden of making family decisions unaided."[38] In such cases, any appearance of power given by the fact of control may be somewhat illusory.

The allowance system differs significantly from the above because it entails the husband keeping control over access to the household income and simply handing over what he considers is sufficient for the domestic income, covering expenditure adjudged to fall within his wife's sphere of responsibility. Although this is typical of working class families, as is the whole wage system, the allowance arrangement correlates with rather higher levels of income. There is also evidence that as income levels rise, control by the husband widens, both in allowance and pooling systems. This has consequences for the amount of money which is handed over, since the wider the sphere of expenditure responsibility which is assumed by the husband, the greater the sum of money retained. In one of Pahl's allowance families, the husband had a bank account in his sole name and gave his wife a weekly amount which was basically just for food, and day-to day household needs, while he paid for the mortgage, fuel, rates, telephone, insurance, hire-purchase on large household goods such as the fridge, washing machine and so on. Her access to the income was therefore heavily restricted and her control minimal. Her one source of independent income was child benefit and she strongly opposed the idea of it being paid into the bank account since that was her husband's and it would then be lost to her as an individual.

As income levels rise, the proportion which must be spent on essentials falls and with the increased discretionary spending comes increased male involvement. The control which the whole wage wife had over her meagre household income is thus lessened as the domestic income is increasingly distinguished from the household income. It must be borne in mind also that some of the wives in allowance systems may not know exactly what their husbands earn. If the husband insists on a flat rate allowance, his personal finances may be increased by pay rises or overtime bonuses which do not necessarily benefit the family - unless he chooses that they should. Since the principal earner is retaining money for "his" collective expenditure it is similarly true that he may retain money for his own personal spending. The amount of money retained by the principal earner tends to increase with skill and income, though it is not always the case that the money would be seen as entirely personal as opposed to collective. One of the most important hallmarks of the allowance system in the context of power and wealth within the family is that a woman who finds her allowance is inadequate must negotiate for more. In a sense it does not matter whether her partner is willing or unwilling to comply with her request since the very act of asking places her in the role of supplicant and dependant. In reality, women may face difficulties in getting a rise in pay, particularly since some men may have little or no idea of how much it costs to run a home. The strategies that women are forced to adopt, from cajoling to dissembling, merely reinforce their subservient status. In the case of a married couple it should also be remembered that, legally, any money which is saved from the allowance does not belong to the wife, but to the spouses jointly. A cohabiting woman may find, if it were ever to come to court, that she is not even joint owner of any surplus but that the intention was that it should revert to her partner.

Joint management or pooling partners seem to be the most equal, there being both equal access to the money and equal responsibility for expenditure. A typical pooling couple would be the dual-earner family with joint wages which allow for a reasonable level of disposable income (since the importance of sole control called for at minimum levels is not so great). Such a couple would fit well into a model of equality and it is the case that joint management apparently increases as incomes rise. But it has also been suggested that male control increases commensurate with disposable income, so the straightforward egalitarian ideal is perhaps too simplistic. Certainly, it is not the case that pooling occurs only in dual earner couples - it may continue after one partner has given up work because of children - but Pahl found that where the wife is not earning there is a tendency for the husband to control the pool so that the wife must approach the husband for access to additional money, which is not entirely consistent with the idea of equality. It is also significant, bearing in mind the legal position in these cases, which is that ownership depends on intention, that control by the husband might militate against a finding that there was an intention to share the money equally. The law has little regard for what happens in practice and it does not, for example, have the flexibility to recognise that the employment pattern experienced by a woman over her working life can have a major effect on the precise arrangement adopted for family finances. Not only may the family lose a contributor to a joint account, it may even be that when a wife ceases to work a pooling arrangement is replaced by an allowance system, which operates until the woman returns to work at a later date. Absence from the labour market thus influences not only the amount of family income and a woman's independent access to wealth, it also directly affects the power relationships within the family and will have possibly unforeseen consequences on the legal ownership of that wealth. Where the wife *is* earning she may control the pool, and this tendency increases as the proportion of her contribution increases. This would suggest, hardly surprisingly, that as a woman's income rises she acquires greater power in the sense of controlling and influencing family wealth, though this may not necessarily lead to greater harmony if the husband feels his dominant, breadwinner role is threatened.

In some cases it may actually be conflict that leads to an independent management system where each keeps their income separate and meets specific expenditure.[39] On the other hand, such an arrangement could result from a wish to signify equality or could be seen as a symbol of the absence of dependence. To that extent it might seem particularly apt for cohabiting couples who have explicitly rejected the dependency notions of marriage (though it is certainly not restricted to unmarried couples). Conversely, independence may be less attractive to some couples precisely because the attachment to an individual arrangement within the partnership could be seen as a lack of commitment. Pahl refers to a couple for whom independent management ceased when they bought a house together and abandoned the idea that independence meant things would be simpler when they split up.[40] This underlines the role of ideology in deciding which system to adopt, quite apart from considerations of size of income and social class. Independent management does seem to correlate with a higher level of income for the *wife*, suggesting that this gives her the power to argue for the split between what is needed for collective costs and what may be retained for personal use. Of course, there are always exceptions and Pahl found a couple where the wife's wages were very low and yet they adopted independent management. Her money was used for her car, clothes and spending money, while he paid most of the household bills, *and* because her income was so low he also gave her money to buy the food, so that this might have been an allowance arrangement except that he had no access to her wages. Such a couple is not typical of independent management who do tend to be in the higher income groups. In a survey in 1987, it was found that 15 per cent of a sample of over 1,000 used independent management, while this rose to 25 per cent in couples whose income was over £18,000. The proportion was even higher for cohabiting couples at nearly 50 per cent.[41]

The variations even within the four categories of money management signal the fact that how couples arrange matters reflects the way they see their relationship and their perceptions of the roles of men and women within the family. Pahl attempts to explain why couples organise their finances in the ways they do and concludes that arriving at a particular pattern of management is the result of a variety of complex variables.[42] She suggests that reasons may be found under four general headings: practical; psychological; socio-economic and ideological. As might be expected the first of these concentrates on convenience: if money is paid into a bank account, who finds it easier to go to the bank; if she does the shopping, she is the one who needs the money and knows what things cost; the self-employed person must have a bank account in his own name rather than a joint account. Psychological explanations attribute choice of arrangement to the personalities of those involved: careful with money, bad at managing etc. Socio-economic reasons depend on the level of wages, whether the wife is earning a significant wage, whether husband is working. Ideological influences are most clearly reflected in notions of equality within a relationship - or conversely that men are meant to be the dominant partner. As Pahl points out none of these can be isolated entirely from the others and in nearly all cases decisions as to how money is managed will result from an amalgam of all of these. Importantly, however, the decisions which couples take, consciously or unconsciously, about how their finances should be arranged rarely seem to have much to do with the wider issues of who owns and controls family property. The law, however, must decide who should have rights in the family home and arrangements based on convenience, personality or inability to work can have far-reaching legal consequences which the parties have never contemplated.

One of the most persistent influences on family life and consequentially on the access that women have to wealth is the notion of the male breadwinner. On one level the responsibility inherent in being the sole provider for a family is a remarkably heavy burden, and indeed some men will chafe under the restrictions this places on their use of the wages they earn. On another level, however, many men take pride in their role as provider, a fact which may lead to problems if unemployment should remove that raison d'être. The breadwinner model has important effects on a woman's status within the family and in paid employment. The assumption that the husband is to provide for his family presumes a wife who is as dependent as her children, with all of them as consumers not earners. Consequent on this is the argument that the wage paid to a man must be the equivalent of a "family wage" or a sum which is notionally sufficient to support the whole unit when it is shared. What those who argued for a family wage may not have recognised, or simply not have acknowledged, is that it leads inexorably to the continued dependence and subordination of women. Not only is there a presumption that the family wage will be equitably shared, but there is also the assumption that the woman's place is in the home, rearing children and performing unpaid and thus invisible work for the benefit of the family. She has no independent income (save and except what the state may provide), must rely entirely on her husband and is thus stripped of any real power. Furthermore, should the woman gain employment outside the home, the primacy of the husband's wage can be used to justify inequalities in women's pay. After all, goes the argument, she is simply earning for extras and his is the important wage.

These ideas have a remarkably tenacious grip on the attitudes which most people bring to their partnerships. This is apparent in the way in which many husbands, and some wives, persistently categorise a wife's earnings as "extra" even when they may be what is keeping them afloat. Surveys in the 1980s found that whereas women work for all kinds of reasons, over a third were working for essentials.[43] Nevertheless women may be complicit in the treatment of their earnings as mattering less than their husband's and this was made very clear in one of Pahl's couples where only the wife was earning and the husband was on benefit. Prior to his losing his job, they had worked an allowance system under which he had kept a substantial sum for himself. Now all income was pooled, but only in the sense that she handed him her entire wage packet and he gave her money to buy food for the weekend, pay bills other than rent, and for "bits for herself" while he did the rest of the shopping and paid the rent. In other words although she had become the breadwinner, they had compensated for the shift in power by her relinquishing control and management to him. Although in that particular couple the husband's unemployment had not deterred the wife from working, this is not always the case and it is not uncommon to find that women involved with unemployed men do give up paid employment, often because their wages will reduce benefits to such an extent that it is not financially worthwhile to continue.[44] This has important consequences, not only for the family income, but also for the position of the woman within the household since she is no longer an independent earner, but entirely dependent on her partner. The withdrawal of such women from the labour market also underlines the continuing perception of women's earnings as somehow less important. A woman gives up work because her employment will affect the benefits claimed by her partner, but why should she relinquish her wage rather than become the breadwinner? One obvious answer might be that her earnings are too low to support the family, but in that case it might be possible to supplement her wages with family credit, to bring them up at least to the level of income support. One study found that this was simply not considered by the couples they interviewed and surmised that this was because it was unthinkable that a woman would be the primary earner.[45] The role reversal which would be entailed in deciding to live on a woman's earnings would have left the husband with no clear definition:

> For a household to move off out-of-work benefits and on to women's earnings would ... leave a man in conceptual limbo and most men found this a hard concept to grasp - as far as they were concerned men were defined by their paid work status, either positively if they were employed or negatively if they were unemployed ... .[46]

Perceptions of women's work and wages as secondary have clear ramifications for the balance of power within a relationship and these are not limited to partnerships where the male earner is unemployed, but spill over even into couples where both are earning. At this point, however, a paradox appears: there is an apparent conflict between the way in which women's wages are regarded and how they are used. It seems that the general practice is for a woman's wage to be added to the domestic income and to be used for the benefit of the household, whether on necessaries or "luxuries" such as holidays and home improvements. Only one of the wives in Pahl's study regarded her wage as her personal spending money and this pattern has been reflected in other studies.[47] In other words, although the status accorded the woman's wage was low, in the majority of cases it was not an unimportant extra and in some families it was absolutely essential. Pahl also identified another instance of conflicting views: when questioned as to how they regarded their own income and their partner's income, the vast majority of men said they saw their wage as belonging to the family, even though many of them did not in practice hand over all their income. Fewer than half of the men identified their wives' earnings as being the family's, but preferred to see it as belonging to the wife, despite the fact that it was used for household purposes, often to augment housekeeping allowances. Conversely, most wives regarded their wage as belonging to the family, and had the same attitude to their husbands' wages which were seen as for collective use. On the other hand, while the wife might regard her husband's wage as for the use of the household, there was a marked reluctance on the part of many women to treat the income as being equally hers, despite the efforts of some of the men to convince them otherwise. Pahl suggests that this might be "because this idea was often linked with an ideology in which the husband's sharing of money was seen as a reward for the wife's domestic work, while her earnings were seen as outside the system"[48] and thus by implication as less important: the husband/breadwinner was not prepared to countenance a diminution in the centrality of his role. Nowhere is this more apparent than in the couple where the working wife commented that her husband liked to think of himself as running the house and being the breadwinner, with her working just because she wanted to, though in practice her earnings paid for the telephone, the car, hire purchase payments and clothes for all five family members. Of course, the pride that a man may feel in the role of provider may be equally important to a woman and it is certainly true that women who work often comment not only on the independence this brings them but also on the pride felt in contributing.

Simply to state that women like to be able to contribute to family finances or experience at least a degree of financial independence is unsurprising and does not necessarily answer questions about power and access to family wealth. There is little doubt that many couples would resent the suggestion that money equals power and that power is concentrated in the hands of men. Their perception of their own relationship would probably be of sharing and equality, even if responsibilities differed. What Pahl and others have shown by their closer examination of what actually takes place within the "black box" is that even in those households where there was a pooling system, the greater earning power of the husband had an important effect on control of the money and access to it. Indeed, the more a husband earns the more likely it is that he will control money within the family, subject to the fact of his wife also earning a reasonable level of wage. Whether the system used is a pool or an allowance, if she earns only a relatively low amount it is likely that her contribution will simply disappear. When used to augment the income available for domestic spending, her wages become as invisible as her other contributions to family welfare. Ironically, whilst women's wages are swallowed up by the black box and categorised as secondary, by and large women contribute a higher proportion of their earned income to the housekeeping. While contributing relatively more, her bargaining position and access to independent wealth is little changed, so that her husband remains in his eyes *and* hers the breadwinner. This shared perception of the roles of the partners within a family is highly significant both publicly and privately, outside and inside the home. Publicly, it has consequences for the way in which the benefits system is organised, assuming that women with partners are dependent and receiving a share of his income and, despite reforms, it has resonances in taxation which currently retains an allegiance, albeit one which is diminishing annually, to the idea of the married couple's allowance. On a practical level, the dependence of women is reflected in the way that women see themselves as secondary, a phenomenon which in some ways might be the most insidious and most resistant to change.

The down-playing of a woman's role in and contribution to the way in which family life is organised and financed is most noticeable in poor families where, as has been noted, women tend to be responsible for managing the budget. Those who have looked at the management strategies employed by women in poor families find that it is the women who come off worst whether in food, clothes or other basics. In other words, when money is really scarce, women budget by sacrificing their own needs, not only to those of their children but also to those of their partners. Mothers miss out their own meals to ensure that the rest of the family is fed, or provide meat only for the husband and children. They buy their clothes from jumble sales in order to afford better ones for the family. They do not light fires or turn on the heating when they are alone in the house. Some of this may be due to altruism, and many a parent would go without to protect his or her children, but the prevalence of this attitude among women is evidence of an ideology which seeks to protect the health and welfare of the breadwinner and in which women have accepted that they are less important. Thus, where the family is poor, the woman is often the poorest and her contribution to family well-being through the personal sacrifices she makes is often overlooked.[49]

A restricted income and constant difficulties in making ends meet means that credit - and debt - become specially important to the wife-manager. Credit is not confined, of course, to low income households - quite the reverse. Allowing for inflation, the amount of credit in the UK nearly doubled between 1981 and 1991, and this figure does not include mortgage borrowing.[50] By 1991 credit from banks accounted for nearly two thirds of outstanding credit and borrowing on bank credit cards showed a marked increase.[51] Bank lending is, however, only part of the story and for many poorer women it has little significance. It is wealthier people who make most use of credit and it is they who are more likely to use bank loans, credit cards and store cards.[52] Further down the income ladder the pattern and source of lending changes and, most importantly, credit becomes more expensive. Associated with credit is debt: this applies not only to consumer purchases but also to housing and fuel costs. Both tenants and owner-occupiers felt the effects of the recession of the late 1980s: rent and mortgage arrears increased and research has shown that a significant number of consumers have difficulties with fuel bills.[53] Parker points out that the position of women within households has consequences for the incidence of debt, the type of credit to which they have access and the sort of debts they incur.[54] Whereas the money going into the household may be adequate, if the husband is retaining a proportion for his personal use and handing over an insufficient amount to his wife, debt may often follow. Problems are exacerbated where the breadwinner has little or no involvement in the running of household finances and thus no idea of the costs, leading to reluctance or refusal to increase housekeeping allowances. In the light of the burdens which fall upon women in poorer households it is adding insult to injury that even the social security system has now taken to lending to the poor via the Social Fund, although the very poorest will not get these loans because of their inability to pay.[55] Other sources of help will be neither so cheap nor so scrupulous.

In households where income is relatively high, the type of credit used tends to centre around bank loans, credit cards and second mortgages; middle income groups favour hire-purchase, loans from finance houses and mail order. At the bottom of the hierarchy, credit becomes less regulated: the poor make use of vouchers and local money lenders. Since the type of credit used depends on income, it is hardly surprising that gender also plays a role: women tend to be concentrated in lower status or lower paid jobs or to be unemployed and this, together with the fewer numbers of women who own their own homes, means that credit cards and bank loans are not realistic possibilities. In any event, wealthier users of credit may be seeking to have immediate access to goods or services which are usually classed as luxuries, or at least not as essentials. Credit is needed only to spread the cost, not because of hardship. In the poorest households, which is where women are more likely to have sole responsibility for managing the family's finances, credit would far more often be required to deal with the necessities of life, whether that be clothing for children or money to pay a fuel bill or rent. Women who are working under the whole wage or allowance system are particularly likely to be budgeting week to week which adds to the problem of finding an appropriate lender and in the end there may be little choice about the source of credit.

Two typical credit sources used by the poor - and thus by women - also show how these can be the most expensive: shopping vouchers or checks and money lenders. The general idea behind shopping checks is that the debtor buys a fixed amount of credit, represented by a card or check, from which is deducted the cost of each purchase.[56] Repayment is usually collected by weekly instalments, and the interest rate can be extremely high. Parker cites one study which found that shopping checks and vouchers can attract rates of up to 200 per cent.[57] Apart from checks and vouchers, there have always been the doorstep lenders or tallymen who offer small-scale credit for clothing and other household goods, collecting repayment weekly by calling at the house. Cash can be obtained from money lenders, often operating locally and, needless to say, the rates of interest are unlikely to be favourable. There is nowadays a good deal of legislation on consumer lending, but it is ironic that those who might be thought to be most in need of protection because their need makes them so vulnerable, are the very people who may not be caught by the protective umbrella of the law. The Consumer Credit Act 1974 classifies any credit agreement for under £30 as "small" and as falling outside the requirements as to formalities dealing with the type of documentation required and the opportunity to cancel the agreement. It is true that certain aspects of these small agreements are still governed by the law (for example, the imposition of extortionate[58] credit rates) but the practical usefulness of such rules is questionable. This can be seen clearly in the area of money lending: although the Act provides that extortionate credit bargains may be challenged, this does not mean that the debtor will be willing to do so. Anyone who is desperate enough to seek out a loan from a lender with such high rates is hardly likely then to jeopardise future loans by taking legal action. As was noted above, the loans taken out by women who are attempting to manage on limited income are more likely to be for day-to-day necessities and families in trouble are reduced to borrowing to pay off earlier debts. Suing the lenders is, literally, to bite the hand that feeds. As Parker comments, "although the need for back-street abortionists has, by and large, disappeared ... the same cannot be said of the money-lender."[59]

Where need is very great women may turn to lending which is less than entirely legal, or even downright criminal as where social security benefit books are used to secure advances, a crime which implicates buyer and seller. Although borrowing does not inevitably lead to problems of indebtedness, there is little doubt that in low income households the progression is much more likely. Parker is of the view that where this happens:

> ... women are both more likely to be involved in coping with it and may also experience its effects more keenly than do men. ... This struggle may lead women to become involved in clandestine credit activity, taking out loans from legal or illegal sources unknown to their partners in an attempt to tide them over financial crises.[60]

Even in families with joint management of income it will normally fall to the woman to feed and clothe the family and in poorer families, where her responsibilities are likely to be wider than just food and clothes, it is women who must turn to credit and women who run the risk of debt. Children do not stop growing and eating just because the breadwinner has lost his job or left home, and it is the pressing need to feed and clothe children which can tip the balance into indebtedness. Poverty does not exempt a parent from the wish to buy a child something for Christmas or to give them a birthday treat, but it is the sudden need for a new pair of shoes or the seasonal expense of Christmas which can require a loan from an expensive lender. Once one repayment is missed, or a repayment is met instead of the rent or the electricity bill, the spiral into debt may have begun and it is very difficult for those already living on a minimum of expenditure to reduce it any further.

Because it is women who still carry the responsibility for *managing* the budget, it is women who are in the front line when things go wrong, even if this is because they are given insufficient by a partner or by the state. Dealing with inadequate resources can lead to even greater problems caused by expensive and short term lending. It is obviously in the interests of those who need credit if they can find it from a cheap and reliable source. Whereas the Social Fund is cheap, it is far from certain that credit would be forthcoming when the applicant needed it and for the purposes for which it was sought. In recent years, another source of non-commercial credit has arrived in the shape of credit unions. These are formed on a co-operative basis to offer members loans out of a pool of funds created by the savings of the members. As non-profit making organisations, set up by neighbours, a church or within a workplace, they can offer very low rates of interest. Although such unions would appear to meet the needs of low income families, it would seem that they are used more by middle income groups who see them as much as savings clubs as sources of credit.[61] For those who are poor there is a real problem in investing the savings that would entitle them to ask for a loan. Apart from this fundamental problem, credit unions do not seem to have made much impact in terms of people actually knowing about them, although this also applies to the existence and availability of the Social Fund and could presumably be addressed if there were both the will and the means to do so.[62]

It is a cruel paradox that those who need cheap and secure loans are precisely those who cannot get them. The poor are last in line, and it is women who make up the bulk of the queue. Few now think of credit as intrinsically wrong (though the older generation may use it less and more reluctantly) and for many it has become a way of life - simply another way of buying goods and ordering finances. To that extent access to credit is as much access to wealth as is earning a wage or owning property. Yet here again women are disadvantaged and it makes little difference that this is not a deliberate ploy by lenders. It may be unlawful to deny a bank loan to a woman because of her sex, but in order to get a loan the bank will want to see an account holder with a good credit record, a reasonably secure income which is sufficient to support the borrowing, possibly together with some asset, such as a house, on which the loan could be secured. Women are not formally excluded from any of those conditions and, undoubtedly, some will meet all of them, but many will not and fewer women than men will ever have a chance of doing so. To that extent this remains an area where women are materially disadvantaged.

The family home

Real property is the term lawyers use to refer to land, and for many people today that means the family home, which they are probably purchasing by means of a mortgage. Not everyone is buying their own home and it is also important to consider the position of tenants in rented accommodation in the public or private sector. Much of the modern law on ownership, occupation and other rights over real property is derived from what happens when marriage or cohabitation breaks down and some sharing of assets is called for. Another large area of law concerns what happens on the death of one of the partners (death rather than divorce still being the most common end to a marriage). These complex issues are dealt with in Chapter 7 whilst here the emphasis is on the continuing relationship and rights within that framework. Although for practising lawyers this has less relevance today, the questions which arise concerning ownership and occupation rights during the relationship are not without significance for those interested in what the law stands for. What the law may or may not grant to a woman who is part of a couple is of clear symbolic importance since any system which denied equality on even a formal level would be perpetuating female subordination and would be considerably out of line with the views of most couples. If the law espouses, even in theory, notions of equality, this may affect the way people choose to organise their lives and it will certainly have an impact on what happens in the event of dispute. The majority of those disputes will concern couples separating but there are occasions when it becomes crucial during the currency of a relationship to decide rights as between competing interests. This happens where a third party becomes involved, perhaps because a lender wishes to call in the loan secured on the family home or where one partner has been declared bankrupt and creditors are seeking payment.

Before tackling some of the details of the law there are some general points to bear in mind. First, as has already been noted, English law has not constructed a special set of rules for dealing with "family" property and this has been re-iterated by the judges on a number of occasions.[63] On the other hand, while the rules themselves are not different, the judges will make allowances for the relationship which exists or existed between the parties, especially when having to decide what the parties intended. To this extent marriage has been given a special status though this does not mean that partners who are married will always be treated differently from mere cohabitees. Although there are some powers of property adjustment which the courts can exercise only on divorce,[64] in other cases cohabitees may be treated as though they were married, provided the relationship had the hallmarks of marriage. Not all couples who live together should expect such treatment, nor indeed would they necessarily wish it. Some relationships are transient, with neither party expecting or giving any commitment to long term investment of an emotional or financial nature. Others, however, may last for years, produce children and involve the purchase of property but, even then, only if the judge is satisfied "that it was intended to involve the same degree of commitment as marriage will it be legitimate to regard them as no different from a married couple."[65] The second general point is that, because there is no special set of rules, many of the concepts used are derived from the traditional rules of land law and equity, some of which sit unhappily with the practicalities of modern relationships. As a result it is necessary to consider at least briefly some of the technical devices peculiar to property law, such as legal and beneficial interests and resulting and constructive trusts, but the technicalities of the law should not disguise the theme of this section which is to examine whether the law supports or hinders the access of women to interests in property.

There are today many areas of law where the traditional division of the English legal system into rules of common law and rules of equity is unimportant, but in property law the difference remains crucial. As far as English law is concerned no individual can own land as it is all, in theory, owned by the crown. The individual is thus granted a mere interest in property, that interest consisting of a bundle of rights and duties in relation to the particular piece of land. The interest is known as an "estate" which may be either freehold or leasehold, the former being of unlimited duration and the latter for a fixed term. Whilst "ownership" is thus a rather dubious term in property law, it is much easier to describe those who have the legal estate as owning the land and that is the terminology adopted here. Although these are the only two legal estates there are clearly many other ways in which rights to property may arise. A simple example is where a house is purchased with the help of a mortgage. The lender must have rights over the property if the borrower defaults on the loan and, during recent years, there has been an increased incidence of banks and building societies resorting to these rights through the repossession of mortgaged properties.[66] Another example is where each partner in a couple provides some of the purchase money for a house, but the house is for some reason placed in the sole name of the husband: the legal estate belongs to him, but the contribution to the purchase price will create an interest in the land for his wife. These rights given to someone excluded from the legal estate may either be *legal* interests (such as the mortgage)[67] or *equitable* interests (also known as beneficial interests). The classic equitable interest arises by way of a trust.

On a very basic level, a trust exists where one person (the trustee) holds property upon trust for another person (the beneficiary). The trustee has the legal estate in the property but holds it for the benefit of the beneficiary and this creates a separation between ownership and enjoyment of the property. Common law would not grant remedies to a beneficiary even if the trustee acted contrary to the beneficiary's interests, but remedies were available in equity. In relation to any property, therefore, there may be two owners: one in law and one in equity. Some trusts are expressly created while others arise from the circumstances of the case and these trusts, which are imposed by the courts, are known as implied, resulting and constructive trusts. It is in this area that property law has seen the most important developments in relation to the protection of women, whether married or cohabiting. It is crucial to note, however, that although the rules of law and equity have long been administered in the same courts there remain important differences, in particular the fact that legal rights are enforceable as of right whereas, with equitable interests, remedies are at the discretion of the court. Although judges are bound by decisions in earlier similar cases, it is more difficult to predict how a case involving an equitable interest will be decided and the judge is allowed to take into account the conduct of the party seeking the equitable remedy so that someone who has himself broken the rules may not be successful in obtaining a remedy ("he who comes to equity must come with clean hands"). The discussion which follows will attempt to avoid legal technicalities if at all possible, but it is an area of law which is highly complex and still in the process of evolution. It should be possible, however, to trace the thread of how old rules have been adapted to meet modern requirements.

For most people today, an interest in land means the family home. The occupier may be purchasing that home through a mortgage (or may have paid off the mortgage and own the property outright) or may be a public or private sector tenant: for the sake of simplicity owners and tenants will be considered separately. During the last half of the twentieth century owner occupation has gone up dramatically and between 1961 and 1992 the number of owner occupied dwellings more than doubled.[68] The trend would also seem to be towards joint ownership since the majority of couples, at least if they are married, place the property in joint names,[69] but until all property is held jointly the rights of some partners will continue to be more precarious. In order to compare the protection given by different arrangements, the approach to the law here is, first, to consider how the property might be owned and who might have interests in it, that is, whether or not there is joint ownership, and whether either party has a beneficial interest in the property. Second, the effects of such ownership and interests must be considered and whether a spouse or cohabitee may be protected against competing claims from a partner or from outsiders such as banks, building societies and creditors.[70]

Land law is beset with formalities concerning the sale and purchase of property, hence the mystique which grew up around conveyancing or the transfer of proprietary interests. Legal titles can be transferred only by the formal documents known as deeds and the transfer of equitable interests must be evidenced in writing.[71] Thus, legal ownership should be evident from the deed of conveyance and it is also open to the parties to declare the position in relation to the equitable or beneficial interests. If the property has been bought jointly and this is reflected in the conveyance, the purchasers are always treated in law as "joint tenants." In equity, however, there is an alternative and the effects are crucially different depending on whether the parties are joint tenants or tenants in common.[72] A declaration of trust may describe the parties as beneficial joint tenants which means that each has equal and identical interests in the property but, perhaps most importantly, when one joint tenant dies, his or her interest passes automatically to the other regardless of any contrary provision in the deceased's will. This rule has a number of obvious advantages for the survivor, though by the same token it can be disadvantageous for others such as the children of a previous marriage: if a father remarries and is a beneficial joint tenant with a new wife, the children from his former marriage will not benefit from his half share of the jointly owned property.[73] If, therefore, there is a conveyance showing the family home in joint names, plus a declaration of trust indicating that the parties intend to hold as beneficial joint tenants, each partner is an equal legal and equitable owner and it is irrelevant who provided what towards the purchase price. To this extent the law recognises both the intentions of the parties and the vulnerability of a financially weaker partner and steps in to effect an equal share of family property and, as will be seen, to provide a degree of protection against third parties.

A joint tenancy may be ended in ways other than by the death of one of the partners, for example by mutual agreement or where one party gives written notice within section 36 (2) of the Law of Property Act 1925 and, in such cases, each again gets an equal share of the property irrespective of contributions, but a "tenancy in common" is then created.[74] This second type of beneficial interest may also be established by an initial declaration of trust, in which case, if it also specifies the shares, then, as with a declaration as to beneficial joint tenancy, there is no problem about establishing respective shares. Tenants in common differ from joint tenants in that they have a right to a specific share which might, typically, be related to the amount contributed to the purchase price of the property. Significantly, however, when a tenant in common dies, his share does not pass automatically to the other co-owner, but instead is regarded as part of his estate (or property) which can be disposed of by will, a fact which could leave the surviving partner in a difficult position. The will may leave the share to someone other than the co-owner or, if there is no will, the rules of intestacy apply and the share will pass to the next of kin. This may not matter quite so much if the parties are married but can have drastic results if they were cohabiting. A cohabitee may find that the bulk of the value of the "family" home now belongs to her partner's family.

Ideally, where there are tenants in common there should be a statement as to their respective shares but if there is no such express indication it would be for the court to decide on the division. It would also be a matter for the court if nothing at all is said about the beneficial ownership. It might be thought that if the *legal* ownership is expressed to be in joint names, the equitable interest would, in the absence of any declaration, follow that pattern, since this would seem to recognise what the partners had intended, but it is not that simple. Admittedly, the court would look to the intention of the parties and it would be strange if joint legal owners were not to be imputed with an intention to share the beneficial interest in some way but this does not necessarily mean equal shares. The court will consider all the surrounding evidence including the situation of the parties and their contributions to the acquisition of the property. So, for example in *Bernard* v *Josephs*[75] an unmarried couple bought a house in joint names, raising the purchase money through a mortgage in joint names, but with no declaration as to the beneficial interests. When the relationship ended Ms Bernard claimed a half share in the property. The court was careful to point out that there is no presumption that parties will always take in equal shares, but, having considered all the circumstances, the court held that in this case it could be inferred that the parties intended to share the beneficial ownership equally: the property was in joint names, it was bought to provide a home for both and there had been a pooling of joint incomes. This latter point is worth noting since, of course, the way in which money is handled within the household is itself a result of a variety of factors, most of which would tend to favour the man. Interestingly, in this case pooling of income occurred in a cohabiting couple, although these are the couples who may be more likely to have separate management.

Although the rules for discovering the intention of the parties are the same for married and unmarried couples, facts may be interpreted differently in different settings: it was in this context that Griffiths LJ in the *Bernard* case commented that:

> There are many reasons why a man and a woman may decide to live together without marrying, and one of them is that each values his independence and does not wish to make the commitment of marriage; in such a case it will be misleading to make the same assumptions and draw the same inferences from their behaviour as in the case of a married couple. The judge must look most carefully at the nature of the relationship, and only if satisfied that it was intended to involve the same degree of commitment as marriage will it be legitimate to regard them as no different from a married couple.[76]

In other words, had they perhaps managed their financial affairs differently under an independent system, it might have weighed against a finding of equal shares.

If there are not to be equal shares, division is heavily influenced by contributions to the purchase price, which by and large would probably favour the male rather than the female partner. Where property is bought with cash there may be little difficulty in apportioning shares, but this would be rare, as most couples would buy the family home with the aid of a mortgage. This has caused some problems for the judges in deciding how to treat liability for mortgage payments and contributions to the deposit. In one case,[77] for example, a couple who were not married bought a house in joint names for £15,900, of which £4,150 was provided in cash by the woman, the rest being raised by joint mortgage. Both were working and pooled their wages, out of which the mortgage was paid. Only sixteen months later they split up and when the dispute over shares came to court, the house was worth £26,000. The judges took the view that the man was entitled to nothing because in the time they were together he had only contributed about £175 towards the £200 which had been paid off the mortgage. This was nothing compared to the money which she had provided and it would be "unrealistic" to decide that any part of the equitable interest should be awarded to him. This happened to benefit the female partner, but the principle at play in the decision is perhaps more likely to benefit the male. In another case concerning a man who was trying to claim an enhanced share, the judge took a rather different approach.

The woman in *Marsh* v *von Sternberg*[78] had to all intents and purposes provided a half of the purchase price (because as a sitting tenant she was entitled to a large discount on the price) and there was a mortgage in joint names. Her partner was at first granted only a very small share (4 per cent) but this was increased on appeal to a quarter share, even though he had actually paid very little in mortgage repayments. The judge took into account not what had been paid, but what were his liabilities under the mortgage agreement, which showed him as the principal debtor. At the time the mortgage was entered into the female partner was unemployed and the judge noted that she would not have got a mortgage but for her partner. On the other hand, the intention had been that they would both contribute to the mortgage (as and when she got a job) and, taking that into account, the judge finally arrived at the 75:25 per cent share. Although this decision takes more notice of what the parties had intended, rather than simply looking at the superficial position of who paid what, it also highlights a common predicament facing women who find that they cannot support, or indeed obtain, a mortgage independently. It should also be borne in mind that few couples give any thought to the *legal* ramifications of exactly who meets which debts. Just because one partner is liable for and paying the mortgage, while the other may pay for everything else is not necessarily the most sensible basis for deciding who owns what.

So far discussion has concerned a couple in respect of whom legal ownership has been expressed in joint names, and where it may or may not be clear about beneficial ownership. The position may be legally more complex where the property appears in the sole name of one of the partners. Whereas the common law deals simply with the application of established rules to a set of facts, equity is, in theory, more concerned with achieving justice between the parties and thus equitable principles play an especially large part in deciding competing interests where it appears that one partner is denied any rights in the family home. In an attempt to achieve justice and to give protection in appropriate cases to the non-owner the courts have developed - and are still developing - the devices of implied, resulting and constructive trusts. Where one party is expressed to be sole legal owner of the family home, one might assume, in the absence of an express declaration of trust, that the legal owner is also the sole beneficial owner and that indeed might be so,[79] with the result that the non-owner has no share at all in the property. An example is *Burns* v *Burns* where the couple were unmarried but had lived together for nineteen years during which she had brought up the children of the family. The house was in his sole name, he had provided the purchase price and had paid the mortgage. For most of the time she had not worked, but when later she did so, her wages were used for housekeeping, including the rates and telephone bills. Such arrangements are common amongst married and unmarried couples, as is evidenced by the research done by Pahl and others. Although Mrs Burns had not made a continuous, significant financial contribution to the family, she had provided her domestic and caring skills. It was held that her contributions did not give her any share in the house. Such a decision ignores the realities of women's lives, and leaves women like Mrs Burns at the uncertain mercy of the law.[80]

The law is, however, not entirely unsympathetic and, depending on the facts, it may be possible to reach a different conclusion and to find that the non-owner does have an equitable interest in the home, either for her sole benefit or jointly with the legal owner. Such an interest is held for her on trust and a good deal of judicial and academic thought has gone into explaining or denying the differences between implied, resulting and constructive trusts. For present purposes it is, happily, not necessary to become acquainted with the details of these debates, but simply to note that, essentially, the court is looking either for evidence from which it is possible to infer a common intention to share in the beneficial interest[81] or for evidence that one partner, having been led to believe that she would have a share in the home, behaved in a way which is to her detriment and which would not have occurred had she not believed that she had an interest in the property.[82] Such judicial "tests" indicate a willingness to consider whether or not a non-owner should have a right to a share in the home but they merely set the scene. Questions then arise as to what the *courts* will accept as being evidence of an intention to share and what sort of conduct will be recognised as creating an interest - in other words what must the woman who is not a joint legal owner contribute if she is to have any rights in the family home? Mrs Burns, for example, was not judged to have made the necessary contribution and it is clear from the cases that the judges are looking for some kind of direct financial contribution or at least something that can be translated into money terms. As one eminent judge has explained:

> When a man (it usually is a man) purchases property and his companion (married or unmarried, female or male) contributes to the purchase price,

or contributes to the payment of a mortgage, equity treats the legal owner as trustee of the property for himself and his companion in the proportions in which they contribute to the purchase price because it would be unconscionable for the legal owner to continue to assert absolute ownership unless there is some express agreement between the parties, or unless the circumstances in which the contributions were made established a gift or loan or some relationship incompatible with the creation of a trust.[83]

How far, then, will such a formulation help the financially weaker party?

The clearest way in which the non-owner can show a contribution and thus establish an interest in the home is to point to a financial contribution to its purchase. A common intention to share the beneficial interest has been recognised as stemming from payment of or a contribution to the deposit, at least where the woman is also able to contribute to household expenses so as to facilitate payment of the mortgage.[84] If the woman not only contributes to the deposit but also makes direct contributions to the mortgage instalments, the argument is even stronger and her share likely to be greater.[85] Theoretically, these rules apply equally to married and unmarried couples although some of the cases seem to suggest that it might be easier to challenge the existence of a common intention in relation to cohabitees. In *Richards* v *Dove*,[86] for instance, the couple bought a house in his sole name. The house cost £3,500 (this was 1974) and Mr Dove paid £350 by way of deposit having effectively been lent £150 by Ms Richards. A mortgage was taken out in his name and he paid household bills except those for food and gas, which she paid. It was held that she had no right to a share in the property and that a cohabitee must be able to show not only a direct contribution but also that it was made with a view to acquiring an interest in the property. In this case her payment towards the deposit was held to be only a loan and her other contributions were not sufficient.

It is always possible to challenge the existence of a common intention to share the beneficial interest by alleging that the contribution to the purchase was intended as a loan or a gift and while this is not restricted to cohabitees, it may be easier in their case to prove the money was simply a loan, given that the courts are more likely to wonder whether the couple who have chosen not to marry see their relationship as permanent and property as a joint investment. Of course, relationships develop and what begins as a loan may change its nature as the years go by and no attempt is made to secure repayment. A cohabitee lent her partner £1,700 subject to ten per cent interest in order to enable him to buy out his ex-wife's interest in the home, and later advanced a further sum to pay off part of the mortgage. In that case it was held that, in the light of the fact that no repayments had been made or sought, she was entitled to a forty per cent share in the property.[87] Contribution towards the initial purchase may take the form of cash or may appear in other guises, one example being *Marsh* v *von Sternberg*,[88] where the woman's status as sitting tenant resulted in a substantial reduction in the price of the property.

A woman may not be in a position to contribute directly or indirectly towards a deposit, but may be able to assist with mortgage repayments and, according to the cases, this may be evidence of an intention to share. From a woman's point of view it is obviously better to have been making these contributions from the outset and to have continued making them without a break, but this is not going to be the case in many families. The judges have recognised that women do have gaps in their working lives and it has been held that contributions do not have to begin immediately or continue unbroken, provided it can be shown that there was some expectation that contributions would be forthcoming when feasible. It is also possible, though not easy, to show that the common intention has changed and that an intention to share resulted from changed circumstances, for example where the woman takes over responsibility for the mortgage payments from her husband.[89] Apart from contributing to the outgoings of the family by making mortgage payments, there is one other area in which a contribution has in the past resulted in a finding that there was an intention to share and that is assistance with the other general expenses of the household. On a common sense level, this is easy to justify: if the wife is paying for fuel, food and clothing this enables her husband to devote his income to the cost of housing or, to put it another way, her income frees his for the mortgage - without her contribution the mortgage could not be supported. Recent decisions, however, have made the precise circumstances in which this will be accepted far from clear.

The view was expressed in *Gissing* that merely because one partner uses income for the benefit of the family, this is not by itself enough to show an intention to share interest in the property rather than simply sharing day to day expenses. In other words, payment of bills had to be referable to acquisition of the property. This might happen where, on moving into the property, the couple rearranged their finances so that the contribution which the husband had made towards household bills ceased because of the high mortgage payments. The Court of Appeal has held on this basis that the wife's contributions to household expenses must be substantial in order to show that this was freeing up money for the mortgage.[90] More recently in the House of Lords an even more stringent view was expressed that it is doubtful that anything other than a direct contribution to the deposit or mortgage payments will suffice to show an intention to share.[91] If this is to be the trend in the law it has important ramifications for both married and unmarried women. Quite apart from the fact that women are frequently not in a position to make a significant contribution to the mortgage (which will often be the major regular expenditure) the discussion of how couples arrange their domestic finances has shown that decisions as to who pays what are rarely taken on any seriously articulated basis, other than convenience, much less with a view to the legal position. This illustrates the artificiality of the law: the judges look for the existence of an intention to share, which should ideally arise at the moment the property is acquired or certainly during the relationship, but in fact disputes generally arise when the relationship has failed and very few couples will have given much thought to what should happen in that event. In the excitement (or stress) of buying a house, not many couples actively arrange matters so as to clarify their respective interests in property which they regard as "theirs" and not "his" or "hers."

There are other important consequences which flow from the courts' apparent insistence on substantial financial contributions to the costs of buying a house. It is considerably less likely that the judges will be willing to put an economic value on the traditional kind of contributions which women make to the home. Failure to acknowledge the non-monetary contributions of a female partner can lead to harsh results as is clearly illustrated in *Burns* v *Burns*,[92] where the woman stayed at home to bring up the children, run the house, and later used her earnings to top up the housekeeping and buy clothes and other items for the family. None of this, despite being over a period of many years, gave her a share in the property when the relationship ended. The same attitude can be seen in relation to wives, as is shown in *Lloyds Bank plc* v *Rosset*,[93] in which the wife had not only supervised building work, but had more or less acted as clerk of works, arranging for delivery of materials, planning the layout of the new rooms, advising on where plugs and radiators were to go, and had done some decorating. It was held that this was trifling compared with the money (£70,000) contributed to the purchase by the husband who also paid for the improvements and anyway, given her anxiety to have the property ready for Christmas, such efforts were "the most natural thing in the world for any wife." (Query whether in that case a cohabitee would have received a more sympathetic hearing!)[94]

Although it would appear from the cases referred to above that a common intention to share the beneficial interest must always be based on financial contributions, it is possible for a trust to arise on rather more flexible grounds. A constructive trust may be created where the common intention has arisen because the non-owner has been promised a share, and in reliance on that has acted to her detriment, though it appears that the acts must be in some way referable to the promise, even if perhaps not to the property itself.[95] A classic example of a woman gaining an interest under these somewhat more relaxed rules is *Eves* v *Eves*[96] in which a cohabitee who undertook heavy physical work on the house, including the wielding of a 14 pound sledgehammer, was held to have done so in reliance on a promise that the house would go into joint names and was awarded a quarter share. If there is no express promise to share it can be difficult to establish the necessary intention to share the beneficial interest. In *Thomas* v *Fuller-Brown*[97] the female owner of the house had provided all the purchase money and also provided her cohabitee, an unemployed builder, with free board and lodging, but he claimed a share in the house on the basis that he had contributed £15,000 worth of labour and materials in improvements. She had not asked him to do this, there was no evidence at all that she had led him to believe he would acquire an interest in the property and it was held that no intention to share could be found or imposed.

The constructive trust allows for recognition of contributions which may not be simply financial but it still requires some intention to share derived from an understanding between the parties. On the basis of a concept known as proprietary estoppel, it is argued that even if there is only conduct by the legal owner which leads the other to believe she has a share in the home, provided this is followed by reliance and detriment, the courts will take the view that it would not be fair or conscionable for the owner to deny that share and evict the partner.[98] The remedy may not always be as wide as actually granting an interest in the property under a trust (which gives a share in the proceeds of sale) but might simply amount to a right to occupy the property, say until the children are grown up. One extremely generous decision concerning cohabitees is found in *Pascoe* v *Turner*[99] where the court took it upon itself to treat the pair almost as if they were divorcing. The parties began as employer and housekeeper then lived as husband and wife until he moved out to live with another woman. He assured her, however, that the house and contents were hers and she spent a good deal of her capital on the property before he claimed it back. Although the court refused to find a constructive trust it was nevertheless decided that ownership of the property should be transferred to her in order to achieve fairness. This is not necessarily a typical decision and it is salutary to compare *Pascoe* with *Coombes* v *Smith*[100] in which a woman who became pregnant by her lover, left her husband and her job to live with him and to look after the house and child, was held not to have acted sufficiently to her detriment to establish an interest in the property. In the view of one judge referring to this case,[101] the law is not so cynical as to assume that a woman will only go to live with a man on the understanding that she will have a share in the house. Perhaps not, but since in *Coombes* she had been told that he would always look after her, it would also appear that women should not readily rely on the promises of their partners.

If all else fails, a non-owner may be able to establish a licence to remain in the property either for a specified number of years or for life. In terms of giving a mere right to occupy these are really of value only to cohabiting couples since married couples are covered by different and more stringent rules preventing eviction either on the basis of common law[102] or statute as in the Matrimonial Homes Act 1983. Recent cases dealing with licences have looked for conduct which would establish what is termed an estoppel.[103] In *Coombes*, above, the court refused to grant even a licence because there was no detriment. In *Bristol & West Building Society* v *Henning*,[104] while it was conceded that the money and effort expended could give the woman a licence to occupy the property against a claim by her lover, it did not operate as against a claim from a third party and so the building society was entitled to possession.

The courts' use of trusts, estoppel and licences makes it clear that the law is not entirely blind to the need to protect a financially weaker partner. Even if a woman does not appear as a co-owner of the property she may be granted a share, provided the court is prepared to give her the benefit of one of the devices developed to achieve that end. Once an interest is established there may still remain the problem of quantifying it and this is particularly the case where the relationship has broken down and the parties want the value of their shares, though it will also arise where there are competing interests from third parties. In such cases a whole new set of rules come into play. It must be decided what proportion each is entitled to (a half, a third, or whatever) and at what point the shares should be valued. In relation to the former, the court will look to see what the parties intended when the property was acquired and in the absence of express statement will look at all the evidence. If the property is in joint names it would suggest half shares; if not, but each has made a direct contribution to the purchase price, the proportion contributed will be a persuasive factor. Sometimes the facts are not too difficult as in *Walker* v *Hall*[105] where the couple had been living in a house which he had acquired before they got together. Their earnings were pooled to meet all expenses including the mortgage. That house was sold and the proceeds were used to buy a new home. It was decided that although she had no interest in the first house, nevertheless her contributions to that mortgage were a contribution to the price of the new house in that they had freed up money to meet the extra costs and she was awarded a quarter share. In other cases the court is forced to take a rather more flexible approach since contributions may be harder to quantify in money terms. It is also possible for the court to conclude that the intention of the parties was that, although the woman is entitled to a share, it should be quantified at a later date (for example on sale) taking into account the totals contributed by each at that point. Actual valuation of the shares will take place only when the proceeds of sale are available.[106]

The law obviously has a good deal to say about how a share in property may be established by a non-owner and how it should be quantified, and it is also clear that this is commonly an issue in divorce and separation at which point the distinction between married and unmarried couples is vital, since some powers of property adjustment are available to the courts only where the parties are or were married: these are dealt with in the next chapter. Here, however, the focus is on the rights of a co-owner where her position is threatened not (or not necessarily) by the breakdown of the relationship but by competing claims from outside it. The obvious examples of where this may arise are where a mortgage lender is seeking to take possession of the property, where a bank is calling in a loan secured on the property or where her partner has been declared bankrupt and creditors are claiming against the property. To what extent may a wife or cohabitee protect herself and her dependents against these claims?

If both partners appear as legal owners on the deeds, neither can sell or mortgage the property without the consent of the other. This appears to grant protection against husbands and cohabitees who wish, say, to take out a second mortgage in order to bolster a faltering business, or pay off debts, but the disputes which come to court tend to arise not where a woman has refused to comply with the request (those will presumably be conducted in private) but where having agreed to the proposal she now wishes to avoid the consequences of failing to meet the debt. If she has signed the deed executing a mortgage secured on the home, the general rule is that the lender may, in the event of non-payment, exercise against both partners rights of possession and sale of the property. Only in very limited circumstances will a woman who repents of her consent be allowed to escape these consequences, for example where her partner has fraudulently misled her or has pressured her into entering an agreement detrimental to her.[107] It is certainly not enough for a woman to say that she did not understand the consequences of what she was signing. On the other hand, if there has been fraud or undue influence or some other wrongful act by the main debtor (for these purposes the husband or partner) the creditor (bank or building society) will not be able to enforce the debt *unless* steps had been taken to ensure that the other partner had entered the agreement freely and with knowledge of the facts.

In a case which involved a wife acting as surety for her husband's debt, the House of Lords has held that the creditor will have taken reasonable steps if the wife or cohabitee has been warned at a separate interview of the amount of the debt, of the potential liability and of the risks involved (for example, losing the family home) and has been advised to take independent legal advice. The husband in *Barclays Bank plc* v *O'Brien*[108] had arranged an overdraft for a company in which he was a shareholder, securing the debt on the home owned jointly with his wife, thus requiring her to become a surety for his debt by signing a document giving the bank a charge on the property. The bank manager instructed that both parties should be made aware of the consequences of signing and should be advised to take independent legal advice if in any doubt, but his instructions were not followed. Both parties signed without reading the papers and when subsequently the bank tried to take possession of the house to meet the debt, the wife claimed first that she had been subject to undue influence from her husband, and second that he had lied to her in telling her that the debt was for £60,000 for three weeks (in fact it was for £135,000 and not limited to three weeks).

Interestingly, it had been argued during the case that married women and cohabitees formed a special class, because the nature of the relationship is such that influence by the husband and reliance by the wife are some of its natural features. Although this was accepted in the Court of Appeal, the House of Lords took a more robust approach, noting that a high proportion of family wealth is invested in the home and that recognition of the equality of the sexes has led to most homes now being in joint names, so that if the house is to be used as security for a debt both partners must agree. Lord Browne-Wilkinson then stated that "society's recognition of the equality of the sexes has led to a rejection of the concept that the wife is subservient to the husband in the management of the family finances," and yet in "a substantial proportion of marriages it is still the husband who has the business experience and the wife is willing to follow his advice without bringing a truly independent mind and will to bear on financial decisions."[109]

Recognition by one of England's senior judges that there is a difference between formal and substantive equality, or between appearance and reality, calls for a balance to be achieved: sympathy for the wife about to lose her home to a bank has to be weighed against the public interest in ensuring that wealth tied up in family homes is not rendered sterile by the wish to protect her interests at all costs. If banks think they are likely to be defeated by wives and partners crying foul, they are unlikely to advance money on the security of the family property. From the judges' point of view protection of the vulnerable must be weighed against continuing economic enterprise and the decision was, therefore, a compromise. Although wives who guarantee their husbands' debts should not be treated differently from others, nevertheless a creditor should take extra care when it is a wife standing surety for her husband's debts (where he has a financial interest in the business but she does not) because such a transaction is not of direct advantage to the wife and there is a risk in such cases that the husband has somehow acted wrongly in persuading his wife to comply. This is why the creditor must take steps to ensure that the consent has been properly obtained and if this is not done the debt cannot be enforced against the wife. It was further held that these considerations apply equally to cohabitees since they are based not on the marriage ceremony but on the emotional relationship between the parties, so where a woman guarantees a debt which is not to her advantage, marriage will not make a difference.

This protection recognises the reality of what goes on, financially, in many relationships but it cannot be taken too far. In another case decided at the same time, *CIBC Mortgages plc* v *Pitt*,[110] it was made clear that where a wife agrees to something which, on the face of it, is for the couple's joint benefit, she will not be allowed to escape so easily. Mrs Pitt agreed, reluctantly and after some pressure, to her husband's wish to raise a second mortgage on their jointly owned home because he wanted to invest on the stock market. The husband told the lender that he wanted the money to buy a holiday home and pay off their existing mortgage and £150,000 was advanced. The wife had signed the papers without reading them; nobody suggested she should take legal advice and she did not do so. She had no idea how much was being borrowed. Once the existing mortgage of £16,700 had been paid off the husband speculated with the rest and eventually got into difficulties. When the lender sought possession of the house the wife claimed she had been subjected to misrepresentation and undue influence. The House of Lords agreed there had been undue influence by the husband, but this did not affect the right of the lender, who was unaware of the undue influence, to call in the loan. As far as the lender was concerned the loan had been for the benefit of *both* parties and the mere fact that they were husband and wife and there was thus a risk of undue influence was not enough by itself to require the plaintiff to do any more. The wife would therefore lose her family home of more than twenty years where her children still lived. Ironically, the house was originally in the sole name of Mr Pitt, but she had objected and it was put into joint names: in the event that proved her downfall, because the advance could then be said for the benefit of both partners. It was pointed out that to hold otherwise would make it extremely difficult for lenders, since on every purchase of a house in joint names the building society or bank would have to speak separately to the wife and advise her to take independent advice. The court felt "that would not benefit the average married couple and would discourage financial institutions from making the advance."[111] Thus where a loan appears to be for the benefit of both partners the considerations which applied in *O'Brien* lose their force. This is the legal position, though whether it accords with the dynamics of many marriages is another question altogether. It is also worth noting that in *Pitt* the court did not expressly include cohabitees within the ambit of its decision, but presumably the same principles would apply to joint owners at least where the relationship had "marriage-like qualities."

In *O'Brien* and *Pitt* the partners were joint owners and this will, of course, often be the situation these days, but there are still family homes in the name of only one of the partners: can the property be sold or otherwise dealt with without the knowledge or consent of the non-owner? A party who is not a legal owner may still have an equitable interest in the property, for example because of the imposition of a trust. The property is then held on what is known as a statutory "trust for sale" which means, amongst other things, that both beneficial owners must agree to a sale;[112] that the legal owner cannot deal with the house without consulting the owner of the equitable interest; and that any rights granted to third parties over the land take effect subject to that interest unless certain formalities are complied with.[113] In particular, if a third party is to acquire the property free of the wife's right to remain in occupation, sale of that property must be undertaken by *two* legal owners.[114] So, if a husband who is the sole legal owner attempts to sell or remortgage the property without the consent of his wife who owns an equitable interest, and the buyer or lender knows or should know of that interest, the wife has a right to stay in the house and the lender cannot, for example, sell the property to meet the debt.[115] Although it is not difficult to show such knowledge in the third party (actual occupation of the home at the time will suffice)[116] this is of practical use in relation to second mortgages rather than the initial mortgage taken out at the time of the purchase. In the latter case it would be unusual to be able to establish occupation at the time the mortgage is executed so that the partner who is not the legal owner will not be able to establish a right which takes priority over the lender.[117] Furthermore, if the sole legal owner does appoint another legal owner, and the sale or mortgage is effected by the two of them, this will override the interests of the partner who has only an equitable interest, even if she is in occupation.[118] Limitations also seem to have developed in the extent to which the courts will allow equitable interests to take priority over the rights of the lender. Where there is a beneficial owner whose interest has arisen by implying a trust, it has been held that if she is aware that a mortgage is being taken out, and has also benefited from the mortgage by living in the property, then it is to be assumed that she has consented to the mortgage and so cannot avoid subsequent possession proceedings.[119] The law does therefore grant some protection to the partner who is not a legal owner but that protection is legally technical and far from watertight.

An even more technical protection is open to wives, *not* to cohabitees, by virtue of the Matrimonial Homes Act 1983. This comes into play either where the equitable interest of a wife has not been sufficient for some reason to provide protection, or where the wife has no legal or equitable interest which she can enforce against third parties. Effectively, the Act confers a right to occupy the house[120] but, if the husband is legal owner of the property, the wife's right of occupation will affect third parties *only* if she has registered it in the legally required manner[121] and since many wives will not know anything about these rules this may deny protection to those who would otherwise have benefited. It is also true that in a happy marriage a wife who does know of the protection offered may see no need to use it or may feel that it would be an unfriendly act. If a charge is registered, it gives a reasonably secure protection, though it is possible for the court to overrule the right to occupy in certain circumstances.[122] This Act does not help cohabitees without equitable interests who are forced back onto the far less reliable device of licences to occupy.[123]

A final threat to the security of wives and cohabitees is the bankruptcy of their partner: one writer has said that "If the husband goes bankrupt the wife and children simply have to cling to the wreckage" and sadly this does reflect the law.[124] When a person becomes bankrupt (that is, has insufficient assets to meet their liabilities and the creditors apply to court for a declaration of bankruptcy) all his property passes to the trustee in bankruptcy whose job is to realise what assets there are and pay off the creditors. In many cases one of the major assets will be the family home. What happens depends on how it is owned: if the wife has an equal share only half will go to the trustee (though this would still entail a sale of the home to realise his share) but if she has no share, it will all go. There is also provision in the Insolvency Act 1986 to set aside transactions within five years of the bankruptcy in which property was transferred to members of the family at an undervalue.[125] This could threaten a wife whose equitable interest in the property is based on something other than monetary contribution or where her contribution does not strictly match the value of the property. Perhaps not surprisingly, the court may also set aside transactions at an undervalue where they were entered in order to protect the property from the bankruptcy - for example, transferring property into the sole name of the wife simply to remove it from the bankrupt's assets.[126] Specifically in relation to the family home, the Insolvency Act gives little more than a breathing space: if the wife has a right to occupy, (even though not a joint owner) the trustee must apply to the court to terminate that right and the court must make an order which is just and reasonable having regard to the interests of the creditors, the needs and resources of the wife, the needs of any children, the conduct of the wife in so far as it might have contributed to the bankruptcy and all the circumstances of the case - though *not* the needs of the bankrupt.[127] This may sound as though the court has the discretion to protect the home from the creditors but it is most unlikely that any possession of the house by the trustee in bankruptcy will be delayed very long and certainly not longer than twelve months, unless there are exceptional circumstances. These must be something more than having to move down market or change schools or any of the other usual consequences of debt. Although the statutory rules apply only to wives and not to cohabitees, the common law is applicable to cohabitees and applies similar rules.[128] The end result is that when a man is declared bankrupt his family will almost invariably suffer with him to the extent of losing their home and there is little that women can do to protect themselves.

The intricacies of the laws relating to owner-occupiers are of no relevance to the many families living in rented property.[129] For tenants, as for owner-occupiers, however, the position will differ according to whether the tenancy is held jointly or in one name,[130] and one very important general rule is that joint tenants are liable for rent both jointly and individually, so that if one tenant stops paying the rent, the landlord can expect the other to pay the whole amount, regardless of what might have been the arrangement within the household. Specific rules will depend on whether tenants are in private or public sector accommodation and when the tenancy was taken out. To some extent the problems which a wife or cohabitee may encounter in rented homes occur, as with owner-occupiers, on family breakdown or the death of a partner. Tenants will not have the problems of second mortgages or raising loans on the security of the property, but issues that might arise during a relationship include the sole or co-tenant who ceases to pay rent or who for some reason gives notice to quit against the wishes of his partner. The Matrimonial Homes Act 1983 which confers a right to occupy the matrimonial home does not depend on whether that home is owned or rented (or whether rented accommodation is public or private sector) but it covers only married couples. The Act may assist wives who are in rented accommodation in a number of ways, provided that it is the matrimonial home and provided there has been no divorce (after which the Act ceases to apply). First, under section 1(5) if a wife is entitled to occupy the property under the Act, any payment of rent by the wife is treated as if it were made by the husband - in other words if the husband stops paying the rent she may simply take his place and carry on with it. This also means that if action for possession is begun she may ask for a delay and undertake to pay the rent and clear the arrears.[131]   Second, if the husband is the sole tenant and gives notice to quit, the wife may remain in occupation and prolong the tenancy. Finally, if the marriage does break down there are provisions in the Act for transferring the tenancy from one party to another.

In the case of cohabitees who are unable to take advantage of the 1983 Act, the provisions are found in the housing legislation, with different Acts applying to public and private sectors. A new regime was introduced for the private sector in the Housing Act 1988, under which tenancies granted after 15 January 1989 are assured tenancies. If cohabitees are joint tenants each has the right to occupy the property and is protected against eviction by the partner (unless by court order). If one joint tenant leaves the property, the position depends on the type of assured tenancy. A fixed term tenancy cannot be brought to an end by one tenant unless the other agrees, but if a fixed term tenancy expires without renewal, it is replaced by something called a statutory periodic tenancy, which may be ended by a notice to quit by only one of the joint tenants, thus ending the right of occupation enjoyed by the other tenant. If the tenancy is in the name of one tenant and he leaves, the occupying partner has little or no protection: the tenancy ceases to be assured and no statutory periodic tenancy comes into force when a fixed term tenancy ends. A cohabitee cannot protect herself by continuing to pay the rent: unlike a wife under the 1983 Act she cannot simply step into the shoes of the tenant.[132]

The law governing the public sector is contained in the Housing Act 1985 which provides for secure tenancies. Where cohabitees are joint tenants, each has equal rights of occupation and protection against eviction by a partner. The right to occupation continues even if one joint tenant leaves but if that partner then gives notice to quit to the local authority, the tenancy will come to an end. If the tenancy is in the sole name of the tenant who leaves, the tenancy will again cease. In both cases the local authority could seek possession against the tenant left behind in occupation, though a deserted cohabitee would be able to apply for a secured tenancy in her sole name. Where a tenant is declared bankrupt it is provided in the Housing Act 1988 that neither assured nor secured tenancies are included in the bankrupt's estate so that the bankrupt is still entitled to occupy the house as the tenant.[133]

This is a necessarily simplified account of how the law regards family property but it should indicate that this area provides a clear example of the traditional reluctance of legislators to intervene in what has been regarded as the private sphere of the home. Where the family unit is functioning normally, and there is no pressure from third parties threatening to upset the status quo, the law is marked by its absence. There is no legal provision for the sharing of resources, whether they are in the form of earned income, social security benefits or bricks and mortar. Only when a problem surfaces in the shape of difficulties within the relationship or financial pressures from outside does the law seek to intervene. It then does so in ways which may pay lip service to the idea of discovering the intentions of the partners, but which in fact may take little note of the actual circumstances of most lives. Because the law is silent on the sharing of wealth within the family, it encourages the failure of most couples expressly to address the issues. Naturally, it would take more than a few legal rules to change the attitudes which underlie the tacit ordering of most family finances, not least the attachment of many men to the breadwinner image and the complicity of many women in maintaining this. Nevertheless, law is an indication of what society believes to be right and to be just. Women may not have achieved equal pay, for example, despite the existence of the Equal Pay Act but at least women know that the law supports them in their legitimate expectation of a wage based on worth rather than sex and the legislation may be used as a bargaining agent. Law is valuable not only in shaping actual behaviour but in raising both consciousness and expectations. The laws which currently govern property rights within the family rest too much on the extent to which male, middle class judges are prepared to recognise the realities of women's lives and not sufficiently on a properly articulated principle of equality.

Notes

1. See Chap. 2.
2. Studies have suggested that between a quarter and a third of lone mothers feel better off alone than they did married because of this element of sole control: Pahl, J. (1985), *Private Violence and Public Policy: The needs of battered women and the response of the public services*; Bradshaw, J. and Millar, J. (1991), *Lone Parent Families in the UK*.
3. See p. 250 et seq.
4. Some of the particular problems facing lone parents are covered in Chaps. 3 and 4.
5. (1994) *Social Trends 24*, Table 2.11. Divorces doubled, ibid.
6. Ibid., Table 2.21.
7. See p. 259.
8. See especially O'Donovan, K. (1985), *Sexual Divisions in Law*.
9. Ibid., p. 107.
10. See Mill, J.S. (1859), *On Liberty*.
11. See pp. 22-29.
12. See also Chap. 7.
13. There have been suggestions that pre-nuptial agreements should be enforceable: (1991)

Maintenance and capital provision on divorce, The Law Society.

14.   Some common law jurisdictions, including Ontario and California, have adopted a sympathetic approach to cohabitation agreements, at least to the extent that they are not automatically void as being contrary to public policy.

15.   See pp. 22-29.

16.   Research in the USA suggested that community property does not necessarily work to the benefit of divorcing wives. Women have been shown to suffer a steep decline in standard of living, in direct contrast to ex-husbands: Weitzman, L. (1985), *The Divorce Revolution*.

17.   For example the extent to which spouses are free to deal with property during marriage and the extent to which couples are allowed to opt out of any scheme. See Glendon, M.A. (1989), *The Transformation of Family Law: State, Law and Family in the United States and Western Europe*.

18.   See Freedman, J., et al. (1988), *Property and Marriage: An integrated approach*.

19.   Property owned before marriage or cohabitation remains the property of the individual. Where there is a gift to the couple ownership depends on the intention of the donor so that it might belong to one or both.

20.   *Hoddinott v Hoddinott* [1949] 2 KB 406 where the point was made that the rule gave no recognition to the skills of management required in creating a surplus.

21.   *Paul v Constance* [1977] 1 All ER 195 (clear statement as to shares); also *Re Densham* [1975] 1 WLR 1519.

22.   See e.g. de Cruz, S. (1985) 135 New Law Journal 797, commenting on the Law Commission's Working Paper No. 90, *Transfer of Money between Spouses - the Married Women's Property Act 1964*.

23.   Assuming a marriage-like relationship: *Bernard v Josephs* [1983] FLR 178.

24.   [1951] Ch 572, at p. 575.

25.   As in *Jones v Maynard*, ibid.

26.   Compare *Heseltine v Heseltine* [1971] 1 All ER 952, where the money was held to belong entirely to the wealthy wife.

27.   Compare *Heseltine v Heseltine* above and *Re Figgis* [1969] 1 Ch 123.

28.   Summary Jurisdiction (Separation and Maintenance) Act 1925.

29.   In any event, the right by one partner to seek maintenance from the other has been overtaken by the growing significance of the presence of dependent children and this applies irrespective of status. See Chap. 7.

30.   Duckworth, P. (1991), *Matrimonial Property and Finance*.

31.   Pahl, J. (1980), 'Patterns of money management within marriage', 9 *Journal of Social Policy*, 313; (1983), 'The allocation of money and the structuring of inequality within marriage', 31 *Sociological Review*, 237; (1988), 'Earning, Sharing, Spending: Married Couples and Their Money', in Walker R. and Parker, G. (eds), *Money Matters*; (1989), *Money and Marriage*. Also: Land, H. (1983), 'Poverty and Gender: the Distribution of Resources within the Family' in Brown, M. (ed.), *The Structure of Disadvantage*; Morris, L. and Ruane, S. (1986), *Household Finance Management and Labour Market Behaviour*; Morris, L. (1990), *The*

Workings of the Household.

32.   Pahl, op. cit., n. 2.

33.   Morris, L. (1984), 'Redundancy and patterns of household finance,' 18 *Sociological Review*, 492.

34.   (1989), *Money and Marriage*, p. 4.

35.   Pahl, J. (1983), 'The allocation of money and the structuring of inequality within marriage', 31 *Sociological Review*, 237.

36.   See for example the discussion of the effects of male and female unemployment in Morris (1990), op.cit., n. 31.

37.   One study found that in a whole wage structure, 86 per cent of the fuel bills were paid by wives, as compared to 68 per cent of fuel bills being paid by the husband in an allowance system: Gray, A. (1979), 'The Working Class Family as an Economic Unit', in Harris, C. (ed.), *The Sociology of the Family.*

38.   Blood, R.O. and Wolfe, D.M. (1960), *Husbands and Wives*, quoted in Morris (1990), *The Workings of the Household*, p. 111.

39.   Or a variant, where each contributes something to a joint pool, but keeps the rest separate.

40.   Pahl (1989), op. cit, n. 31, at p. 75, citing from Katharine Whitehorn in *The Observer.*

41.   Jowell, R. et al. in *British Social Attitudes: 1987 Report*, 6th Report, cited in Pahl (1989), op. cit., n. 31.

42.   Pahl (1989), op. cit., n. 31, Chap. 6.

43.   Martin, J. and Roberts C. (1984), *Women and Employment: a Lifetime Perspective.*

44.   See Chaps. 4 and 5. Note also proposals in relation to jobseeker's allowance and amendments to child support provision which seek to ameliorate this problem.

45.   McLaughlin, E. et al. (1989), *Work and Welfare Benefits.*

46.   Ibid., p. 67.

47.   Pahl (1989), op. cit., n. 31, p. 129.

48.   Ibid., p. 128.

49.   See Graham, H. (1992), 'Budgeting for health: Mothers in low-income households' in Glendinning, C. and Millar, J. (eds), *Women and Poverty in Britain: the 1990s.* Also, Alcock, P. (1993), *Understanding Poverty*, Chap. 8.

50.   See Chart 6.1, (1993) *Social Trends 23*, though there was a fall-off in the increase after 1989.

51.   Ibid., Chart 6.13.

52.   But compare Kempson et al. (1994), *Hard Times: How poor families make ends meet*, in which a number of low income families were found to use up-market credit. This was found to correlate to having a full-time wage earner in the family, or where there had been one when the commitments were entered into.

53.   Parker, G. (1988), 'Credit' and 'Indebtedness' in Walker, R. and Parker, G. (eds), *Money Matters: Income Wealth and Financial Welfare.*

54.   Parker, G. (1992), 'Making ends meet: Women, credit and debt', in Glendinning, C. and Millar, J., *Women and Poverty in Britain: the 1990s.*

55.   See p. 122.

56.   See Parker, G. (1988), op.cit., n. 53.

57.   Parker, G. (1992), op.cit., n. 54, citing Ford, J. (1991), *Consuming Credit: Debt and poverty in the UK.*

58.   See Consumer Credit Act 1974, ss. 137 and 138. Credit is extortionate if the payments are grossly exorbitant or if it grossly contravenes ordinary principles of fair dealing. The court may take into account the pressure which the debtor was under when the loan was taken out.

59.   See Parker, G. (1988), op. cit., n. 53, at p. 191.

60.   Parker, G. (1992), op. cit., n. 54, at p. 234.

61.   Kempson et al. (1994), op. cit., n. 52, Chap. 17.

62.   Ibid.

63.   See for example *Pettit v Pettit* [1970] AC 777; *Gissing v Gissing* [1971] AC 886.

64.   See Chap. 7.

65.   *Bernard v Josephs* [1983] FLR 178, 186, per Griffiths LJ.

66.   In 1991 over 75,000 properties were repossessed: (1993) *Social Trends 23*, Table 8.19. The numbers have since decreased and in 1993 about 32,000 were repossessed: (1994) *Social Trends 24*, Table 8.20.

67.   Law of Property Act 1925, s. 1(2) gives an exhaustive list of legal interests and charges over land.

68.   (1994) *Social Trends* 24, Chart 8.2.

69.   Todd, J. and Jones, L. (1972), *Matrimonial Property*.

70.   Division of property on the ending of a relationship is considered in Chap. 7.

71.   Law of Property Act 1925, ss. 52 and 53(1).

72.   Joint owners of the legal estate are always legal joint tenants (there are no longer common tenancies at law) who hold the property on what is known as a trust for sale for themselves as beneficiaries, see Law of Property Act 1925, ss. 34-36 and below.

73.   This would be subject to Inheritance (Provision for Family and Dependants) Act 1975, and see p. 252.

74.   *Goodman v Gallant* [1986] 1 FLR 513

75.   [1982] Ch 391, [1983] FLR 178. Since many disputes about property arise only when a relationship ends, some of these cases are relevant also to Chap. 7.

76.   Ibid., p. 402 and p. 186.

77.   *Young v Young* [1984] FLR 375.

78.   [1986] 1 FLR 526.

79.   *Burns v Burns* [1984] Ch 317.

80.   When a married couple separates, legislation such as the Matrimonial Causes Act 1973 gives the court wider powers of property adjustment and greater flexibility as to the type of contribution that can be taken into account: Chap. 7, pp. 224-241.

81.   A mere agreement to share is not by itself enough to give rise to these trusts: *Midland Bank v Dobson* [1986] 1 FLR 171.

82.   The modern law stems from two House of Lords decisions, *Pettitt v Pettitt* [1970] AC 777 and *Gissing v Gissing* [1971] AC 886. Subsequently, some decisions were less than

orthodox in applying the principles but, more recently, the courts have signalled a return to a stricter approach: see e.g. *Burns v Burns*, n. 79, and in particular the House of Lords in *Lloyds Bank plc v Rosset* [1991] 1 AC 107.

83.   *Winkworth v Edward Baron Development Co Ltd* [1987] 1 All ER 114, 118, per Lord Templeman.

84.   *Gissing*, n. 82.

85.   *Gissing*, n. 82, *Burns*, n. 79.

86.   [1974] 1 All ER 888.

87.   *Risch v McFee* [1991] 1 FLR 105.

88.   [1986] 1 FLR 526.

89.   *Gissing*, n. 82.

90.   *Burns v Burns* [1984] Ch 317.

91.   *Lloyds Bank plc v Rosset* [1991] 1 AC 107.

92.   [1984] Ch 317.

93.   Ibid.

94.   There are special rules relating to improvements carried out by a husband or wife under which a substantial contribution will grant a share or enlarged share: Matrimonial Proceedings and Property Act 1970, s. 37. This does not apply to cohabitees.

95.   *Grant v Edwards* [1986] Ch 638.

96.   [1975] 3 All ER 768 and see *Grant v Edwards* [1986] Ch 638.

97.   [1988] 1 FLR 237.

98.   Hayton, D. (1990), 'The equitable rights of cohabitees', *The Conveyancer*, 370.

99.   [1979] 1WLR 431. Compare *Greasley v Cooke* [1980] 1 WLR 1306.

100.   [1986] 1 WLR 808.

101.   *Grant v Edwards* [1986] Ch 638, 648, per Nourse LJ.

102.   *National Provincial Bank v Ainsworth* [1965] AC 1175.

103.   This may be very loosely defined as a legal device which prevents (estops) someone from going back on what has been represented as the true position. Estoppels come in various forms with different requirements.

104.   [1985] 2 All ER 606.

105.   [1984] FLR 126.

106.   *Turton v Turton* [1987] 3 WLR 622.

107.   *Kings North Trust Ltd v Bell* [1986] 1 WLR 119 (fraud); *National Westminster Bank plc v Morgan* [1985] AC 686 (undue influence not established).

108.   [1993] 4 All ER 417.

109.   Ibid., p. 422.

110.   [1993] 4 All ER 433.

111.   Ibid., p. 441.

112.   Law of Property Act 1925, s. 26(3). If there is no agreement, a court order must be sought: ibid., s. 30. See also *Bull v Bull* [1955] 1 QB 234.

113.   Law of Property Act 1925, ss. 34-36, 26(3).

114.   Ibid., s. 2(2) and s. 27(2).

115.   *Williams and Glyns Bank Ltd v Boland* [1981] AC 487.

116.   Land Registration Act 1925, s. 70(1)(g).

117.   *Abbey National Building Society v Cann* [1991] 1 AC 56.

118.   *City of London Building Society v Flegg* [1988] AC 54.

119.   *Bristol and West Building Society v Henning* [1985] 2 All ER 606.

120.   A right which also applies against the other spouse: see Chap. 7.

121.   Matrimonial Homes Act 1983, s. 2 and Land Charges Act 1972, s. 2.

122.   See e.g. *Kaur v Gill* [1988] 2 All ER 288.

123.   See above and *Bristol & West Building Society v Henning*, n. 119.

124.   Duckworth, P. (1991), *Matrimonial Property and Finance*, p. 99.

125.   Insolvency Act 1986, s. 339. Or two years if shown that at the time there were assets sufficient to meet liabilities: s. 341.

126.   Ibid., s. 423.

127.   Ibid., s. 336.

128.   *Re Citro* [1990] 3 WLR 880. If the female cohabitee has an interest in the property a sale must be applied for under Law of Property Act 1925, s. 30.

129.   The laws governing rented accommodation are contained in statute and are complex: Housing Act 1985 and Housing Act 1988.

130.   If there is doubt as to whether it is a joint tenancy or not, the court will look for evidence which indicates the intentions of the parties.

131.   The same principles apply to owner-occupiers and mortgage payments.

132.   The law is more generous in relation to the succession of tenancies on death.

133.   Housing Act 1988, s. 117.

7   Ending Relationships

Previous chapters have explored the reasons why economic self sufficiency is such an elusive goal for so many women. Any attempt to achieve a degree of financial autonomy is made more difficult by unequal pay, working practices which conflict with domestic responsibilities and a social security system which, when it recognises women as individuals, provides minimal benefits which discourage efforts to increase the income entering the home. Marriage or cohabitation is one way in which the economic prospects of women can be enhanced since, in theory at least, it gives a woman access to another income. In practice, however, research shows that the way a couple share their income often tends to favour the male partner,[1] and the very fact that the second income is so important to women underlines their inequality and their dependency. Relying on another individual for financial security not only deprives women of power over their lives, it is also precarious. If, for whatever reason, a woman gives up work or accepts part-time employment, the presence of a working partner cushions the immediate financial impact, but she is then dependent on her partner's continued presence and goodwill. Without a partner, many women would struggle to maintain their usual standard of living and some would discover that even financial survival was a problem. If, therefore, a woman loses her partner, either by accident or design, the financial consequences of that "loss" are far-reaching.

Relationships end through death, divorce or separation and this chapter examines how the financial consequences are dealt with by the law and in particular by the courts. Divorce in particular has far-reaching financial consequences not only for the couple who are directly involved but for any future partner or family. A man who is supporting a wife and children from an earlier marriage will have less income to make available to a second family. When he dies, questions may arise over who can claim a share in his estate, and who will be entitled to his occupational pension. As increasing numbers of women cohabit rather than marry, there are further questions of whether cohabitation avoids difficulties or merely creates fresh problems. It is to the law that individuals look for a solution to these complex social issues and there they find that the legal solutions are often inspired by unspoken beliefs and fears about the social changes that have given rise to their particular situation.

Divorce

Statistics clearly show that the number of marriages that end in divorce is increasingly steadily. In 1990, for example, there were 192,000 petitions for divorce in England and Wales as compared with 170,000 in 1981 and 111,000 in 1971.[2] The bleak statistic is that one in every three marriages in the United Kingdom is expected to end in divorce[3] and the trend is reflected throughout the member states of the European Union with the exception of Ireland where the law does not permit divorce.[4] Some commentators attribute the seemingly inexorable rise in the number of divorces to the particular vulnerability of certain types of marriage, for example where the bride is under twenty or where one partner has previously been married.[5] The figures may also indicate a growing tendency, particularly on the part of women - who instigate by far the greater number of divorce petitions - to refuse to tolerate unsatisfactory marriages. Instead of feeling that they must remain married for the sake of respectability or the children, or because they consider that they have no alternative, women are now able to contemplate ending a marriage. The law has responded to that pressure by making divorce easier and simpler.

Financial settlements after divorce - the issues Although when a marriage is dissolved the legal ties between a couple are severed, there remains the question of whether the financial ties between the couple should also come to an end. During a marriage a couple's financial assets fall into three general categories. First, there is tangible property such as the couple's house, car, any jewellery, antiques and general household goods, for example, a washing machine or a hi-fi system. Second, there is the couple's income which can include the income from paid employment as well as investment income from assets such as stocks and shares or the interest on a building society account.   Third, there are the couple's "expectations." This term denotes income or property that a couple might have expected to enjoy at some future date had their marriage not failed. It could include a pension, the benefit from an insurance policy, the equity that might have been released when the matrimonial home was sold, inheritances from parents or other relatives, and money from the realisation of assets such as stocks and shares.

Obviously, there are some married couples whose resources are very meagre indeed and amount to little more than the right to claim social security benefits. There are, however, very few couples who have no resources whatsoever.

Whilst a marriage is in being both parties may expect to benefit from any assets even though they are "owned" by only one of the parties. When an insurance policy matures, for example, the money it produces may be used to finance the purchase of a new car or a holiday which both parties to the marriage can enjoy. Of course, as research into family income has shown, there are a variety of ways in which a couple can arrange their financial affairs[6] and this can include how they choose to spend their own money. The partner who has paid the insurance policy premiums or has bought the winning premium bond may feel that he or she has a better right to decide how that money should be spent and the benefit to the other partner may be minimal or non-existent. Such decisions are not regulated by the law: what goes in inside the home is regarded as private. Nevertheless, though the law is content to allow a married couple to share their assets as they think fit during the currency of a marriage, this is certainly not the case when a marriage ends in divorce. It then becomes necessary to decide how property should be divided.

Perhaps the most obvious solution would seem to be an equal division between the parties of all their assets, with the intention that this should be a once and for all settlement. This approach appears attractive because it is straightforward but its simplicity is deceptive, as it does not take account of what might be the very different needs of the parties. If there are children, the party who assumes the task of caring for them, usually their mother, may have greater calls on her financial resources than the other partner. Nor does an equal and final division of available assets take account of the fact that one of the parties to the marriage might have worked full-time whilst the other forfeited career prospects in order to care for children or to further a partner's career. The former has a half share and a job bringing in an income; the latter has a half share, which may or may not be sufficient to buy a home, and no income with which to convince a bank or other lender that a mortgage could be repaid or a landlord that rent will be regularly forthcoming. Job prospects will have been damaged by time spent out of the labour market and dependent children could hamper the chance of finding full-time employment. Additionally, a very simple division of assets might well be confined to assets to which the couple have access at the time and exclude those assets classed as "expectations" which can often represent substantial sums.

Perhaps most importantly, a final sharing out of property may well suggest that once a marriage ends, so too should any duty on the part of one party to support the other. In an age of supposed equality there is something superficially attractive and logical in the idea that the parties should be expected to support themselves. It seems illogical that after divorce one partner should be able to look to the other for continuing support. There are, however, a number of factors which undermine this argument. Marriage undoubtedly tends to have an adverse effect on a woman's earning capacity, and when her marriage ends that effect does not suddenly disappear. Employment and training opportunities that have been lost in the course of a marriage remain lost. Where there are children, the partner with whom those children reside, in most cases the woman, will continue to feel the impact of her caring responsibilities on her ability to support herself and her children long after the marriage has come to an end. It is arguable, therefore, that the financially more secure partner should contribute to maintaining his or her children and, additionally, should either help meet the costs of child care to enable the ex-spouse to go out to work, or compensate her or him for staying home to care for the children: if a wife continues to care for a couple's children after the marriage has been dissolved, she should be "paid" for performing that task.

There are also problems, however, with an argument in favour of continued support, quite apart from its obvious tendency to reinforce notions of dependency. In particular, it maintains links between a couple when that may be the last thing either of them want. If a marriage has broken down because of a history of violence or abuse, or one party's unacceptable behaviour toward the other, it is understandable if an ex-spouse wishes to sever all contact. Financial support after divorce also explicitly rewards a woman for caring for her children or her family. Whilst some would doubtless see this as quite proper, others would object to it, arguing that such care should attract no payment on the basis that the notion of the family rests on concepts such as mother love, self-sacrifice and the respective roles of husband and wife, and these would be generally undermined if ex-wives were to be paid for performing these tasks. Perhaps more pertinently, it would also distinguish sharply between continuing relationships, where there is no financial recognition of this role, and those marriages which break down. There is a further, practical, reason why the notion of a continuing obligation to support may be problematic. Many people simply do not possess the resources to continue to support an ex-partner and children. After divorce it is quite common for a man or woman to remarry, although the rates for divorced men remarrying seem to be higher than those for divorced women.[7] A man may find that he is supporting a second wife, family and home, leaving him unable or unwilling to continue with any financial support for his first wife and family. A second wife who has paid employment may feel resentful that her earnings are being used in order to "subsidise" another woman and remove from her the obligation to work. Her resentment would be exacerbated if she were herself a divorcee, since it has been assumed that, where a *woman* remarries, she should no longer expect to receive any support from her ex-husband even though she continues to feel the effects of that first marriage on her ability to obtain paid employment and continues to care for the children from that first marriage. By remarrying she is seen to have become another man's responsibility.

If financial support does not come from an ex-partner, it seems inevitable that it will be the state which must take on the obligation in the form of social security benefits paid to the partner who is unable to survive independently. It is far from unusual to find women whose marriages have ended relying on state benefits.[8] This may be because a woman who is awarded care of the children of the marriage is unable to earn enough to support herself and her children, or it may arise where a woman has reached retirement age and has access only to a state retirement pension. This raises the important and contentious question of whether individuals should be allowed to abandon responsibility for their families and expect the state to take over. The debate takes on a moral dimension when feckless fathers and lone mothers find themselves condemned for causing a variety of social ills from vandalism to housing crises. Yet, whatever the rights and wrongs of what is effectively the state subsidising divorce[9] the availability of means-tested benefits and in particular income support and family credit has had a significant impact on the financial arrangements that accompany divorce. The willingness of the state to meet housing costs including mortgage repayments[10] may influence how a couple choose to settle their affairs. A wife may have foregone maintenance payments in return for her ex-husband's share in the matrimonial home in the knowledge that she could rely on means-tested benefits to meet everyday expenses and the cost of any mortgage repayments.

It is tempting to view this kind of arrangement in a purely negative way, and it is true that in one sense it could be said to facilitate men's escape from marriage financially unscathed by forcing the state to assume financial responsibility for ex-partners and children. From a woman's point of view, all she has done is to exchange dependency on her husband for dependency on the state. In so doing she risks being branded as "welfare dependent" and her standard of living is likely to be barely above subsistence level if she is forced to rely exclusively on social security benefits. Unfortunately, a woman may have little choice if the courts are unwilling to award her a realistic share of the couple's resources, which in any event are often limited and are represented in the main by an ex-husband's income from full-time employment. On the other hand, the state's willingness to provide financial support for a divorced woman has the potential to allow her to achieve financial independence if only it were to be employed constructively.

Independence would be encouraged by the state providing an infrastructure of support designed to help both partners, but which in practice would be of particular help to women. If this included, for example, child care and training facilities and generous short term benefits, it would cushion the immediate impact of the loss of a spouse's earnings and allow the ex-partner to place her life on a more secure financial basis. In particular, the aim would be to encourage full-time employment. There would, therefore, be no attempt in the short term to cut benefits pound for pound, to take account of earned income. In this way the state could assist a woman to be become self-supporting rather than helping to trap her into long-term reliance on benefits. According to Maclean, such initiatives have been adopted in France with the consequence that lone mothers there are much more likely to work and work full-time.[11]   There are clear alternatives to lone parents relying on state support but, in the United Kingdom, while the benefit culture is denounced, individuals, and in particular lone mothers, are forced into dependency by the social security system.

Financial settlements after divorce: the practice   Division of assets after divorce could be governed by any one of several principles, although according to some commentators, it is difficult to discern exactly what principle is represented by the English laws which regulate financial settlements:[12]

> ... the court has extremely wide powers over the parties' present capital and future income, and ... those powers are exercised in accordance with a sophisticated legislative prescription. But this is not sufficient in itself to enable us to understand the fundamental character of the regime governing ancillary relief. Perhaps the most striking feature of this legislation is the extent of the discretion which since 1970 has been conferred on the courts; indeed, this is so wide that it may be questioned whether it embodies any principle other than a general requirement to achieve a just solution.[13]

On this view the financial settlement imposed on a divorcing couple does not have to take account of their needs or attempt to share their assets equitably between them. Since the overriding principle is judicial discretion, the settlement may rather represent the perceptions among the judiciary of what are appropriate financial arrangements.

The modern watershed in divorce legislation was the Divorce Reform Act 1969 which aimed to eliminate fault from the decision to dissolve a marriage and rest it instead on the irretrievable breakdown of the relationship.[14] Judged simply on its success in removing the notion of fault the 1969 Act has not been a success. Concepts used within the legislation, such as adultery and unreasonable behaviour, still invite one party to "blame" the other for the breakdown of the marriage. On the other hand, by making irretrievable breakdown a central feature in determining whether to dissolve a marriage, the legislation shifted attention from whether there was evidence of some concrete "offence," such as cruelty, to the parties' belief that their marriage is no longer workable. The probably inevitable consequence is that more and more marriages will, and indeed do, end in divorce.

Looking at these reforms from a woman's perspective, it is tempting to argue that they have empowered women, and certainly a woman is more likely to petition for divorce than a man. This may have some connection with the fact that, as a legal and a social concept, marriage has largely failed to shake off the old notion of dominant husband and subordinate wife. The traditional stereotype is reflected in the philosophy behind much social security law, and the continuing failure to secure equality for women in paid employment or to reward women adequately for caring responsibilities ensures that the majority of marriages are unequal financial partnerships. Whereas in a happy relationship this is a price some would consider worth paying, if indeed they consider it at all, when a marriage fails women may no longer be prepared to tolerate a situation in which their dependence is emphasised.

The continued assumption about a wife's dependency within marriage, begs the question as to whether that is reflected in the financial arrangements made when the relationship is dissolved. When the grounds for divorce were reformed, the laws dealing with how the couple's assets should then be distributed between them were also updated in the Matrimonial and Family Proceedings Act 1970. This was in its turn repealed and the current law is to be found in the Matrimonial Causes Act 1973 and the Matrimonial and Family Proceedings Act 1984. Sections 23, 24, 24A, 25 and 25A of the Matrimonial Causes Act 1973 give the courts the power to order financial relief after divorce. Sections 23, 24 and 24A specify the kinds of order that can be made. For example, section 23 allows the court to order one party to make either periodical payments or a lump sum payment to their ex-partner, or to a specified individual, for the benefit of any children of the marriage. It is, however, sections 25 and 25A which specify the considerations which the courts are to take into account in determining what order to make and for what amount. Since sections 25 and 25A have a crucial part to play in determining the character of the financial settlement a woman might expect when her marriage is dissolved, it is helpful to set them out in full.[15]

Section 25

(1) It shall be the duty of the court in deciding whether to exercise its powers under sections 23, 24 and 24A above and, if so, in what manner, to have regard to all the circumstances of the case, first consideration being given to the welfare while a minor of any child of the family who has not attained the age of eighteen.

(2) As regards the exercise of the powers of the court under sections 23(1)(a), (b) or (c), 24 or 24A above in relation to a party to the marriage, the court shall in particular have regard to the following matters:

(a) the income, earning capacity, property and other financial resources which each of the parties to the marriage has or is likely to have in the foreseeable future, including in the case of earning capacity any increase in that capacity which it would in the opinion of the court be reasonable to expect a party to the marriage to take steps to acquire;

(b) the financial needs, obligations and responsibilities which each of the

parties to the marriage has or is likely to have in the foreseeable future;
(c) the standard of living enjoyed by the family before the breakdown of the marriage;
(d) the age of each party to the marriage and the duration of the marriage;
(e) any physical or mental disability of either of the parties to the marriage;
(f) the contributions made by each of the parties to the welfare of the family, including any contribution made by looking after the home or caring for the family;
(g) the conduct of each of the parties, if that conduct is such that it would in the opinion of the court be inequitable to disregard it;
(h) in the case of proceedings for divorce or nullity of marriage, the value to each of the parties to the marriage of any benefit (for example, a pension) which, by reason of the dissolution or annulment of the marriage, that party will lose the chance of acquiring.

Section 25A, which was a later amendment to the 1973 Act, directs the court's attention to one specific issue, namely, whether any financial settlement between the parties should terminate, either immediately or after a prescribed period has elapsed, the obligations between the parties, thus ensuring a "clean break."

Section 25A

(1) Where on or after the grant of a decree of divorce or nullity of marriage the court decides to exercise its powers under sections 23(1)(a), (b) or (c), 24 or 24A above in favour of a party to the marriage, it shall be the duty of the court to consider whether it would be appropriate so to exercise those powers that the financial obligations of each party towards the other will be terminated as soon after the grant of the decree as the court considers just and reasonable.

(2) Where the court decides in such a case to make a periodical payments or secured periodical payments order in favour of a party to the marriage, the court shall in particular consider whether it would be appropriate to require those payments to be made or secured only for such term as would in the opinion of the court be sufficient to enable a party in whose favour the order is made to adjust without undue hardship to the termination of his or her financial dependence on the other party.

(3) Where on or after the grant of a decree of divorce or nullity of marriage an application is made by a party to the marriage for a periodical payments or secured periodical payments order in his or her favour, then, if the court considers that no continuing obligation should be imposed on either party to make or secure periodical payments in favour of the other, the court may dismiss the application with a direction that the applicant shall not be entitled to make any further application in relation to that marriage for an order under section 23(1)(a) or (b) above.

Over the years the courts have built up a comprehensive body of case-law on how this legislation, and sections 25 and 25A in particular, will be applied in practice. It is the practice of those concerned with the law regulating financial settlements after divorce to review that case law in order to identify any discernible trends or principles. What the courts have to say is important, as it may shape how future cases are handled, but this data must be handled with some caution. There may well be a divergence between the theory and reality of the law.[16] Research indicates that divorce law is one area where the problem of mis-match between practice and theory is particularly acute.[17] A major reason for this is that not every financial settlement between a divorcing couple is imposed on them by the courts. Increasingly, divorcing couples agree a settlement, usually with the help of their legal advisers and the court is then simply asked to approve the settlement though it may question its terms if it appears that one party is not receiving reasonable treatment.

There are positive advantages for the parties who sort out their financial affairs between themselves, not the least being the money they save. If the divorcing couple cannot agree and have to turn to the courts to impose a financial settlement, they will incur significant legal costs. As has been pointed out, if the property in dispute is worth £10,000 but legal costs are likely to be £2,000, litigation may lose its attraction.[18] Legal aid is available to divorcing couples, but the income thresholds are so low that few will benefit.[19] Since a woman's income is likely to be lower than that of a man, there is more chance that *she* will qualify for legal aid but, as some women have discovered to their cost, legal aid is a two-edged sword. The Legal Aid Act 1988 allows the Legal Aid Board, the body which administers the scheme, to place a charge over any property "recovered or preserved."[20] In *Stewart* v *Law Society*,[21] a wife was awarded a lump sum payment of £7,000 but when her legal aid costs of £4,600 were deducted she was left with virtually nothing. There are certain payments from which legal aid costs cannot be recovered,[22] but the danger of money which is recovered being swallowed up in legal costs must act as a disincentive to going to court.

The problems associated with legal aid and litigation mean that some women will accept a settlement offered by their husband or his lawyer, either because they are not eligible for legal aid or fear that any sum that they recover as a result of legally-aided litigation will be absorbed almost entirely in costs. Such negotiated settlements do not necessarily represent the best financial settlement that might have been secured. A criticism levelled at agreements reached privately is that they are vulnerable to the exercise of undue pressure. First, there may be pressure to conclude an agreement and hence to avoid the costs of a trial.[23] Second, there is evidence that women may be tempted to accept settlements which are less than they might have got[24] either because of pressure exerted by their ex-partner or because they believe that they are "entitled" to very little. Research has shown the financial power wielded by a husband whilst a marriage is in being[25] and there is nothing to say that simply because a couple are no longer living together, a wife will cease to feel that she is the junior partner in financial matters. Divorcing couples are inspired by a variety of motives, ranging from a desire to dissolve the relationship as quickly as possible to a wish ensure that the ex-spouse receives very little by way of settlement. Legal advisers are able to bring a degree of impartiality to negotiations, since they are aware of how the courts handle financial arrangements between divorcing couples, but the same advisers also aim to secure the best possible settlement for their clients. The court is thus a safety mechanism for ensuring the fairness of a negotiated settlement and it is the court which must approve any such agreement. In one survey, Eekelaar concluded that there was a willingness to intervene in certain circumstances:

> If any preponderant view emerges, it is perhaps that, subject to the technical correctness of the proposal, registrars are inclined to accept agreements which affect the adults alone *either* if both parties are legally represented *or* if the registrar is satisfied, probably after interviewing the parties, that they have properly understood and genuinely consent to their implications. However, they will be concerned about the adequacy of child support and that the burden of support is not unjustifiably thrown on to the state.[26]

If a divorcing couple thus appear content with a settlement, the court will not intervene simply because one party might seem to be benefiting disproportionately. On the other hand, the desire to protect those who are not directly represented at any negotiations, particularly the children, will, understandably, encourage intervention, although new arrangements regarding child support have curbed the courts' powers to intervene in the interests of any children.[27] The wish to safeguard the interests of the state is rather more problematic. If a husband transfers his interest in the matrimonial home to his wife she may give up any claim to periodical payments. As a result, she could be forced to look to the state for day-to-day support as well as for help with any mortgage repayments. It is difficult to say categorically that the court should reject a settlement which leaves a wife totally dependent on social security benefits for support. If a financial settlement of this nature has been arrived at purely in order to deprive a wife of her legitimate share of the couple's joint assets, it does seem unacceptable. For many women, however, the knowledge that not all men actually honour their commitment to make periodical payments can convince them that they are best advised to extract the largest capital sum from their ex-husbands then turn, where necessary, to the state for support. For such women, dependence on the state is a more secure future, even if possibly less generous. The state cannot turn its back on these women simply because there is no adequate mechanism in place for ensuring that ex-husbands either pay for the support of their children or that social security benefits paid to an ex-wife can be recouped from a defaulting ex-husband.

Whether it is the courts or the parties themselves who determine the content of any financial settlement, there are numerous options as to the form it takes. Importantly, however, the court may only deal with the couple's financial situation as it exists. If they are in poor financial circumstances with numerous debts and few assets, the court has to work within those limits and, it has been claimed, marital breakdown is more common among the lower income-earning sections of the population.[28] The court cannot create wealth where none exists, but simply apportion whatever assets there are between the couple. In doing this, the court has various powers conferred by the relevant legislation. It can, for example, order periodical payments which require one spouse to pay a regular weekly or monthly sum of maintenance to the other. This type of financial settlement articulates the idea that a spouse remains obliged to help to maintain his or her partner and family long after the marriage has been dissolved. A major problem associated with this option is that the party charged with the obligation of making periodical payments can default and fall into arrears. Since periodical payments are most commonly made by an ex-husband to his ex-wife, this can place a woman in a very precarious financial position. Maclean points out that for a female-headed household without other sources of income, a single week's non-compliance can mean a major catastrophe.[29] Even where there are other sources of income, non-compliance may be no less damaging if it disrupts a finely-balanced budget.[30] If an attempt is made to compensate for that shortfall by seeking additional social security payments, the authorities can take a great deal of convincing that periodical payments are no longer being made. Legal action can, of course, be taken to recover maintenance arrears, but litigation is time-consuming and costly.

Some of these problems can, theoretically, be avoided where the court awards secured periodical payments. The idea is that the court tries to guarantee payment by using as security some item of property which is owned by the ex-husband, for example, shares in a company. Failure to pay will give an ex-wife the right to claim what she is owed in the form of a charge on that property. This solution is feasible only where there are assets of sufficient value to be used as security. In addition, it is also possible for an ex-husband to accumulate such arrears of maintenance that the item used as security cannot meet them. Finally, as is the case with unsecured maintenance, the recovery of any arrears is not a speedy process and an ex-wife may find herself in severe financial difficulties during the intervening period.

The next option open to the court is to order a lump sum payment. One ex-spouse will be ordered to pay a defined sum to the other, say £10,000. The sum might have to be paid in full immediately or over a period of time by way of instalments. Lump sum payments embody the philosophy of a once and for all settlement between the parties. They may well be very useful to an ex-wife who can use the money to purchase a house or to make an investment for her long-term future. The court can combine the payment of a lump sum with a periodical payment since the two are not mutually exclusive but a lump sum order can be made only if there are assets which can be realised in order to make the payment. Where, for example, a couple lived in rented accommodation and have no capital, a lump sum payment would not be a viable option.

Another course of action open to the court is to order the transfer of property from one spouse to another. This form of settlement also seeks to achieve a "clean break" between the parties without any continuing long-term financial commitment. A transfer of property order can be used in relation to any property, including, say, a car or a boat or a share-holding. It might seem that such an order would be useful only to couples who are financially well-placed and to some extent this is true, but an order can also be used to transfer the tenancy of rented accommodation, including council accommodation, from one partner to another, even in the face of objections by the local authority or a private landlord.[31] The item of property which is most commonly the object of a transfer of property order is the matrimonial home. If the matrimonial home is owned by one spouse, he or she can be required to transfer it to their partner. If the property is held in joint ownership, one joint owner can be required to transfer his or her share to the other joint owner. Although such an order allows one spouse to gain outright ownership of the matrimonial home, it is not without drawbacks. In particular, if there is a mortgage on the property the spouse gaining ownership will have to meet that liability or risk losing the property. Apart from mortgage repayments, there are many other outgoings on property that have to be met including, for example, council tax and insurance premiums. Without additional financial help, the transfer of ownership of the matrimonial home can actually create more problems than it solves. On the other hand, it does have positive advantages. For many couples the matrimonial home is their most substantial asset and its sale may lead to the realisation of a considerable equity. For example, a couple may have owned their matrimonial home for twenty years and the mortgage may be comparatively small. If a wife were to have the property transferred into her name and were then to sell it she might realise a considerable profit. In the light of the sharp fall in property prices, this may be a less likely outcome than it once was, but it is a factor that the court will take into account, since it might not be regarded as equitable to allow one partner to reap all the gain from the disposition of the matrimonial home. In order to try to avoid this situation, courts have in the past made use of their powers in section 24(1)(b) of the Matrimonial Causes Act 1973.

Section 24(1)(b) allows the court to order that "a settlement of such property as may be so specified, being property to which a party to the marriage is so entitled, be made to the satisfaction of the court for the benefit of the other party to the marriage and of the children of the family or either or any of them." One of the commonest forms of such a settlement was the *Mesher* order.[32] This order, named after the case in which it was first used, tries to give one ex-spouse the benefit of continuing to live in the matrimonial home for a specified period, whilst at the same time providing that when the property is eventually sold any profit will then be divided between the couple in whatever ratio has been agreed. It was commonly used when there were young children and allowed an ex-wife to remain in the matrimonial home until the children reached a certain age, usually eighteen, or she remarried.

As the courts discovered, however, *Mesher* orders created their own problems. Even if an ex-partner is permitted to remain in occupation of the matrimonial home, the resources have to be available to meet the day-to-day costs of running the property, including any mortgage repayments. If this proves beyond the means of the ex-spouse in occupation, (usually the wife), because she loses her job, or her ex-husband fails to make his promised periodical payments, the court cannot substitute an alternative order. It could not, for example, then order the ex-husband to transfer his interest in the matrimonial home to his wife.[33] The only possible course of action in such circumstances is to bring forward the date of sale of the property. It is the very essence of a *Mesher* order that at the end of the prescribed period the matrimonial home will be sold and the proceeds divided. Whenever this occurs, there is no guarantee that the ex-partner in occupation will, as a consequence, realise sufficient capital to enable her to purchase alternative accommodation. It is not difficult to image a situation where an ex-wife has remained in the matrimonial home caring for the children and, therefore, engaging in paid employment only on a part-time basis. Her share of the proceeds of sale of the matrimonial home may not be enough to finance the outright purchase of another property, and her prospects of obtaining a mortgage may be very slim indeed. In the meantime her ex-husband may have been working full-time and may have purchased another property, yet he will still receive his share of the sale proceeds of the matrimonial home. All this has led the courts to advise caution over the use of *Mesher* orders, although whether that advice has been heeded is another matter.[34] An alternative to a *Mesher* order was a *Martin* order.[35] This apportioned the proceeds of sale of the former matrimonial home between husband and wife but postponed the sale until the wife died, remarried, voluntarily left the premises or became dependent on another man. This order had the advantage of allowing a woman to remain in the matrimonial home provided she chose not to form a relationship with another man. Once she did, it was the court's view that her new partner could take over the responsibility of providing accommodation for her. This is, in its way, just as unacceptable as expecting a wife to give up the matrimonial home once any children no longer require her care. A woman is protected in such circumstances only so long as she lives her life in a particular way.

The various powers available to help construct an appropriate financial settlement when a marriage comes to an end give no clue as to what *proportion* of any assets each spouse should expect to receive. Unlike many of their European counterparts, where a divorcing couple receive fixed shares of the matrimonial assets, the United Kingdom courts are given complete discretion in such matters. This introduces a welcome degree of flexibility, but at the same time allows the courts to impose their own views of what would be an appropriate division. These may be shaped by a predominantly male judiciary's perception of the respective roles of husbands and wives. It also means that each case is treated as unique and provides no hard and fast guidance on how a similar situation might be treated. Hence at different times the English courts have adopted different approaches to the whole question of constructing an appropriate financial settlement and from these emerges a picture of how women are perceived by the courts. That perception has not remained constant and its changing nature emphasises the very wide discretion of the English courts in determining financial provision after divorce.

The discretionary powers of the judges derive from the legislation itself and those powers may be narrowed or relaxed as the legislature sees fit. Sometimes the good intentions of the legislators in Parliament are found to be unworkable in practice. For example, section 25 of the Matrimonial Causes Act 1973, as it was originally drafted, instructed the court to exercise its powers so "... as to place the parties, so far as it is practicable and, having regard to their conduct, just to do so, in the financial position in which they would have been if the marriage had not broken down and each had properly discharged his or her financial obligations and responsibilities towards the other." For the majority of divorcing couples this was a practical impossibility since the resources needed to allow a couple to live in comfort, for example, in their own home with a car and frequent foreign holidays, will not be sufficient to allow two individuals living separately to enjoy exactly the same standard of living. That instruction to the court has now been repealed.[36]

Sometimes the judges themselves attempt to lay down guidelines and, in the past, decisions on financial settlement between a divorcing couple have referred to the one-third principle.[37] When a marriage was dissolved and the question arose as to how exactly any capital and revenue-producing assets should be divided, it was a rule of thumb that, so far as the parties to the marriage were concerned, the revenue-producing assets and the capital assets should be shared on the basis of one third to the wife and two thirds to the husband. Although this so-called rule was intended to provide the courts with no more than guidance, and there were circumstances when it would be disregarded, for example when a couple were very rich and it would provide over-generously for the wife, it undoubtedly implied that a wife should expect to receive less from a financial settlement than her husband. The reason given for allowing this unequal division was the perceived roles of husbands and wives:

When a marriage breaks up, there will thenceforth be two households instead of one. The husband will have to go out to work all day and must get some woman to look after the house - either a wife if he remarries or a housekeeper if he does not. He will also have to provide maintenance for the children. The wife will not usually have so much expense. She may go out to work herself, but she will not usually employ a housekeeper. She will do most of the housework herself, perhaps with some help. Or she may marry, in which case her new husband will provide for her.[38]

A wife was, therefore, perceived as having less claim on the family assets because she might be expected to cook and clean whereas a husband would not. There is evidence that the one-third rule now commands less support amongst the judges than was previously the case, though cases still occur which make reference to it.[39]

The traditional expectation that a wife will perform domestic tasks has elicited an ambivalent attitude from the courts. On the one hand, because it is seen as part of her natural role, it has been used to justify awarding her a smaller share of the couple's total assets. On the other hand, a wife's contribution, in the form of caring for her husband and family and performing various household duties, has in the past gained her a share in property to which she might have made no financial contribution:

> ... the wife who looks after the home and family contributes as much to the family assets as the wife who goes out to work. The one contributes in kind. The other in money or money's worth. If the court comes to the conclusion that the home has been acquired and maintained by the joint efforts of both, then, when the marriage breaks down, it should be regarded as the joint property of both of them, no matter in whose name it stands. Just as the wife who makes substantial money contributions usually gets a share, so should the wife who looks after the home and cares for the family for 20 years or more.[40]

A willingness to recognize the importance of a wife's unpaid work in the home was welcome, but it had unexpected consequences. It raised the expectation that a wife had to "earn" her share if she was basing it on her work in the home. The shorter the duration of the marriage the less likely it was that she would be regarded as having done enough. It also gave the court the chance to find that "unwomanly" conduct meant that a wife could forfeit some of her share. A wife who left her husband and four children after fifteen years of marriage was said by the court to have "left the job unfinished" and hence not earned a one-third share.[41] Ultimately, the one third principle provided no more than a starting point for calculating an appropriate financial settlement. There are so many instances where it might not provide a workable solution - when, for example, a couple are excessively wealthy or in straitened circumstances - that it has become "to some extent at least, marginalised."[42]

Other factors which now figure prominently in arriving at a financial settlement are the welfare of any children and the clean break principle. Section 25(1) of the Matrimonial Causes Act 1973 specifically instructs the court "to have regard to all the circumstances of the case, first consideration being given to the welfare while a minor of any child of the family who has not attained the age of eighteen." This suggests that a settlement must aim to secure the financial future of the children. If so, this should work to the benefit of women since it is usually the ex-wife who is the partner charged with the care of any children, and it would seem self-evident that only by securing the financial future of the partner with responsibility for caring for a child can one guarantee that child's financial future. The view that the interests of the child are and should be paramount is widely held as is illustrated by Eekelaar's comment in *Family Law and Social Policy*:

> The primary purpose of the divorce process therefore should be to provide a mechanism to plan for the best future for the children of those families which break down, once all hope of reconciliation is exhausted.[43]

In practice, however, it seems that the children's welfare is simply one of the considerations taken into account by the court and not the deciding factor in how any settlement should be structured. Indeed, some of the issues that the court is directed to have regard to in section 25(2) of the Matrimonial Causes Act seem to run counter to a child's interest. The court can, for example, take account of the conduct of the parties in certain circumstances. If the court chooses thereby to penalise a wife financially because of her "conduct" this is bound to affect any children living with her.

The clean break principle is specifically mentioned in section 25A of the 1973 Act which charges the courts with the task of considering whether any financial settlement should aim to settle once and for all the financial dealings between the parties (as opposed to maintenance for children). This does not mean that a clean break settlement cannot require the making of periodical payments, but that any such payments would be for a defined period. A clean break settlement might be thought most appropriate where a marriage has been of short duration and there are no children. The couple's assets could be split between them and any periodical payment might simply be intended to allow the financially more vulnerable partner time to adjust. In practice the courts have made it clear that the presence of children does not completely rule out a clean break settlement, though it might raise doubts about how appropriate such a solution is.[44] Neither does the fact that a couple are childless or that their children have left the matrimonial home make a clean break settlement inevitable. If the court believes that a woman's future looks uncertain or that, given her circumstances, including her age, she is unlikely to be able to provide for herself, then an order for periodical payments might be made in her favour.

Whilst it is possible to indicate the circumstances in which the courts might think it undesirable to make a clean break order, there is no guarantee that an ex-wife who requires some form of continuing financial support will in fact receive it. Research has shown that maintenance orders in favour of ex-wives are becoming less common.[45] Eekelaar suggests that this might be partly explained by the limited resources of divorcing couples. Once a husband has been instructed to make child support payments, the court might feel that it would be unfair or unrealistic to ask him to make periodical payments to his wife:

> So where the couple have not entered the "property-owning democracy", it is unlikely that the income resources will stretch far enough to allow a significant order for the former wife; if they have, the former wife (usually) will prefer to forgo her maintenance in favour of an interest in the house.[46]

The ability of an ex-spouse to claim social security benefits may also be another factor which leads to the negotiation of a clean break settlement in circumstances where it might not appear at first sight to be appropriate.

A willingness by ex-wives to forgo maintenance for themselves, at least where they receive a share in the matrimonial home and child support payments, may have had some unlooked for effects. The court has absolute discretion in arriving at a settlement and there is no formula which must be applied. In particular, the amount awarded as child support has never been calculated so as to bear some relation to the actual costs of raising children. This means that when maintenance payments to an ex-spouse disappear from the total financial package, as increasingly seems to be the case, the partner with care of the children may be in a very difficult financial position. In these circumstances, women are increasingly forced to look to the state to support them, their families and any mortgage repayments on the family home. The decline in the incidence of spousal maintenance might also be attributed to women's increasing participation in the labour market. Why should a woman look to her ex-husband for support when she can engage in full-time employment? This argument appeals to ideas of equality but is badly weakened by the lack of child care facilities and the generally low level of women's wages when compared to those of men.

Perhaps it was because the courts failed to address these fundamental problems associated with child support that the policy makers decided to remove from the courts the power to award child support and entrust it instead to a special agency which would calculate payments in line with a specific formula.[47] This was a solution adopted by other jurisdictions in an effort to ensure adequate levels of child support and to enforce payment.[48] In theory, the scheme has much to commend it. In practice, it has given rise to massive controversy, especially, though not only, because many suspect that its introduction owes more to a desire on the part of government to save money than to a commitment to promote the interests of children and fairness between divorcing couples.

Apart from general considerations such as the clean break principle, the Matrimonial Causes Act 1973 lists a whole range of factors which the courts can ignore or apply as they see fit. One result of this is that the picture that emerges of financial settlements following divorce is an increasingly confused one since the legislation, taken as a whole, does not seem to be designed to achieve any particular policy objective.   Section 25(2), for example, has a very specific list of considerations which the court can take into account. The first of these is the "income, earning capacity, property and other financial resources which each of the parties to the marriage has or is likely to have in the foreseeable future." Cases illustrate that the courts are willing to take a broad view of what constitutes resources. If, for example, it is clear that one of the parties to a marriage stands to benefit under the terms of a will then the courts can take this fact into account,[49] though in cases where there is no more than a possibility of an inheritance the courts are more reluctant to regard this as part of the couple's assets.[50] Compensation that a spouse may have received because of injuries suffered in a road accident have also been considered a resource falling within the terms of section 25.[51]   A business that is owned by one of the spouses represents a substantial asset, but there is the difficulty that it cannot easily be disposed of without threatening an individual's livelihood. The court would not make an order which did that, but would instead look for some other way of allowing an ex-spouse to benefit from an asset of this nature, if it deems that to be appropriate.

Inheritances and damages are clearly exceptional resources, and for the majority of couples it is their earning power which is their major asset. Usually each of the parties will provide details, which may or may not be accurate, of their financial affairs including what, if anything, they are currently earning. The court can question any information it receives, particularly if it feels that it is not obtaining a true picture of the couple's finances. There have been a number of cases where a spouse clearly had a lifestyle that was incompatible with his declared annual earnings. The disparity resulted from the existence of other sources of income available to augment annual earnings, including loans made against property and support from wealthy relatives. In such cases the courts have been prepared to assess what they regard as the spouse's *real* income.[52]

Conversely, in times of high unemployment the court may have to deal with a couple where either or both are unemployed and receiving state benefits. The court should not make value judgments in these circumstances and proceed on the basis that the partner could find work if only he tried a little harder.[53] Neither, however, should it be assumed that a partner receiving social security benefits cannot be ordered to make periodical payments, though the courts will not demand a level of payment that brings a spouse below subsistence level. In situations where periodical payments are deemed appropriate the court may make a nominal order, say five pounds a year. This can then be adjusted by the courts when and if the spouse in question obtains employment.

Wives may not be in full-time paid employment, or in employment at all. This could be due to child care responsibilities or because they cannot find a job. If there are children, the courts are unlikely to take the view that a wife should be working. If the children are grown up, the courts may then feel that a wife should seek paid employment, though this has to be weighed against the feasibility of her finding such employment. The court's view on what is appropriate may, of course, influence the final shape of any settlement. If, for example, the view is that a wife should be working, she could receive a smaller share of any assets. A wife's earning capacity is thus a problematic factor in the eventual settlement and how the court structures a settlement may reflect its views on how a wife should behave. There is less opportunity for this kind of judgment when the court is assessing the earning capacity of a husband: the assumption is that he should be in full-time work if such work is available.

One final issue that the courts may consider when assessing a couple's financial situation is the prospect of remarriage. There are, supposedly, a number of reasons why this is relevant. If a man intends to remarry almost immediately after he has obtained his divorce the court may consider how this will affect him financially. His new family may represent an additional call on his resources. Alternatively, a second wife who is in full-time paid employment may be meeting certain expenses, such as a share of the mortgage repayments on a new property, which otherwise an ex-husband would have to meet. A second wife's earnings cannot, however, be regarded as a resource from which maintenance payments may be made. So if a husband is unemployed but his second wife is in full-time employment she will not be expected to finance any maintenance payments to his ex-wife.[54] If an ex-wife intends to remarry, however, any maintenance payments *she* receives will cease on re-marriage, since the presumption is that she will be supported by her new husband.

The next consideration which section 25(2) states should be taken into account is the existing and future "financial needs, obligations and responsibilities" of the parties. The court will need to consider the outgoings of each spouse on items such as housing, food, travel and heating costs. Once again the existence of a second family created by remarriage will be relevant. The problem with assessing outgoings is that one spouse may well be unwilling to compromise his or her lifestyle in order to make payments to the ex-partner. Therefore, if when a couple have separated, the husband has taken on a number of new commitments, (and he is the partner more likely to do so because he will often be in full-time employment), there is little the courts can do but take these commitments into account. In this way, one ex-spouse can thwart the legitimate financial expectations of the other. In *Delaney* v *Delaney*,[55] for example, a couple with three children divorced and the ex-wife sought maintenance for herself and the children. Her ex-husband was unemployed for a period but then found a job. He lived with a woman whom he hoped to marry in a one bedroomed flat and then bought a three bedroomed house in order that his children by the first marriage could visit him, though the mortgage repayments substantially increased his outgoings. At first instance it was held that he had incurred unnecessary expenditure in the light of his obligations to his first wife and family. On appeal, however, the court held that any orders requiring the husband to pay maintenance would place him in severe financial difficulties. In the court's view he had behaved in an acceptable manner and his first family had the option of claiming social security benefits:

> Whilst this court deprecates any notion that a former husband and ... father may slough off the tight skin of familial responsibilities and may slither into and lose himself in the green grass on the other side nonetheless this court has proclaimed and will proclaim that it looks to the realities of the real world ... and that among the realities of life is that there is life after divorce. The respondent husband is entitled to order his life in such a way as will hold in reasonable balance the responsibilities to his existing family which he carried into his new life, as well as his proper aspirations for that new future.[56]

Section 25(2) instructs the court to have regard to the family's standard of living before their marriage broke down. This is not in order to preserve that standard of living in any post-divorce financial settlement, since in the case of most couples, with the exception of the very wealthy, this is simply not possible. It is almost inevitable that there will be a drop in living standards, since the income used to support one household now has to support two. The purpose of the subsection is to ensure a fair apportionment of that drop in standard. Whether the court is actually even-handed is not clear. Should the couple have children, it would be hard to deny that the spouse given day-to-day care of those children will need a greater share of the couple's resources. That spouse will have to pay for the children's food, clothing and accommodation (subject to child support payments) as well as suffering a loss in income if the ability to work is affected. Since the spouse with day-to-day care is normally the wife, one might expect her to receive more in order to ensure that any drop in her standard of living is no greater than that of her husband's. In practice, it is difficult to believe that the court does take this objective seriously when, in the past at least, it has regarded a one third/two thirds split between wife and husband as fair.

Section 25(2) next specifies that the court must consider the age of the parties to the marriage and the duration of the marriage. This is relevant because, as a general principle, the younger the couple and the shorter the duration of the marriage the more likely it is that the court will try to achieve a clean break settlement, particularly if there are no children. The court will assume that a young woman will be able to obtain full-time paid employment and support herself. If the court is willing to award her any periodical payments, this is likely to be a short term arrangement. In contrast, the older a couple are and the longer they have been married, the harder it may be for them to lead independent lives. A wife's employment prospects may have suffered because her domestic responsibilities including child care have meant protracted periods out of the labour market or only intermittent employment. The traditional non-working wife who has devoted herself to her husband and family may excite a desire on the part of the court to compensate her for being a "loyal" wife. Individuals in their forties and fifties may find it harder to borrow money in order to finance the purchase of alternative accommodation, and they may also be contemplating their retirement from paid employment in the not too distant future. The kind of financial settlement that would suit them may, therefore, be very different from that which is appropriate when the court is dealing with a younger couple.

Also relevant, according to section 25(2) is any mental or physical disability from which one of the parties to the marriage may be suffering. Clearly, if one spouse is suffering from a serious illness such as multiple sclerosis, their day-to-day living costs will be very different from those of an able-bodied individual. They may require special transport, a special diet or around the clock care. Any financial settlement should, in so far as it is possible, reflect those special needs.

Whilst it may be comparatively easy for the court to assess disability, it also has to evaluate the contribution each spouse has made to the welfare of the family. The inclusion of caring responsibilities as a relevant factor in determining financial arrangements has, not surprisingly, worked to women's advantage. In the past it has earned them a share in such major family assets as the matrimonial home, even though their husband might be the legal owner of the property and might meet any mortgage repayments. With more and more couples purchasing the matrimonial home in their joint names, a woman may have to rely less on her contribution "in kind" in order to claim a share in the matrimonial home. There are, however, still instances where this can prove a useful provision. If a husband has substantial personal assets, for example the ownership of a lucrative business, a wife can argue that her assumption of the entire burden of caring for the family or indeed her help in building up a business entitles her to benefit, perhaps by being awarded a lump sum payment.[57] The courts have used this factor, however, only when they felt that a wife had "earned" some additional financial reward. This could involve a judgment on how "good" a wife she has been.

The factors listed in section 25(2) focus for the most part on the current personal circumstances of the divorcing couple in order to arrive at an assessment of their financial needs. In requiring the court to take account of the contribution each has made to the welfare of the family, the emphasis turns to the couple's behaviour whilst the marriage was in being. Section 25(2) continues this theme by permitting the court to evaluate the couple's conduct, if the court is of the view that not to do so would be inequitable. Conduct is hardly a precise term but in this context it has been interpreted to include any matrimonial misconduct that might have contributed to the breakdown of the couple's marriage. In reality the courts are reluctant to penalise a spouse financially simply for behaviour which broke up the marriage and there is little evidence of the courts utilising this particular power though the parties to the divorce might feel it is a relevant factor.[58] The view seems to be that only in exceptional circumstances will the behaviour that accompanies the breakdown of a marriage be such as to warrant the imposition of a financial penalty when an appropriate financial settlement is being negotiated. Exceptions have been made, however, where an individual's behaviour has been viewed as particularly repugnant,[59] although behaviour which the courts have been prepared to condemn might not seem worthy of that description to those outside the judiciary. A wife has, for example, suffered a financial penalty for committing adultery with her father-in-law.[60] Moreover, what might appear obvious and gross to one generation of the judiciary might be considered less outrageous behaviour by the next. There is little to justify the inclusion of this factor, given the subjectivity of the judgments involved. It presents the prospect of continuing friction between the couple and represents an ideal opportunity for a disgruntled spouse to avoid financial responsibilities.

The final factor that the courts may take into account is the value of any benefit, such as a pension which, if it were not for the divorce, would have been enjoyed by both parties. The wife is the spouse more likely to be affected by the loss of pension rights since women find it more difficult to fulfil the contribution conditions needed to obtain a pension.[61] There is a question, therefore, whether it should be possible to allow an ex-partner to share in a pension and, if not, how best to compensate her for that loss, as pensions represent a significant financial benefit. In the case of the basic retirement pension a woman can rely on her ex-husband's national insurance contribution record in order to claim a pension in her own right.[62] The same is not true, however, if an ex-partner is entitled to either the State Earnings Related Pension (SERPS) or an occupational pension. Occupational pension schemes as well as SERPS are linked to salary and aim to guarantee a comfortable standard of living on retirement. Should the beneficiary of such a pension die and leave a widow, she may continue to receive benefits. When a couple divorce, if the assets accruing under a pension scheme are likely to be realised in the foreseeable future then, under the terms of section 25(2)(a) of the Matrimonial Causes Act 1973, the court may be willing to order that a share of those assets are transferred to an ex-wife.[63] If the assets represented by an occupational or earnings related pension are not available in the foreseeable future, an ex-wife is best advised either to seek an adjournment of her application for a lump sum order or alternatively to delay it.[64] In practice, therefore, many women have little hope of enjoying any share of their husband's occupational pension. For women who have no occupational pension of their own this can mean a very uncertain financial future on retirement. An ex-partner could, of course, be given a larger share of a couple's current assets in order to try to compensate for this future "loss" but this depends on there being assets available to do this. It is also possible for a woman to try to prevent her husband from obtaining a divorce by alleging that the dissolution of the marriage will result in grave financial hardship[65] which can include the loss of a benefit.[66] It seems unlikely, however, that many women would wish to take advantage of this special defence, even if it is available to them, since it would preserve an unhappy marriage. If the stage has been reached where a husband is seeking divorce, financial hardship may seem preferable.

Pensions, or more specifically, occupational and earnings related pensions, represent a significant financial asset which the courts currently have no practical way of dealing with. They cannot normally order the pension provider to pay out a share to an ex-partner when the pension eventually matures even if this were a viable option. Various solutions to this particular problem have been canvassed,[67] but it is not one which is easily resolved. Pensions are intended to provide the contributor with a secure retirement, but they are not limitless. If a divorced man remarries he, his current wife and his ex-wife could all be seeking to rely on that single pension. Even if an ex-husband does not remarry, a single pension may have to support two households instead of one. Pension providers may also resist any changes to the law which will mean greater administrative efforts and cost for them. The problem may gradually lessen as more women have access to occupational pensions in their own right but there is always likely to be a substantial minority of women who have no occupational pension. It is probably the case that the solution lies not in a single strategy but in a range of solutions, including more realistic state retirement pensions and a better mechanism for "dividing" an occupational pension when a couple divorce.

Surviving divorce

It is apparent that many ex-wives will find themselves in an extremely precarious financial situation following the breakdown of their marriage. It is not obvious that the law is entirely responsible for this, but the lack of a coherent policy regarding post-divorce financial arrangements must take some of the blame for the difficulties faced by many ex-wives.[68] The courts are given a wide-ranging discretion and the way in which they exercise it with its unscientific assessment of needs combined with a desire for a clean break seems designed to force a great many women into financial hardship and reliance on the state. At the same time, the resources available for division between a divorcing couple could be regarded as more a matter of chance and hence beyond the law's influence. The income which might have kept a *couple* afloat while they were married may not stretch to supporting two households after divorce. An ex-husband may not have sufficient income for himself, his ex-family and in many cases a second family. His ex-wife, on the other hand, might not be capable of earning enough even to maintain herself and their children. The equation is not equal. An ex-wife's potential inability to support herself is a comment on women's lower earning power as compared with men, and also on the law's failure to deal with this. If she is caring for children her earning potential is reduced even further, and she may be forced to rely on social security benefits with their natural tendency to perpetuate dependency. Her marriage may have brought her very little in the sense of financial gain since, whilst her earning potential might be affected, the law takes no steps to regulate what is perceived as an essentially private relationship so far as questions of money are concerned. When a marriage ends the law is concerned that the parties reach an appropriate financial settlement, but this does not address the law's earlier failure to ensure women's financial well-being both before and during the currency of any marriage.

The end of cohabitation

One of the hallmarks of divorce is the wide-ranging, discretionary powers which the courts have in order not only to declare who owns what, but also to redistribute property to reflect what the court believes is a proper financial settlement. When a couple who have been cohabiting split up the situation is very different. No matter how marriage-like the relationship, nor how long they may have been together, nor how many children the relationship may have produced, the parties are not married and thus the Matrimonial Causes Act 1973 will not apply. This means that the court is denied those statutory powers which allow it to redistribute property and to a large extent it is a matter of deciding who is entitled to what according to the general principles of law, in particular, those which operate in the law of equity. A cohabitee who may be in exactly the same position as a wife, in that she has devoted many years to the family and has not been in paid employment, is at a distinct disadvantage in that she, unlike the wife, has no right to claim maintenance for herself. When it comes to deciding her future financial and property rights, much will depend on whether there are children.

If there are no children a cohabitee is forced back on the general principles which apply in deciding disputes as to the ownership of property. Chapter 6 was concerned with property rights which arise during a relationship, but the principles outlined there are relevant also when it breaks down. Where property is owned in joint names a cohabitee should have some protection in relation to establishing a share in the property when the relationship ends.[69] It is more problematic if the property is in the name of one partner only since in those cases the non-owner must rely on being able to establish a right which arises by way of trust or estoppel. In such situations the position of the non-owner is far less secure.[70] Everything which was true about the difficulties faced by wives in making equal contributions to household finances and the purchase of property applies with equal force to cohabitees, with the additional drawback that women in this situation do not benefit from the special status afforded to wives. It may also be more difficult to convince the court that there was a common intention that the non-owner should have a beneficial interest in the property.

If the cohabitees lived in rented property and there are no children, the position is even less favourable when the relationship ends. Essentially, the situation is governed by the ordinary rules of landlord and tenant and the law provides no special powers simply because the tenants were living together as husband and wife. The end result, depending on the type of tenancy and who has rights of occupation, may be that (unless there has been domestic violence) there is no legal mechanism for deciding who should go and who should stay. Furthermore, it is quite possible, given the complexities of landlord and tenant law, that the departure of one tenant will result in a woman losing her home.[71]

Where there are children of an unmarried couple, the law does provide for more flexibility, but does so for the benefit and protection of the child, rather than for the parent who has custody. For many years, the law distinguished between legitimate and illegitimate children in ways which subjected the latter to significant disabilities. The policy now is that such children should not be penalised and as more and more couples choose not to marry it would be wrong to treat the children of such relationships in a discriminatory fashion. It is possible for the parent of a child from an unmarried relationship to apply for maintenance for the child in ways which are similar to those applicable to those who were once married. Under the Children Act 1989, Schedule 1, orders may be made for either periodical or lump sum payments for the benefit of the child to be paid to the applicant (very likely to be the mother). In addition, the court may order that property may be transferred or settled for the benefit of the child. As with married parents, the property which is available for transfer is likely to be the family home. Although there is no power to make property adjustments as between the parties themselves, this mechanism does mean that, in practice, a cohabitee with a child of the relationship does stand the chance of acquiring some protection, at least as far as the occupation of the family home is concerned. It is probably inevitable, however, that the unmarried mother will find that the transfer is only for a temporary period - say, until the child is eighteen (in other words, a type of *Mesher* order). Nevertheless, given that the parent with care is probably going to be the mother and that she is probably less financially secure than her ex-partner, the existence of this power is extremely important.

It does, however, suffer from some of the same drawbacks as those applicable to ex-wives: transfer of property rights also brings obligations, including payment of rent or mortgage. There is also one consideration which does not apply to ex-wives. The court has no power to order maintenance for the ex-partner, even if she is a parent with care responsibilities which preclude employment. Moreover, the court may, in deciding the value of the property to be transferred for the benefit of the child, take into account that it is not supposed to benefit the ex-partner. Since any move to protect the child's home will, inevitably, benefit the parent who lives there, the courts may be less generous than they would be in divorce cases. It is especially noticeable that, while the criteria for making orders in these cases clearly echo section 25 of the Matrimonial Causes Act 1973, there are some significant differences and, in particular it is not stated that the welfare of the child is to be the "first consideration," simply that it is a factor to be taken into account. On the other hand, the criteria do include the financial needs of the parent with care which could allow consideration of the fact that she cannot work, or that if she does she must pay for child care.

There is little doubt that the law has been gradually moving towards an assimilation of the married and unmarried family. In general, this will lessen the vulnerability of the cohabitee who finds herself alone and unsupported. It remains the case, however, that public policy may demand that some distinctions are maintained between marriage and cohabitation and the courts may thus continue to afford greater protection to the ex-wife than to the ex-cohabitee in order to signify recognition of the commitment represented by marriage. There is, perhaps, one way in which a cohabitee may choose to remain unmarried and yet achieve a position very close to that of the ex-wife and that is by entering a cohabitation contract.

It was noted in Chapter 6 that such contracts may raise their own problems. There are difficulties in relation to their enforceability - at least under English law[72] - and there are also problems about the satisfactory protection of the weaker party. In the past, they would have been regarded as contracts to promote sexual immorality and even now they might fail because they lack the consideration which is a vital feature of contracts. On the other hand, such agreements would have definite advantages, particularly when cohabitation breaks down since a properly constructed contract would deal with questions of property division and maintenance (for the partners as well as any children). A contract could provide for rights which the law would not otherwise recognise, including, for example, the use of credit cards and even methods of birth control. Such binding agreements would be of advantage to a properly advised female partner. The latter point is of course crucial: without legal advice it is most unlikely that an agreement would cover the important aspects or would be sufficiently certain to be enforceable.

In some jurisdictions in the United States and Canada the law has recognised the validity of cohabitation contracts. In the United Kingdom the cohabitation contract tends to be regarded with a mixture of amusement and distrust, since they do not accord with the notion of a loving, sharing couple. An attempt has been made to legislate for validity of these contracts by the introduction of a bill which would have legalised them in England and Wales.[73] The status of such agreements is therefore still a matter for argument and this does little to encourage their increased use. As an alternative to cohabitation contracts, some countries have spelt out the general consequences of a breakdown in cohabitation, one example being the New South Wales De Facto Relationships Act 1984.

Child support

Child support is an issue which straddles the divide between the married and the unmarried. Although courts have far fewer powers of property adjustment in relation to separating cohabitees, where there are children of the relationship questions of maintenance for those children were dealt with by the courts in much the same way as for the maintenance of children of a divorcing couple. The difficulty in all cases was that child maintenance was dealt with by a range of bodies, generally courts, with the power to make an award. There was no set formula to ensure consistency and, in general, the level of awards was low - on average £16 per week per child. Many lone parents - and in reality this meant lone mothers - found themselves in a financial predicament. Their need to care for their children meant that they were unable to work or alternatively unable to work full-time. As a consequence they were forced to turn to the benefit system for support. Any child maintenance they might receive was unlikely to enable them to break free of their dependency on the benefits system. Perhaps because they were unhappy with the courts' performance or, as seems more likely, worried by increasing demands on the social security system, the policy makers tried an alternative approach. Instead of allowing the *courts* to set child support, it was decided to hand over this task to a governmental body, the Child Support Agency (CSA). The courts' responsibility for setting child maintenance was to be phased out, though they would still retain other powers in relation to children such as determining care arrangements and making property adjustments.

Under the provisions of the Child Support Act 1991, it is the task of the CSA to calculate maintenance payments for children using a specific formula whose terms are set out in the legislation.[74] On the face of it, this attempt to set child support at a more realistic level has much to recommend it. While the courts were responsible for calculating child maintenance payments, they appear not to have paid much, if any, attention to the actual costs involved in caring for a child. The number of divorced women forced to exist on social security benefits was indicative of the fact that either maintenance payments were not being set at a realistic level, or were not being honoured by ex-partners. The legal machinery for enforcement was also unsatisfactory, being slow and expensive. By choosing to entrust the task of assessing and collecting child support to the CSA, there appeared to be a good chance of improving the financial situation of women. The child support formula used by the CSA was also to include an element designed to take account of the value of caring by making an allowance to the carer for performing this task.

In the short time the CSA has been operational[75] the system has been the subject of wide-spread criticism and vociferous condemnation. The fairness of the formula has been constantly attacked and reports have appeared of how ex-husbands are hounded, sometimes to the stage of suicide, for sums which they claim they are totally unable to pay. There has been a well-orchestrated and well-publicised campaign to secure the abolition of the Child Support Act. It is difficult to avoid the conclusion that some of the resistance which the Act has provoked has been inspired by fathers asked to make rather more realistic contributions to their children's maintenance and finding themselves with less disposable income to spend as they would wish. If this were the sole cause of unhappiness with the legislation and it could be demonstrated that the lot of lone mothers and their children had improved appreciably as a consequence, a claim could be made that a major shift of resources from men to women had been achieved. This is not the case. Both absent parents and those with caring responsibilities have valid grounds on which to criticise the Act. The perfectly legitimate principle that absent parents should make adequate contributions to the maintenance of their children has been brought into disrepute as a consequence of the confusion surrounding the operation of the Act. Indeed, the motivation behind the legislation seems to be a desire to make savings on the social security budget rather than ensure a fair financial settlement.

From a woman's point of view the most fundamental criticism of the new system is that for women who are receiving social security benefits, it brings little or no financial gain. For those women who are employed and receiving family credit there is a limited financial incentive in that the first £15 of any maintenance received is disregarded in calculating entitlement to family credit. For those women who are not working but are receiving income support there is no corresponding disregard. Their benefit is reduced pound for pound with the payment of maintenance. In their case the payment of child support simply reduces the financial burden on the state rather than raising their standard of living. Moreover, if the receipt of child support means that a woman no longer qualifies for benefit, it may rob her of certain related advantages such as free school meals and prescriptions which means that overall she is in a *worse* financial situation. The chance for a substantial number of women and children to enjoy a more comfortable existence by actually receiving some, if not all, of any child support has been lost because of the government's desire to save money. A further cause for complaint has been that some women claiming social security benefits have been further penalised under the new system. If a woman refuses to co-operate with the CSA by failing to provide them with details of her ex-partner the amount of benefit she and her children receive can be reduced by 20 per cent for the first six months and 10 per cent for the following year.[76] A woman may have very good reasons for wishing to avoid contact with her ex-partner. He may, for example, have subjected her or their children to abuse. In such extreme circumstances a woman might be able to justify her non-cooperation by alleging that to do otherwise would cause harm or undue distress to her or her children.[77] If, however, her refusal to supply information rests simply on unwillingness to resume contact with a former partner, it is unlikely to prove acceptable to the CSA. This creates a sub-class of women who are in receipt of benefit and whose very dependence on the state is used as a form of blackmail to extract the information necessary for the cost-cutting strategy of the government. The counter argument is that if there were no sanction there would be numerous women who would refuse to cooperate with the CSA and former partners would be able to escape their obligations to their children. According to the CSA the power to reduce benefits has been used very sparingly and on comparatively few occasions - 22 up to the end of September 1993. This does not change the fact that by its very existence benefit reduction may force a very vulnerable group to provide information in circumstances where they would prefer not to do so.

There are other criticisms of the legislation, not the least being that since the assessment of the amount of child support to be paid is formula-based, it is inflexible, leaving little room for any discretion in its application. Many absent fathers, for example, criticised the formula for not taking into account the costs of access (for example, travel expenses), or any second family. There is one factor in particular - the existence of a clean break settlement - whose omission from the formula has provoked major resentment amongst divorced fathers. A divorcing couple may have agreed that in return for the transfer of the matrimonial home into the wife's name, the husband is to make nominal child support payments. This is line with current legislative policy which is keen to see a once and for all financial settlement between the parties. Although an agreement of this nature might have been concluded before the Child Support Act came into force, if the partner with care of the child claims benefit, the CSA can and will pursue the absent parent for child support, which is likely to be considerably higher than anything paid previously. The court will not, however, set aside the clean break settlement. In the court's view, whilst the parties to a marriage are free to achieve a clean break settlement as between themselves, they cannot do so in respect of any child. Both parents possess a continuing legal obligation to maintain any child.[78] As a result fewer men may be willing to transfer the matrimonial home to their ex-wives, if they know that this will not be taken into account in any subsequent assessment of child support by the CSA.

Another result of applying the original formula in the Child Support Act is that in almost all cases the absent parent, normally the father, would find himself paying much higher amounts in maintenance. Once certain allowances have been made in accordance with the formula, 50 per cent of whatever sum remains is available to meet child support payments. To many absent parents the unfairness of the formula was not their only objection to the system. In the case of those whose ex-partners were claiming income support, their increased contribution to their children's maintenance simply allowed benefit payments to be reduced without any corresponding benefits to their children.

The perceived unfairness of the new system may actually hamper the achievement of its objectives if more men dispute the fact that they are the father of the child in question. If this occurs the matter is referred to court to resolve the issue of paternity.[79] The mother of the child then faces questions on her personal life both from the CSA and the courts. Once more it will be women who rely on social security benefits who will have little choice but to submit to this questioning.

As a consequence of a campaign of sustained criticism of and opposition to the CSA, the government has been forced to reconsider the operation of the child support scheme. The situation has been exacerbated by the difficulties experienced by the CSA in handling the workload. The 1991 Act contemplated that, eventually, *all* cases involving child support would be handled by the CSA. Initially, the Agency was to handle only those cases where the parent with care is claiming benefit. It seems, however, that even with this restricted workload, the CSA finds it difficult to cope. There is evidence of delay in handling cases, and the CSA has been criticised for concentrating its efforts on those parents who were already making maintenance payments to their ex-partners, rather than absent parents who were making no contributions whatsoever.

In an effort to salvage the scheme the government has put forward a set of proposals for change in the White Paper *Improving Child Support*[80] in which many of the criticisms made of the formula are addressed. Account will be taken of clean break settlements, as will costs related to second families, whilst the amount of available income that can be used for child support payments will be reduced to 30 per cent. These changes will work principally to the advantage of the absent parent and offer no financial gain to the parent with care. Indeed, the only financial inducement offered to the parent with care, usually the mother, is an incentive to those who are claiming income support to return to work. From April 1997, a parent with care who is receiving maintenance and who is also claiming income support will be allowed to accumulate "maintenance credit" at a rate of £5 per week up to a maximum of £1,000. The money will be credited from the amount of benefit clawed back by the Treasury and will be paid as a lump sum if and when she obtains a job which involves working at least 16 hours per week. Although this might provide some incentive for lone mothers to return to work, it does not compare well with the £15 disregard allowed to those women who work and claim family credit. It seems to suggest that lone parents could work if they put their minds to it and that they simply need some kind of inducement to persuade them of this fact. The fact that work might not be available, nor may help with childcare is absent from the equation.

Indeed, there is one proposal in *Improving Child Support* that seems to work against the notion of encouraging lone parents back to work. Plans for the CSA to take over all child support cases are amended so that in future the CSA will not deal with those parents who have care of children but who work and do not claim benefits. Instead, their claims for maintenance will continue to be handled by the courts. One of the reasons for removing the question of child support from the courts was the low level of payments and poor enforcement record. This would seem to suggest that a two tier system of maintenance will be created. Much lower sums may be awarded by the courts as compared with those awarded by the CSA which will still be using its formula, albeit in a modified form. This may persuade some women who are working that they would be better off claiming benefits, as their case will be handled (eventually) by the CSA and a more realistic level of child support might be awarded and enforced.

Death

The property rights and financial provision which a wife can claim on the death of her husband depend on whether he has left a will and whether there are other surviving relatives. If a husband dies intestate, that is without leaving a will, then by operation of law his widow is entitled to a prescribed share of his property. Under the terms of the Administration of Estates Act 1925 the wife of a childless marriage takes the whole of her spouse's estate. If, however, the deceased has certain relatives who are still living, for example, a parent, or if no parent, brothers or sisters, they are entitled to a share. The widow takes all her husband's personal belongings, the first £125,000 of the estate and half of any balance. The remainder of the balance goes to the parents or brothers and sisters. If a married couple own any property as joint tenants, as is commonly the case with the matrimonial home, this goes automatically to the surviving owner and is not part of the estate. Where there are children of the marriage the widow will again take all her husband's personal possessions, the first £75,000 of the estate and a life interest in one half of the balance, with the other half going to the children. The result of these arrangements is that in the majority of cases, except where the estate is very large, the wife takes the whole estate on her husband's intestacy. This means that, in principle at least, wives are very well provided for on their husband's intestacy.

The same is not true if a couple are cohabiting. In the absence of a will, the law distributes a deceased's property among his relatives according to the rules governing intestacy and his partner will not be legally entitled to a share. In certain circumstances the financial consequences of someone dying intestate may not be as serious for a cohabiting partner as at first appears to be the case. If the cohabiting couple have acquired property as joint tenants, the surviving partner automatically inherits. If the deceased was a contributor to an occupational pension scheme and he has nominated his partner to receive the benefits that accrue on his death, this too should ameliorate the unfortunate financial consequences of intestacy, provided the trustees of the pension fund comply with the nomination. Whether these steps have been taken is, however, a matter of chance and may depend on how a couple chose to organise their financial affairs during their lifetime. A cohabiting partner, as compared with a wife, has no automatic right to inherit. As a last resort, however, she can make an application to the court requesting that adequate financial provision be made for her out of her partner's estate.[81]

If a husband chooses to make a will, one might assume that he would make adequate financial provision for his wife. Unlike many European systems, however, the law in England gives a testator complete freedom to dispose of his property as he wishes. He is thus not bound to leave prescribed shares of his property to his wife and children and there is a chance, therefore, that on her husband's death a wife may discover that he has bequeathed his entire estate to charity, (or elsewhere) leaving her with little or nothing. In these circumstances a surviving wife may apply to the court under the terms of the Inheritance (Provision for Family and Dependants) Act 1975 alleging that her husband has failed to make reasonable financial provision for her.

A surviving wife who has not been provided for in her husband's will is not, however, the only person who can make use of the legislation. A former wife who has not remarried is also included among the list of individuals who can apply to the court. When a couple divorce, any provision in an ex-husband's will that benefits his ex-wife lapses as a matter of law.[82] This does not, however, prevent her making a claim under the 1975 Act. In addition, persons being maintained either wholly or partly by the deceased are permitted to make a claim. If, therefore, a couple has been cohabiting, a woman may make a claim on her partner's death if she is not adequately provided for and she may do so not only where the deceased has left a will but also where he dies intestate. A cohabitee can therefore make use of this procedure when her partner dies intestate but if she does resort to the court, she will experience difficulties that do not face a wife or an ex-wife. She must demonstrate that immediately before the deceased's death she was being wholly or partly maintained by him, which means, according to the 1975 Act, that the deceased was making a substantial contribution in money or money's worth towards the reasonable needs of that person otherwise than for full, valuable consideration.[83] In other words, the court is looking for the individual to show that she was dependent on the deceased. Any contributions she made to the couple's relationship, whether they were financial or in the form of services, must not be equal to or outweigh those of the deceased: if they are, the claim will fail.[84] Changes to the law have been suggested which would put the emphasis on a couple living as husband and wife rather than the dependency of one individual upon another.[85] As the law stands at present, however, a cohabiting partner has to prove her dependency whilst a wife pursuing a claim under the 1975 Act does not.

The manner in which the court goes about determining whether or not a widow, an ex-wife or a cohabitee has a valid claim is complex. As a consequence any action is likely to prove costly and is not recommended if the estate is small, since costs will be deducted from it.[86] There is a two stage procedure. The first stage requires the court to consider objectively whether or not reasonable financial provision has been made for the applicant. In order to answer this question the court will consider the situation in its entirety. If the answer is "no" then the court moves on to the second stage of the process in which it is decided whether, in the discretion of the court, it will order financial provision to be made for the applicant.

The 1975 Act sets out a list of general and specific considerations which must be taken into account by the court in reaching its conclusion. They include the means of the applicant, the applicant's circumstances as compared with other applicants and beneficiaries under the will, the deceased's obligations towards the applicant, the size of the estate, any disability suffered by the applicant and any other matter including the applicant's conduct. The specific considerations vary according to the individual who is making the claim. In the case of the wife, the court is told to have regard to what the wife would have been entitled to if there had been a divorce, her age, the duration of the marriage and the contribution she made to the welfare of the deceased's family. There is a good deal of similarity between these and the factors taken into account when reaching a financial settlement after divorce. Once again, a woman who makes a successful claim must show not only need but also that she has somehow "earned" that entitlement.

A former wife who has not remarried will find it difficult to pursue a successful claim since financial provision will have been made for her at the time of the couple's divorce. Indeed, if there has been a clean break settlement the court may have barred the wife from making a claim under the 1975 Act. Because the court uses its discretion it is difficult to predict with any certainty when the court might be prepared to make an order. It has been prepared to do so, for example, where an ex-husband failed to make agreed maintenance payments.[87]

A cohabitee must show that the deceased made a substantial financial contribution towards her reasonable needs. If a couple pool their resources and provide for each other, as is increasingly the case with modern relationships, a claim may not succeed.[88] There are instances when a cohabitee has been able to bring a successful claim, but since each case is judged on its particular circumstances, it is difficult to decide why some succeed and others do not or to deduce any general principles. The orders that the court can make if an application succeeds are basically the same that are made on divorce; they include periodical payments, lump sum payments and a transfer of property order.

With the exception of a wife whose husband dies intestate, a woman who has not been adequately provided for out of the deceased's estate may have difficulties in rectifying the situation. The machinery is there but it is expensive to use, entrusts the court with a great deal of discretion and emphasises past conduct. It might be simpler and fairer if a husband was obliged to leave his wife a fixed share of his estate, though this would leave open the question of how a cohabitee would be treated, particularly if the deceased also had a wife.

Breaking up: a fair division?

The treatment that women receive when a relationship breaks down is a product of the law's perception of the relative standing of the partners and their roles. Women's general inability to make as great a financial contribution as men to the relationship is assumed to be justification for awarding them less when the relationship ends. Indeed the power that superior earning-ability gives a man whilst a relationship is in being may be used by the law as indicating a desire on the part of the couple to organise their financial affairs in a particular manner. Moreover, the unpaid services that women commonly perform in the course of a partnership seem to be expected of them and do not necessarily receive acknowledgement in any financial settlement. Such attitudes merely reflect the traditional view that women are the junior partners in any relationship. The very fact that women generally have less access to wealth because of their lower rates of pay and their inability to provide for their own financial security is used by the law as proof of their inferior status within a relationship. The belated acknowledgement by the law that a man should make proper financial provision for his child even though he and his partner no longer live together has been subverted from a device with the potential to improve the financial circumstances of women to one that makes their financial situation worse. When a relationship is ended by death, the law's attachment to the notion of women's dependency becomes especially clear, even though in the case of cohabiting women it demands they prove it, whilst for wives it is prepared to assume it.

The problems posed by questions of inheritance raise the general issue of how the law should deal with cohabitation. It is not necessarily the solution to say that cohabitation should be treated as if it were a marriage. Indeed, since many couples deliberately choose to live together rather than marry, it is neither logical nor satisfactory to do so. On the other hand, when cohabitation ends, the consequences may be exactly the same as the dissolution of a marriage. This in turn raises the issue of whether a wife should not enjoy greater rights than a cohabitee since, if both are treated equally, there would be little point to marriage. The public commitment required by marriage, still leads some to the conclusion that a wife deserves more because of her willingness to make that commitment.

Whatever the conclusion about the difference, if any, between marriage and cohabitation, there needs to be some clear indication of what are the results, including the financial results, of opting for such a relationship. A *wife* can expect the law to take account of her special status when dealing with the consequences of divorce or death, including the financial consequences. Cohabiting partners find themselves in a much more uncertain situation. In particular, a woman may discover that she has to *prove* her right to a share in the couple's assets, either by demonstrating that she has made a contribution or by alleging that she was dependent on her partner. There are ways in which a cohabiting couple can provide for the ending of their relationship at some future date, but these tend to depend on the parties having access to legal advice and being able to pay for it. The inevitable conclusion is, that being a wife currently has financial advantages when a relationship ends. The law's unwillingness in this context to treat cohabitation as if it were a quasi-marriage seems at odds with its willingness to do so in other circumstances, most particularly when a cohabiting couple are claiming social security benefits.

Notes

1.   See pp. 185 et seq.
2.   (1993) *Social Trends 23*, Table 2.14 p. 30.

3.   Maclean, M. (1991), *Surviving Divorce*, p. 12.

4.   Eurostat (1991), *A Social Portrait of Europe*, p. 25.

5.   Eekelaar, J. (1984), *Family Law and Social Policy*, p. 28; (1993) *Social Trends 23*, p. 30.

6.   See pp. 185 et seq.

7.   (1993) *Social Trends 23*, Table 2.13 p. 30.

8.   In May 1992, 194,000 lone parent families headed by a divorced woman were claiming income support. The corresponding figure for men was 15,000: *Department of Social Security Statistics 1993*, Table A2.15, p. 19.

9.   Davis, G. Cretney, S. and Collins, J. (1994), *Simple Quarrels*, p. 27.

10.   See p. 112 and note that there are proposals to tighten up on the eligibility rules.

11.   Maclean op. cit., n. 3, pp. 114-119.

12.   Davis et al. (1994), op. cit., n. 9, p. 8.

13.   Ibid., pp. 7-8.

14.   See now the Matrimonial Causes Act 1973, s. 1(1). In a White Paper, (1994), *Looking to the Future: Mediation and the Ground for Divorce*, Cmnd 2799, the government acknowledges grounds on which current divorce law may be criticised: paras 2.12-2.30. Proposed changes to the law would include delaying the granting of a divorce for twelve months, during which time couples would be encouraged to seek advice through family mediation, to determine whether reconciliation was possible. If it was not, they would be expected to settle issues regarding access to children, financial provision and property during that period.

15.   The government proposes to consider financial provision after divorce as part of its review of the family justice system. No date has yet been set for this.

16.   See p. 22.

17.   Davis et al. (1994), op. cit., n. 9.

18.   See *Keller v Keller and Legal Aid Board* in *The Independent*, 21 October 1994.

19.   Legal Aid Act 1988, s. 15.

20.   Ibid., s. 16(6).

21.   [1987] 1 FLR 223.

22.   For example periodical payments. Civil Legal Aid (General) Regulations 1989, S.I. 1989, No. 339, reg. 94; amended, S.I. 1991, No. 2036.

23.   Davis et al. (1994), op. cit., n. 9.

24.   Ibid., p. 82.

25.   See pp. 185-196.

26.   Eekelaar, J. (1991), *Regulating Divorce*, p. 154.

27.   See p. 247.

28.   Eekelaar, J. (1984), *Family Law and Social Policy*, p. 29.

29.   Maclean, M. (1991), *Surviving Divorce*, p. 25.

30.   Ibid., p. 26.

31.   *Lee v Lee* [1984] FLR 243.

32.   *Mesher v Mesher and Hall* [1980] 1 All ER 126.

33.   *Carson v Carson* [1983] 1 All ER 478.

34. *Clutton v Clutton* [1991] 1 All ER 340: Eekelaar, op. cit., n. 26, p. 71, p. 74.
35. *Martin v Martin* [1978] Fam 12.
36. Matrimonial and Family Proceedings Act 1984, s. 3.
37. *Wachtel v Wachtel* [1973] 1 All ER 829.
38. Ibid., p. 839.
39. Eekelaar, op. cit. n. 26 p 61.
40. *Wachtel v Wachtel* [1973] 1 All ER 829 at p. 837. See also Chap. 6.
41. *H v H* [1975] 1 All ER 376.
42. Hoggett, B. and Pearl, D. (1991), *The Family Law and Society*, p. 271.
43. Eekelaar, J. (1984), *Family Law and Social Policy*, p. 34.
44. *Suter v Suter and Jones* [1987] 2 All ER 336.
45. Eekelaar, op. cit., n. 26, p. 68.
46. Ibid., p. 70.
47. Child Support Act 1991. See p. 247 et seq.
48. In Australia, for example.
49. *B v B* [1988] 2 FLR 490.
50. *K v K* [1990] 2 FLR 225.
51. *Wagstaff v Wagstaff* [1992] 1 FLR 333.
52. *Wachtel v Wachtel* [1973] 1 All ER 829.
53. *Williams v Williams* [1974] 3 All ER 377.
54. *Brown v Brown* (1981) 3 FLR 161.
55. [1990] 2 FLR 457.
56. Ibid., p. 461.
57. *Gojkovic v Gojkovic* [1990] 2 All ER 84
58. Davies, G. et al, op. cit., n. 9, p. 51.
59. *Wachtel v Wachtel* [1973] 1 All ER 829
60. *Bailey v Tolliday* (1982) 4 FLR 542
61. See pp. 156-159.
62. Salter, D., (ed.), (1992), *Pensions and Insurance on Family Breakdown*.
63. Ibid., Chap. 4. The foreseeable future tends to be regarded by the courts as the three to five years following divorce.
64. Ibid.
65. Matrimonial Causes Act 1973, s. 5 and s. 10.
66. Ibid., s. 5(3).
67. Salter (1992), op. cit., n. 62, Chap. 8.
68. It is suggested (see (1994) Cmnd 2799) that reforms will force couples to address these issues more seriously and less antagonistically. This will supposedly be achieved by family mediation and the need to settle the issues before a divorce is granted. The laws relating to financial provision will, however, remain the same.
69. See, for example, *Bernard v Josephs* [1982] Ch 391, above Chap. 6.
70. *Burns v Burns* [1983] FLR 178, and Chap. 6.

71. See, for example, *Greenwich LBC v McGrady* [1983] 81 LGR 288.

72. Courts in the USA have recognised cohabitation contracts and several provinces in Canada have legislated to allow them. The Council of Ministers of the European Union adopted a recommendation in 1988 that member states should not prevent the enforcement of cohabitation contracts dealing with money and property simply on the ground the parties are unmarried.

73. The Cohabitation (Contract Enforcement) Bill, introduced in June 1991 by Teresa Gorman as a ten minute rule bill. It was unsuccessful.

74. Child Support Act 1991, s. 11 and Schedule 1.

75. From 5th April 1993.

76. Child Support Act 1991, ss. 6, 46. Child Support (Maintenance Assessment Procedure) Regulations 1992, S.I. 1992 No. 1813.

77. Child Support Act 1991, ss. 6, 46.

78. *Crozier v Crozier* [1994] 2 All ER 362 at pp. 370-371.

79. Child Support Act 1991, s. 27.

80. (1995) Cmnd 2745.

81. Inheritance (Provision for Family and Dependants) Act 1975 s. 1.

82. Wills Act 1837, s. 18A.

83. Inheritance (Provision for Family and Dependants) Act 1975, s. 1(3).

84. *Jelley v Iliffe* [1981] 2 All ER 236.

85. Law Commission (1989), *Distribution on Intestacy* No. 187, paras. 58-62.

86. [1979] 2 All ER 820 at p. 828, Buckley L.J.

87. *Re Farrow (deceased)* [1987] 1 FLR 205

88. *Re Beaumont* [1979] 3 WLR 818

8　For Richer For Poorer

This book set out to demonstrate that, despite decades of formal equality, women remain economically unequal and, more specifically, to investigate the particular role of the law in this equation.　Proof of inequality is everywhere - from the segregated world of paid work to the isolation of unpaid carers, from the statistics on women's pay to those on poverty.　Whilst it is not difficult to identify the products of a gendered society, it is less easy to arrive at a consensus on how true equality of opportunity may be achieved.　Admitting that the law has played and still plays a key part in the continued dependency of women - whether on the state or on partners and family - does not necessarily rule out the use of law to redress the balance.　The anti-discrimination legislation, including the Equal Pay Act and the Sex Discrimination Act may not have been unqualified successes, but it is clear that some of the positive developments in the last twenty years can be traced to the existence of these and similar measures.　Women in the United Kingdom who are in paid employment may have the least generous maternity rights in the European Union, but without the laws which result from our membership of that Union, they would probably have nothing at all.　As lawyers and as feminists, the writers believe that the law can help to increase the access which women have to wealth and that, just as it was used to protect the status quo in the past, so it may be used to engineer social and political change for the future.　This begs the question as to what measures would secure a more equal future for women and how their passage is to be achieved.

There is, however, a logically prior question to any discussion of how to achieve women's economic equality and that is, why bother?　Some might argue that the most important task facing policy makers today is to generate sufficient wealth through a well run economy that, even though there may remain inequalities, everyone is better off than they were before as a result of the "trickle-down" theory.

If there is a buoyant and wealth-creating economy in which breadwinners earn sufficient to feed their families and the welfare state operates to catch those on the margins, does it really matter if certain sections of society are not enjoying equal rights or that some people remain dependent on others? Such debates serve only to emphasise, however, that arguments about equality are, ultimately, arguments about human rights. If adherence to principles of political and civil liberties is to mean anything at all, it must mean the chance for all citizens to participate in the life of their society. This does not just mean the traditional fundamental rights such as freedom of speech and religion, the right to found a family, or to have a fair trial, it means the recognition that in order to exercise citizenship, every individual must have access to resources which guarantee the basic needs of life in the late twentieth century. If there are misgivings about the "dependency culture" engendered by the welfare state, these should extend also to those adults who must depend on others for the necessities of life. Women will not have equal rights of citizenship if they are *forced* into dependency on partners or social security payments by underpaid employment or an unpaid caring role.

Redressing the balance and creating equality of opportunity implies some redistribution of wealth (in its widest sense), since one of the hallmarks of contemporary British society is the growing divide between the rich and the poor. It is access to wealth in the form of waged work or adequate benefits for the unwaged which is the key to a more equal society, since it is financial independence which underpins equal citizenship. This is not restricted to women - it extends to all of those who are currently discriminated against, including the disabled, ethnic minorities, the homeless and the unemployed of either sex - but it is of particular importance in the context of this book that all women, of whatever class, colour or age are enabled to live as independent actors in a fairer world.

Distributing resources in equal shares is not, of course, a recipe for making everyone rich, but it does contribute towards giving the same starting point for all. Equality need not mean identity, in the sense of all being the same and, in as much as individuals have different abilities and personalities, it is likely that, even if equality of opportunity were achieved, some would prosper more than others. It is not axiomatic that redistribution of wealth calls for identical treatment for all, rather it requires a recognition of the different needs of different groups and a commitment to meeting those needs at levels which do not condemn the beneficiaries to a standard of life which the majority would find at worst unacceptable and at best unpleasant. Not everyone would agree that such redistribution is possible (for instance, because it is too expensive) or indeed desirable (because it smacks of interventionism and "nannying"). Nevertheless, without such intervention, especially that of the law, it is unlikely, given the way society is currently ordered, that women can attain equality. As the earlier chapters have illustrated, despite moves towards equality, the legal framework serves to maintain women's situation of dependency and, whilst it would be exaggerating to claim this as a deliberate male conspiracy, it remains a significant obstacle to the final emancipation of women.

The verdict on the law

Feminists have charged the law with obstructing and frustrating the aspirations and legitimate expectations of women. The evidence marshalled against the legal system and the rules it imposes includes the allegation that the law perceives women as men perceive women.[1] Since, it is alleged, men have always perceived women primarily in terms of their sexual and reproductive functions, the law does likewise. Women's own desires are subordinated to their role in society as defined by men. Their potential as sexual partners, mothers and those best suited to rear the next generation forces upon them a set of unsatisfactory compromises. One method of enforcing those compromises is the alleged dichotomy which is created between the public and private spheres.[2] The public sphere represents those areas of activity and human behaviour where legal regulation is thought appropriate. The private sphere contains those aspects of everyday living in relation to which legal intervention is believed to be inappropriate and it is argued that matters are best left to the individuals concerned. The boundary between public and private is, however, not fixed and the law has increasingly encroached upon areas which would have been thought of as sacrosanct.[3] Regulation, by legislators and/or by the judges, is now found in relation to what might have been thought of as amongst the most intimate of matters, including, for example, the behaviour and choices of pregnant women, in whose case the right to intervene is claimed in the interests of health and safety or the well-being of the foetus. Despite its increasingly blurred nature the public/private divide remains significant for feminists, if only because it is a prime example of how laws can be manipulated to the disadvantage of women. It is too easy to explain the absence of legal regulation of household finances between husband and wife by asserting that this is "private" or to try to excuse the lack of state nurseries by saying that women who choose to work must make "private" arrangements for child care. Women denied income by their partners and unable to work outside the home to earn their own wage are thereby effectively excluded from the public sphere. On the other hand, once a woman does wish to claim state benefits, she will find that her private life is anything but private.

The case against the law includes also its willingness to define and exclude. It uses superficially gender-neutral standards to define sex discrimination in the workplace but, in practice, the law condones the marginalisation of female experience. It does so on the basis that such experience relates to the family and is therefore a matter of private choice rather than public and thus legal concern.

Women are expected to conform to male patterns of working hours and availability and are not supposed to carry with them into the workplace the responsibilities that they have elsewhere. Even the ECJ, which in many ways has been the champion of women workers, has not been prepared to take account of their domestic responsibilities in defining concepts such as equal pay.[4]

The charges made against the law by feminists have, undeniably, provided telling insights into the manner in which laws and legal systems function. Feminist analyses of law tend, however, to be uni-dimensional in their approach and there is also a tendency, having exposed one particular flaw or weakness, to blame that for all the inadequacies of the legal system. The aim of this book has been to subject the laws which regulate access to wealth to an analysis aimed at identifying the major reasons why women are not men's financial equals. Some of the shortcomings which have emerged add weight to the analyses offered by feminist writers such as MacKinnon; others reveal fresh reasons as to why the law fails women.

The range and number of the defects identified within the law and the legal system is itself important. Feminism is sometimes accused of lack of method, or even of a central argument and of being instead a loose collection of complaints and issues which, taken together, describe rather than explain the misfortunes of the female sex. The challenge is to demonstrate that feminism systematically converges upon a central explanation of sex inequality through an approach distinctive to its subject yet applicable to the whole of social life, including class.[5]

Rather than simply listing the complaints which feminists legitimately have about law, this book has examined different laws in an effort to throw light on the central issue of how, in various ways and by various means, those laws are failing women, not least by not taking account of the salient features of women's lives. It is part of the task of feminist writers to ascertain what women need from the law, to determine what is preventing them from attaining that objective and to suggest how best the reforms may be achieved. To say, as some feminists have, that there is a "central explanation of sex inequality" is reassuringly simple but overly naive. Feminist analysis is better employed in concentrating on how well or otherwise legal rules meet women's needs, rather than seeking to identify the one reason behind the law's apparent acceptance of the unequal status of women. The efforts expended in seeking to allocate blame may simply persuade women not to resort to law at all on the basis that the system will never work satisfactorily for them. If women were, however, to take a leading role in the law- and policy-making process, which they have thus far not succeeded in doing, it might well be the case that whilst matters would not change overnight, the legal and bureaucratic systems would be more responsive to measures which would advance the status and independence of women.

The analysis undertaken here suggests that it would be an over-simplification to condemn the law simply on the basis of its "maleness" or even because of its inherent conservatism which tends to create an attachment to the status quo. Each chapter illustrates that the law's failure to secure for women equality in the guise of economic independence arises from a mixture of motives which are political, economic and pragmatic in origin and often, it would appear, completely contradictory. In Chapter 1 it was suggested that if women are to become truly independent, there are certain fundamental issues which must be addressed. These related generally to paid employment, the welfare system and the apportionment of wealth within the family. The first of these requires an investigation of the extent to which the laws regulating access to paid employment take account of women's domestic or caring responsibilities, while the second concentrates on the status of women within the welfare system and inquires whether they are seen as individuals or as members of a unit, as workers or as carers. The final question encapsulates many of the issues raised elsewhere, since it could be argued that it is women's dependence within the family which colours and controls their lack of independence outside it. None of these issues is self-contained, nor will the achievement of equality in one sphere be sufficient without changes in the others. For centuries women were regarded as being dependent on men. Economic independence for women can be achieved only when all of these wider issues are addressed in ways which recognise, not only in theory but also in practice, the legitimacy and the validity of women's claims.

It is hardly surprising that feminists' allegations about the law's fundamentally gendered attitudes have some truth to them, since it is apparent that the law has always been the instrument of those best placed to make their needs and desires heard. The history of women's access to wealth, as Chapter 2 emphasises, is one in which women played no part, except as objects of the law's attention. They took no direct part in the law-making process and were accommodated only to the extent which male law makers believed was necessary, and in a manner which men thought appropriate. This was not entirely a matter of *sex* discrimination, since the ruling class, though male, was nevertheless an elite. Though the requirements of men may have been the driving force behind the law, they were the requirements of a particular group of men. The laws that allowed men to take control of their wives' property were of greatest significance to those whose wives owned property. Since, at least until Victorian times, property owners were a minority, the law was used for the benefit of a privileged minority of men who had control of the law and policy-making processes.

Though the social divisions of the nineteenth century may be unsurprising, it is remarkable that even now that women have secured equal political rights, there are many occasions when they struggle to have their particular concerns placed prominently on the legal and social agenda.[6] Chapter 3 makes clear that women are playing an increasing role in the workplace and it is true that the law offers working women a guarantee of equal treatment with men. It is at least arguable, however, that the equality on offer is on male rather than female terms, since there has been no effective challenge to the use made of the paradigm of the male worker in assessing discrimination. Women are *unlawfully* discriminated against only if they receive less favourable treatment than a man, but it is not unlawful where an employer refuses to offer flexible hours or term-time working to *all* of the employees. The lack of such facilities is not a major issue because these have not, traditionally, been seen as terms of employment which are of importance to the typical male worker. The same is true of child care facilities, career breaks, and, obviously, enhanced maternity provisions. Such matters are still too often thought of as women's issues, as expensive extras and even as proof that women are problematic employees.   Even a woman who seeks to establish indirect discrimination must prove that proportionately fewer women than men are able to meet the employer's requirements, thus lending support to those who argue that women are less adaptable or less well qualified or less committed to their work. When women argue for changes in working practices or for laws which would call for acknowledgement of their different responsibilities and the constraints which these place on them, they are criticised for demanding *special* treatment rather than equal treatment, even though at the moment they are denied an equal chance in the competition.

Perhaps it is the absence of women from the law-making process which has contributed to the narrow and unsatisfactory nature of the definition of discrimination, which has succeeded only in achieving formal rather than substantive equality. While it is no longer legally permissible to state expressly that women are better fitted to perform certain tasks and should be excluded from others which are within the male domain, the law concedes equality only provided that women are prepared to behave as men. If they are unable or unwilling to fit the male pattern, this is presented as a matter of choice (which, moreover, men are said not to have). It is true that equality would be more attainable if the law was used to help women comply with the male standards, since more women could achieve financial self-sufficiency. On the other hand, turning women into economic men is not necessarily the best way forward for either women or men. Measures which assist women to combine work and family should be seen as both advantageous and essential for both sexes. With this end in view, child care facilities and family-friendly working practices must cease to be seen as a matter of private choice (for women) rather than something which concerns the state. It is currently the case in the United Kingdom that whilst employers may have their attention drawn to "good practice" in the context of the inter-relationship between work and family, there are no mechanisms for imposing such practices on reluctant organisations. In a general atmosphere of deregulation, the decision to have children is presented as one that involves the parents being prepared to assume the burden and costs of caring for those children. In this way, the public/private divide is quite openly manipulated in a way that is antipathetic to women's needs.

The review of the social security system in Chapters 4 and 5 examined the extent to which that system meets women's needs as individuals rather than as part of a unit such as the family. In this area the traditional view of men as breadwinners and women as carers remains exceedingly and surprisingly persistent. It is true that social security systems are complex structures which cannot respond swiftly to change, nor can they easily be changed in any radical fashion too often. They represent long-term commitments for both government and for individuals. The current social security system still retains overtones of its origins in the Britain of the 1940s and as a consequence it reflects male attitudes towards women and how they should behave. It has not entirely shaken off the assumption that women will be the carers and homemakers supported by male breadwinners. It is also the case that anti-discrimination legislation has had much less of an impact in the context of social security than in the area of waged work generally. The European Union is working towards the harmonisation of social security laws and the ECJ has done its best to anticipate this development by insisting, for example, that occupational pensions constitute pay.[7] Such developments do little, however, to correct the discrimination that is so integral a part of the United Kingdom's social security system. The availability of social security benefits is based on particular work patterns and the key position occupied by the family unit. The work pattern that guarantees the maximum benefit is the traditional male pattern of long-term, well-paid, full-time work. Women find it hard to meet these prerequisites since they are not as well-paid as men, are much more likely than men to work part-time and voluntarily take career breaks. That said, there are increasing numbers of men who for different reasons, most particularly redundancy and unemployment, find it hard to satisfy these conditions. The criteria used to secure maximum benefits follow a traditionally "male" pattern which may no longer match the working lives of either men or women, but they cannot be challenged as discriminatory if they are applied to both sexes. The European Union, for its part, has not defined the term worker in measures such as Directive 79/7 dealing with equal treatment in statutory social security schemes so as to include those individuals, mainly women, who undertake unpaid caring tasks.[8]

The other crucial feature of social security benefits, particularly means-tested benefits, is that whilst they are paid to individuals, they are assessed on the basis of family income and assets. This has a natural tendency to force one family member into dependency on another and in many cases it will be a woman who is forced to depend on a man. A woman who loses her job may be unable to claim social security benefits if her partner is in employment and if the family income is above the levels set for such payment. If her partner is unemployed it may not be economically worthwhile for her to take a job if the result is that the family will lose an equivalent amount in benefit.[9]   Paying benefit to the family unit also assumes that whoever receives that benefit within the unit will be prepared to share it with other members.   Women without partners are not hampered by the concept of aggregation but they are far from immune from the poverty trap created by trying to improve upon the low level of welfare benefits by securing paid employment. While the introduction of allowances for child care costs are welcome, they are not enough.   There must be a radical overhaul of a system which gives few incentives to lone mothers to find a job and to aim for financial independence.   Parents without partners are also those most affected by the lack of child care - it is likely that many more mothers would be seeking employment if they could be assured of adequate care for their children.   This in itself raises questions about whether the state is sincere in its desire to move claimants off benefits.   Although there is much talk about reducing the levels of unemployment and the use of training to produce a better skilled workforce, there is some ambivalence in the minds of many about whether the mothers of young children should be encouraged to leave those children in the care of others in order to work outside the home.   The answer, of course, is that motherhood will not be a properly valued role in life until it is recognised as such in something other than rhetoric.   It is hypocritical to talk of the important work that mothers do in maintaining a stable family environment and rearing the next generation while refusing to recognise that contribution in any concrete way.   If the promotion of motherhood is simply a smoke-screen for discouraging the employment of women and a way of driving them back into the home, it is most unlikely to succeed.

Comparison of the social security system and the system of taxation in the United Kingdom elicits some interesting parallels and contrasts.   Whereas both systems aim to allocate resources to groups within the population, the recipients of social security benefits, and in particular of means-tested benefits, are generally regarded as being less deserving than the recipients of tax allowances.   Mortgage tax relief, personal allowances and concessions to savers, cost money in the same way as do social security benefits.   Moreover, the state's decision to subsidise certain activities such as saving, house-purchase or marriage, helps only a certain proportion of the population which, in many cases, is predominantly male.

In contrast, the current government's determination to cut the costs of its social security budget has meant that welfare benefits, including contributory benefits, now represent some of the lowest in Europe.[10]   It is apparent that many women find themselves forced to rely on the social security system for a whole variety of reasons.   On divorce, for example, a woman may find, especially if she has dependent children, that the only way she can survive financially is by turning to the state for help, including help with her housing costs.   What help she receives is grudgingly provided and subject to what might be regarded as unacceptable intrusion into her private life.   The negative images associated with the social security system are a particular problem for women with nowhere else to turn and contrast with the positive image of those benefiting from tax allowances and tax incentives.

The negative connotations of being forced to rely on social security benefits may derive, in part at least, from the fact that the claimants are perceived as failing to fulfil their role in society. This is true for both men and women. The former are seen as not performing the breadwinner role, while women, particularly if they do not have a partner, are seen as exploiting the welfare state. Those who receive tax relief are regarded as successful, at the same time that the recipients of social security benefits are disempowered by their very need. The law plays its part by neatly and easily reinforcing a particular view of how individuals are to function in society. It is thus particularly sad that the laws regulating these benefits do not also provide incentives to move from claimant to tax payer. The potential loss in benefit discourages any real moves to self help and again the main victims are often women whether as lone mothers or as part of a couple. The law positively encourages dependency even though welfare dependency is the subject of so much criticism.

An important part of any solution to this is to recognise that much of the law on social security benefits has been influenced by the law's construction of the family. The way in which a couple, married or cohabiting, choose to organise their financial affairs appears superficially to be an issue which falls within or is relegated to the private and hence legally unregulated sphere. This is to misconstrue the true position. Although there is no law to say which partner shall have what share of any income coming into the family unit, the laws regulating social security and personal taxation undoubtedly exert an influence. They may deter one or both partners from working and may dictate how any assets that are available are shared. The existence of personal tax allowances may mean that it is more advantageous to place certain resources in one partner's name than another.

The unregulated nature of the "happy" family unit is in direct contrast with what happens when that unit breaks up, at which point there is an excess of legal rules directing how any assets should be divided. Yet, as Chapter 7 demonstrates, there is no real guiding principle indicating how the courts should approach this task: instead there is discretion. It is left to the couple and their legal advisers and occasionally to the court to decide what will amount to satisfactory financial arrangements. The appearance of legal regulation is thus somewhat illusory and in this case the lack of regulation may once more work to women's disadvantage. The very pressures which, during the course of a marriage may ensure that the husband is the dominant partner in financial matters, may still be at work when a marriage is in the process of dissolution. The financial sacrifices required of a husband may be alleviated by the existence of social security benefits. An ex-spouse may be forced to exchange her financial dependency on her husband for dependency on the state and with it the knowledge that it is exceedingly difficult to break free from such dependency.

It is only in relation to children that the law now demands that adequate financial arrangements be made. However this switch from the courts to an administrative agency employing a precise formula in order to calculate the appropriate rate of child support has been, from all angles, an unmitigated disaster.[11] The principle behind the legislation is unassailable in demanding realistic levels of maintenance by the absent parent. In practice, that principle has been sacrificed in favour of savings on the social security budget. A measure that could have ensured greater independence for women has served only to emphasise how dependent many of them are on the continuing support and good-will of the state. Once the threat is made to withdraw that support and good-will many women are faced with a choice of either complying or facing reductions in their benefit payments.

The sharing out of property required when someone dies is another example of how there can be an illusion of legal regulation. There appears to be a good deal of law concerning the succession to property but on closer examination it becomes apparent that the law is really peripheral in most cases. Only when a husband dies intestate will a wife automatically be entitled to a share of his property. If a couple are cohabiting, there is no automatic share for the surviving partner. Should a husband choose to make a will, he can, if he wishes, leave his property to whomever he likes, knowing that there is no obligation imposed on him by the law to make satisfactory provision for his wife. Her only legal redress in these circumstances is to prove to the court's satisfaction that she was dependent on her husband and thus needs to be provided for out of his estate. In other words, women who have been able to establish their financial independence will be penalised. The law does not acknowledge that where a couple have lived together the accumulation of individual wealth may be due in no small measure to the existence of that partnership, and therefore demand that some share should automatically go to the surviving partner. Although married women can find themselves excluded from enjoying a share in their husband's estate, the position is even more precarious when a couple cohabit. The law has yet to determine how to treat cohabitation. In many respects it is treated in the same fashion as marriage which seems crass given that many couples cohabit in order to avoid the legal consequences of marriage. There is ambivalence over whether a cohabiting couple should be allowed to define for themselves the parameters of their relationship in a cohabitation contract.

That kind of ambivalence may, indeed, be the key to understanding why the laws currently regulating access to wealth do not address the needs of women as successfully as those of men. The law demands a "say" in the ways in which people organise their lives, and rightly so, since without intervention on the part of the state, all manner of unfairness could result. Yet, that intervention carries no guarantee of coherence. It may occur in order to save money, to promote greater efficiency, to ensure fairness, to permit the redistribution of wealth or to uphold certain values, including political values, such as the well-being of children, the family, equality or a free-market economy. Indeed, the absence of legal regulation can be as much as product of those forces as its presence. It is certain, however, that any such intervention will be inspired by and will seek to further the preoccupations of those who are closest to the policy-making and decision-taking process. As a consequence, legal systems will be adversely affected in a number of ways. First, ambivalence and lack of coherent and compatible policies produce a less than efficient legal system where the benefit of one policy may be cancelled out by a conflicting policy in another context. To take a simple example, laws that protect pregnant workers from dismissal and guarantee their continuing employment seek to address a specific instance of sex discrimination and are inspired by the policy of equal treatment. But much of the benefit that could be produced by such legislation is wasted as there is no corresponding law placing a duty upon employers or local authorities to provide child care facilities. Calls for steps to be taken to rectify this are met by arguments concerning cost, the proper way in which to raise children and the suggestion that this is an area best left to private choice. Second, the absence of certain groups such as the poor, the disabled, ethnic minorities and women from the decision-making process ensures that what is important to them may be low on the agenda of those who control this process, particularly if seen as incompatible with objectives or values that are important to the decision-makers. Even if those who exercise power within the state are prepared to promote the interests of under-represented groups, there is no guarantee that their view of what is needed will match the aspirations of those groups. A man's view of what is good for women is not necessarily the same as a woman's view. Finally, even if the decision-makers are willing and able to intervene and do so sympathetically, there is every likelihood that the impact of a single measure will be minimal in the context of the legal system as a whole.

The way forward

It would be difficult to disagree with the authors of the Report of the Commission for Social Justice[12] who state:

> Work is central to our lives. Paid or unpaid, it is the way in which we meet needs, create wealth and distribute resources. It is a source of personal identity and individual fulfilment, social status and relationships. It is the heart of wealth and welfare. ...[P]aid work remains the best pathway out of poverty, as well as the only way in which most people can hope to achieve a decent standard of living.[13]

Nevertheless, such sentiments serve to highlight the special problems faced by women in the context of access to such wealth. These include the persistently gendered nature of the workforce; the resultant undervaluing of women's work and the inevitable consequence of women's unequal pay.

As seen in Chapter 3, there is a persistent sex stereotyping within the workforce. This disadvantages both women and men. For women, it means that they are still under-represented in certain sectors and in the higher reaches of most occupations. Although women now make up a half of the workforce in the United Kingdom, many of them work part-time, in jobs in which women predominate. The gendering of the labour market has been one important reason for the limited success of the Equal Pay Act, which has proved unequal to the task of persuading employers to value the work done by women as highly as that done by men. Women are cheap to employ and until recently part-timers have been cheap to get rid of - a truly flexible workforce. It is in these areas that such growth in employment that exists is occurring but, because women's work is both undervalued and underpaid, men who have lost their jobs in the declining sectors of heavy industry and manufacturing are reluctant to compete with women for the jobs.

Some of this stems from the reluctance on the part of many men to relinquish the idea of the male breadwinner and his dependent family. To improve the position of women in the labour market a concerted programme is needed to educate both employers and workers about the importance of abandoning traditional notions of women's work and men's work. The move towards fairer pay for women will be given a welcome impetus if their work is properly valued and one way of helping to achieve that goal is for the jobs they do to cease to be seen as a female preserve. There would be little point in doing this, of course, if the only consequence was that men took over those sectors where women have predominated and pushed women out of the market. Along with the abandonment of sex stereotyping in relation to the jobs which men and women do, there must be a real commitment to the combining of work and family, *for both sexes.* There is nothing wrong with part-time employment per se, provided it is proportionately and adequately rewarded. Workers in the United Kingdom tend to work longer hours than their counterparts in the European Union, and it is at least arguable that if working hours were reduced, not only would it create extra jobs but would also make it easier for workers of both sexes to spend more time with their families. A move away from long hours and overtime for both men and women might make employers more willing to accept that the desire to devote time and energy to home and family is not necessarily a sign of lack of commitment to the job nor a peculiarly female attribute. Nor are such developments inimical to employers' commercial interests: lower hours and flexible patterns of work can be of real advantage to an employer - and are indeed what makes part-timers so attractive a proposition.[14]

For those with family or other caring responsibilities, part-time employment may currently be the only way to combine paid work with those other obligations. In striving for women's economic equality, such employment should not necessarily be discouraged, but rather there should be a move to ensure that all forms of "non-standard" employment patterns are adequately rewarded and protected by employment legislation. Nor should these be the preserve of women: men should be encouraged to take their share of family duties, including unpaid work in the home. Flexibility must not be seen, however, as the preserve of the employer and as no more than a way of acquiring cheap labour. For an employer who wishes to have the advantages of a flexible work force there are concomitant obligations. Part-time employment and job-sharing schemes are not the only requirements on employers if workers are to be able to combine work and home.

As traditional industries decline and the service sectors increase, it becomes increasingly obvious that there are patterns of work other than those we have been used to, not simply in relation to hours of work but also to periods in and out of work. While some employers now recognise that it is both feasible and cost effective to allow *women* career breaks, and although the law does confer some rights upon pregnant employees, the next legal hurdle is to extend these to parents, that is, to include fathers as well as mothers and to encourage the realisation that child care is something which either sex may choose to undertake. The European Commission's draft Directive on Parental Leave was first proposed in 1983 and provided for at least three month's unpaid leave for a worker, to be taken by either parent at the end of maternity leave. When the draft reappeared in 1993, the United Kingdom voiced its implacable opposition on grounds of cost and on the basis that it was the wrong time to add to the burdens placed on businesses, which would put jobs at risk. The United Kingdom is, however, one of only four member states not to offer parental leave and many of the schemes already in operation are considerably more generous than that proposed in the draft Directive. It would appear that the draft Directive will itself be overtaken by events since the European Commission's more recent proposals are further reaching. In *European social policy - a way forward for the union*, which sets out the next phase of social policy development, for 1995-1999, the Commission announces that it is to investigate the introduction of a framework Directive which deals with issues of reconciling professional and family life, including, but not restricted to, parental leave. In the meantime, the Parental Leave Directive remains a live issue, since it has been decided that with eleven members in favour, the proposal will be taken forward under the social Protocol which will allow qualified majority voting, rather than a unanimous vote. On the other hand, even if adopted, it would not apply to the United Kingdom because of the opt out agreement.

Such refusal on the part of the British government to countenance any assistance to combine work and parenthood prejudices workers of both sexes and creates a workforce in the United Kingdom which will lag further and further behind their

European colleagues.[15] Nor is it only those with children who have responsibilities outside the workplace: there should be recognition also that those caring for adult dependents should have similar access to more flexible forms of employment in order to increase the income available to carers and their dependants.[16] The arguments that such policies increase costs are not necessarily borne out in practice. One example of how family friendly working may actually save costs is in the area of staff training and retention. Costs expended on training employees are not lost to the same extent since the employees are encouraged to stay in employment following the birth of a child or similar life changes.

The basic requirement, however, must be that all workers are paid wages which fairly reflect their value to the employer. One of the reasons people work is to enable them to live independent and satisfying lives. Far more working women than men are paid wages which, apart from the fact that they bear no relationship to the value of the work done, are simply inadequate for survival. This applies to part-time and full-time employees. Whereas those who do not work full-time cannot expect the same take-home pay as their full-time colleagues, the hourly rates of part-time employees are often derisory and the lack of properly structured welfare benefits either discourages part-time work altogether or leaves poorly paid workers dependent on their partners. Economists and politicians will continue for the foreseeable future to argue about the advantages and disadvantages of a statutory minimum wage, but one thing is for sure: the last ten years or so have shown that an unregulated market and high unemployment forces wages down to levels which are below subsistence level. Moreover, this is a particular problem for women, who, as has been shown, make up most of the low paid in this country. Because of the segregation in the labour market, the attempts to improve their pay by use of equal pay legislation have met with limited success. A minimum wage would, almost inevitably, boost women's wages at the lower end of the scales: this is apparent from the effects of the previous wages councils system, under which the gap between men's and women's wages in the wages councils sector was lower than that generally. The disappearance of the Wages Councils and with them any regulation of minimum rates of pay has patently worked to women's disadvantage. Women tend to work in the very industries where low wages are endemic and these rates have fallen further with the disappearance of minimum wage regulation. Whilst there may have been no deliberate attempt to focus on women as a target for disadvantage, a philosophy was nevertheless applied which tolerates wages below subsistence level, even though these must be then subsidised in some other way.

The principal argument against the minimum wage is that which was used against the Wages Councils, namely, that it would reduce employment because employers would be forced to pay wages that they cannot afford. The abolition of the Wages Councils does not seem to have boosted employment, but simply to have driven wages in low paid work even lower. It is essential for women's financial independence and security that the law tackles not only inequalities in pay between the sexes, but also the lack of any regulation at all in the setting of wages. Even if a minimum wage were to be judged politically unacceptable or economically unjustifiable, there should at least be a revival of some form of protection of wages in the most vulnerable sectors - hotels, catering, retail, clothing, cleaning. Otherwise, the women who make up the bulk of those workers will never achieve anything approaching a living wage.

There is another reason why wages should be set at levels which allow a reasonable standard of living for the recipients: for those whose wages are below subsistence level it is the state who picks up the bill in the shape of family credit. Although the present Conservative administration may oppose a minimum wage on the grounds, inter alia, that it is too expensive for employers, it is that same government which is subsidising paltry wages through the benefits system. For women, however, the relationship between social security and wages is considerably more complex, since their route to independence through waged work can be jeopardised by the unemployment or the low wages of their partner. Thus, although women's employment has been increasing steadily, this is not true of some groups of women, including lone mothers and the partners of unemployed men. If a woman's partner is unemployed, her wages reduce his benefit. Some limited steps are proposed to address this particular problem, in that the new jobseeker's allowance, which will eventually replace unemployment benefit, attempts to encourage those who are unemployed and their partners to take part-time employment.[17] As well as a disregard of £5 where a single person is working and £10 for a couple, those claiming jobseeker's allowance and their partners will be allowed to accumulate a so-called bonus payment. If one or both are working part-time, although benefit is reduced by every pound earned, fifty pence of each pound is notionally set aside up to a maximum credit of £1,000. Any such sum accumulated can be claimed if and when the hours of part-time work are increased to a sufficient number. The ability to benefit from such an incentive does, of course, depend on work being available and it being possible, especially in the case of a woman, to work more than the prescribed number of hours.

These changes, however limited, are welcome. The traditional approach has led to a real disincentive for women to work where a partner is unemployed or where he succeeds in finding work, but the wages are so low that family credit is payable, since her wages would again reduce the benefit payable. It has been noted that whereas employment rates for mothers with employed partners increased from 48 to 64 per cent during the 1980s it actually *fell* among mothers with unemployed partners from 27 to 21 per cent.[18] The Report of the Commission for Social Justice comments that the current operation of the benefits system means that "there is little point in pursuing the best route to a decent standard of living which is to have two (not necessarily full-time) earners." The Report goes on to note that:

> In essence, Income Support and Family Credit, both dependent upon a family means-test, are preventing no-job families from becoming one-job families and one-job families from becoming two-job families.[19]

Hardly surprisingly, the Report recommends changes in the benefits system, one of the most important in this context being that there should cease to be automatic aggregation between partners, in the sense that women should have individual benefits in return for individual contributions, so that one partner's wages do not affect the other's benefits. This is vital if women are to be encouraged to throw off the dependency culture of the current welfare state. It also begins to address the issue of poverty *within* the family, rather than just *of* the family. The more women are recognised as being separate and independent within the partnership, the more likely they are to have independent access to wealth.

Although paid employment may be the obvious route to financial independence, it remains the case that not all women work and for many the reason is that they prefer to or are forced to put domestic responsibilities first. One of the most outstanding examples of discrimination in the way wealth is distributed is that caring within the home by family members is not rewarded - financially at least - and since it is women who provide most care, they are the ones who are penalised. Staying at home to provide care for children or other dependants is not an easy option. Quite apart from the adverse effects which it has on the financial security of the individual carer, it can bring isolation, stress and reduced prospects of employment because of prolonged absences from the labour market. Unpaid carers are saving the state enormous sums of money but are themselves getting very little in return. The social security payments available to the carers of disabled people are pitifully small and are nowhere near what would be needed to replace earnings. Furthermore, they are tied in to the benefits received by the disabled person him- or herself. It seems a particularly cruel irony that a benefit to one can affect the levels of payments to the other.

In relation to those who care for children, there is child benefit, a sum set at a level which, as any parent knows, is ludicrously low. The future of this benefit is constantly threatened, from all shades of political opinion. The idea that it might be taxed for the better off fails completely to acknowledge the purpose of the payment or to recognise that it is one of the few sources of money which belongs specifically to a female partner. Child benefit is paid to the people most directly responsible for bringing up the next generation. It should not depend on *family* income, nor even on the mother's income. It is the last vestige of any acknowledgement not only of the cost, but also of the importance, of rearing tomorrow's workers and carers. If proposals to tax child benefit where *either* partner is paying higher rate tax were to be implemented, not only would this deprive women of an important symbolic source of income, it would also undermine female independence, by stressing the family income (which, as has been seen, is not at all the same thing as money in the mother's hands) and would incidentally take the taxation system back to the days of joint assessment. A mother is far less likely than her partner to be paying higher rate tax but if he comes into that tax band, *her* income is reduced by the imposition of tax on the child benefit. The motive behind such taxation may be to increase the money available for other benefits, but this is not an acceptable way of raising that income.

Whether in employment policies or in reform of the welfare system, there is enormous scope for law reforms which would enable women to avoid both dependence and poverty. One of the greatest obstacles to such reforms is that the political climate has been antipathetic to such moves. The current network of legal rules pays lip service to the ideal of the family without going so far as to provide any real support for most of those living within it. Although single mothers are criticised and the "normal" family held up for approval, there is little effort to ensure that within the traditional family there is equity. Pahl's work on money within the family emphasises that there is no guarantee that each member of a family benefits equally and fairly from the household income.[20] Although this phenomenon is well documented and long established[21] there has been little evidence of any intention to attempt to tackle the problem. There is a marked reluctance to open Pahl's "black box" to discover what exactly is happening inside. It is certainly true that during the 1980s there was a resurgence of the Beveridge principle which holds that families would benefit from policies to encourage full-time employment amongst *men*.[22] Implicit in such notions is the idea that the male breadwinner will - naturally - support a dependent wife and children. This takes account neither of women's desire for independence nor the incidence of marital breakdown. A similar picture emerges from the community care policies - it is assumed that there will be someone to care for, say, an elderly relative and moreover that the carer herself (since it is usually a woman) will have someone on whom she can depend, since welfare benefits alone are insufficient.[23]

The thrust of the arguments in this book have concentrated on women as individuals and not as members of the family unit. It is not necessary to renounce the family in order to call for a legislative programme which, having recognised the needs of women as evidenced by the lives they lead, will create a framework in which it is possible to achieve substantive equality for women whilst at the same time having the potential to improve the lives of women, children and men. A first step would be to improve and strengthen the anti-discrimination laws. The amendments proposed by the Equal Opportunities Commission and rejected, almost totally, by the government would be a good starting point.[24] Any attempt to impose equality will, necessarily, involve greater intervention or regulation. A provision which was repealed by the Conservative government during the 1980s is resurrected in the Social Justice Report, namely, the idea of contract compliance within the public sector. Local authorities and other public employers can have significant impact on other employers by virtue of the imposition of particular requirements on those with whom it chooses to do business. A local authority which invites tenders for cleaning services or catering in schools could insist on evidence that the firm to whom the contract is awarded is an equal opportunities employer. Lack of such a policy means inability to tender for lucrative contracts and is thus meant to have an impact on the employment practices of private sector employers. The scope of contract compliance was radically curtailed in the Local Government Act 1988 which prohibits local authorities from taking into account "non-commercial matters" when awarding contracts. These matters include the rates of pay of women and the number of women employed. The only exception is in relation to certain vetting functions which allow the authorities to comply with their obligations under the Race Relations Act 1976 - there is no exception in relation to sex discrimination. The Social Justice Report recommends the reintroduction of contract compliance in order to:

> ... harness the huge purchasing power of the public sector through central and local government in order to accelerate the effect of anti-discrimination and positive equality measures in recruitment, promotion and access to training.[25]

Contract compliance is simply one aid to the achievement of equality, working through market mechanisms rather than legislative requirements. One of the difficulties inherent in such an approach - apart from charges of interference with a free market - is that its coverage is necessarily somewhat patchy. At least legislation can be drafted so that it is universally applicable. It is tempting to suggest that the law should become involved in those areas in which voluntary action has been slow and insufficient. A classic example of this is child care. Although the law now grants a period of maternity leave, there is no legal requirement for an employer to make it feasible for a woman to return by offering care facilities or cash assistance. Some employers have acted, many others have not and the lack of affordable child care is certainly one important factor in the decisions women must make about their lives. An employer which claims to be an "equal opportunities employer" but which does not provide or help with child care is trading under false colours. Whilst a proper network of creches and nurseries would, of course, cost money, without them women will not be able to earn the money they and their families need.

Concluding thoughts

Identifying the ways in which the law prevents women from being men's equals financially makes it clear that it is vital that the persistent inequalities and contradictions are tackled, and tackled quickly, since financial autonomy is the key to full citizenship and a fulfilling existence. Some of the suggested solutions, such as wages for housework may seem merely to emphasise women's traditional role as carers, but a proper reward for the performance of such tasks could well enhance the status of carers generally. Other solutions such as the provision of help with child care might be said to force women into work and penalise those who wish to be full-time mothers. Arguments over what might be "best for women" should not, however, be allowed to assume the negative character which they had in the past when men were only too keen to tell women what to do (and some would argue still are). The law should be responsive to women's needs and as far as possible allow them choice, so that they can use the solution that suits them best. The law does not presently do this. Instead, it forces women, and indeed men, to make compromises over the balance between work and home. Those women who cannot obtain adequately-paid employment, particularly if they are lone parents, may now have no choice but to construct complex economic survival packages which combine income from paid employment, from welfare benefits or from other sources such as child support payments. Married women are disadvantaged by the law's current conception of marriage which does not automatically allow a woman a share in any family resources, leaving a couple free to organise their financial affairs as they see fit. This may compel women to accept arrangements which exploit the weakness of their financial position as compared with men. The law is, however, quite prepared to intervene when the relationship ends and is not then averse to using a woman's behaviour whilst the marriage was on-going as a basis for distributing assets. If there is a theme to the laws which govern women's access to wealth, it is one of lack of power and marginalisation, rather than choice. This book is an argument for increasing the choices available to women in order to augment their access to wealth in its widest sense.

Notes

1. MacKinnon, C. (1989), *Toward a Feminist Theory of the State*.
2. O'Donovan, K. (1985), *Sexual Divisions in Law*.
3. An interesting example is the legal history of marital rape: see Barton, L.J. (1992), 'The Story of Marital Rape', 108 LQR, p. 260.
4. *Bilka-Kaufhaus GmbH v Weber Von Hartz* Case 170/84 [1986] ECR 1607.
5. MacKinnon, C. op. cit., n. 1, p. 108.

6.   This is certainly true in the United Kingdom, though the European Union has shown a willingness to tackle a number of social issues.

7.   *Barber v Guardian Royal Exchange Assurance Group* Case 262/88 (1990) 2 All ER 660.

8.   Sohrab, J. (1994), 'An Overview of the Equality Directive on Social Security and its Implementation in Four Social Security Systems', *Journal of European Social Policy* 4(4), p. 263.

9.   Jobseeker's allowance, due to replace unemployment benefit, makes a limited attempt to tackle this problem. A woman will not jeopardise her partner's benefit if she works for up to 24 hours a week. It is also possible to accumulate a 'back to work bonus' if either or both work part-time. Earnings will cause a pound for pound loss of benefit, apart from a small disregard, but there will be a credit of 50 pence for every pound lost up to £1,000. This is paid when either the unemployed person or partner increase their working hours to over 16 for the claimant and over 24 for a partner: (1994) Cmnd 2687.

10.   *Social Protection in Europe 1993*, Commission of the European Communities, 1994.

11.   See however (1995), *Improving Child Support*, Cmnd 2745, and see pp. 247-251.

12.   Commission for Social Justice/Institute for Public Policy Research (1994), *Social Justice: Strategies for National Renewal*.

13.   Ibid., at p. 151.

14.   Some employers have already taken the plunge: employees in the German government sector may choose to work part-time, full-time or job-share: Ormerod, P. (1994), 'Why Western employment policy is going around in circles' *Demos Journal* 2/1994, cited in op. cit., n. 1.

15.   See, e.g., the rights granted to parents in France and outlined in (1994) *Equal Opportunities Review* No. 58, at p. 5.

16.   See Dex, S. and Taylor, M. (1994), 'Household employment in 1991', *Employment Gazette* 102 (No. 10), p. 353: households with lowest resources and income were those accommodating an elderly person.

17.   (1994), *Jobseeker's Allowance*, Cmnd 2687.

18.   Harrop, A. and Moss, P. (1994), 'Working parents: trends in the 1980s', *Employment Gazette* 102, (No. 10), p. 343 at p. 347. The authors suggest that the effects of the social security system are insufficient to explain the fall. The employment rates for lone mothers also fell.

19.   Op. cit., n. 1, at p. 227.

20.   See Chap. 6.

21.   Rowntree referred to 'secondary poverty' in *Poverty: A Study of Town Life*, published in 1902.

22.   See Smart, C. (1987), 'Securing the family: Rhetoric and policy in the field of social security' in Loney, M. (ed.), *The State or the Market*, p. 99.

23.   See Wicks, M. (1987), 'Family matters and public policy,' ibid, p. 115.

24.   See p. 82.

25.   Op. cit., n. 1, at p. 195.

Cases

Legislation

Bibliography

A Strategy for Justice: Publicly Funded Legal Services in the 1990s (1992), Legal Action Group.

Alcock, P. (1993), *Understanding Poverty*, Macmillan, Basingstoke.

Allen, S., and Wolkowitz, C. (1987), *Homeworking: Myths and Realities*, Macmillan Education, Basingstoke.

Andrews, K. and Jacobs, J. (1990), *Punishing the Poor*, Macmillan, London.

Annual Hours, Incomes Data Study No 544.

Annual Report of the Department of the Environment (1991), Cmnd 1508, HMSO.

Annual Report of the Supplementary Benefits Commission (1978), Cmnd 7725, HMSO.

Are fair rents losing their appeal?' (1993), *Independent*, 14 October.

Atkins, S. and Hoggett, B. (1984) *Women and the Law*, Basil Blackwell, Oxford.

Baldwin, J., Wikeley, N. and Young, R. (1992), *Judging Social Security: the adjudication of claims for benefit in Britain*, Clarendon Press, Oxford.

Barlow, A. (1992), *Living Together: A Guide to the Law*, Fourmat Publishing, London.

Bartholomew, R., Hibbett, A. and Sidaway, J. (1992), 'Lone parents and the labour market: evidence from the Labour Force Survey', *Employment Gazette*, 100, no. 11, 559-578.

Beveridge, W. (1942), *Social Insurance and Allied Services*, Cmnd 6404, HMSO, London.

Bird, D., Beatson, M. and Butcher, S. (1993) 'Membership of trade unions', *Employment Gazette* 101, no. 5, 189.

Blackstone's *Commentaries on the Laws of England* (1765), Vol. 2, Part 1 p. 129.

Blood, R.O. and Wolfe, D.M. (1960), *Husbands and Wives*, Free Press, Glencoe, Illinois.

Bradley, H. (1989), *Men's Work, Women's Work*, Polity Press, Cambridge.

Bradshaw, J. and Millar, J. (1991), *Lone Parent Families in the UK*, Department of Social Security Research Report, no. 6, HMSO.

Brannen, J. and Moss P. (1991), *Managing Mothers: Dual Earner Households after Maternity Leave*, Unwin Hyman, London.

Breadline Britain - 1990s (1991), see Mack J. and Lansley, S.

British Social Attitudes: 1987 Report (1989), see Jowell et al.

British Social Attitudes: 9th Report (1992), see Jowell et al.

Bromley, P.M. (1966), *Family Law* (3rd edition), Butterworths, London.

Bromley, P.M. (1971), *Family Law* (4th edition), Butterworths, London.

Bryson, A. (1989), *Undervalued, underpaid and undercut: The Future of the Wages Councils*, Low Pay Unit, Pamphlet 53.

Burn E.H. (1994), *Cheshire and Burn's Modern Law of Real Property*, (15th edition), Butterworths, London.

Cadbury, E. Matheson, M.C. and Shann, G. (1980), *Women's Work and Wages*, Garland, New York.

Callender, C. (1993), 'Redundancy, unemployment and poverty' in Glendinning, C. and Millar, J. (eds), *Women and Poverty in Britain: the 1990s*, Harvester Wheatsheaf, New York.

Cary, E. and Peratis, K. (1977), *Women and the Law*, National Textbook Company, Illinois.

Central Statistical Office, *Family Expenditure Surveys*, HMSO.

Central Statistical Office's Social Trends 24 (1994), HMSO.

Checkland, E. and S.G. (1974), *Poor Law Report of 1834*, Penguin, Harmondsworth.

Cioni, M.L. (1985), *Women and Law in Elizabethan England with Particular Reference to the Court of Chancery*, Garland, New York.

Clark, A. (1992), *Working Life of Women in the Seventeenth Century*, (3rd ed.), Routledge, London.

Cohen, R. and Tarpey, M. (eds) (1988), *Single Payments: The Disappearing Safety Net*, Child Poverty Action Group, London, Poverty Pamphlets 74.

Cook, D. (1989), *Rich Law, Poor Law: Different Responses to Tax and Supplementary Benefit Fraud*, Open University Press, Milton Keynes.

Cook, J., and Watt, S. (1992), 'Racism, women and poverty' in Glendinning, C. and Millar, J., (eds) *Women and Poverty in Britain: the 1990s*, Harvester Wheatsheaf, New York.

Coyle, A. (1984), *Redundant Women*, The Women's Press, London.

CPAG Handbooks, *Rights guide to non-means tested benefits, National Welfare Benefits Handbook* (published annually), Child Poverty Action Group, London.

Cranston, R. (1985), *Legal Foundations of the Welfare State*, Weidenfeld and Nicolson, London.

Creighton, W.B. (1979), *Working Women and the Law*, Mansell, London.

Davies, B. and Ward, S. (1992), *Women and Personal Pensions*, HMSO, London.

Dean, M. (1991), *The Constitution of Poverty: toward a genealogy of liberal governance*, Routledge, London.

Department of Employment (1992), *New Earnings Survey*, HMSO.

Department of Employment (1993), *New Earnings Survey*, HMSO.

Department of Employment (1994), *New Earnings Survey*, HMSO.

Department of Social Security (1992), Households below Average Income, A Statistical Analysis 1979 - 1988/9, HMSO.

Department of Social Security (1994), Households below Average Income: A Statistical Analysis 1979 to 1991-92, HMSO.

Department of Social Security *Statistics 1993*, HMSO.

Dewar, J. and Parker, S. (1992), *Law and the Family*, 2nd ed., Butterworths, London.

Dex, S. (1987), *Women's Occupational Mobility*, Macmillan, Basingstoke.

Duckworth, P. (1991), *Matrimonial Property and Finance*, Longman, London.

Eekelaar, J. (1984), *Family Law & Social Policy* (2nd edition), Weidenfield and Nicholson, London.

Eekelaar, J. (1991), *Regulating Divorce*, Clarendon Press, Oxford.

Ellis, E. (1991), *European Community Sex Equality Law*, Clarendon Press, Oxford.

Employment Gazette 102 (1994), (No. 7), LFS2.

Employment Gazette 102 (1994), (No. 1), LFS7.

Employment Gazette 102 (1994), (No. 3), 75.

Employment Gazette 102 (1994), (No. 6), LFS4.

Employment Gazette 102 (1994), (No. 7), LFS1.

Equal Opportunities Review 45 (1992).

Equal Opportunities Review 48 (1993).

Equal Opportunities Review 49 (1993).

Equal Opportunities Review 51 (1993).

Equal Opportunities Review 52 (1993).

Equal Opportunities Review 57 (1994).

Equal Opportunities Review 58 (1994).

Equal Treatment for Men and Women - Strengthening the Acts and *Equal Pay for Men and Women - Strengthening the Acts*, (1988, 1990), EOC.

Equal value update (1993), *Equal Opportunities Review* 51.

Equality in State Pension Age, (1993) Cmnd 2420, HMSO, London.

Esam, P. and Berthoud, R. (1992), *Independent Benefits for Men and Women: An enquiry into treating husbands and wives as separate units in the assessment of social security*, Policy Studies Institute, London.

Eurobarometer Survey, 1990, Commission of the European Communities.

Eurostat (1991), *A Social Portrait of Europe*, European Communities, Luxembourg.

Field, F., Meacher, M., Pond, C. (1977), *To Him Who Hath: A Study of Poverty and Taxation*, Penguin, Harmondsworth.

Finch, J. and Groves, D. (eds) (1983), *A Labour of Love: Women, Work and Caring*, Routledge, London.

Ford, J. (1991), *Consuming Credit: Debt and poverty in the UK*, Child Poverty Action Group, London .

Foster, H., (ed.) (1994), *Employee Benefits in Europe and the USA*, Longmans, London.

Freedman, J., et al (1988), *Property and marriage: An integrated approach*, Institute of Fiscal Studies.

General Household Survey 1992 (1994), HMSO.

Glendinning, C. (1987), 'Impoverishing women' in Walker, A. and Walker, C. (eds), The Growing Divide: a social audit 1979-87, CPAG, London.

Glendinning, C. (1992), '"Community care": The financial consequences for women', Glendinning, C. and Millar, J., (eds), *Women and Poverty in Britain: the 1990s,* Harvester Wheatsheaf, New York.

Glendinning, C. and Millar, J. (eds), (1992), *Women and Poverty in Britain: the 1990s,* Harvester Wheatsheaf, New York.

Glendon, M. A. (1981), *The New Family and the New Property*, Butterworth & Co, Canada.

Glendon, M.A. (1989), *The transformation of Family Law: State, Law and Family in the United States and Western Europe*, University of Chicago Press.

Graham, H. (1992), 'Budgeting for health: Mothers in low-income households', in Glendinning, C. and Millar, J. *Women and Poverty in Britain: the 1990s*, Harvester Wheatsheaf, New York.

Gray, A. (1979), 'The Working Class Family as an Economic Unit', in Harris, C. (ed.), *The Sociology of the Family*, University of Keele Sociological Review Monograph, University of Keele.

Groves, D. (1992), 'Occupational Pension Provision and Women's Poverty in Old Age,' in Glendinning, C. and Millar, J. (eds), *Women and Poverty in Britain in the 1990's*, Harvester Wheatsheaf, New York.

Haavio-Mannila, E. and Kauppinen, K. (1992), 'Women and the Welfare State in the Nordic Countries,' in Kahne, H. and Giele, J.Z. (eds), *Women's Work and Women's Lives: The Continuing Struggle Worldwide*, Westview Press, Boulder, Colarado.

Hakim, C. (1987), *Home-Based Work in Britain: a report on the 1981 National Homeworking Survey and the Department of Employment research programme on homework*, Department of Employment Research Paper No 60, HMSO.

Hannah, L. (1986), *Inventing Retirement: the Development of Occupational Pensions in Britain*, Cambridge University Press, Cambridge.

Harris, N. (1989), *Social Security for Young People*, Avebury, Aldershot.

Harrop, A. and Moss, P. (1994), 'Working parents: trends in the 1980s,' *Employment Gazette* 102 (No. 10), 343

Haskey, J. (1994), 'Estimated numbers of one-parent families and their prevalence in Great Britain in 1991,' *Population Trends*, 78, Winter, HMSO, London.

Hayton, D. (1990), 'The equitable rights of cohabitees,' 54 The Conveyancer, 370.

Hills, J. (1988), *Changing Tax*, Child Poverty Action Group.

Holcombe, L. (1983), *Wives and Property: reform of the married women's property law in nineteenth century England*, Martin Robertson, Oxford.

Improving Child Support (1995), Cmnd 2745, HMSO, London

Industrial Relations Services (1991), *Pay and Gender in Britain, A Research Report for the EOC*, IRS.

Industrial Relations Services (1992), *Pay and Gender in Britain: 2, Second Research Report for the EOC*, IRS.

Jobseeker's Allowance (1994), Cmnd 2687, HMSO, London.

Johnson, N. (1990), *Reconstructing the Welfare State: A Decade of Change*, Harvester Wheatsheaf, New York.

Joshi, H. (1992), 'The Cost of Caring,' in Glendinning C., and Millar, J. (eds), *Women and Poverty in Britain: the 1990s*, Harvester Wheatsheaf, New York.

Jowell, R., Brook, L., Prior, G., Taylor, B. (eds.) (1992), *British Social Attitudes*, 9th Report, Dartmouth, Aldershot.

Jowell, R., Witherspoon, S. and Brook, L. (1989), *British Social Attitudes: 1987 Report*, Social and Community Planning Research, Dartmouth, Aldershot.

Kahne, H. and Giele, J.Z. (1992), *Women's Work and Women's Lives: The Continuing Struggle*

Worldwide, Westview Press, Boulder, Colarado.

Kempson, E., Bryson, A. and Rowlingson, K. (1994), *Hard Times: How poor families make ends meet*, Policy Studies Institute, London.

Kessler-Harris, A. (1990), *A Woman's Wage: Historical Meanings and Social Consequences*, University Press of Kentucky, Lexington.

Kiernan, K. (1992), 'The roles of men and women in tomorrow's Europe,' *Employment Gazette* 100 (No. 10), 491.

Labour Research (1994), September, October.

Land, H. (1983), 'Poverty and Gender: the Distribution of Resources within the Family' in Brown, M. (ed.), The Structure of Disadvantage, Heinemann.

Land, H. (1992), 'Whatever Happened to the Social Wage?' in Glendinning, C. and Millar, J. (eds), *Women and Poverty in Britain: the 1990s*, Harvester Wheatsheaf, New York.

Landsdown, G. (1994), 'Respecting the rights of children', *Poverty* 86, 9-11.

Legal Action Group (1992), *A Strategy for Justice: Publicly Funded Legal Services in the 1990s*, LAG, London.

Leighton, P. (1986), 'Marginal Workers' in Lewis, R. (ed.), *Labour Law in Britain*, Basil Blackwell Ltd, Oxford.

Lewis, J. (1984), *Women in England 1870-1950: Sexual Divisions and Social Change*, Wheatsheaf Books Ltd, Brighton.

Lewis, J. (1992), *Women in Britain since 1945*, Blackwell, Oxford.

Lewis, J. and Piachaud, D., 'Women and poverty in the twentieth century' in Glendinning, C., Millar J. (eds) (1992), *Women and Poverty in Britain: the 1990s*, Harvester Wheatsheaf, New York.

Lister, R. (1992), *Women's Economic Dependency and Social Security*, EOC, Manchester.

Looking to the Future: Mediation and the Ground for Divorce (1994), Cmnd 2799, HMSO, London.

Mack J. and Lansley S. (1985), Poor Britain, Allen and Unwin, London (updated in the television series *Breadline Britain - the 1990s*, 1991, LWT).

Mackinnon, C. (1989), *Toward a Feminist Theory of the State*, Harvard University Press, Cambridge, Massachusetts.

Maclean, M (1991), *Surviving Divorce*, Macmillan, London.

Maintenance and capital provision on divorce (1991), The Law Society.

Marsh, A. and McKay, S. (1993), *Families, Work and Benefits*, Policy Studies Institute, London.

Martin, J. and Roberts, C. (1984), *Women and Employment: A Lifetime Perspective*, HMSO.

McLaughlin, E. (1991), *Social Security and Community care: The case of the invalid care allowance*, Department of Social Security Research Report No. 4, HMSO.

McLaughlin, E., Millar, J., Cooke, K. (1989), *Work and Welfare Benefits*, Avebury, Aldershot.

Merit pay, performance appraisal and attitudes to women's work, (1993), Institute of Manpower Studies and EOC.

Mill, J.S. (1859), *On Liberty*, Harmondsworth: Penguin, 1983.

Millar, J. (1992), 'Lone Mothers and Poverty,' in Glendinning, C. and Millar, J. (eds), *Women and Poverty in Britain: the 1990s*, Harvester Wheatsheaf, New York.

Millar, J. and Glendinning, C. (1989), 'Gender and poverty', 18 *Journal of Social Policy*, 363-81.

Minford, P. (1987), 'The role of the social services: a view from the New Right', in Loney, M. (ed.), *The State or the Market?*, Sage, London.

Morris A.E., and Nott, S.M. (1991), *Working Women and the Law: Equality and Discrimination in Theory and Practice,* Routledge, in association with Sweet and Maxwell.

Morris, A.E. and Nott, S.M. (1992), 'The Legal Response to Pregnancy' 12 *Legal Studies* 54.

Morris, A.E. and Nott, S.M. 'The Law's Engagement with Pregnancy' in (1995), Millns, S. and Bridgeman, J.C. (eds), *Law and Body Politics*, Dartmouth, Aldershot.

Morris, L., 'Redundancy and patterns of household finance' (1984), 18 *Sociological Review*, 492.

Morris, L. (1990), *The Workings of the Household: a US-UK comparison*, Polity Press, Cambridge.

Morris, L. and Ruane, S. (1986), *Household Finance Management and Labour Market Behaviour*, Work and Employment Research Unit, Durham.

National Welfare Benefits Handbook, 23rd ed. (1993) CPAG.

Nobles, R. (1993), *Pensions, Employment and the Law,* Clarendon Press, Oxford.

O'Donovan, K. (1985), *Sexual Divisions in Law*, Weidenfeld and Nicolson, London.

Ogus, A.I., Barendt, E.M. (1988), *The Law of Social Security*, 3rd Edition, Supplement (1991), Butterworths, London.

OPCS General Household Survey 1980 (1982), HMSO.

Oppenheim, C. (1993), *Poverty: The Facts*, Child Poverty Action Group, London.

Pahl, J. (1980), 'Patterns of money management within marriage', 9 *Journal of Social Policy*, 313.

Pahl, J. (1983), 'The allocation of money and the structuring of inequality within marriage', 31 *Sociological Review*, 237.

Pahl, J. (1985), *Private Violence and Public Policy: The needs of battered women and the response of the public services*, Routledge and Kegan Paul, London.

Pahl, J. (1988), 'Earning, Sharing, Spending: Married Couples and Their Money' in Walker R. and Parker, G., (eds), *Money Matters*, Sage, London, in association with University of York Social Policy Research Unit.

Pahl, J. (1989), *Money and Marriage*, Macmillan, Basingstoke.

Parker, G. (1988), 'Credit' and 'Indebtedness' in Walker, R. and Parker, G. (eds), *Money Matters: Income Wealth and Financial Welfare*, Sage, London, in association with University of York Social Policy Research Unit.

Parker, G. (1992), 'Counting Care: numbers and types of informal carers', in Twigg J. (ed.), *Carers, Research and Practice*, HMSO.

Parker, G. (1992), 'Making ends meet: Women, credit and debt', in Glendinning, C. and Millar, J. (eds), *Women and Poverty in Britain: the 1990s*, Harvester Wheatsheaf, New York.

Parry, M.L. (1993), *The Law Relating to Cohabitation,* 3rd edition, Sweet and Maxwell, London.

The Pastons (1981), The Folio Society, London.

Patterns of pay: results from the 1993 New Earnings Survey', (1993), *Employment Gazette* 101, no. 11, 515.

Pay and Gender in Britain: A Research Report for the EOC from the Industrial Relations Services, (1991), IRS.

Pay and Gender in Britain: 2 A Second Research Report for the EOC from the Industrial Relations

Services (1992), IRS.

Pearson, P. and Quiney, M. (1992), Poor Britain: Poverty, inequality and low pay in the nineties, Low Pay Unit.

Pearson, P. (1993), *More Crime and Still No Punishment, Wages Councils and illegal underpayments*, Low Pay Unit.

Plumer, A-M. (1992), *Equal Value judgments: objective assessment or lottery*, University of Warwick, Industrial Relations Research Unit, Warwick papers in industrial relations, No 40.

Pollock, F. and Maitland, F. W. (1968), *History of English Law Before the Time of Edward 1*, Cambridge University Press, Vol. 1, 485.

Poynter, J.R. (1969), *Society and Pauperism: English ideas on poor relief 1795-1834*, Routledge and Kegan Paul, London.

Poynter, R. and Martin, C. (1993), *Rights Guide to non-means tested benefits*, Child Poverty Action Group, London.

Prechal, S. and Burrows, N. (1990), *Gender Discrimination Law of the European Community*, Dartmouth, Aldershot.

Priest, J. (1993), *Families Outside Marriage*, 2nd edition, Family Law, Bristol.

Public service, private hardship' (1994), *The New Review*, April/May.

Rathbone, E. (1924), *The Disinherited Family 19*, Arnold, London.

Reform of Social Security (1985), Vols. 1 & 2, Cmnd 9517 and 9518, HMSO, London.

Reform of Social Security Programme for Action (1985), Cmnd 9691, HMSO, London.

Rights guide to non-means-tested benefits, 16th ed. (1993), CPAG.

Rowntree, B.S. (1902), *Poverty: A study of town life*, Macmillan.

Rubery, J. (1992), *The economics of equal value*, EOC.

Sabine, B.E.V. (1966), A History of Income Tax, Allen and Unwin.

Scutt, J. A. (1990), *Women and the Law*, The Law Book Company, North Ryde, N.S.W.

Sly, F. (1993), 'Women in the labour market', *Employment Gazette* 101 (No. 11), 483.

Sly, F. (1994), 'Ethnic groups and the labour market', *Employment Gazette* 102 (No. 5), 147.

Sly, F. (1994), 'Mothers in the labour market', *Employment Gazette* 102 (No. 11), 403.

Smart, C. (1989), *Feminism and the Power of Law*, Routledge, London.

Smart, C. (1992), *Regulating Womanhood*, Routledge, London & New York.

Social Trends 23 (1993), HMSO.

Social Trends 24 (1994), HMSO.

Sohrab, J. (1994), 'An Overview of the Equality Directive on Social Security and its Implementation in Four Social Security Systems', *Journal of European Social Policy* 4(4).

Snell, K.D.M. and Millar, J. (1987), 'Lone-parent Families and the Welfare State: past and present' in *Continuity and Change*, Vol. 2. Cambridge University Press, Cambridge.

Spicker, P. (1993), *Poverty and Social Security*, Routledge, London.

Staves, S. (1990), *Married Women's Separate Property in England 1660 - 1833*, Harvard University Press, Cambridge, Massachusetts.

Stone, L. (1977), *The Family, Sex and Marriage in England 1500-1800*, Weidenfeld and Nicolson, London.

Stone, L. (1990), *Road to Divorce England 1530-1987,* Clarendon Press, Oxford.

Szyszczak, E. (1990), *Partial Unemployment: The Regulation of Short Time Working in Britain,* Mansell, London.

Taking the Bloom off Youth' (1992), *New Review of the Low Pay Unit,* No. 15.

Thane, P. (1982), *The Foundations of the Welfare State,* Longman, London.

Todd, J. and Jones, L. (1972), *Matrimonial Property,* HMSO.

Townsend, P. and Gordon D. (1990), 'Let Them Eat Cake' Low Pay Unit, London (The text from *The new review,* No 4).

Vogel, U. (1992), 'Whose Property? The Double Standard of Adultery in Nineteenth-century Law,' in Smart, C. (1992), *Regulating Womanhood,* Routledge, London & New York.

Walker, R. and Parker, G. (eds) (1988), *Money Matters: Income Wealth and Financial Welfare,* Sage, London.

Watson, G. and Fothergill, B. (1993), 'Part-time employment and attitudes to part-time work', *Employment Gazette* 101, no. 5, 213.

Webb, S.J. and B. (1910), *English Poor Law Policy,* Longmans, London.

Webb, S.J. and B. (1963), *English Poor Law History,* Cass, London, reprinting Longmans, London 1927-29.

Webb, S. (1993), 'Women's Incomes: Past, Present and Prospects', *Fiscal Studies,* Vol. 14, no. 4, 14-36.

Weitzman, L. (1985), *The Divorce Revolution,* The Free Press, New York.

Who Needs the Wages Councils? (1983), Low Pay Unit, 11.

Women and Men in Britain 1992, EOC.

Women in the unions' (1993) *Equal Opportunities Review* 48, 34.

Yeandle, S. (1984), *Women's Working Lives: Patterns and Strategies,* Tavistock, London.

Index